RESEARCH METHODS
Science and Diversity

ANDREA SPATA
Molloy College

WILEY

JOHN WILEY & SONS, INC.

SENIOR ACQUISITIONS EDITOR	Tim Vertovec
MARKETING MANAGER	Kevin Molloy
SENIOR PRODUCTION EDITOR	Patricia McFadden
SENIOR DESIGNER	Kevin Murphy
PRODUCTION MANAGEMENT SERVICES	Hermitage Publishing Services

This book was set in Times Roman by Hermitage Publishing Services and printed and bound by RR Donnelley, Inc. The cover was printed by Lehigh Press, Inc.

This book is printed on acid-free paper. ∞

ISBN 0-471-36912-8

Printed in the United States of America

10 9 8 7 6 5 4 3 2 1

PREFACE

My primary motive for writing a research methodology textbook was to impart to students my genuine love and enthusiasm for the subject matter. It all began with a discussion in my experimental psychology class, when a student made the statement that most textbooks are written as though professors were writing for each other, rather for the average student. The student's statement then lead to a class discussion about what makes a good textbook, one that the students actually enjoy reading. After listening to the various comments, I felt that there was a need for a concise, clearly written text that offered a blend of interesting and relevant examples, appropriate level of language, and an approach that makes students appreciate the importance of understanding basic research principles and techniques.

On the basis of student input, I attempted to write a textbook that contains concise, to-the-point chapters that cover the important concepts with good examples, but without a lot of "padding." In addition, the textbook is easy to read, in that it states concepts clearly and provides concrete real-life examples to which the students can relate. It contains examples of classic research studies from various areas of psychology, as well as the most recent examples of cutting-edge research. In addition, I believe that my writing style engages the student, and attempts to explain difficult topics without being dry, intimidating, or pedantic. In general, I believe that my text is more accessible and student-friendly than others I have reviewed and/or used in the past.

The level of presentation is appropriate for all undergraduates (except freshmen), as well as for first year graduate students who might need a good review of basic experimental designs, principles, and methods. In writing this textbook, I also assumed that the students have a background in elementary statistical concepts and analyses. Pedagogical features include an outline at the beginning of each chapter, a summary of key concepts at the end of each chapter, and an appendix containing a full glossary. Students can also test their knowledge and understanding of the material by completing a set of questions at the end of each chapter. Since students typically do not find the questions at the end of chapters helpful unless the correct answers are provided, an appendix contains all the answers to the end-of-chapter short answer questions.

The textbook is divided into five major sections. Part I covers the scientific process, with Chapter 1 introducing the role of science and the scientific method; Chapter 2 discusses the basic elements of an experimental study; Chapter 3 covers the concept of validity and control procedures; Chapter 4 deals with ethical issues; and Chapter five contains topics on measuring behavior. Part II covers descriptive statistics (Chapter 6) and inferential statistics (Chapter 7), and Chapter 8 reviews some popular statistical te... analysis. Part III discusses various types of true experiments, while Part I...

nonexperimental approaches such as correlational studies, field studies, and quasi-experimental studies. Part IV fully discusses the research process, from getting ideas and conducting library research (Chapter 16) to writing up the research project following the recommendations set forth in the American Psychological Association (APA) style manual (Chapter 17.) The final chapter (18) introduces important methodological issues unique to researching human diversity. Included in this chapter are some of the problems the researcher may encounter when comparing different groups with regard to gender, ethnicity, culture, or subculture.

My main reason for including Chapter 18 was that since we live in an increasingly diverse world, the issue of researching human diversity and the methodological issues and problems that accompany such endeavors needed to be addressed. No textbook that I have reviewed and/or used addressed this topic. While a single chapter is admittedly inadequate to fully acquaint the student with this topic, it at least introduces it and makes the student aware of the various "pitfalls" and shortcomings of researching diversity.

My main objection to most research methodology texts is their in-depth coverage of nonexperimental designs before introducing true experiments. I admit that this may very well be a personal preference, but in my opinion students should have a solid understanding of what an experiment is and what it can establish, before being introduced to nonexperimental techniques and their limitations. I find it hard to discuss the weaknesses and limitations of nonexperimental designs when the students do not understand what a true experiment is. For this reason, I also object to the appearance of an ethics chapter or a library research/where to get ideas chapter before students even understand what research is. In addition, texts that do not introduce the concept of independent and dependent variables until Chapters 5 or 6 are not very useful for professors whose students are also taking a laboratory course. If students are conducting experiments early in the semester, they cannot wait several weeks to be introduced to these crucial terms.

Another of my pet peeves with the majority of textbooks is the relegation of statistics to either the closing chapter(s) or to an appendix. In my experience, even if the students have had a formal course in statistics, they tend to remember very little of the material. This makes it necessary for me to review important concepts and analyses. Again, this is a personal issue, and some professors may like more or less statistical coverage in a methods text. I, for one, prefer to have a better coverage and review of important concepts, especially as it relates to hypothesis testing: the crux of experimentation. In addition, students rarely remember which statistical analysis is appropriate for which type of design; for this reason, my text includes a section on appropriate statistical tests for the particular design under discussion. While statistics is a required course for psychology majors, in my experience, the majority of students have difficulty not only remembering the various tests, but also seeing how these procedures are related to various experimental designs. In this text, the statistics chapters can easily be skipped by the instructor if so desired; however, a major advantage of this text over others is that the discussion of each research design is followed by an "appropriate statistical analysis" section. This way, students can see the connection between the statistical tests they studied in one course, and the research design they are studying in another.

I attempted to organize the material so that continuity was maintained not only between concepts and elements within a given chapter, but between chapters as well. I believe that important themes, ideas, and concepts need to be returned to and reiterated so that that the student sees a continuity between these ideas and concepts. In my experience, most texts introduce the important elements, but never return to them in later chapters to show how these elements are related to those later concepts or ideas. I firmly believe that this is necessary; the majority of students in my experience tend not to see the connections or make those connections on their own. On the other hand, while the connection between chapters is stressed and reiterated throughout the textbook, Chapters 6, 7, and 8 in Part II dealing with statistics may be skipped entirely without affecting the continuity should the instructor wish to do so. In addition, should the instructor wish to cover library research and writing reports using APA style, Chapter 16 and 17 may be covered early in the semester without affecting the textbook's continuity.

I am indebted to the following reviewers of this textbook for their helpful suggestions and comments:

Tim Brockes (Nazareth College)
David Conner (Truman State University)
Susan Heidenreich (University of San Francisco)
William Lieberman (California State University—Northridge and Los Angeles)
Mary Jo Litten (Pittsburgh State University)
Joel Warm (University of Cincinnati)

All the suggestions were greatly appreciated and if some of the recommendations were not followed, it is not because I did not take them into consideration. Thank you for trying to make this textbook the best it could be.

In addition, a big thank you to the editorial and production staff at Wiley. In particular, I would like to thank Ellen Schatz, Tim Vertovec, Anne Smith, Joan Petrokofsky, and Kristen Babroski.

A thank you is owed to all my students who have, over the years, helped me to become a better teacher by voicing their opinions and concerns, and by making countless suggestions and recommendations on what makes a textbook enjoyable.

Finally, I would like to thank my husband, Michael Spata, who supported me all the way, and who patiently and ungrudgingly put up with me spending months upon months in the basement while completing this textbook.

SUMMARY TABLE OF CONTENTS

CONTENTS

THE SCIENTIFIC PROCESS

THE ROLE OF SCIENCE AND THE SCIENTIFIC METHOD

- Why do we dream?
- What attracts people to each other?
- How can she do something like that?
- Why can't he say what he means?
- Why do I always react that way?
- Why do I have such a lousy memory?
- What makes people tick, anyway?

IF YOU have ever asked any of these questions, or questions similar to them, you have already taken the first step toward becoming a researcher. Research is driven by the human need to know—to discover answers to questions we might have about ourselves, our world, and others. As human beings, we all share an important characteristic, which is the need to make sense out of our environment and our experiences. In other words, we all share the desire to discover the "truth." This search for the truth regarding human behavior is the hallmark of researchers in the field of psychology, and research is the scientific process that is initiated by the questions asked. A major goal of the researcher is to develop satisfactory explanations for behavior.

So, how do we go about obtaining knowledge? Research based on the scientific method is one route, but it is not the only route. Before we discuss the scientific method, let's take a look at some alternative approaches.

APPROACHES TO KNOWLEDGE

The Method of Authority

- A 5-year-old pulls his hand away before touching a hot stove because Mommy said it was dangerous.
- An 18-year-old college student is repeating his professor's explanation for why toddlers throw temper tantrums.
- A 27-year-old graduate student is citing a leading expert's view in her dissertation.
- A 40-year-old cut down on salt in her diet because her doctor said that it was bad for her blood pressure.

What do all these people have in common? They are all relying on the **method of authority,** one of the oldest approaches to knowledge. You accept that certain things are true because "they" said so. "They" are the authorities, or the experts in a particular field. When you were a child, you accepted the explanations offered by your parents because they were authority figures. As an adult, you turn to doctors, lawyers, teachers, and psychologists (just to name a few) for answers or advice. Each time you look in an encyclopedia, consult a textbook, or listen to an expert on a particular topic, you are relying on the method of authority. In your daily life, you are constantly bombarded with information from experts or authority figures: you are told to stop smoking and stop eating diets high in fat because they lead to cancer or heart disease; you are told that four out of five dentists recommend a certain toothpaste to prevent cavities; or you are informed that scientists have discovered a new gene linked to depression. If you stop smoking, switch to a different brand of toothpaste, or feel optimistic that a cure for depression is just around the corner, you have accepted the word of the experts without actually confirming these "facts" for yourself.

Relying on the method of authority is a part of human existence. For example, most people believe that atoms exist, though few people have ever seen one. People accept the notion that a high level of cholesterol is bad for the heart, although they have never tested it for themselves. Scientists also rely on the method of authority. Before beginning a research project, scientists review the literature in that particular area, accepting certain statements and theoretical positions, while treating others with skepticism. It is precisely this ability to accept some things while challenging others that is so important in scientific inquiry. It would be foolish to treat all findings with skepticism; after all, who has the time, ability, and energy to test everything? Even if you were able to test everything for yourself, it would be a waste of resources since instead of furthering a body of knowledge, you would be merely reinventing it. On the other hand, without skepticism and challenge, science and human knowledge do not advance.

The method of authority, therefore, has its advantages. You can save yourself time by drawing on an existing knowledge base, and you can rely on it as a stepping stone for further inquiry. But it has its disadvantages as well. Experts and authority figures may be quite impressive, but they are still human and human beings are not infallible. As such, experts may be biased, authority figures may abuse their power and status, and there are even times when the authorities or the experts are just plain wrong. In addition, experts frequently disagree. When each side in a court case provides an expert witness, which expert's view or explanation is correct? When two doctors offer two different diagnoses or methods of treatment, which one should be accepted?

When searching for information on the Internet, you must be especially careful, since anyone can publish a web page on any subject. A great deal of information is available, but it is important that you keep in mind the following criteria while doing online research. First, you need to ensure that the author is *qualified* to write on this particular topic. Are his or her qualifications listed on the web page? Make sure that the authors give an address, phone number, or e-mail address so that you can contact them to verify the information. Second, determine who is the intended *audience* of a particular web page. Articles written with an academic audience in mind tend to be more scholarly and contain more technical terms than articles written for a general audience. Third, is the information *current?* If the source is reliable, the authors tend to list the date for when the information was posted. In addition, the web page should display the date on which it was created and updated. Web sites or pages that are not frequently updated tend to have outdated information. Fourth, is the information *accurate?* Editors check printed publications for accuracy; Internet publications are self-published, and therefore the information may not be accurate. It is best to be on the safe side and to check the information obtained from the Internet against a printed source. Finally, make sure that the information is *unbiased* and impartial, and not merely the opinion of the author or advertisers. If the web page contains advertising that is related to the information being presented, the information may be biased in favor of the product being advertised.

As you can see, the method of authority, though an important and necessary approach, requires you to tread carefully and with a critical eye. Some questions to ask when faced with information from experts or authorities are: (a) is the source reliable? (b) is the information based on scientific testing? (c) have the findings been replicated? (d) is there a consensus among the experts?

The Rational Approach

Rationalism proposes that knowledge and the ultimate truth regarding various phenomena can be arrived at through reasoning alone. Therefore, according to this approach, experimentation or scientific testing is unnecessary, since pure reason alone is enough to demonstrate the self-evident truth of a discovery. A truth is considered to be self-evident because it is logical. If it were not logical, it would not be a truth.

Such arguments certainly have their place in the realm of philosophy, but to support their arguments scientists must rely on empirical observation through experimentation. Take, for instance, deductive logic, or syllogistic reasoning. This system of reasoning, introduced by Aristotle, proposes that arguments can be validated through deductive logic. Syllogistic reasoning includes a major premise, a minor premise, and a conclusion. You are probably familiar with the following famous syllogism:

Major premise:	All men are mortal.
Minor premise:	Socrates is a man.
Conclusion:	Therefore Socrates is mortal.

Note that in order to arrive at a valid or true conclusion, the major premise must be true and correct. If the major premise is false and incorrect, the conclusion is also incorrect. For example, look at the following syllogism:

Major premise:	All men are moral.
Minor premise:	Hitler was a man.
Conclusion:	Therefore Hitler was moral.

This example demonstrates why deductive reasoning alone is not enough; the conclusion we arrive at may seem logical, but if it is based on a false assumption, it is simply incorrect. Though used extensively by scientists in all fields of research, deductive reasoning and logic are not sufficient by themselves to offer scientific explanations for events and behavior. It is precisely the empirical nature of the scientist's approach to knowledge that allows it to be called the scientific method.

The Common-Sense Approach

- They spent money researching that? I could have told them.
- I'm not surprised by their results. It's just common sense.
- A child could have figured that out. They didn't need to spend time on an experiment.

At one time or another, you might have read or heard about the findings of a long, involved, and expensive research study and made a comment similar to the ones above. Why? Because most people pride themselves on having good common sense. Folk wisdom and popular sayings are frequently based on common sense. For example, take the saying, "birds of a feather flock together." The idea that the more similar people are, the more likely they are to be friends makes good common sense, right? Think about that for a moment. Now what about the alternative saying, "opposites attract?" Which one is correct? Similarly, we have the contradictory sayings, haste makes waste and he who hesitates is lost. Again, each one makes good sense, so which one is the "truth"? The point is, no matter how much sense an idea makes, until it is tested systematically, there is no way to know whether it is correct or under what conditions it is correct. Incidentally, social psychologists have found that opposites may attract, but the relationship tends not to last (Jamieson, Lyndon, & Zanna, 1987; Meyer & Pepper, 1977).

Common sense may also lead to the wrong conclusion. Consider the following question: If a person were to suddenly suffer a seizure and collapse on a street, would he or she be more likely to get help quickly on a crowded street or on a fairly deserted one? If you are like most people, you probably intuitively thought, a crowded street. In a series of experiments, Darley and Latane (1968) demonstrated that just the opposite is true, and they called the phenomenon the *bystander effect*. Their studies employed a confederate—someone who is "in on" the experiment but pretends to be a participant along with the other participants in the study. In one of the Darley and Latane studies, the confederate suddenly gasped and pretended to be having an epileptic seizure. The question of interest was how quickly the actual participants attempted to call for help. The study found that helping behavior decreased as the group size increased. If only one other person was present, help was immediate, whereas when five people were present, the participants hesitated for three full minutes before attempting to get help for the confederate.

As you can see, common sense may not always make as much sense as you think. However, it tends to be accepted at face value simply because it seems to make such good sense. Common sense does have a place in science; for example, it can serve as a stepping stone for setting up a research project in order to test an idea that seems to make perfectly good sense. However, as with reason and pure logic, common sense by itself is insufficient to arrive at the "truth." Does something strike you as good common sense? Terrific! Now put it to the test. Until you do, you just never know. The next approach does exactly that.

THE SCIENTIFIC METHOD

What Is Science?

Before you read any further, define the word "science." Although you are certainly familiar with the term and most likely use it correctly in conversation, you are probably finding it difficult to give a good definition. Maybe you said that science is biology, or chemistry, or nuclear physics. If that is the case, you were naming examples, or areas, of science rather than giving a precise definition of the term itself. Scientists themselves disagree on the proper definition of science. Tavris addressed this issue at the Annual Convention of the American Psychological Society in 1999 by saying that some define science by its goal, others define it by its tools, while still others define it by its subject matter. For example, according to Tavris, those who define science by its subject matter consider studying something tangible such as brain science, whereas studying intangible psychological states such as love or wisdom is not science. Similarly, the person who defines science by its tools may consider gaining information through a positron emission tomography (PET) scan science, while gathering information through an interview is not science.

Conant (1951) defined science as a connected series of theories and concepts derived from observation and experimentation that can lead to further experimentation and observation. Science, therefore, can be viewed as the process of searching for explanations, or for the causes of events, and it is defined by its method: the **scientific method.**

The method of authority, the rational approach, common sense, and the scientific method all share two important characteristics: each one is based on observation, and each one attempts to search for explanations and to discover the "truth" regarding human nature.

The scientific method incorporates important aspects of the other approaches. Scientists rely on the existing body of knowledge put together by experts in their field, and they rely on the deductive, logical reasoning of the rationalist. In addition, a scientist without common sense would not get very far. However, scientists go one step further: they gather empirical evidence to support or refute their ideas.

The scientific method is a systematic, empirical approach used by all scientists, be they physicists, biologists, astronomers, or psychologists. It is the methodical process of observation, prediction, experimentation, explanation, and refining of explanation. The refining of explanation typically leads to further observation, prediction, experimentation, explanation, and so on, as the scientist gathers more and more answers for the questions under consideration. The major goal of the scientist is to understand and explain behavior. What that particular behavior happens to be depends on the scientist. For a biologist, it may be the behavior of viruses; for an astronomer, the behavior of stars; and for a chemist, the behavior of molecules. Psychologists, naturally, study the behavior and mental processes of people, and at times of animals. But regardless of their fields of specialty, all scientists follow the same basic approach to reach those goals of understanding and explanation, and that approach is made up of a number of important elements.

The Basic Elements of the Scientific Method

You read in the previous section that, like all other approaches, the scientific method begins with *observation.* The scientist observes that certain events, called variables, tend to occur together. In other words, these events seem to be related in some way. The next step is to make a prediction on the basis of this observation, and the scientist formulates a **hypothesis.** A hypothesis is a tentative statement regarding the relationship between the variables. The hypothesis formulated must be testable, and the scientist conducts a *research study* during which empirical evidence is gathered through *scientific observation.* The empirical evidence gathered is what scientists call **data,** and it is the analysis of the data at the end of an experiment that allows the scientist to conclude that the hypothesis has either been supported or not supported.

Scientific observation is the step that differentiates the scientific method from rationalism or common sense. For no matter how logical or rational the relationship between certain events or variables seems, or how much common sense a relationship may make, until it is tested scientifically, there is no way to know for certain that there is in fact a cause-and-effect relationship. Scientific observation differs from casual observation in that it must meet certain restricting criteria. The first criterion is that the observation must be *empirical,* which means that it must be objective and measurable. The second criterion is a logical extension of the first one. If an observation is real and measurable, then others must be able to observe it as well. In other words, the observation must be *public;* it cannot be a private event that only the researcher can see. But if an event is public and observable by others, then it follows that the observation should be *repeatable,* which is the final criterion. Research findings that cannot be replicated do not contribute as much to the body of knowledge as do findings that can be confirmed by others. A "one-shot" observation that can never be repeated may indicate that chance, coincidence, or random events are operating.

For example, suppose I tell you that I have observed that I have ESP. Hopefully, before you believe this claim and stand in awe of me, you would like to verify it through scientific observation. First, you would want to measure my ESP ability by asking me to identify cards you are holding up outside of my view. By counting how many "hits" or correct responses I make as opposed to "misses" or incorrect ones, you can gain some measure of the extent of my talents. In addition, by measuring my ability to identify cards, you are verifying my original private observation; my performance is now public. However, suppose I get an impressive number of hits, should that convince you? That's right, it shouldn't. In order for me to truly have ESP, I should be able to repeat my amazing performance at least several times in order to rule out coincidence, chance, lucky guesses, or even cheating.

The Scientific Method in Action: An Example

Let's say that a psychologist casually *observes* that her children seem more aggressive in their play after watching violent cartoons. This tends to be a fairly consistent observation and over a period of time leads her to believe that there is a relationship between the two events: violent cartoons and aggressive play. Based on this apparent relationship, she makes a prediction. She *hypothesizes* that violent cartoons increase aggression, and therefore children watching such shows would be more aggressive than children watching nonviolent cartoons. In order to find support for her hypothesis, the psychologist conducts a carefully controlled *experiment,* in which she systematically examines the effects of different types of cartoons on children's play behavior. She is now engaging in *scientific observation;* during the experiment she collects *data,* which are measurements of the children's behavior during play time, following the cartoons. For example, the data may represent the number of times the children hit or pushed each other. Once all the data have been recorded, she selects the appropriate statistical method to *analyze* them, and, depending on the results of the analysis, her hypothesis that violent cartoons increase aggression will either be supported or refuted.

It is important to remember that, even if the data support the hypothesis, the psychologist cannot claim that this "proves" that violent television increases children's aggression. No matter how convincingly the data support the hypothesis, the hypothesis is never "proven" to be true; the data can only confirm or disconfirm the hypothesis. Why is that? As you will see in Chapter 7 (or may recall from your statistics class), prior to beginning the study, the experimenter limits the probability that the observed differences between conditions are due to chance or error. Therefore, even if statistical analyses show that this critical level of probability for error has not been exceeded, there is always the possibility that the observed differences were in fact due to chance. This concept is fully explained in Chapter 7, which discusses inferential statistics and hypothesis testing.

Nothing is more exciting than finding that an experiment worked out, that is, that the original hypothesis was supported. However, the research process does not end there. In fact, a successful experiment generates additional hypotheses which, in turn, must be tested. Figure 1.1 shows the steps involved in the research process.

The Assumptions of the Scientific Method

In their quest for knowledge, scientists make some basic assumptions about the world. The three major assumptions are **order, determinism,** and **discoverability.**

The first assumption is that there is a basic pattern to the occurrence of events due to an *order* in the universe. In other words, it is assumed that our world is ordered, rather than

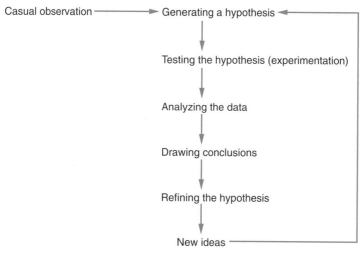

FIGURE 1.1 Steps in the research process.

chaotic, and that events, be they physical or psychological, do not occur randomly or haphazardly. If scientists did not assume that events occur in an orderly, systematic way, following some logical sequence, it would be futile to attempt to theorize about causality or to make predictions regarding any events.

A logical extension of the assumption of order is that all events must therefore have a cause. *Determinism* is the belief that for every event there are preceding events, or causes, although these antecedent circumstances may not be readily apparent. If you find your favorite crystal vase in pieces when you get home, you may not have seen what happened, but you will still assume that the breakage didn't happen out of the blue or by magic. You might begin to formulate some logical possibilities for why your vase broke: maybe it was the cat, maybe it was the curtain blowing in the wind. Scientists engage in research because they, too, assume that the event they wish to explain has a logical determinant that can be uncovered.

The final assumption goes hand in hand with the assumptions of order and determinism. If there is an orderly pattern to the occurrence of events, and all events are caused by other, preceding events, then it can also be assumed that each step in the causal chain can be traced and *discovered.* We may lack the knowledge, skill, technology, time, or money needed to answer certain questions, but that does not mean that there are no answers or that those answers are unknowable. For this reason, many scientists share the fundamental belief that given enough of the above-mentioned resources, the answers could be, and will be, discovered.

RESEARCH METHODS

Experimental vs. Nonexperimental Approaches

In their attempt to understand behaviors and mental processes, psychologists rely on various techniques or research methods. Each method has its advantages and limitations, as you will see when each approach is discussed in detail in later chapters.

Scientific research falls into two basic categories: **true experiments** and **nonexperimental designs.** The method the researcher ultimately chooses depends on the topic under investigation and on the questions being asked. *True experiments* entail systematic manipulation of one or more variables and observation of the effects of this manipulation on other variables. Systematic manipulation involves deliberately changing one or more variables and then observing the effects of this change on other variables. The question of interest is: Will changes in one variable produce changes in another variable? For example, if you want to see how room temperature affects learning, you can manipulate the first variable by changing the temperature in a room from cool to warm to hot. You can then observe the effects of each change in temperature by measuring the amount of learning under the different temperature conditions.

Because of this deliberate manipulation of variables, and the measurement of changes produced on another variable as a result of the manipulation, true experiments can demonstrate *cause-and-effect relationships.* It is this ability to attribute causality and to explain behavior from a causal perspective that makes true experiments the strongest research method. The example provided on the effects of violent cartoons on children's behavior was a true experiment. The psychologist manipulated one variable—the type of cartoon she showed the children—and observed the effects of this manipulation on another variable— the children's play behavior. If the children who watched the violent cartoons acted significantly more aggressively than the children who watched the nonviolent cartoons, it would be reasonable to attribute the different levels of aggression to the type of show watched.

In *nonexperimental research,* variables are not actively manipulated. Instead, the researcher observes events as they occur, with no deliberate interference. Since no manipulation is involved, causality cannot be established. Nonexperimental designs are considered *descriptive* in that they can describe behaviors or events, but they cannot make claims regarding the causes of those behaviors or events. Although "weaker" in this sense than true experiments, there are occasions when only a nonexperimental approach is appropriate, or even possible. Suppose you wished to study the mating habits of Canadian Geese, or the grooming behavior of adolescent girls, or the effects of x-ray exposure on birth defects, or the effects of alcohol consumption during pregnancy, or the way brain chemistry affects schizophrenic symptoms. Suppose you wished to find out how the average working mother feels about daycare, how college students regard required courses, or what African-Americans think about current race relationships. There are countless topics or behaviors of interest, and many of them cannot be approached with a true experiment. Three frequently used methods that qualify as descriptive rather than experimental are **naturalistic observation, survey research,** and **correlational studies.** Table 1.1 summarizes commonly used research methods.

Descriptive Studies

If a scientist did wish to study the mating habits of Canadian Geese, or the grooming behavior of adolescent girls, or the play behavior of children, he or she would most likely engage in what is called *naturalistic observation.* In such studies, the aim of the researcher is to collect data on the behavior of interest as it occurs in its natural setting and to accurately describe the behavior. The ability of the researcher to make predictions regarding the behavior under investigation is limited, as is the ability to attribute causality.

TABLE 1.1   RESEARCH METHODS

Research Method	Experimental	Survey Research	Naturalistic Observation	Correlational Studies
Purpose	To demonstrate cause-and-effect relationships between two or more variables.	To gather information about people's attitudes, opinions, behaviors, etc.	To collect data on the behavior of interest as it occurs in its natural setting.	To establish whether two or more variables are related and to describe the relationship.
Example	Studying the effect of practice on the number of errors made on a motor task.	Surveying the religious beliefs of college students in the United States.	Observing the toy preferences of children.	Studying the relationship between self-esteem and college GPA.
Limitations	Impossible, or unethical, to study certain variables experimentally.	Limited in its usefulness to make predictions or to explain the causes of behaviors.	Same as surveys. In addition, there is no control over outside factors.	Low to moderate control over outside factors. Cannot establish cause-and-effect relationships.

Survey research, on the other hand, gathers information about people's feelings, opinions, beliefs, attitudes, and behaviors through self-report questionnaires. To find out what attitude of African-Americans have about race relationships, or how working mothers feel about daycare, or what freshmen think about required courses, the researcher could administer a survey. The data collected represent people's responses to a series of questions, and as with naturalistic observation, the data are used for descriptive purposes only. Although a well-constructed survey can gather a large amount of useful information relatively inexpensively and quickly, it is still limited in its usefulness to make predictions or to explain the causes of behaviors.

Correlational studies are useful for establishing whether two (or more) variables are related, how they are related, and how strong that relationship is. In addition, they can be useful in making predictions regarding those variables. For example, graduate programs in psychology frequently have more applicants than openings. How do these programs determine which applicant would make a more successful Ph.D. candidate and which one would not? The correlational method can be useful in such an instance in making a fairly accurate prediction. First, the researcher can determine whether there is a relationship between certain characteristics of the applicants such as grade point average (GPA) or scores received on the Graduate Record Exam (GRE), and success in graduate school. If there is a relationship, or *correlation,* between those variables, then we can say that GRE scores or a student's undergraduate GPA can predict success in graduate school and that schools can use those criteria for admission. Notice once again that the stress is on description. You can say that there is a relationship between GPA, or GRE scores, and success in graduate school; you can say that the higher the GPA or GRE score, the greater the success; you can even say that this relationship is strong and that these are valuable predictors. What you cannot say is that success in graduate school is determined by a high GPA or high GRE scores. You can't say that because it is very possible that outside factors such as motivation and interest in the subject matter cause success in graduate school.

Correlational studies, therefore, have the same limitation as surveys and naturalistic observation in that they cannot determine the causes of behaviors. However, it is crucial to point out that this limitation does not imply that correlational studies are unimportant or have no place in science. Correlational studies are useful in investigating behaviors that could not be studied otherwise. For example, to examine the effects of alcohol consumption during pregnancy, it would be necessary to conduct correlational research. Even if researchers could find pregnant women who would agree to be in a true experiment where they would be systematically exposed to varying amounts of alcohol, it would be grossly unethical to conduct such a study. In Chapter 14, you will examine correlational techniques and their uses, and look at several important studies that were based on this method.

SAMPLES VS. POPULATIONS

- Twenty-six percent of high school seniors use marijuana (Treaster, 1994).
- Different areas of the brain are associated with different cognitive tasks (Farah, 1988).

How did researchers arrive at such conclusions? Did they survey all adolescents and high school students? Did they test all people on all cognitive tasks? The answer is clearly, 'no'. That would be not only impractical but downright impossible. Whether the investigator is engaged in experimental or nonexperimental research, the actual study is conducted on a **sample** drawn from the **population** of interest. The *population* is a set of all the people (or animals, objects, events) the researcher is interested in knowing about. For example, the population for the preceding statements would be, respectively, all adolescents; all high school seniors; all human beings. These would be the groups of individuals about whom the researcher wishes to make generalizations.

The *sample,* on the other hand, is a subset of the population. Samples are the individuals who were selected from the population to participate in the research project. For example, the adolescents, the high school seniors, and the participants in the cognitive experiment who were selected for the study constituted the sample. Research is conducted on the sample, and the results are generalized to the population.

Psychologists make an important assumption when they engage in the process of generalization. They assume that the results obtained from a sample of the population accurately reflect the population. For example, let's say that a psychologist conducts a survey on 500 working mothers in the United States, wishing to find out the income and level of job satisfaction of the typical working mom. The psychologist who conducts the survey assumes that the 500 women "speak for" the population of all working mothers. Can the psychologist make this assumption? The answer is: that depends. If the sample is *unbiased,* or **representative** of the population, then the answer is, yes. On the other hand, the results of a study based on a biased sample cannot be generalized. A *biased* sample is one in which the participants are not representative of the population of interest. Consider that hypothetical sample of 500 working mothers. If the sample includes mothers who do not work, working women without children, or women who neither work nor have children, the sample will not yield results that can be generalized to the population of working mothers. Similarly, since the main issue of interest is income and job satisfaction, if the sample is made up primarily of women with very high incomes, or conversely, mostly of women who make just the minimum wage, it will not be representative of the population where we can assume all economic strata are represented. Along the same lines, if the sample is made up of predominantly one ethnic group, we may not be able to generalize the findings to members of other ethnic groups.

The best way of obtaining an unbiased, representative sample is to randomly select participants from the population. Random sampling ensures that all members of the population have the same chance of being selected; therefore, the chance that only certain people, let's say minimum wage earners, would be selected is statistically slim. However, obtaining a representative sample is not as simple as it seems, and quite a bit of attention has been given to the issue of just how valid are the generalizations that researchers make regarding human behaviors. This issue becomes especially important when the researcher wishes to generalize across race, gender, or cultures. This important topic is addressed in Chapter 3, along with the major sampling techniques used.

THE ROLE OF THEORIES IN THE SCIENTIFIC METHOD

A **theory** is an organized body of statements or assumptions that generates hypotheses and attempts to explain behaviors within a specific framework. Theories are built on data gathered in the past, and they allow scientists to make predictions about future events. Therefore, theories are dynamic in that they are continually tested, refined, and revised, as new experimental evidence is gathered.

You have most likely learned in a General Psychology class that there are many schools of thought in psychology. A *school of thought* is essentially a group of psychologists who share a theoretical orientation. You may recall that one major school of thought in psychology is behaviorism, founded by John Watson (1878–1958). Behaviorists explain some learning within a specific theoretical framework that differs from how psychologists who follow the psychodynamic school of thought would explain it. For example, one theoretical view of the behaviorists is that learning occurs through principles of operant conditioning, namely, positive and negative reinforcement and punishment. This theory in turn generates several hypotheses that enable us to test the concept of learning through reinforcement. One possible prediction generated by this theory is that children given positive reinforcement for performing a task should learn the task in fewer trials than children not given positive reinforcement. Notice that this prediction can be tested. If the experimental results support this hypothesis, then another piece of evidence is added to the body of knowledge in support for the theory of learning through operant conditioning. On the other hand, if consistent testing fails to produce results that support the theory, then the theory will have to be revised or discarded.

Since the field of psychology is still divided into various schools of thought, it is considered to be in the pre-paradigmatic stage (Schultz & Schultz, 1992). A **paradigm** is a model, or a system, that is followed by the majority of the scientists within a given discipline, who agree upon major theoretical and methodological issues. An example of a field defined by a single paradigm is physics, where most scientists follow the Einsteinian paradigm. Once psychologists no longer belong to various schools of thought, but follow a common theoretical system, then the field of psychology is defined by a paradigm. Currently, each major school of thought attempts to explain human behavior and mental processes within its own theoretical framework, using its own tools and methodologies. Therefore, competing theories of learning, memory, motivation, abnormal behavior, and so on have arisen.

Even if the majority of the psychologists were to agree on a single paradigm, however, it is important to realize that paradigms change over time. Although the current paradigm in physics is Einsteinian, for nearly 300 years the accepted paradigm in physics was Newtonian, and the majority of scientists in the field worked within the Newtonian framework.

SUMMARY

- As human beings, we are driven by the need to understand events and behaviors around us, and in our search for knowledge and explanations we can take several routes.
- The method of authority entails relying on the word of experts or authorities on the topic of interest. However, unquestioning or exclusive reliance on this approach may stifle experimentation and the advancement of knowledge.
- The rational approach relies on logic and reason alone to arrive at explanations. Although logic is an important aspect of experimentation, by itself it is insufficient.
- Common-sense explanations tend to be taken at face value because they seem to make such good sense. However, common-sense explanations can turn out to be wrong, and without empirical evidence to support them they cannot be relied upon to fully explain events or behaviors.
- The scientific method incorporates aspects of the method of authority, the rational approach, and common sense, but it goes one step further by empirically testing hypotheses. Because of this additional step, it is a more reliable approach to knowledge.
- The elements of the scientific method are: casual observation, hypothesizing, scientific observation, data analysis, and theory updating.
- Scientific observation is empirical, public, and repeatable.
- The scientific method assumes that the universe is ordered; that events and behaviors are determined or caused by other events and behaviors; and that these causes are discoverable.
- The experimental method entails the systematic manipulation of variables. The effects of these manipulations on other variables are observed and measured. Because of the manipulation of variables, cause-and-effect relationships can be established.
- In nonexperimental studies, variables are not manipulated. Instead events are observed as they occur naturally, with no deliberate interference. Some frequently used nonexperimental approaches are correlational studies, naturalistic observation, and survey research. Causality cannot be inferred in nonexperimental studies.
- The population contains all the individuals the researcher wishes to study or know about, whereas the sample is a subset of the population selected for the research project. The sample must be unbiased and representative of the population in order for the results of the study to be generalizable to the population of interest.
- A theory is an organized body of assumptions that generates hypotheses and explains behaviors within a specific framework. Theories are said to be dynamic in that they are continually tested, refined, and revised in light of new experimental evidence.

KEY CONCEPTS

Correlational Studies   Hypothesis   Order   Scientific Method
Data   Method of Authority   Population   Survey Research
Determinism   Naturalistic Observation   Rationalism   Theory
Discoverability   Nonexperimental   Representative Sample   True Experiments
Experimental Studies   Designs   Sample

QUESTIONS

Short answers can be found in Appendix A.

1. Briefly describe how the method of authority differs from the scientific method.

2. Identify the approach to knowledge used in the following statements:

   a. Accepting a professor's explanation for human aggression without question

   b. Testing the effects of music on plant growth by exposing a group of plants to music and comparing their growth to that of plants not exposed to music

   c. Believing that noise interferes with concentration because it makes good sense

   d. Accepting that Socrates was mortal since all men are mortal and he was a man

   e. Excusing the negative behavior of boys as normal because "boys will be boys"

3. Were the following most likely experimental or nonexperimental designs?

   a. Studying the effects of room temperature on learning

   b. Studying the effects of crack cocaine on fetal development

   c. Studying the mothering behavior of gorillas

   d. Studying the effects of practice on the number of errors made

   e. Studying the relationship between education level and income

4. Identify the population and the sample in the following statements:

   a. A group of 50 fifth graders from New York State was selected for the study.

   b. There were 120 college freshmen participating in the project.

   c. A group of 120 dentists was surveyed from Detroit.

5. State the criteria for scientific observation.

6. Were the following results most likely obtained by a survey, naturalistic observation, a correlational study, or a true experiment?

   a. There was a strong relationship between drug abuse and memory loss.

   b. By increasing the noise level, we obtained a decrease in task accuracy.

   c. In our sample, 250 women stated that they work full time.

   d. On the playground, children seemed to prefer playmates of the same gender.

   e. When the music volume was increased, concentration was affected.

VARIABLES AND VARIANCE

WHY DO some students do so well on exams? Is it due to innate intelligence, motivation, good study skills, exceptional memory for information, the subject matter itself, or to the professor's ability to transmit the material? As you can see, there are many potential causes for getting good grades. Each of these potential causes, as well as the grades received by students, are **variables.** A variable is any condition, situation, object, event, or characteristic that may change in quantity and/or quality. For example, students differ in the amount and type of intelligence they possess, memory skills, level of motivation, and study skills. The amount of time spent studying for exams also varies, professors differ in their ability to transmit information, and some subject matter is difficult and abstract, while other materials are simpler and more concrete. In addition, grades received by students can also vary. **Constants,** on the other hand are events, objects, or situations that do not vary. The number of pennies in a dollar, the height of the Empire State Building, or the date for Valentine's Day, for example, does not vary.

DEFINITION OF VARIABLES

In Chapter 1, you read that in true experiments the researcher manipulates one variable and observes the effects of this manipulation on another variable. In other words, what the researcher is attempting to do is establish a cause-and-effect relationship between two variables. The variable being manipulated is the suspected "cause" in the relationship, whereas the variable being affected by the manipulation is the "effect." All true experiments, therefore, involve at least two variables: the **independent variable** and the **dependent variable.**

The *independent variable* is the factor or event that the experimenter thinks will *affect* another factor or event. To affect something is to influence it or change it in some way—for example, increase it, decrease it, bring it about, eliminate it, improve it, or worsen it. The independent variable, therefore, is the one that the experimenter *manipulates.* To manipulate is to assign different *levels* (amounts or types) of the independent variable. The levels are also called *conditions.*

Every experiment must have at least two levels of the independent variable so that comparisons may be made to see if the manipulation of the independent variable had any effect. For example, if you wish to see whether memory for information is affected by how people are tested, you could manipulate test type (the independent variable) by assigning at least two levels: recall and recognition. In the first level, or condition, participants are asked to recall information, whereas in the second level, or condition, the participants are asked to recognize information.

Independent variables may also be called *treatment variables* in that some form of treatment is administered to the participants. The treatment may be a new medication to treat schizophrenic symptoms, a new program designed to aid developmentally delayed children, or a new teaching method to improve student performance. In the simplest study, one group is exposed to the treatment, while another group does not receive any treatment. The group exposed to the treatment is called the **experimental group,** and the group that does not receive the treatment is the **control group.** As you can see, there are still at least two levels or conditions in the study.

So far we have discussed independent variables that the experimenter can actively manipulate by assigning different levels. She or he can even assign levels or conditions that indicate the absence of treatment, such as the control condition. To return to the student grades example, it is simple to manipulate study time, the type of material studied, even the teaching method used in order to observe any effects these manipulations may have on grades received. But what about factors such as intelligence, level of motivation, or memory? These are important factors that may play a large role in the grades students receive, yet the experimenter cannot actively manipulate these characteristics. Individual characteristics such as age, gender, race, ethnic background, motivation, intelligence, and personality are called **subject variables.**

Subject variables are by definition nonexperimental in that the researcher *selects* for these characteristics rather than *manipulates* them. For example, if you suspect that intelligence plays a large role in grades received, you may select groups of participants on the basis of scores received on an intelligence test. Keep in mind, however, that research involving subject variables cannot establish cause-and-effect relationships. Since participants for the study are selected on the basis of possessing or lacking some characteristic, trait, or ability, it cannot be assumed that aside from the particular trait, characteristic, or ability they were selected for, the participants are equivalent in all other aspects.

The following example may help to illustrate this important point. Let's say that a researcher is interested in studying the effects of smoking crack cocaine during pregnancy on babies' birth weight. In a true experiment, some pregnant women would be randomly assigned to a crack cocaine condition, others to a no crack cocaine condition, and both groups would be treated exactly the same except for the independent variable of crack. Obviously, such a study could not be conducted. Even if some pregnant women were willing to participate in the study, it would be grossly unethical to subject pregnant women to crack cocaine. Therefore, the researcher would need to locate a group of women who smoked crack cocaine while pregnant and another group of women who did not use the drug. Once their babies were born, the birth weights would be compared to see if there was a significant difference. But let us suppose that a difference in birth weight is found. Could the researcher assume that it was the crack use during pregnancy that caused it? No, he could not because most likely the two groups of women differed not just in the drug use, but also in terms of other variables such as receiving prenatal care while pregnant, diet and nutrition, and stress levels. Therefore, the difference in birth weight may have been caused by differences in diet, prenatal care, stress levels of the mothers, or a combination of factors. In other words, alternate explanations for the low birth weight could not be ruled out.

As you will see later in this chapter, careful control over outside factors, or variables, is the hallmark of the true experiment, and it is this control that allows experimenters to draw conclusions about cause-and-effect relationships. Without this ability to control for variables other than the independent variable, cause-and-effect conclusions are not possible, since alternative explanations cannot be ruled out.

Although subject variables are nonexperimental, for the sake of convenience they will be referred to as independent variables throughout the textbook.

The dependent variable in the experiment is the suspected "effect" in the relationship between two events. It is the behavior, or event, that the experimenter thinks will be affected, or changed in some way, by the manipulation of the independent variable. It is called a dependent variable because its measure or value is believed to be *dependent* on what the researcher does to the independent variable. For example, grades received by students may depend on intelligence, level of motivation, study skills, time spent studying, memory, type of material studied, or professors' ability to teach. As such, the grade received is the dependent variable. It is the variable the experimenter believes will be affected by the independent variable manipulations. To affect a variable is to change it in some way: increase it or decrease it, improve it or worsen it, bring it about or eliminate it, heighten it or lower it, and so on.

One simple way to remember the difference between independent and dependent variables is to keep in mind that the independent variable is what the experimenter controls, whereas the dependent variable is what the participant does. Before we go any further, see if you can identify the independent and dependent variables in each of the following statements without looking at the correct answers that follow:

1. Hunger has an effect on the aggression of cats.
2. Practice increases learning on spatial tasks.
3. Teaching method has an effect on grade received in statistics.
4. Medication reduces schizophrenic symptoms.

5. Motor performance is lowered by threat of punishment.

6. Imagery increases vocabulary.

7. Positive reinforcement leads to an increase in prosocial behaviors.

8. Short-term memory is reduced by marijuana consumption.

9. Attention is affected by room temperature.

10. Alcohol impairs reaction time.

The correct answers are:

Independent Variable	Dependent Variable
1. Hunger	Aggression
2. Practice	Learning
3. Teaching method	Grade received
4. Medication	Schizophrenic symptoms
5. Threat of punishment	Motor performance
6. Imagery	Vocabulary
7. Positive reinforcement	Prosocial behaviors
8. Marijuana	Short-term memory
9. Room temperature	Attention
10. Alcohol	Reaction time

Now see if you can identify which of the following studies involved manipulated independent variables and which involved subject variables:

1. Genetic background influences artistic ability.

2. An increase in room temperature leads to a decrease in learning.

3. Is there a gender difference in creativity?

4. Children solve problems differently than adolescents.

5. Concrete words are easier to recall than abstract words.

6. A computerized method of teaching improves math performance.

7. There was no difference between African-American and white children in a maze learning task.

8. There is no relationship between religious affiliation and income.

9. SAT scores are successful in predicting college performance.

10. Low-imagery words are harder to remember than high-imagery words.

The correct answers are:

1. Subject variable

2. Manipulated variable

3. Subject variable

4. Subject variable

5. Manipulated variable

6. Manipulated variable

7. Subject variable

8. Subject variable

9. Subject variable

10. Manipulated variable

OPERATIONAL DEFINITIONS

A researcher states that she is studying the effects of imagery on memory. By now you should be able to recognize that in this study imagery is the independent variable and memory is the dependent variable. But what exactly does she mean by "imagery"? vivid pictures shown to a participant? line drawings? images thought of by each participant? Furthermore, what does the researcher mean by "memory"? Is she referring to the ability to recall or recognize information? If yes, what type of information? Does she mean pictures, words, or sentences? Is she interested in long-term or short-term memory? As you can see, without additional information it is difficult to tell what exactly she is investigating. Any time you hear terms such as learning, anxiety, intelligence, child abuse, or shyness, to name only a very few variables researchers are interested in studying, if you find yourself asking, "what do they mean by intelligence, learning, anxiety, child abuse, or shyness?" you are asking the right question. Variables are not defined identically by all scientists; there are no universally agreed upon and acceptable definitions. Instead, each researcher must carefully and precisely define his or her experimental variables. These precise definitions are called **operational definitions.**

Operational definitions give clear, precise definition to variables, including how they are measured. In the previous example, "imagery" may be operationally defined as colored photographs accompanying words, and "memory" may be operationally defined as the number of words recalled after a five-minute delay period. On the other hand, a second researcher studying imagery and memory may operationally define "imagery" as line drawings illustrating a story and "memory" as the number of ideas recalled from the story one week later. As you can see, different researchers may choose different definitions for their variables.

Operational definitions can also explain how two studies may result in different findings. Let us say that a researcher reports that practice on a difficult motor task did not improve learning, whereas another researcher reports the opposite. The first researcher operationally defined learning as the amount of time it took the participants to complete a mirror-drawing task, whereas the second researcher defined learning as the number of errors made on the task. The first researcher found that participants in both the practice and the no practice conditions finished the task in about the same time, and concluded that practice had no effect on performance. The second researcher, however, found that the practice participants completed the task with significantly fewer errors than the no practice participants, and concluded that practice is important for learning. At times, the careful selection of an operational definition means the difference between having your hypothesis supported or not supported. The importance of operational definitions will be elaborated in Chapter 5.

VARIANCE

Variance is defined as observed differences in measures of the dependent variable. If, for example, you conduct a study on the effect of study time on grades received, the differences you observe between the grades of the participants is called variance. In a perfect world, any observed changes in the dependent variable would be due to the effects of the independent variable, and *only* the independent variable. In other words, the participants' grades should vary due to your manipulation of study time, and not to other, outside factors such as differential treatment of participants or individual differences in intelligence, motivation, and memory. Unfortunately, we don't live in a perfect world, and experimenters must be able to distinguish between variance due to the manipulation of the independent variable and variance due to outside, unwanted factors. In fact, one of the most important aspects of experimentation is controlling for sources of unwanted variance.

There are three major types of variance: **primary variance, secondary variance, and error variance.** Only the first type of variance is desirable, and, as you will see in Chapter 3, researchers take great care to control for the unwanted effects of secondary and error variance.

Primary variance is the observed differences in the dependent variable scores due to the manipulation of the independent variable. It is typically the reason research is conducted. The experimenter manipulates the independent variable and hopes that this manipulation will cause a change in the dependent measure. As such, primary variance is wanted, since it shows that the independent variable had an effect. In the earlier example, if you were to observe differences in the grades of the participants, hopefully this difference would represent primary variance, variance that is due to your manipulation of study time. Primary variance is also called *systematic variance* or *between-groups variance,* and in most cases the experimenter wants and predicts this kind of variance. All other forms of variance are unwanted and will affect the researcher's ability to draw conclusions about the results.

Secondary variance results from extraneous, outside factors that the experimenter did not recognize and/or control for. These extraneous variables may have an effect on the dependent variable, but the experimenter may not be interested in selecting these variables for an independent variable. For example, both meaningfulness and word frequency are known to affect memory (Cofer, 1971; Hall, 1954); however, a researcher may choose to study only the effects of word frequency. In this instance, word frequency is the independent variable, and meaningfulness is an extraneous, secondary variable that must be controlled. Conversely, the experimenter may select meaningfulness as the independent variable, in which case it is word frequency that she must control. What differentiates an extraneous, secondary variable from the independent variable is the experimenter's intent. Any secondary variable may be chosen as the independent variable. On the other hand, any variable whose effects the experimenter is not systematically examining is considered a potential source of secondary variance. Therefore, one researcher's independent variable may be another researcher's unwanted secondary variable, and vice versa.

Variables that lead to secondary variance may change the dependent variable scores in a consistent way, either elevating or depressing the dependent measures. When the secondary variable interacts with the independent variable, it is called a **confound.** Since the confounding variable consistently co-varies with the independent variable, it is difficult to separate the effects of the independent variable from those of the confounding variable.

For example, let's say that you are interested in testing the hypothesis that concrete words such as table, chair, and lamp are easier to remember than abstract words such as mercy, poverty, and injustice. Unfortunately, you only have two hours in the morning and two hours in the evening to conduct the study, and so you test all your concrete words-condition participants in the morning and all your abstract words-condition participants in the evening. You find that, indeed, recall of concrete words was significantly better, and so you conclude that your hypothesis is supported.

Is this a logically compelling conclusion? The answer is no, because the unrecognized secondary variable, time of day, is confounded with the independent variable of word type. Yes, it is possible that concrete words are easier to remember, but it is equally possible that the participants are fresher in the morning, and therefore their ability to learn and remember is enhanced. In other words, the variable of time of day may be having a differential effect on the levels of the independent variable: enhancing performance in the concrete condition, while impairing it in the abstract condition. At this point, it is impossible to tell whether the observed variance in recall is due to the independent variable of word type, to the secondary confounding variable of time of day, or to both variables.

Not all confounds are considered serious threats to the integrity of the experiment. Secondary variables that have minimal or no effect on the dependent variable will not pose serious problems. What determines the degree to which a researcher should be concerned with a confounding variable is the degree to which that variable is known to have an effect on the dependent variable. For example, if you have more male participants in one condition and more female participants in the other condition, it will not pose a problem if the dependent variable is not affected by gender. Unfortunately, the researcher may not always know the degree to which a confound will affect the dependent variable; for this reason, it is best to be vigilant and to treat all outside variables as potential confounds.

Error variance is the last source of variance, and it is also called *within-groups variance*. Unlike secondary variance, which has a consistent effect on the dependent variable, error variance affects the dependent variable in an *inconsistent* manner. Error variance may occur as a result of inappropriate or inconsistent measuring devices, incorrect data recording or analysis, or inconsistent treatment of the participants. For example, using a stopwatch to measure reaction time may be inappropriate if the watch is not sensitive enough to measure time in milliseconds. Similarly, if the computer presenting the stimuli is not programmed correctly, it may show some stimuli for 1 second, others for 1.5 seconds, and still others for 2 seconds. Careful experimenters calibrate and test their equipment prior to conducting the study, and they ensure that every instrument is in proper working condition.

Experimenters should also make every effort to treat all participants the same, especially in terms of explaining instructions and allowing practice trials prior to the actual experiment. For example, if some participants are given written instructions that they may take as much time as needed to read while others are given a rushed verbal explanation, this may lead to error variance. Similarly, if some participants are allowed practice trials prior to beginning the experiment while others are not, then the participants who practiced may perform better, leading to inconsistent variability in scores.

Treating all participants with the same level of patience, courtesy, and consideration may seem like common sense, but researchers are human and by the time they get to the twentieth participant of the day, patience and courtesy may be at a minimum. The temptation to be a little less thorough in explaining the instructions than to earlier participants may be fairly great. However, deviation from consistent treatment may lead to inconsistent scores, which in turn will make it impossible to isolate the effect of the independent variable.

Error variance may also stem from individual differences. Participants in experiments are individuals, and as such they have their own history, genetic makeup, personalities, abilities, environments, skills, expectations, and competencies, just to name a few possible sources of individual differences. Any and all of these differences may lead to inconsistencies in scores, giving rise to error variance. However, individual differences may also lead to secondary variance. When these individual differences have a consistent effect on the scores, they are considered sources of secondary variance. When the individual differences have an inconsistent effect, they are sources of error variance.

KERLINGER'S PRINCIPLES OF CONTROL

How do you ensure that the variance you observe in scores is in fact due to your manipulation of the independent variable and not to secondary, or error, variance? In 1973, Kerlinger proposed the following: (1) Maximize primary variance, (2) control secondary variance, and (3) minimize error variance.

Maximizing Primary Variance

Essentially, maximizing primary variance means that you take every step to ensure that your independent variable will have an effect. Remember, this is "good" variance; it is variance that you predict and hope to obtain as a result of your manipulation of the independent variable. Furthermore, you want to be able to say that the differences you observe between groups or conditions are due to the independent variable, and not to confounding or error. You want to obtain as large a between-groups (or conditions) variance as possible, since this "good" primary variance is going to be competing with "bad" variance, as you will see later in the chapter on statistical tests of significance. It is the ratio of "good" variance to "bad" variance that ultimately determines whether your hypothesis turns out be supported or not supported. There are three steps you may take to ensure that you get large primary variance.

First, choose *extreme levels* for the independent variable; that is, do not select levels that are very close or similar to one another in quality and/or quantity. For example, suppose that you are interested in studying the effects of caffeine on reaction time, and you predict that people will be significantly faster in the caffeine condition than in the no caffeine condition. You give participants in the caffeine condition a glass of soft drink known to contain caffeine, and then you compare their reaction time to that of participants in the no caffeine condition. You find no significant difference and conclude that caffeine has no effect on reaction time. What is the problem here? Well, it is very possible that the two levels of the independent variable were too close to each other in value. Most likely a glass of soft drink does not elevate caffeine levels in the body enough to produce a significant difference in reaction time.

A similar problem may occur if the researcher is examining the effects of practice on a difficult task, with one group receiving five practice trials and the other receiving no practice trials prior to performing the actual task. Once the number of errors are compared, the researcher finds no significant difference in performance and concludes that practice has no effect on reducing errors. As with the previous example, the lack of primary variance is most likely due to the researcher not having chosen extreme levels. For a difficult task, five practice trials may simply not be enough to produce a significant effect.

There are times, however, when choosing extreme levels is not possible or advised. Studies involving drugs or alcohol, for example, may endanger the welfare of the participants if extreme levels are chosen. Even with the above example of investigating the effect of practice trials, it is possible that by the time the participant finishes 25 practice trials on a difficult task, he or she is fatigued, bored, or annoyed to the point where performance on the actual task will suffer. In such cases it is more prudent to use the second method of maximizing primary variance: choosing *optimal levels*. This is easier said than done, since frequently researchers do not know what the optimal levels are. Of course, the experimenter could keep running a series of studies with just two levels of the independent variable until the optimal level was found, but this would be time consuming, not to mention inconvenient.

The simplest way of locating the optimal level is to employ the third method of maximizing primary variance, which is to assign *several levels* to the independent variable. This method of assigning several levels is advantageous for three reasons. First, as stated earlier, it can lead to determining the optimal levels for the independent variable. Second, it increases the probability that a significant difference will exist between at least two of the conditions. In other words, the more levels your independent variable has, the more you have maximized the probability that there will be a significant difference between at least two of those levels. Finally, having more than two levels of an independent variable enables the researcher to detect a *curvilinear relationship* between the independent and dependent variables, should one exist. Although curvilinear relationships are discussed in Chapter 6, a brief description here may be helpful. The relationship between the independent and dependent variables is said to be curvilinear when an increase in the independent variable value leads to an increase in the dependent variable measure but only up to a point: then the dependent variable measure starts decreasing. Of course, the opposite is also true: an increase in the independent variable leads to a decrease in the dependent variable up to a certain point, after which the dependent variable measure starts increasing. When the independent variable has only two levels, curvilinear relationships cannot be detected.

Controlling Secondary Variance

Controlling secondary variance is one of the most important aspects of good research methodology. Once the potential sources of secondary variance are identified, they should either be eliminated or held constant. Holding constant means maintaining consistency across all the experimental sessions. Essentially, all participants are treated exactly the same, with only the independent variable varying between them. Holding extraneous, secondary variables constant means that all the participants, in all the conditions, are exposed to them in the same way. If, for example, you suspect that room temperature may have an effect on learning, and you are not interested in systematically examining the effects of room temperature—in other words, it is not your independent variable—then make sure that all the participants are tested under the same temperature condition. By holding temperature constant, you are controlling a source of secondary variance.

Let us look again at the previous example of the study that examined the effects of word type on memory. Remember that you had only two hours in the morning and two hours in the evening to test the participants' memory for abstract and concrete words. If all the concrete condition participants are tested in the morning, and all the abstract condition participants are tested in the evening, there's confounding of time of day with word type. One way to deal with this potential source of secondary variance would be to give up one of the experimental sessions, either the morning or the evening one, and to test all the participants at the same time of day. This would extend the time it would take to finish the experiment, but the extra time would be well worth it. On the other hand, suppose you had a deadline to meet and could not, or would not, give up valuable time. What would you do in that case? If you said, Test half the participants in each condition in the morning, and the remaining participants in each condition in the evening, you were correct. This way, if the participants in the concrete condition still recall more words, no one could say that it might be due to being fresher in the morning.

In the next chapter you will learn about the potential sources of secondary variance and the steps experimenters take to control them.

Minimizing Error Variance

Kerlinger's final principle of control is to minimize error variance. Error variance may be minimized, but as you will see in Chapter 3, it can never be eliminated. No matter how careful the researcher, how strong and appropriate the research design, how meticulous the data collection and analysis, there will always be a certain amount of random error, or "noise," in an experiment. It is the experimenter's skill that allows him or her to separate the effects of the independent variable (primary variance) from that produced by random sources of error variance.

A Sample Problem for Review

Now that you have a basic understanding of variables and variance, let's review this chapter by revisiting the example used in Chapter 1 on the effects of television on children's aggression.

A researcher hypothesized that violent television increases children's aggression. She randomly assigned 20 children into a violent condition (Group I) and 20 children into a nonviolent condition (Group II). Each group consisted of 10 male and 10 female children. Group I watched 30 minutes of a cartoon rated as violent by independent adult observers, while Group II watched 30 minutes of a cartoon rated as nonviolent. Both groups were tested in the early afternoon by the same experimenter. The children were not allowed to have any candy, soda, or "junk food" while watching the show. Following the viewing of the cartoons, both groups of children were given a 20-minute play period, during which the experimenter recorded the number of times the children hit, kicked, or pushed each other. Analysis of the data showed that Group I committed a significantly greater number of aggressive acts than Group II, supporting the hypothesis.

At this point, you should be able to answer the following questions. Try to do so without peeking at the answers.

1. What was the independent variable?
2. What were the levels?
3. How was the independent variable operationally defined?
4. What was the dependent variable?
5. How was the dependent variable operationally defined?
6. What measures did the researcher take to control for extraneous variables?
7. Can we rule out alternative explanations for the children's aggression?

Now let's take a look at the answers to see how successful you were:

1. The independent variable was the type of television show the children watched.
2. The levels were violent and nonviolent.
3. Thirty minutes of cartoons rated as violent or nonviolent by independent adult raters. Note that "violent and nonviolent television show" needed to be clarified. It could have meant any type of show: a war movie, action adventure, police drama, or just about anything shown on television. In this study, it was defined as cartoons. In addition, what is violent to one person may not be to another; therefore, independent adult raters were asked to view each show and rate them for violence.
4. The dependent variable was aggression.
5. The number of times the children hit, kicked, or pushed each other. Note that "aggression" needed to be defined. Did the researcher mean physical or verbal aggression? Here, it was limited to physical aggression.
6. Same experimenter, same time of day, same amount of television (30 minutes), same amount of play time (20 minutes), no snacks, same number of boys and girls in each condition.
7. Pretty much. Notice that factors that may have compromised the experiment were carefully controlled for. For example, gender was balanced across the conditions to eliminate the potential confound of there being more boys or girls in either condition. Also, just in case aggression increases due to the boredom of sitting watching television, both groups watched the same amount. Regarding junk food, it was eliminated altogether, just in case there is something to the so-far-unsupported hypothesis that sugar increases hyperactivity. In addition, except for gender, the children were *randomly* assigned into conditions, which theoretically equated the two groups in terms of individual differences in aggression. Therefore, the alternative explanation that perhaps Group I had more aggressive children to begin with is unlikely. The concept of random assignment is crucial and will be fully explored in the next chapter.

SUMMARY

- In the majority of experiments, the researcher attempts to establish a cause-and-effect relationship between two or more variables.
- A variable is any condition, situation, object, event, or characteristic that may change in quantity and/or quality.
- The experimenter manipulates the independent variable, and the effects of this manipulation are then observed on the dependent variable.
- To manipulate a variable is to assign several levels or conditions. There must always be at least two levels or conditions, so that comparisons may be made between them. At the most basic level, there is typically a treatment condition and a control condition.
- The independent and dependent variables must be operationally defined, which gives a precise definition of these variables, including how they are measured.
- Once the independent variable has been manipulated, all other sources of variance must be controlled either by eliminating them or holding them constant.
- Holding a variable constant means maintaining consistency in the experimental sessions. All participants are treated the same, with only the independent variable varying between them.
- Variance is the observed differences in measures of the dependent variable. There are three major types of variance: primary variance, secondary variance, and error variance. Only primary variance is desirable.
- According to Kerlinger's Principles of Control, the researcher should maximize primary variance, control secondary variance, and minimize error variance.
- Primary variance may be maximized by choosing extreme levels, optimal levels, or several levels of the independent variable.

KEY CONCEPTS

Confound	Dependent Variable	Independent Variable	Secondary Variance
Constants	Error Variance	Operational Definitions	Subject Variables
Control Group	Experimental Group	Primary Variance	Variables

QUESTIONS

Short answers can be found in Appendix A.

1. Identify whether the following are variables or constants:
   a. The height of the Chrysler Building
   b. The temperature in July
   c. The weight of a participant
   d. The method a professor uses to teach psychology
   e. The number of errors made on a spatial task
   f. The imagery used in advertisements
   g. The ethnic background of participants

2. Identify the independent and dependent variables in the following statements:
   a. The mood of the participants depended on the weather.
   b. An increase in print size led to an increase in memory for words.
   c. Grades in statistics were affected by the software used in class.
   d. There was a decrease in errors when training was given.

e. The race of the participants had no effect on their product preferences.

f. Absence makes the heart grow fonder.

g. Performance improved as a result of verbal feedback.

h. The reaction time of males was significantly faster than that of females.

3. How would you operationally define the following variables?

   a. anxiety

   b. depression

   c. intelligence

   d. memory

   e. aggression

   f. learning

   g. helping behavior

4. Identify the experimental and control groups in the following statements:

   a. In order to examine the effects of alcohol on driving ability, Group 1 was given alcohol, while Group 2 received no alcohol.

   b. In a study on the effects of practice on performance, Group 1 did the task without practice, while Group 2 received 20 practice trials.

   c. To investigate the effects of imagery on learning, Group 1 saw 40 words with pictures below them, while Group 2 saw the same words without pictures.

   d. To demonstrate the negative effect of marijuana on motor skills, Group 1 performed a motor task after being exposed to marijuana, while Group 2 performed the same task without marijuana.

   e. In an experiment on the effect of music on mood, Group 1 sat in silence for 20 minutes, while Group 2 listened to music for 20 minutes.

5. List, explain, and give examples for how you would maximize primary variance.

6. An investigator wants to see whether packaging information affects the way people rate colognes. The same cologne is put into three boxes: a brown box that says, Be mysterious; a blue box that says, Be romantic; and a yellow box that says, Be unforgettable. In this study,

   a. the type of cologne is confounded with box color.

   b. packaging info is confounded with box color.

   c. packaging info is confounded with type of cologne.

   d. everything is valid.

7. An experimenter conducted a study on the effects of stress on the ability to learn a difficult motor task. Group I learned the task while being interrupted every two minutes, while Group II learned the task without interruption. The researcher counted the number of errors made on the task. As expected, Group I made significantly more errors on the task.

   a. State the independent variable.

   b. How was the independent variable operationally defined?

   c. State the levels of the independent variable.

   d. State how the dependent variable was operationally defined.

VALIDITY, CONTROL, AND GENERALIZING

IN **CHAPTER 2,** you learned that a crucial feature of experimentation is the need to control for unwanted sources of variance. If secondary variance is not controlled and error variance is not minimized, then the validity of the experiment is compromised. In 1957, Campbell distinguished between internal and external validity. Ideally, researchers should aim for both. However, as you will see, one paradox of experimentation is that by maximizing internal validity, the researcher may be reducing external validity and vice versa. On the other hand, depending on the experimenter's intent, this tradeoff between the two types of validity may not be a serious concern.

INTERNAL AND EXTERNAL VALIDITY

Internal Validity

Internal validity refers to the researcher's ability to state that the relationship she or he predicted between the independent and dependent variables does indeed exist, and that this relationship is due to the effects of the independent variable and not to extraneous, uncontrolled variables. Simply put, if the study is well designed and well controlled, and if alternative explanations for the results can be ruled out, it is said to have internal validity. It is crucial to understand the concept of alternate explanations. In every experiment the researcher forms a hypothesis, or a prediction for the outcome of the experiment. When the study is finished, that hypothesis is either supported by the data or it is not supported. If the data support the hypothesis, the researcher needs to be able to say that the results are due to the manipulation of the independent variable, and not to outside factors such as extraneous variables. In other words, alternative or rival explanations need to be ruled out.

Let us return for a moment to the memory experiment example presented in Chapter 2, where you learned that if you tested all the participants in the concrete condition in the morning and all the abstract condition participants in the evening, you would have confounded your study. The presence of the confounding variable—the time of day when participants were tested—would not allow you to rule out alternative explanations for your findings. The superior performance in the concrete condition may be due to participants being more alert and refreshed in the morning, and not to the effects of the independent variable.

Extraneous, uncontrolled variables lead to alternate explanations for the outcome of the experiment, which is why control procedures are so crucial. The more alternative explanations exist, the less validity the study has. Thoughtful researchers deal with this problem right from the start, when they first design the experiment. Once the independent variable has been selected and its levels have been determined, potential alternative explanations are considered. In other words, the researcher asks, "What other factors could affect my dependent variable? What other explanations would be possible for the experiment's outcome?" Once these potential threats to internal validity have been identified, the researcher makes every effort to eliminate or control for them, even if it means having to redesign the experiment.

External Validity

External validity refers to the *generalizability* of the study. Recall that in Chapter 1 you read about samples and populations. The researcher selects a sample of participants from the population of interest, conducts the study, and then generalizes the findings from the sample back to the population. The extent to which the experimenter can make generalizations about the results is external validity. If the researcher can extend the findings beyond the experimental setting and the sample of participants tested, then the study is said to have external validity. In sum, external validity is the extent to which the observed relationship between the independent and dependent variables in the experiment can be generalized to other settings, other people, and other circumstances.

For example, let's say that a researcher was interested in developing a new method for teaching vocabulary words to elementary school children. She hypothesized that children taught with vivid imagery would learn the words faster than would children taught without imagery. She randomly assigned 30 children to the imagery condition and 30 children to the no imagery condition. In the imagery condition the children saw a list of words with a picture next to each word, while in the no imagery condition the children learned the same list of words but without the pictures. As predicted, the children learned significantly more words in the imagery condition. At this point, if the researcher can generalize the findings from her *sample* of 60 participants in the experiment to elementary school children in *general,* then the study has external validity. In other words, if imagery truly enhances learning, then elementary school children from a wide variety of schools should benefit from learning vocabulary words accompanied by imagery.

Internal vs. External Validity

Earlier in the chapter you read about the possibility of a tradeoff between internal and external validity. By now you know that the more carefully you control the experiment, the more internal validity the study has. However, the stricter you control conditions in a laboratory setting, the less the laboratory setting may resemble real life and the less you may be able to generalize your findings. Should this be a concern? The answer depends on the type of research that is being conducted: **basic research** or **applied research.**

Basic research involves the testing of hypotheses generated by a particular theoretical framework. The purpose of basic research is to gather a body of "evidence" or knowledge that supports a given theoretical position. Although it would be an added bonus for the scientist to be able to apply his or her findings to real-life situations, this ability to go beyond the laboratory setting is not the primary goal of the researcher. For example, let's say that you are interested in the Levels of Processing (LOP) theory of human memory (Craik & Lockhart, 1972). According to Craik and Lockhart, the more deeply the information is encoded, or processed, during study time, the greater the ability to retrieve the information during test time. Given this condition, you may decide to test this theoretical position by hypothesizing that participants who were given a deep level of encoding instructions during the study phase would recall more words than participants who were given a shallow level of encoding instructions. At this point, you may not be concerned with the applied value of the LOP theory, but only with finding support for it in the laboratory. Therefore, you would be less concerned with trading off external validity for strong internal validity.

Applied research, on the other hand, is conducted in order to predict behavior in the real world (as opposed to the laboratory) or to solve real-life problems. If the intent of the researcher is to predict behaviors in their natural setting, or to solve problems in the real world, then the researcher should be concerned with external validity. In general, applied research strives for external validity: the ability to apply the findings to real-life situations and settings.

The fields of basic and applied research are not necessarily two separate and distinct dichotomies. Frequently they overlap and, even more frequently, applied research is founded on basic research. An example of this overlap, or interrelationship, can be seen in an area of psychology known as *human factors.* Human factors research is the application of knowledge regarding human abilities such as memory, learning, perception, attention, and so on, to the design of tools, machines, or manuals used by people in the real world. In other words, scientists engaged in human factors use the knowledge derived from basic research on human abilities in order to design, among other things, more user-friendly computers, software, aircraft cockpits, telephones, and answering machines.

This is not to imply that basic research has nothing to do with the real world or that scientists engaged in basic research have no interest in how their findings may apply to real life. It is merely to point out that whether the researcher is willing to compromise external validity for the sake of internal validity, or vice versa, depends on the primary goal of the research project. In fact, the long-held belief that external validity is compromised by strengthened internal validity has been questioned recently (Anderson, Lindsay, & Bushman, 1999).

Anderson, Lindsay, and Bushman conducted a massive study that compared the findings of laboratory research and field research articles. They analyzed 288 articles published in psychological journals, and their question of interest was whether the effects of the same independent variables on the same dependent variables were consistent in laboratory and field settings. They were interested in seeing whether the results found in a laboratory were comparable to results found in real-world or field research settings. Their results showed a high consistency between laboratory and field settings, indicating that the artificial controls applied in the laboratory did not compromise external validity. Anderson et al. (1999) offer the following statement regarding the concern over the internal and external validity tradeoff:

> As long as scholars in both settings keep in mind the complementary pitfalls of too little control over extraneous variables (leading to low internal validity) and of overgeneralizing from the specific features of a specific study (leading to low external validity), we believe the psychological research enterprise will continue to succeed. (p. 8)

SECONDARY VARIANCE AND CONTROL

Secondary variables can affect both the internal and external validity of the experiment, depending on their source. In the previous chapter you were introduced to the concept of secondary variance and to Kerlinger's Principles of Control. According to Kerlinger, secondary variables should be eliminated when possible or, if that is not possible, held constant. In addition, secondary variables can also be randomized and in certain instances even be made into or considered an additional independent variable. The following section lists some potential sources of unwanted variance. As you study these sources, keep in mind that whether the experimenter should worry about a particular source of secondary variance depends on the research design.

Sources of Secondary Variance

Factors that affect internal validity include the following:

- **Nonrandom assignment** of participants into the conditions. If the participants are not randomly assigned into the conditions, all the "competent" participants may end up in the experimental condition, while the "less competent" ones may end up in the control condition. In this instance, the scores of the experimental group will be superior to the scores received by the control group, regardless of how the independent variable was manipulated.

- **Maturation** of participants, which refers to how participants change over time. As the experiment progresses, especially if it is a lengthy one, people grow tired, frustrated, hungry, or bored. As such, the dependent variable measure may indicate maturation effects rather than effects of the independent variable. In addition, as you will see in a later chapter, when the experimental design entails pretest and posttest measures, the possibility that maturation is confounded with the independent variables is a possibility, if the experimenter does not control for it.

- **Order or pretest effects,** which occur when performance on a second task is affected by the first task regardless of the independent variable. For example, students may do better on the Scholastic Assessment Test (SAT) the second time due to practice effects, not because they enrolled in a training course. In a similar vein, participants may make more errors on the second task not because it is more difficult than the first task, but because of fatigue or boredom.

- **Regression toward the mean,** which is a statistical phenomenon that tends to occur when participants are selected on the basis of extreme scores on some measure. For example, let's say you are interested in studying low- and high-sensation seekers. If you select participants on the basis of their extremely low- or extremely high-sensation seeking score on a personality inventory, over time the high scorers will regress toward the mean or average sensation-seeking score. Therefore, if you were to assess their sensation seeking a second time, they would tend to have lower sensation-seeking scores even if they were not exposed to any treatment between test 1 and test 2.

- **History,** which refers to the passing of time between multiple observations. Studies that entail a before and after measure—meaning before and after the introduction of the independent variable—may have history as a potential confounding factor. Events that occur between the multiple measures (test 1, test 2, and so on) may affect the dependent variable and mask the true effects of the independent variable. For example, let us say that an investigator was interested in seeing whether people's attitudes regarding the treatment of prisoners could be manipulated by showing a film. On Friday, he measured the participants' initial attitude toward the treatment of prisoners, and on Monday, he showed a film that was contrary to the initial attitude. Following the film, the participants' attitude was once again measured. Unfortunately for the experimenter, on Saturday there was a major prison riot, which was covered extensively by the media. As you can imagine, any change (or for that matter, no change) in the participants' initial attitude might be due to this intervening event rather than to the effect of the film.

- **Subject mortality,** which affects studies that are either longitudinal, meaning long term, or require several experimental sessions. Participants may drop out of the study altogether or may not show up for a subsequent session. This tends to affect the more tiresome, difficult, or frustrating experimental condition, resulting in differential loss of participants. For example, if the independent variable is stress, and the experimenter is measuring the number of errors made as a function of stress, it is highly probable that it will be the high-stress condition participants who will not return to complete the study.

- **Different time and place** of testing, which should be held constant for all participants.
- **Differential treatment** by the experimenter which could refer to any factor that is not held constant. For example, all participants should receive the same instructions, the same number of practice trials, if any, and the same amount of time to learn the task.

Factors that can affect the external validity of a study include:

- **Pretest sensitization,** which occurs when the pretest alerts the participants to the hypothesis and/or treatment variable. This sensitization then leads the participants to respond differently on the posttest than they might have if there had been no pretest. For example, let's say that you are given a pretest to assess your attitude toward abortion, and then you are exposed to the independent variable, which is a film on abortion. It wouldn't take you long to put two and two together and think that the experimenter is interested in seeing whether the film could change your initial attitude. When it's time to take the posttest attitude measure, you might respond differently than you would have, had you not linked the pretest to the independent variable. As you can see, in pretest sensitization the pretest interacts with the treatment.
- **Reactive effects,** which refer to the participants' awareness that, since they are taking part in an experiment, their behaviors are being observed and measured. As a result, the participants' behaviors or responses may not be "natural," or true to real-life situations. For example, if you are being observed as you complete a difficult task, you may take more care in avoiding errors than you would in a more natural, real-life situation. In addition, the strictly controlled, artificial setting of the research laboratory may affect the experimenter's ability to generalize the findings. In other words, the external validity of the experiment may be reduced. Reactive effects are covered in detail in the next chapter.
- **Multiple-treatment interaction,** which affects experiments in which each participant experiences every level of the independent variable, or variables. If having participated in one condition changes the way a participant responds in the second condition, then we can say that there is multiple-treatment interaction. For example, if the researcher is studying the effects of alcohol and marijuana on reaction time, then a participant's consumption of alcohol in the first condition may interact with the marijuana in the second condition. If the participant had both alcohol and marijuana, the researcher would not be able to tell whether the participant's reaction time reflected the effects of alcohol, marijuana, or an interaction of the two.

As mentioned earlier, it is the research design that determines whether any of the above-mentioned sources of unwanted variance should be of concern to the experimenter. For example, pretest sensitization is not a problem if the design does not include a pretest. Similarly, if the study is not long term (longitudinal) or does not involve multiple sessions, subject mortality is not a potential source of unwanted variance. In later chapters, you will revisit many of these potential sources when the particular type of design that might be affected is discussed.

CONTROLLING SECONDARY VARIANCE

Eliminating Secondary Variables

Whenever possible, eliminating unwanted variables is an excellent way of dealing with secondary variance. For example, one potential source of unwanted variance arises when the participant is aware of, or even thinks she is aware of, the hypothesis and/or the desired treatment effect. Suppose that a group of psychologists is clinically testing the effects of a new drug on depression. They give the drug to 20 participants who have been diagnosed with depression, while a control group of participants receives no treatment. Following the treatment phase, both groups are assessed for depression and it is found that the treatment group has improved but the control group has not. At this point, can the researchers conclude that the drug is effective in reducing depression? No, they cannot because alternative explanations for the improvement cannot be ruled out.

For example, it is possible that the participants improved simply because they *expected* to improve. In other words, if the participants believed that the medication would improve their mood, the belief and the accompanying expectation might have been what caused the improvement, and not the drug at all. In a similar vein, it is also possible that the control group did not improve simply because they knew that there was no reason for them to improve. Since they did not receive any medication, they had not expected to improve. In addition, if the psychologists themselves were aware of the treatment conditions and the identity of the participants in those conditions, then they, too, had expectations. For example, they may have erroneously observed more depressive symptoms in the control group and fewer symptoms in the treatment condition. The cliché, "We see what we want to see," can become a real source of secondary variance. However, such *expectancy effects* can be eliminated.

Think for a moment: How would you eliminate both subject and experimenter expectancy effects in the preceding example? The best way to eliminate the problem would be to use a **double-blind** placebo design. In such a design, a placebo pill, usually made of sugar, is used in order to control for expectancies. The **single-blind** version means that the participants are not aware of whether they are receiving the actual drug, or the placebo. In the double-blind version, neither the participants nor the administrators of the drug know who receives the drug and who receives the placebo. Therefore, both subject and experimenter expectancies are eliminated.

In general, the best way to eliminate subject expectancies is to keep the participants from being aware of the hypothesis and to make sure they remain ignorant of the treatment effects you are expecting in terms of the experimental conditions. For example, don't say to the participant, "You will see both pleasant and unpleasant words, and I am predicting that you will remember more of the pleasant ones."

Holding Secondary Variables Constant

When the elimination of secondary variables is not possible, then hold these variables constant. Treat all participants in the same way, and test them under the same conditions. For example, if the room where you are conducting your study is unpleasantly warm and you fear that the temperature will adversely affect the participants' ability to remember, test everyone under the same temperature condition. This way you can assume that the temperature affects everyone's score equally, and thus the effect of this secondary variable is held constant.

Random Assignment

Random assignment of participants into conditions is one of the most common ways of dealing with a source of unwanted variance: subject factors or individual differences. Participants are individuals and therefore come with their own unique "history," their own unique characteristics, traits, and abilities, and their own unique ways of seeing and analyzing information. In other words, individual differences will always be a source of secondary variance. Are all sources of individual differences a problem? No, because the particular characteristic you should worry about depends on your topic under investigation. For example, individual differences in visual acuity are a problem if you are studying visual discrimination of colored lights but not if you are studying auditory discrimination between different pitches of sounds. Similarly, individual differences in verbal abilities may be a problem in a memory study but not in a study examining spatial skills.

In general, one of the best ways to handle individual differences is to randomly assign the participants into conditions. Random assignment theoretically *equates* your groups prior to the introduction of the independent variable. With random assignment, each participant has an equal chance of being assigned to any of the conditions. Therefore, it is unlikely that all the really "good" participants will end up in one condition and all the not so "good" participants in the other condition. The probability of equating the groups by random assignment increases as the sample size increases. For example, let's return to the earlier example of violent television and aggressiveness. One major individual difference between the children is their own level of aggression prior to exposure to the independent variable. Some children are simply more aggressive than others, but, by randomly assigning them, it is unlikely that you will end up with all the more aggressive children in the violent condition and with all the less aggressive or not aggressive children in the nonviolent condition. It is more likely that both conditions will have children who are aggressive and children who are not as aggressive.

Typically, researchers want an equal number of participants in each condition, but with true random assignment it is possible to end up with 40 participants in one condition and only 20 participants in the other condition. For example, if the researcher decides to randomly assign participants by flipping a coin, where "heads" go into one condition and "tails" into the other, it is possible to obtain mostly "heads" and very few flips with "tails." If the researcher desires the same number of participants in each group, then random assignment is carried out within limits of equal cell sizes. Cell sizes refer to the number of participants in each condition. Equal cell sizes means that once all the participants have been randomly assigned to one condition, the remaining participants automatically go into the other condition.

As you will see in later chapters, randomization is possible not only with participants, but also with stimulus materials, treatment conditions, and the order in which stimuli are presented.

Systematizing the Secondary Variable

When you systematize the secondary variable, you make it an independent variable. This way, you can systematically observe and measure its effects, not only by itself, but also in conjunction with your original independent variable. For example, let's say that you are interested in studying the effect of a training course on performance on a standardized test. Being aware of the literature on differences between male and female performance on standardized tests (Steele, 1997), you worry that gender might be a potential source of secondary variance. Well, you can always make gender an additional primary variable. As you can see in Table 3.1, you will need four groups of participants.

When the study is over, you can look for the effects of the training, for gender differences, and even for an interaction between gender and training. Interactions are covered in detail in later chapters, but briefly, an interaction would occur if the levels of the independent variable of training affected the genders differently, for example, facilitating performance for males but not for females.

MINIMIZING ERROR VARIANCE

Recall from Chapter 2 that error variance leads to inconsistent fluctuations in the dependent measure, and it may arise from individual differences, observation and measurement errors, or even during data entry and analysis. There will always be some error variance, or "noise," in an experiment, no matter how careful experimenters are with their designs and methodologies, and the best that a careful researcher can do is to take every step to minimize it.

Individual differences, as you saw earlier, can be minimized by randomly assigning the participants into conditions and by increasing the sample size. When the effects of individual differences are consistent, they produce secondary variance. When the effects are inconsistent, they produce error variance.

Measurement errors may occur if the researcher is careless or inconsistent with the observations and/or data gathering. Today, the use of computers in the laboratory to present stimuli and to record responses has greatly reduced this potential source of error variance. For example, many studies use reaction time as the dependent variable, and, when participants are tested on a computer, it is the computer that records the reaction times. This eliminates the worry that the timing may be inaccurate or that the experimenter may have missed a response from the participant due to distraction or inattention. In general, the more automated you make the experiment, the less you need to worry about variability and inaccuracy in stimulus presentation and response measurement.

TABLE 3.1 SYSTEMATIZING A SECONDARY VARIABLE

	Training	No Training
Males	Group I	Group II
Females	Group III	Group IV

Data analysis error may occur if the researcher enters the data incorrectly into the computer for analysis or selects the wrong statistical procedure. The availability of computerized statistical packages such as SPSS, MyStat, and Minitab, to name a few, has greatly reduced the chance for errors in calculations. However, to date no statistical package exists that enters the data and selects the appropriate procedure for the experimenter. As you will see in Chapter 8, different experimental designs and different dependent variable measures require different types of statistical analyses. The inappropriate statistical procedure can lead to erroneous conclusions. In addition, entering hundreds of data points (participant responses) into a computer is a lengthy and tedious procedure. Methodical researchers carefully check their data entry prior to analysis to ensure that no errors were made.

In summary, good research requires good control procedures. Secondary variance may be eliminated or held constant, and error variance may be minimized. However, since we don't live in a perfect world, there will always be some random "noise," or error variance in all research studies.

SAMPLING TECHNIQUES

Earlier in this chapter you learned about external validity, which is the ability to generalize from the experimental sample to the population of interest. One important factor to keep in mind is that this ability to generalize is greatly affected by the sample of participants in the study. If the sample is not representative of the population, then the ability to generalize, or external validity, is compromised. A **representative sample** is one in which the characteristics of the participants reflect the characteristics of the population. For example, if you were interested in the attitude of North American women toward abortion, you would need a sample of North American women representative of the population. A sample of women chosen from a religious organization would be as nonrepresentative and biased as a sample of women chosen from a political feminist organization.

> One issue of concern is that, given that the majority of research studies are conducted on college students (Sears, 1986), to what extent can we generalize the findings of research studies? Can we assume that these participants are representative of the population? College students may differ from the population in terms of age, level of education, socioeconomic status, cognitive skills, and intelligence, to name a few potential variables. In addition, as our population becomes increasingly diverse, gender, race, and ethnicity are important variables and, as some investigators point out, not taking these variables into account can also result in a non-representative sample. (Denmark, Russo, Frieze, & Sechzer, 1988)

Just how concerned should the researcher be, then? Once again, the answer is that it depends on the purpose of the research study. If the purpose is to accurately describe population characteristics, then the answer is, very concerned. On the other hand, if the aim of the research is simply to establish a relationship between the independent and dependent variables, or to test hypotheses derived from various theories, then the concern to be able to apply the findings to all people, everywhere, may not be so great. However, keep in mind that, regardless of the purpose of the study, having both male and female participants, as well as participants from diverse racial and ethnic backgrounds, can only improve the external validity of the research project.

Sampling techniques fall into two major categories: **probability sampling,** and **non-probability sampling.** Depending on the purpose of the research project, an experimenter may opt for either type of sampling technique.

Probability Sampling

When the aim of the study is to describe or make inferences about population characteristics, then the researcher must use *probability sampling techniques.* In probability sampling, we can calculate the probability that a specific member of the population will be selected to participate in the study. Survey research in particular demands that a probability sampling technique be used, since the researcher's aim is to accurately describe population characteristics from the basis of the sample. Opinion polls, surveys about religious or moral beliefs, and questionnaires regarding political and social attitudes, for example, must be administered to a representative sample if the researcher wishes to accurately describe how the population at large thinks or feels about the issues addressed in the survey. Two commonly used probability sampling techniques are **random sampling** and **stratified random sampling.**

In *random sampling* every member of the population has an equal chance of being selected for participation. For example, if the population of a hypothetical city is 2 million people, every member has a probability of 1 in 2 million of being selected. Random sampling is ideal in some instances, for it is the most unbiased way of selecting participants. Random sampling may be attempted by having a computer select people by their social security numbers. Since all documented residents in the United States must have a social security card, it would be considered random selection. Additional ways of selecting randomly would be to rely on a random numbers table, where you would select a number, let's say 124,003, then go to the telephone book, turn to page 124, and select the third name on the page. You would continue this until all participants had been selected.

But random sampling does not always guarantee that the sample you selected is truly representative. For example, suppose that you are interested in studying the population of the hypothetical city mentioned earlier, and you know that the ethnic makeup of the city is 75 percent White, 10 percent African-American, 10 percent Hispanic, and 5 percent Asian. Notice that by using true random sampling, Asians have the least chance of being selected for the study, while Whites have the greatest chance of being selected. Therefore, if you wanted a sample of 200 people, there is a good chance that your sample would contain mostly White participants. So, what is a researcher to do?

Stratified random sampling ensures that the sample matches the population on certain characteristics such as gender, race, ethnicity, religion, or any other factor that is known about the population. Given the example above, knowing the makeup of the city you would randomly draw participants from each ethnic *stratum* until you had a sample that mirrored the population. For example, you would randomly select 150 Whites, 20 African-Americans, 20 Hispanics, and 10 Asians, and you would end up with a sample of 200 people, with each ethnic group represented in proportion to the population.

Nonprobability Sampling

You read in the previous section that, depending on the purpose of the research study, an experimenter may choose either a probability or a *nonprobability sampling technique.*

Although probability sampling may result in the most unbiased and representative sample, a much more common technique is nonprobability sampling. In nonprobability sampling the probability of a given member of the population being selected for participation is not known because the sampling is based on convenience. Therefore, there is always a possibility that the sample is not truly representative of the population, and external validity may be reduced. A large percentage of experimental research in psychology takes place on university or college campuses, where students majoring in psychology are required to participate in experiments. This ready-made *subject pool* is the reason why it was mentioned earlier that the typical participant in a research study tends to be a college student.

If, as noted earlier, the purpose of the research project is to demonstrate a relationship between the independent and dependent variables, the researcher might not be interested in generalizing the findings to all members of the population of interest. Therefore, the expensive and time-consuming process of probability sampling may be undesirable or unattainable. Furthermore, should the experimenter find a relationship between the two variables under investigation in the laboratory, an interesting question would be: Is there a reason to assume that this relationship would not exist in the real world? For example, suppose you find that the participants in your study recalled more concrete words than abstract words. Is there a compelling reason to assume that, just because your participants were college students, the population at large would not recall more concrete words as well? As you read earlier in the chapter, there is evidence that a strong relationship exists between laboratory and real-world findings, which supports the validity of experimental samples in general.

Nonprobability sampling techniques include the **available sample** and the **quota sample.**

The *available sample* is also called a *haphazard sample,* or a *convenience sample.* As Cozby (1997) called it, it is a "take-them-where-you-find-them" approach to gathering participants. This approach may take advantage of subject pools, such as psychology students at colleges and universities who are required to participate for course credit, or it may depend on *volunteers* who are willing to participate in the study. In addition, some experimenters pay individuals for their participation. Keep in mind that college students who are required to participate are still, in a sense, volunteers; the students must give informed consent to participate, and they typically have a series of experiments from which to choose. For example, most colleges and universities have sign-up sheets posted on a board outside the research laboratories. Students can read over the various studies and choose one over the other. Therefore, some students may opt for a social psychology research project, while others may choose experiments in cognitive psychology. In addition, participation is not an absolute requirement in most institutions in that the students are typically given the option to write a research paper instead. However, given that students have a choice of experiments, it is important to keep in mind that certain topics will attract certain participants. As such, the sample may not be as representative as the researcher hopes.

Volunteer characteristics have been studied extensively (Rosenthal & Rosnow, 1975), and several factors have emerged that may make these participants different from the population in general. For example, regardless of where the volunteers are found, they tend to be female, more educated, have a higher socioeconomic status, higher intelligence in general, and a higher need for approval. In addition, they tend to be more curious, unconventional, and less authoritarian than nonvolunteers. In terms of religion, Catholics are the least likely to volunteer, and Jews are the most likely to volunteer.

In general, as our population becomes more diverse, there is hope that college students and volunteers will become more diverse as well. Also, as you read in Chapter 1, an important hallmark of experimentation is the ability to replicate the findings. If the findings can be replicated at other colleges and universities, with other samples, then the concern about limited generalizability is mitigated.

Quota sampling is similar to stratified sampling, except that the members of the subgroups of interest are not randomly selected from the various strata. To return to the example given under stratified sampling, if you wanted to ensure that your sample accurately reflected the proportion of various ethnic groups in the city, you would still need 150 Whites, 20 African-Americans, 20 Hispanics, and 10 Asians. However, these participants are chosen not randomly, but on the basis of their availability and/or willingness to participate. In other words, the participants will be chosen haphazardly rather than randomly, and, as such, this method will have the same limitations as a haphazard or available sample.

SUMMARY

- Internal validity refers to the researcher's ability to state that the relationship she or he predicted between the independent and dependent variables does indeed exist and that this relationship is due to the effects of the independent variable and not to extraneous, uncontrolled variables. If the study is well controlled and alternative explanations for the results can be ruled out, it is said to have internal validity.

- External validity refers to the extent to which the results of an experiment can be generalized to other settings, other people, and other circumstances.

- A major paradox of research is that by strengthening internal validity, external validity may be compromised. Depending on the purpose of the research study, an investigator may be more concerned with internal validity than external validity and vice versa.

- Basic research is typically driven by theory-generated hypotheses, and therefore the researcher may be less concerned with external validity. The aim of applied research, on the other hand, is to solve real-life problems outside of the laboratory. As such, applied researchers need to be concerned with external validity.

- Secondary variables can affect both the internal and external validity of a study, depending on their sources. To control secondary variance these unwanted variables should be eliminated, held constant, or systematized.

- Secondary variables that affect internal validity include nonrandom assignment into conditions, maturation, order or pretest effects, regression toward the mean, history, subject mortality, and differential treatment of participants.

- Secondary variables that affect external validity include pretest sensitization, reactive effects, and multiple-treatment interaction.

- Error variance may arise from individual differences or measuring error. Individual differences can be controlled by randomly assigning the participants into conditions. Measurement error can be minimized by using care in data collection and data analysis procedures.

- Random assignment theoretically equates the groups prior to introducing the independent variable. In random assignment, every participant has an equal chance of being assigned to any of the conditions.

- The external validity of a study depends on the sample. If the sample is biased, and/or nonrepresentative of the population, the external validity of the study is compromised. In a representative sample, the characteristics of the sample accurately reflect population characteristics.

- Sampling techniques fall into two major categories: probability or nonprobability sampling. In probability sampling the probability of a given member of the population being selected can be determined, whereas in nonprobability sampling the probability of being selected is not known.
- Random and stratified sampling belong to the category of probability sampling, whereas available samples and quota samples represent nonprobability sampling.
- Attempts should be made to ensure that the sample represents the diversity of the population in terms of gender, race, and ethnicity.

KEY CONCEPTS

Applied Research	Individual Differences	Order or Pretest Effects	Regression Toward the
Available Sample	Internal Validity	Pretest Sensitization	Mean
Basic Research	Maturation	Probability Sampling	Representative Sample
Differential Treatment	Multiple-Treatment	Quota Sample	Single-Blind
Double-Blind	Interaction	Random Assignment	Stratified Random
External Validity	Nonrandom Assignment	Random Sampling	Sampling
History	Nonprobability Sampling	Reactive Effects	Subject Mortality

QUESTIONS

Short answers can be found in Appendix A.

1. Identify whether the following factors affect the internal or external validity of the study.
   a. nonrepresentative sample of participants
   b. pretest sensitization
   c. practice effects
   d. subject mortality
   e. reactive effects
   f. maturation

2. A teacher gave her fifth grade class a reading test in September, introduced a new teaching method for reading, and gave the class another reading test in June. Since the reading scores were higher in June, she concluded that the new teaching method was effective. Which of the following is a possible explanation for the improved scores? Check as many as apply.
   a. effective teaching method
   b. maturation
   c. history
   d. practice effects
   e. pretest sensitization

3. Explain basic and applied research. Give two examples for each.

4. Explain how you would control for expectancy effects (both subject and experimenter) in a study on the effect of alcohol on reaction time.

5. What are reactive effects? Define and give an example.

6. In a study on verbal learning, participants were randomly assigned to a recall or recognition condition. Both groups saw the same words, which were presented by a computer at the rate of one word per every two seconds. Each group was given five minutes to recall or recognize as many words as possible, depending on the experimental condition. In the recall condition, the participants entered their responses into a computer, and in the recognition condition, the participants were asked to highlight as many words on the computer screen as they could recognize as having been seen before.
   a. Explain how the experimenter controlled secondary variance.
   b. Explain how error variance was minimized.

7. Identify the type of sampling method used in the following:
   a. Asking people to fill out a survey as they are coming out of a department store
   b. Asking for volunteers by posting fliers around a college campus

c. Contacting all the people whose phone numbers were selected by a computer-generated program

d. Identifying the proportion of Catholics, Protestants, Jews, and Muslims in a city, and then randomly selecting participants from each category so that the sample represents the religious makeup of the city

e. Asking for volunteers from the African-American, Asian, and Hispanic communities so that the sample will represent the proportion of each group in the population

f. Asking every fifth person leaving a high school cafeteria to fill out a questionnaire.

ETHICAL CONSIDERATIONS IN RESEARCH

IF THE UNIVERSITY or college you are attending conducts psychological research, as a psychology major, you have probably participated in at least one research investigation. If you have participated, you likely remember signing the consent form that the researcher handed you prior to beginning the experiment. The consent form most likely told you something about the nature and purpose of the study, what would occur during the experimental session, whether any risk was involved, and assured you that all data collected from you would be coded to protect your identity and privacy. In addition, it probably informed you that you were entitled to a summary of the outcome of the experiment. Was the researcher simply being considerate and helpful by keeping you informed? No, because **informed consent** to participate is one of the major hallmarks of modern ethical research.

As a research participant, you may have wondered about how these experiments get posted on the sign-up board, a familiar fixture in most research laboratories or psychology departments. If your institution does not conduct research, or if you are not yet acquainted with the sign-up procedure, the sign-up board is where all the available experiments are listed along with a brief description. Students who are required to participate in experiments read over the various studies posted and then select the one that seems most interesting. How do these experiments end up on the sign-up board? Is it up to the particular professor whose research it is to simply post it? Does it require prior approval from the departmental chair? Is there a committee that decides whether a project is ethical and worthwhile to be posted? At the majority of colleges and universities, there is an institutionwide committee that makes the decision. Provided that your institution receives government funding, which is the case for the majority of colleges and universities, your institution must have an **institutional review board** (IRB) that must approve a study before it can be conducted using human participants.

A BRIEF HISTORY OF ETHICAL CONCERNS

Between 1932 and 1972, 400 Black males, who were known to be infected with syphilis, participated in a study that withheld treatment for the disease. The study was first known as "The Tuskegee Study of Untreated Syphilis in the Negro Male" (Smith, 1996) and was conducted in Macon County, Alabama. The purpose of the study was to determine the damage caused by syphilis if left untreated.

During World War II, at infamous concentration camps such as Auschwitz, SS doctors carried out the most heinous "medical" experiments on captive men, women, and children. The experiments included deliberate breaking of bones until no healing was possible, sterilization of women without anesthesia, and use of twin children, one of whom served as "control" while the other was subjected to various atrocities.

As these examples so starkly remind us, ethical guidelines and principles for conducting research with human participants (and nonhuman ones as well) are clearly needed. Both the American Psychological Association (APA) and the U. S. Department of Health and Human Services (HHS) have established guidelines that all researchers in the United States and its auspices must follow.

The key principles of ethical guidelines regarding the use of human participants can be traced back to the Nuremberg trials that tried the Nazi war criminals following World War II. When the war ended and the Nazi atrocities fully came to light, those responsible were tried at Nuremberg, Germany, for crimes against humanity. An outgrowth of the Nuremberg trials was the **Nuremberg Code,** which became the foundation for future ethical guidelines regarding the use of human participants. Although ethical concerns had been under discussion by the APA since the 1930s, it was not until 1953 that the APA's first ethical code was accepted and published. In this guideline, the APA adopted several of the Nuremberg Code's major principles. Since then, there have been several revisions, the most recent one in 1992. In addition, in 1982 the HHS issued its own guidelines, which apply to all institutions receiving government funds.

ETHICAL PRINCIPLES

For a full version of the APA guideline, read "Ethical Principles of Psychologist and Code of Conduct" published in the *American Psychologist, 47* (1992). The following summarizes some of the key principles put forth by the APA. Included in the summary are issues raised by the HHS regarding the IRB requirements in their "Guidelines for Use of Humans as Research Participants" (1982).

Planning Research

In planning and conducting research, as well as in reporting research findings, experimenters have to fulfill several obligations in order to meet the ethical standards set forth by the APA. First, the research project must be planned so that the chance for misleading results is minimized. Second, the project must be planned so that it meets ethical acceptability. Any doubts the researcher may have regarding questionable ethical procedures or methods must be resolved through peer review or through consultation with appropriate parties such as the IRB. Third, steps must be taken to protect and ensure the dignity and welfare of all participants, as well as those who may be affected by the results of the research project.

Responsibility

Psychologists, as well as their assistants, are responsible for maintaining the dignity and welfare of all participants. This obligation also entails protecting them from harm, unnecessary risks, or mental and physical discomfort that may be inherent in the research procedure. Research that poses potential harm, risk, or danger to the participant is not allowed, unless the benefit of the research outweighs the risks and full informed consent is given. Psychologists and their assistants are also responsible for conducting themselves ethically and for treating the participants in an ethical manner at all times. In addition, psychologists and their assistants may only perform those activities or tasks for which they are appropriately trained. If special populations are needed, for example, children, the elderly, or clinical populations, it is the researcher's responsibility to consult with those who have expertise with those populations.

State and Federal Laws

All research conducted by psychologists and their assistants must comply with state and federal laws and regulations. For example, if the state in which the research is conducted prohibits the consumption of alcohol by anyone under the age of 21, the research project cannot involve giving alcohol to participants under the legal age.

Inducement to Participate

If the researcher offers financial or other inducement to participants in order to obtain participants for the project, the same full disclosure policy regarding the purpose and nature of the study, including the use of deception, applies as when no inducement is made. For example, just because the participant receives $5.00 for taking part in a research project, the experimenter must still inform the participant about the nature of the study, including any risks or harm that the study may create. In addition, inappropriate or excessive inducement is unethical. For example, if I am desperately in need of participants for a research project (which has happened on occasion), I cannot "bribe" the students in my psychology classes by saying that anyone who participates will receive an automatic "A" in the class.

Reporting Results and Plagiarism

Ethical researchers do not *fabricate* or *falsify data* in their publications. If the experimenter discovers that the data published are erroneous, it is the experimenter's responsibility to correct the error through retraction, an addendum, or other appropriate means. In addition, ethical researchers do not present the work of others as their own, or do not fail to give appropriate credit for the work of others through citations.

Institutional Approval

In the United States, all institutions that conduct research and receive federal funding must have an institutional review board (HHS, 1982). At universities and colleges, the IRB is made up of individuals from a wide variety of departments so that the board will not have a vested interest in any particular research project. For example, an IRB cannot be made up of members of the Psychology Department only. If it were, then it would be more difficult for it to remain neutral when evaluating a particular research proposal by a psychology department faculty member.

Prior to conducting the study, the researcher prepares a proposal, which is then submitted to the IRB for approval. The proposal includes a description of the purpose and nature of the study, how the participants will be acquired and treated, and what they will be told to expect in the study. In addition, a sample consent form is also required at most institutions. A sample IRB proposal can be seen in Figure 4.1, although proposal forms do vary from institution to institution.

Once the IRB receives the proposal, it is reviewed for ethical considerations. For example, does the project have scientific, educational, and/or societal value? If it involves some risk, is the risk to the participant justified by the benefit of the knowledge gained? Is the proposed study ethical in terms of respecting the participants' welfare and dignity and their right to privacy and confidentiality? Is deception used, and if the answer is yes, is the

---

HUMAN SUBJECT RESEARCH PROPOSAL

I. IDENTIFYING DATA:

Name(s) of Researcher(s): _____

Title of Project: _____

II. DESCRIPTION OF HUMAN SUBJECTS SAFEGUARDS AND RIGHTS:

A. Possible psychological or physical risk or discomfort involved in research?
_____ Yes   _____ No (If no, skip to Item B)

If yes, answer the following:

  1. Why necessary:

  2. Possible consequences:

B. Answer the following questions on collection of data:

  1. When will it take place?

  2. Length of time needed (minutes/hours):

  3. Period of time needed (days/weeks/months):

  4. Specific place(s) within institution:

  5. Population required, including number of subjects:

  6. Name of instrument to be used for data collection:

  7. Methodology to be used:

C. Explain procedure for obtaining subjects' voluntary informed consent to be participants in research study:

D. What will be told to subjects about the research project both before and after participation? Be specific about oral and/or written conditions.

E. Indicate how subjects can, if they wish, withdraw from the study:

F. Specify how subjects' anonymity will be achieved, if applicable, and/or how confidentiality will be maintained:

G. Will subjects be given research results if they so request? _____ Yes _____ No

H. Describe how data will be used:

III. PLEASE SUBMIT SIX COPIES OF

A. Proposal abstract

B. Consent form

C. Proposal form

SIGNATURE(S) OF RESEARCHER (S): _____

DATE: _____

FIGURE 4.1   Sample IRB proposal form.

deception justified? When and how will the participants be informed about the deception? After all the questions have been satisfactorily answered and the IRB has approved the study, the experimenter is typically free to begin his or her research. However, the IRB sometimes rejects a study, in which case the experimenter should either revise the project to meet ethical standards or abandon it altogether.

It is important to remember that the IRB is not infallible. Studies conducted by the General Accounting Office (an agency of the U.S. Congress) and the Office of Inspector

General of the HHS show that the IRB frequently operates without appropriate resources (Greenberg, 1999). As a result, some institutional review boards are forced to rush through the process of evaluating research projects, which leads to "rubber stamping" approval rather than careful evaluation. In addition, the studies found that rejection by the IRB is rare, as are requests for modifications of projects, and in some cases, the scientists applying for approval are members of the IRB.

Informed Consent

According to the APA ethical guidelines, certain research projects do not require the informed consent of participants. Such projects may entail the use of anonymous questionnaires or simple naturalistic observations where the participants cannot be personally identified or harmed in any way. In addition, archival research, which relies on published, publicly available data, does not require informed consent. All other research projects mandate the informed consent of participants, which is typically achieved by having them sign a consent form.

The consent form embodies several key principles of the APA guidelines. The participants are told about the general nature of the study as well as about any potential harm or risk that the study may cause. They are assured of confidentiality, and they are also told that they are free to decline participation. In addition, they are offered the opportunity to receive a report about the results and conclusions of the research project.

Consent forms vary from institution to institution, as do IRB proposal forms. A sample form can be seen in Figure 4.2. Notice how the consent form briefly describes the study by stating that the participants will take part in an experiment on human memory. Note also that it assures the participants that there are no risks involved and that the study was approved by the IRB. It also tells the participants what they can expect to occur and what is expected of them as participants. The statement regarding the coding of the data to protect the participants' identity is intended to alleviate concerns about privacy and confidentiality. In addition, the participants are told that they may withdraw from the study at any time without penalty and that the results of the experiment will be made available to them should they wish to receive them.

Consent and Cyberspace

An interesting recent development is the ability to conduct research on the World Wide Web (WWW). Since the participants log on to an experimental site either from home or from their college campus, they cannot of course be handed a consent form to sign prior to participation. However, as E. Miller (1999) points out, this issue has been successfully resolved through electronic consent forms, which the participants read online prior to agreeing to participate in the study. The electronic consent form can be signed or initialized electronically, or it can be accepted by default. Therefore, whether the participation takes place online or in the laboratory, the participants are still informed about the nature of the project and must give their consent prior to data collection. In addition, at the end of the experimental session, the participants are given the option to electronically transmit their data or not to transmit.

CONSENT FORM

The study you are about to participate in is part of a series of studies on human memory. It is a test of memory processes only and is not a test of your intelligence or personality. The study employs standard laboratory tasks that have no potential harm to participants, and has been approved by the Institutional Review Board for ethical standards.

Should you agree to being in the study, you will be asked to participate in a variety of verbal tasks such as: deciding if a word is pleasant or not, and stating the first word that comes to mind upon seeing another word.

All data collected from you will be coded in order to protect your identity. Following the study there will be no way to connect your name with your data.

Any additional information about the study results will be provided to you at its conclusion, upon your request.

You are free to withdraw from the study at any time. Should you agree to participate, please sign your name below, indicating that you have read and understood the nature of the study, and that all your inquiries concerning the activities have been answered to your satisfaction.

Complete the following if you wish to receive a copy of the results of this study.

_____   _____
Signature of participant and date   Signature of researcher and date

Name: _____

Address: _____ (Street)

_____ (City, State, and Zip)

FIGURE 4.2 Sample consent form.

THE USE OF DECEPTION IN RESEARCH

One concern that arises with consent forms is that, on the one hand, the participants need to be informed about the nature of the study, but on the other hand, it is important not to give away the hypothesis. Therefore, the consent form must be so worded that while the participant is given a brief, general discussion, the hypothesis, or the true purpose of the study, is not revealed. But what about studies that use **deception** in order to avoid revealing the true nature of the study? If the participants are given false information regarding the nature of the experiment in the consent form, are they truly giving their informed consent to participate?

Two famous experiments have used deception; one of them, the Darley and Latane (1968) experiment on the bystander effect, has already been mentioned. In their experiment, the true purpose of the study was to see whether group size had an effect on helping a victim. However, the participants in the experiment were told that they were taking part in a group discussion on personal problems that students may experience as part of college life. Clearly, this was deception, but suppose that Darley and Latane had informed the participants that they were studying helping behavior. Most likely, this would have biased the participants' behavior, and there is a good chance that everyone would have responded in a helpful manner. Were Darley and Latane, therefore, justified in using deception?

The other famous experiment that used deception was Milgram's study of obedience to authority in 1963. Milgram was interested in seeing how far ordinary participants would go in administering painful shocks to another, if told by an authority figure that they must do so. Though certainly an interesting topic worthy of investigation, the problem was that the participants were deceived about the nature of the experiment. When they arrived at the laboratory, Milgram told the participants that they were taking part in an experiment on learning and that they, the participants, would be the "teacher." Their role as "teachers" was to administer electric shocks to the "learners" every time the "learners" made a mistake. Unbeknownst to the "teachers," the "learners" were confederates, who only pretended to be shocked and in pain. (Recall from Chapter 1 that a confederate is someone who is "in on the experiment" but pretends to be a participant.) The intensity of the shocks (which were actually fake) varied from mild to severe, and Milgram was interested in seeing what percentage of the participants would be willing to administer the highest level of intensity if urged on by the authority figure, the experimenter. Milgram found that 65 percent of the participants were willing to go to the highest level of shock, despite the fake cries of pain from the "learners." Again, the important question is whether Milgram was justified in using deception, considering that full disclosure of the true nature of the study would have biased the participants' behavior?

When Is Deception Used?

Before we go any further, it is important to point out that the majority of research studies do not make use of deception. For example, experiments on learning, memory, and cognition, or sensation and perception, rarely require outright deception. Frequently, studies that do rely on deception tend to be in the area of social and personality psychology, where behaviors such as altruism, honesty, prejudice, helpfulness, and obedience are investigated. If you think about it for a moment, if the researchers were to inform the participants that they were interested in studying such behaviors, they would most likely find that no one was prejudiced, everyone was honest, altruistic, and helpful, and obedience would only go as far as the participants' conscience would allow. In addition, at times the knowledge or information sought cannot be obtained in a straightforward manner. For example, look at the following classic study by Rosenhan (1973).

Rosenhan was investigating the accuracy of diagnoses in psychiatric settings and published his findings in an article called "On Being Sane in Insane Places." In his study, eight pseudopatients (not mentally ill, only pretending to be) were admitted into different hospitals complaining of hearing voices, which is a typical symptom of schizophrenia. Indeed, with one exception, all pseudopatients were diagnosed with schizophrenia. Once admitted, the pseudopatients ceased faking any symptoms and behaved in a perfectly "normal" and ordinary manner. Nevertheless, the "patients" were held for an average of 19 days, and each was discharged from the hospital with the psychiatric label "schizophrenia in remission." The study demonstrated that once labeled, no matter how "sanely" one acts, the label sticks. In other words, the hospital staff could not differentiate the mentally healthy from the mentally ill. Was the deception justified by the knowledge gained?

Deception and the APA

The following summarizes the APA's "Ethical Principles and Code of Conduct" regarding the use of deception:

- Deception is not allowed unless it is justified by the study's scientific, educational, or applied value, and when alternative means that do not employ deception are not feasible.
- Deception is never allowed if full disclosure of the nature of the study (potential harm, risk, discomfort, or unpleasant emotional experience) would alter the participants' willingness to take part in the study.
- Deception and its purpose must be fully explained to the participants following the conclusion of the experimental session or, at the latest, at the conclusion of the research project.

The first statement refers to whether the knowledge gained from the study justifies deceiving the participants. This is a difficult ethical question and one that scientists themselves may disagree on. In addition, it requires that alternative procedures be considered first and be ruled out as infeasible. The ultimate decision rests with the institutional review board, which carefully reviews the proposal, the purpose and nature of the study, and the rationale for deception, and then makes its decision on the basis of the inherent scientific value of the study. Think back, for a moment, to the Milgram, Darley and Latane, and Rosenhan studies, and ask yourself the following two questions. Did the knowledge gained justify the use of deception? Can you think of alternative ways of getting the information that would not require deception?

The second statement ensures that participants are not deceived into participating when full knowledge of the experimental procedures would have resulted in their declining to participate. For example, if the participants know in advance that they are going to be subjected to electric shocks, they may decline participation out of fear of pain or discomfort. The experimenter is not allowed to lie to the participants or to omit information about the shocks simply because he or she fears that they would then decline to participate. In other words, if the use of deception, either by outright lying or by omitting information regarding risk, harm, or discomfort alters a person's willingness to participate, it goes against the APA principles.

The last statement refers to an experimental procedure known as **debriefing.** Debriefing is mandatory in research studies that employ deceptive techniques. During debriefing the true nature of the study is revealed, and the purpose of the deception is explained. For example, at the conclusion of the Darley and Latane study, the participants were told that the true purpose of the study was to examine the effect of group size on helping behavior and that the "victim" of the epileptic seizure was actually a confederate.

Aside from informing the participants about the nature and purpose of the deception, the debriefing process seeks to remove any negative or unpleasant impact of the experimental manipulation. For example, in the Milgram study, debriefing was necessary not only to explain the deception itself, but also to restore the participants' sense of self-esteem and self-worth, which may have suffered a bit from the knowledge that they were willing to inflict pain on a fellow human being.

An interesting recent development regarding deception and informed consent is a proposal by the APA's Ethics Code Task Force, a group of individuals responsible for reviewing the existing 1992 revision of the APA Ethical Principles and Code of Conduct and proposing certain changes and/or additions. The Task Force proposed that the next revision of the ethical guidelines include a provision allowing participants to withdraw "informed consent retroactively upon debriefing in deception research" (Martin, 1999, p. 44).

Many experimenters use debriefing procedures for all types of research studies, even for those without deceptive techniques. For example, Figure 4.3 shows a sample debriefing form that I used in a verbal learning study. Note how the study is now fully explained rather than in the general terms stated in the consent form. In addition, the participant is asked not to discuss the study with anyone because prior knowledge may affect the future response of other participants. Although Figure 4.3 shows a printed debriefing form handed out to all participants at the conclusion of the experimental session, other researchers may conduct extensive debriefing sessions, depending on the nature of the project.

Even if the study follows the APA principles regarding deception and extensive debriefing is used, it does not mean that all experimental psychologists condone deception in research. Some researchers do not approve of deception and do not see it as justified (Krupat & Garonzik, 1994; Oliansky, 1991; Ortmann & Hertwig, 1997). Others, such as Kelman (1967), caution that the widespread use of deception may ultimately harm the research process by making participants suspicious and distrustful of psychology and psychologists. This suspicion and mistrust can lead to unwanted sources of variance, such as demand characteristics and subject expectancies.

Interestingly, the use of deception in research has declined in recent years (Epley & Huff, 1998). For example, Epley and Huff reviewed articles published in the 1996 volume

---

DEBRIEFING FORM

The study you have just participated in was conducted in order to examine the effects of priming on a variety of tasks. Priming is when a previously seen word influences the way you perform later tasks, such as completing a word, or a word association. In particular, we were interested in whether making relatedness decisions in the first part of the study would influence how you performed on later tasks such as word associations and stem completions.

Research shows that when we see a word it activates our mental concept for that word. This activation then improves our performance on later tasks that are similar in concept to the original one. By making relatedness decisions, it was assumed that the underlying concepts for those words were activated. Later, when doing word associations, it was expected that you would use those words that were related to the association words. For example, you saw the words "VIRUS-DISEASE" and said "YES" to their being related. Later on the word association you were asked to come up with the first word that comes to mind when seeing the word "CANCER." It was expected that you would now say "DISEASE" since you were primed for it by the original relatedness decision.

Studies like this are important to science as they help us gain understanding of human memory. Thank you for participating. Should you wish to receive a copy of the final results, I will be happy to provide you with one.

FIGURE 4.3   Sample debriefing form.

of *Journal of Personality and Social Psychology* and found that 42 percent of the studies entailed deception, down from 58 percent in 1971. Whether the modest decrease is due to greater ethical awareness in general, to stricter institutional review boards in particular, or simply to changes in the variables of interest under investigation, for example, from social and personality factors to cognitive ones, is yet to be determined.

(Note that the review by Epley and Huff only focused on articles published in the area of social and personality psychology, and not research articles in general. In other words, one should not get the idea that 42 percent of ALL research used deception.)

The Effects of Deception

If you have participated in a research study at your college or university, it is possible that the study involved deception. The experimenter may have simply kept some information from you in order to protect the validity of the experiment and to keep you from knowing the hypothesis, or you may have been given a cover story, or may even have been lied to outright. If this happened to you, how did you feel after you were debriefed? Were you resentful? Did you feel duped or taken advantage of? Did the experience make you suspicious of psychological research in general? Do you anticipate being deceived again? If in the future an experimenter tells you that the study you are about to participate in does not entail deception, will you believe her?

Some studies on the effects of deception indicate that, in general, participants in deceptive research tend to accept and understand the reason behind it, and experience little, if any, negative effects from being deceived (Christensen, 1988; Epley & Huff, 1998; Smith & Richardson, 1983). Interestingly, even in the controversial Milgram experiments only 1.3 percent of the participants reported negative feelings about their participation (Berscheid, Baron, Dermer, & Libman, 1973).

A study by Sharpe, Adair, and Roese (1992) found that when participants were asked to rate the trustworthiness of psychologists and the educational value of participation, there was no significant difference between participants who had been deceived and those who had not been deceived. In addition, both the deceived and the not deceived participants were equally positive about their role in psychological research, and in general they endorsed the idea that deception may be necessary. In terms of ethical considerations, the participants in the Sharpe et al. study considered deception ethical if the benefit outweighed the cost, and they rejected the notion that deception is an ethical violation of the participants' freedom.

On the other hand, Kelman's (1967) proposition that the increasing use of deception would lead to increased suspiciousness among participants was partially supported by Epley and Huff (1998). In their study, participants who were deceived reported high levels of suspicion even after a three-month followup. In contrast, participants who had not been deceived reported no suspicion about psychological research. The suspicion, however, was not accompanied by negative feelings about the experience.

Some researchers disapprove of deceptive techniques regardless of what effect, if any, the deception has on participants. Authors such as Krupat and Garonzik (1994) base their argument not so much on the consequences of deception, but on concerns for human rights. As such, they believe that it is the researcher's duty not to deceive participants, even when it can be demonstrated to have no negative effects.

Alternatives to Deception

What is a researcher to do? As stated before, human behaviors and characteristics such as prejudice, discrimination, altruism, honesty, obedience, bigotry, and tolerance, need to be studied and understood. If the researcher is straightforward about the topic under investigation, the results will most likely be affected by the participants' awareness of the research project. On the other hand, deception, especially lying to a participant outright, does raise important ethical considerations.

Campbell (1969) proposed that, early in the semester, colleges and universities should inform every member of the subject pool that he or she may be asked to participate in a project that entails deception. In this way the participants would be aware of the existence of deceptive experiments, and therefore participation would be with full consent. Although this is an interesting proposal, the early "warning" would very likely make the participants even more suspicious, leading them to expect deception at every turn. Since students can fulfill their experimental participation requirements without encountering any deceptive projects, Campbell's proposal would raise suspicion even in students who would not have had any reason to be suspicious in the first place.

Other proposals have included handing out questionnaires to students and asking them to check off all the various types of research in which they would be willing to participate (Gamson, Fireman, & Rytina, 1982). The questionnaire would list research that entails deception. Thus, the questionnaire would enable the researcher who needs to rely on deception to contact only those students who answered that they would be willing to participate in deceptive projects. Unfortunately, selecting only those who are willing to participate in deceptive research may lead to an unrepresentative sample that can affect the validity of the study.

As you can see, solutions are scant and far from perfect. The best that researchers can do is to think creatively about their studies and to consider ways of conducting the project that would avoid deception. If that is not possible, the omission of details (unless, of course, the details have to do with stress, harm, or risk) is preferable to outright lying. Finally, researchers need to think carefully about the cost-benefit ratio of the deceptive study. If the benefit is minimal or nonexistent, then deception is not justified.

ETHICAL RESEARCH USING ANIMALS

Why Use Animals in Research?

A research psychologist may choose to conduct experiments with animal subjects for several reasons. First, some researchers believe that by studying animal behavior, we can gain an understanding of human behavior. In a similar vein, by understanding the impact of various environmental factors such as crowding, cognitive stimulation, enrichment, or deprivation on animal behavior, by extension we may also understand how these environmental factors affect human behavior.

For example, you have most likely studied the work of Harlow and Zimmerman (1959), Harlow and Harlow (1962), and Suomi and Harlow (1970) on attachment formation in infant monkeys. In their experiments, infant monkeys were separated from their natural mothers and raised under two different surrogate conditions; in one condition the surrogate "mother" was constructed of wire with a wooden head, while in the other condition the wire was covered with terry cloth to provide softness and warmth. The experimenters were interested in seeing whether the primary function of attachment to the mother was simply survival: she provides food. What the studies found was that, regardless of which "mother" provided the food, the baby monkeys spent more time clinging to the terry cloth "mother." This led the investigators to conclude that attachment is not merely for survival (food) but for contact comfort: something warm and soft to cling to. However, the studies also found that, regardless of which type of surrogate the monkeys had, all developed problems later on. They were either inappropriately aggressive or timid, and the females tended to neglect or abuse their own young.

Can we conclude from this study that attachment between human infants and their mothers also goes beyond the simple need for food and survival? In other words, can we generalize the findings of the Harlow et al. studies to human children and hypothesize that a lack of opportunity for contact comfort, or attachment, will also have an adverse effect on human development? It is difficult to say, but there is some evidence to support that notion.

In a classic paper, Dennis (1960) reported that children raised in an Iranian orphanage were severely delayed in terms of development. Of the 90 children examined, Dennis found that only 42 percent of the children between the ages of 1 and 1.9 could sit up unsupported (as compared to 100 percent of home-reared children) and only 4 percent could stand while holding on. Between the ages of 2 and 2.9, only 8 percent of the children could walk alone, whereas 100 percent of normal, noninstitutionalized children walk by that age. In terms of social development, the children did not smile and would cry when they were picked up. In addition, they showed fear when Dennis or his assistants approached them.

Before you conclude that it was the orphanage experience itself that caused the severe delay in development, it is important to point out that the situation of the children in this particular orphanage was unique. For example, there was very little handling of the children at the orphanage, except for when they were being bathed. There was no rocking, cuddling, or holding. Even during meal times, the bottle was propped on a pillow, rather than the child being held while being fed. The children spent the entire day lying in a crib, with no toys to play with and very little human contact. There was no opportunity to play, to learn, to explore; the children received only the most minimum of care such as bathing and feeding. Whether the developmental delay of the children was due to the lack of opportunity for movement and exploration, to the lack of opportunity for attachment or contact comfort, or to a combination of the two is inconclusive.

Another reason animals may be used in research is a very simple one: animal behavior is interesting in and of itself. Many psychologists are interested in understanding animal behavior without extending their findings to human behavior. As such, they may study the mating habits of Canadian Geese, the maternal behavior of gorillas, or the social hierarchy of herd animals. These studies tend to be largely naturalistic observation, or field studies.

Still another reason for using animals is that human beings cannot be subjected to certain procedures and experimental conditions. The studies conducted by Harlow et al., for example, could not have used human participants for obvious ethical reasons. Similarly, researchers in the area of neuroscience cannot subject human beings to various surgical procedures to determine the effects of brain lesions on learning, motivation, memory, and behavior. In addition, to examine the effects of various environmental factors on neural development, at the end of the study the animals may have to be sacrificed so that their brains may be examined.

Of course, some maintain that subjecting animals to procedures and conditions that would not be used on a human being is unethical and should be discontinued (Singer, 1990). However, as Perkins (1990) so eloquently points out, without animal research millions of diabetics and cancer patients would be dead due to no insulin and no chemotherapy. Diseases such as tuberculosis, scarlet fever, and polio, not to mention high blood pressure, would continue to claim millions of lives. In addition, many of the treatments developed through the use of animal research are used to treat animals themselves. According to Perkins, 90 percent of the animals used in research are rats, mice, and fish, and are bred solely for research purposes. Eliminating animal research would not set these animals "free"; they would simply not exist at all.

Misguided attempts to free the animals can also have tragic consequences for the animals themselves. For example, in a recent attack on the animal research laboratory at the University of Minnesota, the animals were "liberated" and set free on a field near the school. Many of the animals were found wandering by the road, hardly a safe environment for animals, and several of the stolen rats were found dead (Azar, 1999).

Regardless of where one may stand on this issue, animal research does continue, and it is governed by ethical guidelines much the same as research involving human participants is regulated. Naturally, there is no informed consent or debriefing, but the psychologist is still under obligation to treat all animals subject ethically and to weigh the cost-benefit ratio carefully while planning the research project. The following presents some of the major principles stated in the APA guidelines regarding the use of animals in research.

APA Principles

- Psychologists who conduct research with animals are obligated to treat the animals humanely. They are responsible for complying with state, federal, and local laws regulating how the animals are acquired, cared for, used, and disposed of.

- Psychologists must be trained in methods appropriate for animal research and must have experience in taking care of animals. They have the responsibility of supervising the procedures involving the animals, and they must ensure that steps are taken to protect the animals' comfort, health, and humane treatment.

- The responsibilities of individuals who are assisting in the research project must be commensurate with their competencies and abilities.

- Psychologists must make every effort to minimize the discomfort, pain, or illness of the animals under their care.

- Subjecting animals to pain, discomfort, stress, or deprivation is permitted only if alternative means of obtaining information is unavailable, and if the study is justified by scientific, applied, or educational value.

- All surgical procedures must entail the use of anesthesia, and care must be taken to minimize pain and the risk of infection during and after surgery.

- If the animal's life is to be terminated, it must be done rapidly, with minimum pain, and must follow accepted procedures.

Alternative Approaches

Some alternatives to using animals in research have been proposed, such as *in vitro studies* or *computer simulations.* In vitro, which literally means "in glass," refers to a technique that uses tissue samples or cultures rather than living animals. For example, an in vitro study may tell us how lead-based paint affects brain tissue or how a certain drug affects cell division. In general, in vitro studies are appropriate for biological and/or medical research; however, they have very limited (if any) application in behavioral research. Even within medical research they have their limitations; we may find out what the lead-based paint does to the tissue itself, but we may learn nothing about how it affects behavior in general.

Computer simulations involve programming a computer to predict various events or behaviors, given certain factors or predictors. Although this may be theoretically sound, a computer program is only as good as the information on which it is based. The information, on the other hand, may need to be obtained from prior research on live animals. If little information is available, the program will have limited ability to predict behavior accurately. As Perkins (1990) points out, results from research based on computer models are very likely to be incomplete and may lead to faulty, or even dangerous, conclusions.

The alternatives mentioned here are far from perfect, and until a more viable method is discovered animal research will continue. All research, whether it uses human or animal subjects, must be justifiable on the basis of scientific, educational, or applied value, and must be conducted with the utmost ethical consideration of its participants. As Macy (1990) points out, no one is arguing the benefit of animal research to humanity, but when an animal's life is spent needlessly on frivolous or unnecessary research, then the practice becomes abhorrent.

Just as there are psychologists who do not condone the use of deception with human participants under any circumstances, there are those who oppose the use of animals, regardless of the benefits from knowledge gained.

SUMMARY

- Ethical guidelines regarding the use of human participants are based on the Nuremberg Code, which is an outgrowth of the Nuremberg trials following World War II.

- The Nuremberg Code set forth a series of principles regarding the use of human participants in research. This was in response to the atrocious medical experiments conducted at Nazi concentration camps that came to light during the Nuremberg trials.

- The most recent revision of the APA's "Ethical Principles and Code of Conduct" (1992) governs all research conducted with human and animal subjects.

- The majority of institutions have an IRB that reviews and approves research projects and ensures that all research procedures meet ethical standards.

- According to the APA, all participation by humans must be voluntary, and participants must give their informed consent prior to participation. In addition, participants must be allowed to withdraw from the study at any time without penalty, and they have the right to obtain the results of the study if they so wish.

- Participants must be treated with dignity, and their rights and welfare must be protected. If the research poses potential harm or risk to the participant, the participants must be informed of these factors prior to giving their consent.

- There are times when the researcher cannot reveal the full purpose of the study because the internal validity of the experiment would be compromised. Typically, these studies are in the area of social and personality psychology, and prior knowledge of the hypothesis or purpose of the study may alter the way the participants respond. In such cases, researchers may have to rely on misleading or misinforming the participants.

- According to the APA, deceptive research is not allowed unless justified by educational, societal, or scientific value, and unless alternative ways of gaining information are not available. Deception is not permitted if full disclosure of the nature of the study would alter the willingness of the participants to participate.

- Debriefing at the end of the experimental session is mandatory if deception was used. During debriefing, the participants are informed of any deceptive procedures that were used, and the true nature and purpose of the study are explained. Many researchers choose to debrief their participants even if no deception had been used in the study.

- Although some investigators have expressed concern over the use of deception, most studies on the effects of deception show no lasting detrimental effects. However, some investigators consider deception unethical under any circumstances.

- Research using animal subjects is also governed by ethical guidelines that are similar to those governing the use of human participants.

- All animal subjects must be treated humanely, and experimenters must comply with state, federal, and local laws regarding the use, care, and disposal of animals.

- Animal research is typically conducted when it would be unethical to expose human participants to certain treatments or conditions. In addition, some scientists use animals in research because animal behavior is inherently interesting.

- Alternative procedures to animal research such as computer modeling and in vitro studies have been proposed, but these methods are far from perfect.

- Some scientists consider procedures or conditions that are deemed unethical for humans to be unethical also for animals.

KEY CONCEPTS

Debriefing
Deception
Informed Consent

Institutional Review
   Board
Nuremberg Code

QUESTIONS

Short answers can be found in Appendix A.

1. Explain what role the Nuremberg trials played in the development of ethical guidelines governing research with human participants.

2. Summarize the key principles of the APA regarding ethical reserach with human participants.

3. Summarize the key principles of the APA regarding ethical research with animals.

4. What is the IRB? Explain its function.

5. Deception in experiments is
   a. not permitted under any circumstances
   b. allowed if the truth would alter people's willingness to participate
   c. allowed only if justified by educational/scientific/ applied value
   d. permitted in most experiments

6. Which of the following is true regarding deception?

   a. The majority of studies use it.

   b. It is used mostly in social psychological research.

   c. It is used mostly in order to get people to participate willingly.

   d. There is no need to explain deception unless the study causes harm.

7. Which of the following is necessary according to the APA ethical guidelines?

   a. Participants must give informed consent prior to participation.

   b. Participants must be told what to expect, including any potential harm or risk.

   c. Participants must be assured of confidentiality.

   d. All of the above

8. Identify which of the following practices is unethical according to the APA. Check as many as apply.

   a. Not revealing the hypothesis of the study

   b. Offering your students an extra 25 points on an exam if they participate in your study

   c. Concealing the true nature of the study because if the participants knew the true purpose they would not sign up for the project

   d. Running out of consent forms but promising the participants that you will put one in their campus mailbox as soon as possible

   e. Not debriefing the participants after a session that did not involve deception

   f. Not debriefing the participants after a session that involved deception because you worry that they may tell other prospective participants about the true nature of the study, which would bias the results

CHAPTER 5

MEASURING BEHAVIOR

CHOOSING DEPENDENT VARIABLES

According to Keppel and Saufley (1980), the researcher should adopt the following criteria when choosing the dependent variable: The dependent measure should be readily observable, easily transformed into numbers, and economically feasible. Although these criteria are certainly important, additional factors should be considered when choosing a dependent measure. The dependent measure must be *reliable* and *valid,* and the researcher needs to consider the adequacy of its *operational definition.* In addition, it is important to be aware of potential *range effects.*

Measurement Reliability

Think of a friend you would describe as reliable. What is this person like? Most likely the trait **reliability** implies that he or she is dependable, trustworthy, stable, and consistent. A person who acts in such a highly unpredictable manner that you never know what to expect from moment to moment is not someone you would typically characterize as reliable.

The same holds true for the reliability of measurement. If the device you are using to measure the dependent variable produces consistent results each time it is used, you can say that it has reliability. The measuring device may be a questionnaire or survey, a personality test such as the Minnesota Multiphasic Personality Inventory (MMPI), the Wechsler Adult Intelligence Scale (WAIS), a computer that records responses, a stop watch, or just about anything that is appropriate to assess the dependent variable of the study. Imagine if the first time you took the WAIS your IQ score was 110, indicating that you were in the normal range, the second time a 170, indicating that you were a genius, and the third time a 60, indicating that you were mentally retarded. Obviously, the test could not be considered a reliable measure of your IQ.

Reliability refers to the ability of the measuring device to yield similar results when repeated measures are taken under identical testing conditions. Why do I say similar instead of exact results? Because, as you will recall from the previous chapter, there will always be a certain amount of error variance in measurement. In other words, you can expect variability in the scores due to fluctuations in the behavior or trait being measured, the time of day of testing, subject factors such as hunger, fatigue, or boredom, and environmental influences such as room temperature or noise. In addition, there will always be a certain amount of variability in the measuring device itself, since no measuring device is perfect.

A certain amount of variability is expected and accepted, but remember that the more variability you observe, the less reliable is your measuring device. What is acceptable variability? It depends on the type of study being conducted and on the measuring device itself. For example, one common technique for assessing the reliability of psychological tests or inventories is to administer the test twice and then correlate the two sets of scores by calculating a **correlation coefficient,** the Pearson *r.* The higher the numerical value of the Pearson *r,* the greater the reliability. Various techniques may also be used when we want to ensure that there is **interrater reliability** between observers, meaning that the ratings or judgments of the observers are reliable. In survey or questionnaire studies where the researcher is interested in estimating population characteristics from the basis of the sample response, a **margin of error** is calculated.

Validity of Measurement

Imagine, for a moment, that you are taking an intelligence test and you come across questions such as, what is your shoe size, what religion are you, do you like the color blue, and how much money did you make last summer? Would you consider the score you receive to be an accurate reflection of your intelligence? Or suppose that your experimental psychology professor's next exam asks you to write an essay on the French Revolution and its effect on the economic status of the nineteenth-century working class. Would you be satisfied that your grade was a valid assessment of your knowledge of experimental psychology? Chances are, of course not. Most likely, you would wonder what questions about your shoe size, color preferences, or religion had to do with intelligence, or what your knowledge about the French Revolution and economics had to do with experimental psychology. It would seem that neither test was measuring what it was supposed to measure.

The simplest, most basic definition of **validity** is the extent to which a measuring device measures what it was intended to measure. Most frequently, the issue of validity tends to apply to psychological tests or inventories and their ability to measure various psychological constructs or attributes such as intelligence, motivation, achievement, or extraversion. However, all tools of measurement should be valid in that they must be appropriate for measuring the dependent variable in the study. For example, if you were interested in measuring response time in milliseconds, where 1000 milliseconds equal 1 second, you would not use a wristwatch. Similarly, you would not use a bathroom scale to measure weight in milligrams. Just as the wristwatch was not designed to measure milliseconds (at least not the typical wristwatch), the bathroom scale was not intended for measuring minute amounts of weight. In other words, neither device is appropriate, or valid, for the task at hand.

Table 5.1 summarizes the major types of validity that apply to psychological tests and inventories. They will be discussed in greater detail in Chapter 15.

TABLE 5.1 TYPES OF VALIDITY

Type of Validity	Definition	Example
Face	The test appears to measure what it is supposed to measure.	The questions on an intelligence test that appear to be assessing intelligence.
Content	The items on a test constitute a representative sample of all possible items for a given category or area.	The questions on an intelligence test form a representative sample of all the possible questions that may be used to assess intelligence.
Criterion-Related	Performance on a test correlates with other measures used to assess a particular behavior.	There is a relationship between the scores received on an SAT test and the student's grade point average.
Construct	The measuring device produces results that are consistent with the construct being measured.	A person who received a high score on an intelligence test should behave in a highly intelligent manner.
Predictive	The measuring device should be able to predict a future event or behavior.	Scores received on the Graduate Record Exam (GRE) predict a student's performance in graduate school.

Adequacy of Operational Definitions

In Chapter 2 it was mentioned that choosing the right operational definition for the dependent variable could mean the difference between the hypothesis being supported or not supported. To be able to detect a significant effect of the independent variable when one truly exists, the choice of operational definitions for the dependent measure may be crucial.

For example, in my experimental psychology class, students investigate the concept of positive transfer by learning to complete two mazes without making any errors. Perhaps you are familiar with this laboratory exercise. The participants are blindfolded, their finger is placed at the starting point, and they are told to make their way through the maze until they reach the finishing point. Depending on the operational definition of learning, the experimenter records either the number of errors made or the number of trials it takes the participants to complete the maze without any errors. Once the participants finish the first maze without any errors, they are given the second maze, and the process is repeated. Positive transfer of learning is indicated if the participants learn the second maze with fewer errors or trials, depending on the operational definition. What we frequently find is that, while the mean number of trials needed to complete the two mazes does not differ significantly, the participants tend to make fewer errors on the second maze.

What is the significance of these findings? Well, if we define learning in terms of errors, then the hypothesis of positive transfer of learning from Maze 1 to Maze 2 is supported. However, if we define learning in terms of number of trials, we do not obtain positive transfer. In other words, frequently it is the operational definition of learning that determines whether the hypothesis is supported or not supported.

In a similar vein, most experiments that entail reaction time as a dependent measure also record information about accuracy. This is due to a well-known phenomenon called the speed-accuracy tradeoff, which refers to the sacrifice of speed for accuracy, and vice versa. For example, suppose that you are studying the effects of practice on learning. Prior to doing a difficult motor task, one group receives 20 practice trials, while a second group receives no practice trials. Both groups then perform the task, and you measure the time it takes each group to complete it. When you analyze the results, you find that the opposite of what you predicted happened: the no practice group was significantly faster. Should you conclude that, contrary to expectations, practice hinders performance on a difficult task? Well, it depends on the error rate for each group. If there is no significant difference between the errors made by the practice and no practice groups, then you could conclude that practice is detrimental to performance. On the other hand, if there is a significant difference in error rates, you could not conclude that practice hinders performance.

Choosing the right dependent variable also means that the behavioral measure should be sensitive enough to pick up subtle changes or differences in behavior that are due to the manipulation of the independent variable. In the next section you will read about a potential problem known as **range effects.**

Range Effects

Suppose your teacher gave an exam that no one passed. Would that indicate that the students in that particular class were spectacularly untalented? Could it mean that no one studied? Is it possible that the teacher had absolutely no ability to teach or transmit information? Or could it mean that the test was so difficult that it could not differentiate between good students and poor ones, those who studied and those who did not, the academically talented and the untalented? In a similar vein, suppose everyone received a grade in the high 90s. Should the teacher rejoice that she is blessed with an unusually brilliant group of students? Should she assume that her talents as a teacher are quite remarkable? Or should she assume that the test was so simple that even those who did not study or were not particularly gifted academically were able to do well.

Both examples reflect the inability of the measuring device, in this case the exam, to measure subtle differences in students with respect to learning, knowledge of the material, and memory for information. In the first instance we have what is called a **floor effect,** and in the second instance we have a **ceiling effect.** Floor and ceiling effects occur when the participants quickly reach a variable's lower and upper limit, respectively. If, for example, you notice that, regardless of the experimental condition, the majority of your participants are performing at or about 100 percent, then you know that you have a ceiling effect. On the other hand, if the majority of the participants are performing near the lowest value or limit of the variable, you have a floor effect.

Floor effects occur when the task is so difficult that no one can do well, regardless of the independent variable manipulations. For example, let's say that you were interested in studying the effects of word relatedness on memory, and you hypothesize that significantly more related words would be recalled than unrelated words. However, you selected such low-frequency, seldom used words for your stimulus materials that whether they were paired with a related or unrelated item, the participants were only able to recall a few of them. Hence, you found no significant difference in recall as a function of word relatedness. The problem here was that the task was so difficult that the participants were performing at floor level. Everyone did poorly, regardless of relatedness.

On the other hand, consider the following hypothetical study. An experimenter investigated the effects of speed of presentation on memory. In the high-speed condition participants were shown 10 words, with one word shown every second. In the normal speed condition, participants were shown the same 10 words, but this time each word was shown for two seconds. In the slow speed condition, the 10 words were presented at the rate of one word per three seconds. Once all the words were shown, the participants were asked to recall all the words they could remember. No differences were found between the three conditions, leading the experimenter to conclude that speed of presentation had no effect on memory.

What do you think of this conclusion? Hopefully, you noted that the experiment involved only 10 words; therefore, the task was very simple. There is a good chance that regardless of what was manipulated, the participants would have no difficulty recalling most of those 10 words. In other words, the participants' performance was at ceiling. *Ceiling effects* occur when all the participants reach their maximum level of performance due to the simplicity of the task.

Range effects are troublesome because they distort the data, which in turn may lead to erroneous conclusions. First, range effects minimize the difference between the means of the various conditions, and therefore it is possible that no statistical difference will be found between the conditions. As such, the researcher may incorrectly conclude that the independent variable had no effect. Second, range effects minimize the variability of scores: most scores are high or low. Since some statistical tests rely on the variability of the scores within the treatment conditions to estimate variability due to chance, the reduced variability in the scores may lead to an underestimation of variance due to chance or random error. In other words, the probability that the observed differences between conditions are due to chance is underestimated when there are ceiling or floor effects. The topic of drawing erroneous conclusions about the results of a research study is discussed in detail in Chapter 7.

How does a researcher avoid floor and ceiling effects? The best approach is to research the literature, looking carefully at methodologies used by others. If prior research on your particular topic is scant or unavailable, sit through your own experiment and look at it from the participants' point of view. This is always a good idea, regardless of worries about range effects. If you find the task too simple or too difficult, there is a good chance that so will the participants. Finally, conducting a pilot study with just a few participants may add extra time to your schedule but would be well worth it if you were to discover that they were performing at ceiling or floor. If that should happen, better to have spent some time testing 20 participants than 120, only to find that your data were distorted due to range effects.

TYPES OF DEPENDENT VARIABLE MEASURES

Although a researcher may choose from an almost limitless number of potential dependent variables, all dependent variable measures can fall into three major categories: behavioral measures, physiological measures, and self-report measures.

Behavioral Measures

Behavioral measures involve observing and recording overt behaviors. In a study on the effects of violent television on children's aggression, the number of aggressive acts is recorded. In an experiment on whether babies prefer to look at familiar or unfamiliar photographs, the researcher may record the length of time a baby gazes at each type of photograph. In a word decision study, the experimenter measures how long it takes the participant to respond from the time the stimulus was presented.

Clearly, the type of behavioral measure that is taken depends on the nature of the experiment. Some behavioral measures represent *frequencies,* meaning how often the participant responds or how many responses are made. In the preceding example, the number of aggressive acts committed by the children would represent frequency data. Similarly, the number of words recalled in a memory experiment, the number of errors made on a task, the number of lever presses a pigeon made in a conditioning study, or the number of college students choosing Coke versus Pepsi, all represent frequencies of responses.

On the other hand, the operational definition of the dependent variable may necessitate that the researcher measure the *duration* of the response. In this instance, the question of interest is, how long does the behavior last? For example, in the babies' preferential looking experiment, the researcher is measuring how long babies look at different types of photographs in order to determine their interest in novel versus familiar stimuli. Similarly, how long (as measured in time) a rat takes to learn to run a maze without an error, how long a temper tantrum lasts if no attention is paid, or how long a seizure lasts are all measuring the duration of the response.

Finally, if the researcher is measuring the time it takes a participant to respond to a particular stimulus, then what is being measured is *response latency*. Examining latency, as measured by *reaction time,* is common in cognitive psychology experiments on learning and memory. For example, Meyer and Schvaneveldt (1971) tested the semantic organization of human memory by having participants perform a lexical decision task. In a lexical decision task, participants are shown letter strings, for example, DOGTEM, or DOCTOR, and are asked to decide if the string is a word or a nonword. The behavioral measure is reaction time, meaning how long it takes the participant to press the appropriate key from the time the letter string is presented. Over a series of trials, Meyer and Schvaneveldt showed the participants two letter strings, where the letter strings formed two words, two nonwords, or one of each. Where the letter strings formed words, they were either related, for example, DOCTOR-NURSE, or unrelated, for example, DOCTOR-TULIP. They hypothesized that, if the memory system is highly organized, with semantically related information stored together, then participants will be faster in deciding that two letter strings formed words when the words were related. Meyer and Schvaneveldt found that participants were significantly quicker in their decisions when the letter strings formed two related words.

Latency measures were also used in the Darley and Latane (1968) study on group size and helping behavior. In their experiment the manipulated variable was the size of the group, and the dependent variable was how long it took the participants to get help for the "victim" as measured in minutes from the onset of the "epileptic seizure."

Physiological Measures

Overt behaviors are frequently measured in research, and, depending on the nature of the study, it is the appropriate measure to use. However, the researcher is interested not in overt behaviors but in underlying physiological processes. For example, a cognitive neuroscientist may want to "map the brain"—that is, identify areas of the brain that are active during memorizing word lists, thinking of a pleasant experience, playing video games, or solving a problem. In such cases, the type of measure sought is not directly observable from a participant's overt behavior. Similarly, if you are interested in seeing whether biofeedback can lower blood pressure, you will not be able to determine it by relying on overt behaviors.

Some types of physiological measures have been in use for a long time. For example, you are most likely familiar with the galvanic skin response (GSR), the electroencephalogram (EEG), and the electrocardiogram (EKG). The GSR measures emotional arousal as indicated by skin conductivity. When a participant is aroused, for example, when he or she is lying, the skin conductivity changes as a result of sweating. The GSR, incidentally, is a basis of the lie detector test. The EEG maps brain waves and indicates the electric activity of cortical brain cells. It may be used to monitor arousal, interest, drowsiness, dreaming, or relaxation. The EKG, on the other hand, measures heart rate and can also be used as an indicator of arousal.

Suppose, for a moment, that you wished to study infant learning and memory. Obviously, you cannot ask an infant what he or she knows, nor can you show babies a list of items and then ask them to recall them. How would you go about doing such an experiment? The solution to the problem is ingenious, and it is one of the most widely used techniques to study infant learning and memory. The experimental technique is called orientation-habituation, and the dependent variable measure is, naturally, physiological. During the study, the infant is shown a stimulus, and, provided it is a novel stimulus, meaning that the infant is not yet familiar with it, an orientation response is observed. When the baby orients, the pupils of the eye dilate, respiration rate decreases, blood vessels in the brain dilate, and the EEG shows an increase in arousal. After repeated exposures to the same stimulus, this orientation, as measured by changes in physiological responses, no longer occurs. At this point, the baby is said to have habituated to the stimulus. In other words, we could say that the infant has learned the stimulus and it is no longer novel.

More recently developed methods such as brain imaging techniques include functional magnetic resonance imaging (fMRI), positron emission tomography (PET), magnetoencephalography (MEG), and magnetic source imaging (MSI). These techniques allow scientists to identify with impressive accuracy exactly which areas of the brain do the most work during psychological processes such as reading, learning, memory, and language processing. For example, Richard Haier (as cited in Solso, 1998) at the University of California (Irvine) used PET scans to determine the activity of the brain of two people playing a computer game. One of the players was experienced, while the other was a novice. The PET scan revealed that the brain of the novice player was significantly more active, indicating that the more experienced player burned less energy and was more neurologically efficient. Haier also found that while learning to play the game, people with higher IQ scores had less active brains, presumably due to their ability to process information more efficiently than those with lower IQ scores.

An interesting recent finding using PET may support Freud's original theory of dreams and their purpose (Carpenter, 1999). You are most likely familiar with Freud's proposal that the function of dreams is to express unacceptable sexual and aggressive urges. In other words, dreams serve a wish-fulfilling function. This theory came under fire when scientists in the 1960s discovered that the brain mechanism that controls the REM stage is the pons, which is responsible for lower-order physiological functions such as temperature regulation, respiration, and cardiac activities. Since the emotional and motivational areas of the brain were not involved during REM, dreams could not have anything to do with wishes, feelings, and memories. However, using PET, Braun, a neurologist, and his colleague, Hersovitch (1998) recently discovered a high level of activity in the limbic and paralimbic areas of the brain during REM sleep. These areas of the brain control emotion and motivation. In addition, the decreased activity found in the prefrontal cortex, an area that controls short-term memory, attention, and logic, further supports Freud's theory. This finding of deactivation in the prefrontal cortex "may be consistent with Freud's ideas of encoding wishes into dream imagery, emotional disinhibition and instinctual needs" (Carpenter, 1999, p. 19).

In a similar vein, Kosslyn, Thompson, Costantini-Ferrando, Alpert, and Spiegel (2000) used PET scans to determine whether hypnosis can modulate color perception. There are two schools of thought regarding hypnosis; one side views hypnosis as a legitimate, altered psychological state, and the other side sees it as not much more than acting out a role adopted by the participant. In order to determine whether hypnosis is a genuine psychological state or merely role-playing adopted by the participant in order to cooperate with the hypnotist, the authors hypnotized the participants and asked them to view colored and gray patterns while undergoing a PET scan. The rationale was that "people cannot voluntarily alter the workings of the neural mechanisms that underlie a specific experience—

for example, those involved in perception—unless they have the experience" (Kosslyn et al., 2000, p. 1280). In other words, if the appropriate brain mechanisms become activated when the hypnotized participants are shown grayscales (stimuli drained of color), but they believe that they are perceiving colors, then hypnosis can be viewed as a legitimate psychological state, and not simply as role-playing. The results of this study were that the color areas of the left hemisphere showed activation whether the hypnotized participants were shown colors or grayscale. On the other hand, activation decreased when the participants were told that they were looking at grayscale, whether the stimuli were in color or grayscale. According to the authors, the findings that subjective experiences were accompanied by corresponding changes in neural activation indicate that hypnosis is in fact a genuine psychological state.

Although these technological advances greatly increase the types of physiological measures available to the researcher, they are very expensive to acquire and maintain, and therefore access to them by the average researcher is limited.

Self-Report Measures

Self-report measures are common in survey or questionnaire research, as well as in psychological testing. As the name implies, through self-report measures the participants report their responses to various stimuli or questions. The questions may require a simple yes or no, or true or false, response, or participants may be asked to rate or evaluate certain events, stimuli, or experiences on a scale. In addition, self-reports may involve answering questions dealing with hypothetical or future situations, for example, "How would you feel if someone cut in front of you in a line," or questions dealing with the past, such as "How did you feel when a friend lied to you."

At many colleges or universities, professors often ask students to evaluate them and their course at the end of the semester. The evaluation forms used are based on a technique called the **rating scale.** The participant is presented with a series of questions and is asked to respond by selecting from two or more alternatives on the scale. For example, a question on the teacher evaluation form may ask you to rate the professor's clarity of speech on a scale of 1 to 5, with 1 representing not at all clear and 5 representing very clear. Or you may be asked to rate the quality of instructions, with 1 representing poor quality and 5 being outstanding.

Take a look at the examples of rating scales in Figure 5.1. Example 1 in Figure 5.1 shows the **Likert scale,** where participants place a check mark in the appropriate place. The Likert scale is used when the researcher is interested in the degree to which participants agree or disagree with various statements. A modified version of the Likert scale can be seen in Example 2. Notice how in the modified version rather than using check marks, the participants are asked to circle the most appropriate response. Example 3 shows a rating scale using labels for all the response choices (points on the scale), while Examples 4 and 5 show three and two labels, respectively.

How many points should a scale have, and should all points be labeled or only some of them? There is no set answer. Typically, rating scales do not exceed 10 points or go below 5 points. As for labeling the points, if all points are labeled, the participant is not left wondering what the numbers stand for; the points are clearly defined. However, it is not always necessary to label each point, and it may be enough to give the participants the lower and upper limits, as in Example 5.

Example 1	Strongly				Strongly		
	Agree	Agree	Neutral	Disagree	Disagree		
Likert scale							
	____	____	____	____	____		

Example 2	Strongly				Strongly		
	Agree	Agree	Neutral	Disagree	Disagree		
Likert-type scale	1	2	3	4	5		

Example 3	Strongly		Slightly		Slightly		Strongly
	Favor	Favor	Favor	Neutral	Oppose	Oppose	Oppose
Fully labeled Rating scale	1	2	3	4	5	6	7

Example 4	Strongly						Strongly
	Favor			Neutral			Oppose
Rating scale with 3 points labeled	1	2	3	4	5	6	7

Example 5	Strongly						Strongly
	Favor						Oppose
Rating scale with 2 end points labeled	1	2	3	4	5	6	7

FIGURE 5.1   Examples of rating scales.

Although self-reports are easy to use and, to a certain extent, easy to score, they do have their problems. For example, unconsciously, the participants may be answering with their ideal self—the way they think they ought to be, and not their true self—the way they actually are. Another problem may be that the participants are deliberately not telling the truth or are attempting to place themselves in a positive light by trying to give socially desirable answers.

In addition, when the self-report asks participants to reflect back on some past event or experience, it is difficult to tell the extent to which the memory accurately describes the event. Memory is reconstructive (Bartlett, 1932); our mind is not a camera that records events faithfully, so that all we need to do to remember an event is to replay it in our mind. Rather, with time, we add some details and forget others, and when it's time to retrieve a memory we tend to reconstruct it, based on how we interpreted the event, how long ago it occurred, and what other events have occurred since. As such, memory for past events may be highly inaccurate; this is especially true if the memory is for some emotionally charged event or experience. Similarly, asking participants to hypothesize about some future event may not lead to accurate reporting. How we think we will act or feel about something is not necessarily the same as how we really would act or feel when faced with the actual situation.

SCALES OF MEASUREMENT

To paraphrase Stevens (1951), measurement is the assigning of numbers to objects or events according to rules. We can expand on this definition by saying that measurement is the assigning of values to variables in research studies. For example, if you are measuring male and female responses, males may be assigned the numerical value of 1, while females are assigned the numerical value of 2. In a similar vein, participants may be rated as first, second, or third on a maze completion task.

There are four basic scales of measurement, and they depict relations between the variables and the numerical labels assigned to them. The type of scale used depends on the nature of the variables under study, as well as on how much and what type of information is sought. In addition, the type of scale used may determine which statistical analysis is appropriate and may affect the researchers' conclusions about their results. There is some disagreement between scientists regarding this issue (see Stevens, 1975; Velleman & Wilkinson, 1993).

The four major measurement scales posited by Stevens are the **nominal, ordinal, interval,** and **ratio** scales, with the nominal scale being the lowest level and the ratio scale the highest. A given scale of measurement possesses one or more mathematical attributes, such as magnitude, equal interval spacing between units, and an absolute zero. The four scales differ in terms of their mathematical attributes, but each higher level of measurement incorporates all the mathematical attributes of the lower ones. Table 5.2 summarizes the four major scales of measurement.

Nominal Scales

The lowest level of measurement, the nominal scale, is typically used with variables that are qualitative rather than quantitative. Nominal scales do not possess any mathematical

TABLE 5.2   SCALES OF MEASUREMENT

Scales	Description	Example	Limitation
Nominal (categories)	Assign labels	• Males and females • Children and adults • Coke and Pepsi	Can't say there are quantitative differences between categories.
Ordinal (categories and ranks)	Establish rank order	• Rank order in class • Order of finishing a race	The magnitude of difference along the scale is not known.
Interval (categories, orders, and equal interval scaling)	Equal interval spacing	• Temperature • IQ scores • Standard scores on a test	There is no absolute zero. Can't say that a temperature of 0 degrees Fahrenheit or Celsius indicates an absence of temperature.
Ratio (categories, orders, equal interval spacing, and an absolute zero)	The zero on the scale indicates an absence of what is being measured.	• Weight • Number of errors made on a task • Number of lever presses	No limitation

attributes; they have no magnitude, rank, equal interval spacing, or an absolute zero. They merely label or define *discrete categories* to which the variables can be assigned. Therefore, measurement along this scale entails classifying objects, events, or people by labeling them. Gender, social class, race, religion, and product preferences by consumers are all examples of variables that are "measured" (named or labeled) by the nominal scale. If you were interested in studying different religious groups, you could classify each person as belonging to the Catholic, Protestant, or Jewish faith. Similarly, you could ask people about their preference for Coke or Pepsi, whether they were pro-choice or anti-abortion, or what they were majoring in as college students.

The nominal scale involves no ordering of values since the classification is merely descriptive. In other words, there are no quantitative differences between the categories. For example, you can't say that, in terms of religion, being Protestant is "more" or "greater" than being Catholic or Jewish, just as you can't say that Crest is more of a toothpaste than Colgate. The categories are merely different along qualitative dimensions. Although for coding purposes you may assign the numerical value of 1 to males and 2 to females, the numbers are used simply for identification; you could not say that the numerical value of 1 (being male) is less than 2 (being female).

The observations, or data, collected under each category are the number of occurrences, or frequencies, that belong to that particular category. For example, you may find that 35 students at a university are majoring in English and 42 are majoring in Spanish. While the observed frequencies may allow you to conclude that more students are majoring in Spanish than English, they do not allow you to conclude that Spanish is a quantifiably better major.

Ordinal Scales

One level of measurement above the nominal scale, the ordinal scale does possess some mathematical property of magnitude. As the name "ordinal" implies, the ordinal scale allows for the *ranking* or *rank ordering* of variables. Therefore, observations can be ranked below, above, or equal to another observation. For example, saying that Juan is nicer than Darryl, that Susan came in after Maria in a race, or that Lakisha is first in her class, all involve measurement along the ordinal scale. With ordinal scales, objects, people, animals, or events are ranked according to how much of the attribute that is being measured they may possess. For example, if you are judging college debate teams, you may rank the teams as number 1, number 2, or number 3, depending on articulateness, ability to argue logically, or knowledge of the topic. Although we can say that coming in first is better than coming in second, or that being third is worse than being first or second, we cannot say by how much. The magnitude of difference along the scale is not known. For example, we cannot say that the debating team that was ranked number 1 is twice as knowledgeable, articulate, and logical than the team that was ranked number 2. In addition, the spacing of values, or the magnitude of difference, between units on the scale is not equal. We cannot say that the magnitude of difference between coming in first and second in the debating contest is the same as between coming in second and third. The difference in logic, articulateness, and knowledge of the topic between the first and second team may not be the same as the difference between the second and third team. In other words, ordinal scales do not possess the mathematical property of equal interval spacing between adjacent units.

We can say that something is less than, equal to, or more than another thing, but we cannot say by how much.

Interval Scales

The interval scale is higher than the ordinal scale, which in turn is, higher than the nominal scale. The interval scale has the mathematical properties of *magnitude* and *equal interval* spacing. However, the zero on the scale is arbitrary; there is *no absolute zero* point. (An absolute zero point indicates a total absence, or lack of the property, or attribute under consideration.) The best example of an interval scale of measurement is temperature (Fahrenheit or Celsius). The spacing of values between adjacent units is equal, but there is no absolute zero, which would indicate a total lack, or absence, of temperature. For example, we can say that 80 degrees is 20 degrees warmer than 60 degrees, which in turn is 20 degrees warmer than 40 degrees. Zero degree, however, does not imply an absence of temperature; therefore, we cannot say that 40 degrees is twice as warm as 20 degrees.

Other examples of interval scale measurement include IQ test scores, scores received on personality inventories, and other psychological tests. For example, let's say that you administered a depression inventory to Timothy, who scored a 60, and to Jason, who scored a 30. Although you could say that Timothy scored 30 points higher than Jason, you could not say that he is twice as depressed.

Ratio Scales

The highest level of measurement, the ratio scale, has the same mathematical properties as the interval scale and in addition has an absolute zero point. For example, if participants are required to respond to stimuli by pressing a lever, then the measure is on a ratio scale. If the number of lever presses for Keith is 20, for Tyrone it is 10, and for Mario it is 0, we could say that Keith had twice as many lever presses than Tyrone, while Mario made no lever presses at all. Similarly, if the dependent variable in a learning task is the number of errors made, then zero errors would indicate a complete absence of errors.

MEASUREMENT AND REACTIVITY

Effects of Being Observed

In the 1930s, two psychologists investigated the effects of working conditions on productivity at the Hawthorne plant of the Western Electric Company (Roethlisberger & Dickson, 1939). They systematically manipulated various environmental conditions such as illumination, wage rate, breaks from work, and so forth, and then observed the productivity of the workers. They found that, regardless of what was altered, worker productivity increased. Did productivity increase because of the effectiveness of all the manipulated variables, or simply because the workers knew that they were in an experiment and being observed? The correct answer is the second one, and this phenomenon became known as the **Hawthorne effect.**

The Hawthorne effect is a good illustration of how being in an experiment and being measured along some behavioral dimension may alter the participants' behavior. As mentioned in Chapter 3, this phenomenon is also known as a *reactive effect*—the participants react to being in an experiment where they are observed, evaluated, or measured on some attribute or behavior. Since the experimental session is essentially social in nature in that the experimenter and the participants interact with each other, the participants' behavior may at least partially reflect their reaction to you and your study.

Reactive effects may include the participants' suspicion about the true nature of the experiment, resentment or hostility for being experimented on, anxiety about performing well, and desire to please the experimenter (Jung, 1971). Suspicion, for example, may easily arise if a person has participated in previous experiments that have used deceptive techniques. If participants had been lied to in prior studies, they may expect to be deceived, regardless of how straightforward the current experiment is.

Resentment and hostility, on the other hand, may well develop if the college or university has mandatory research participation requirements (Adair, 1973). Although most institutions do offer an alternative to participation, such as writing a term paper or research paper, most students realize that it takes considerably less time to fulfill experimental requirements than to write an extensive paper. Therefore, few students opt for the paper over the participation requirement, at least in the author's experience.

Apprehension over being evaluated may cause the participants to strive harder to do well in the laboratory than they would in real life. For example, they may make a special effort to remember the items in a memory study, or they may be extra careful to avoid making errors on a task. In addition, the participants may be anxious to appear as "good participants" and will attempt to please the experimenter (Adair, 1973).

As noted in Chapter 3, additional factors such as expectancies may operate at any given time. As stated previously, if the participants know, or think they know, the purpose of the study, or think that they have figured out the hypothesis, they may act accordingly.

Experimenter Effects

According to Rosenthal (1966; 1969), the behavior or characteristics of the experimenter may affect the behavior of the participants, and vice versa. Characteristics such as gender, race, age, or even the physical appearance of the experimenter may affect different participants differently. For example, Maccoby (1990) found that individuals act differently in the presence of males or females, while Graham (1992) raised the issue of White experimenters studying the behavior of African-American participants. Although some researchers found that White experimenters did not have a negative effect on African-American participants (Graziano, Varca, & Levy, 1982), Graham remains concerned about **experimenter effects:**

> *In the absence of careful controls on race of E [experimenter], we simply do not know what effect a White experimenter has on an African-American child who is required, for example, to read a passage in perfect Standard English, choose between a Black and White doll, solve a puzzle in the wake of induced failure, or realistically estimate the likelihood of going to college. (p. 635)*

One example of how the appearance and gender of the experimenter can alter the participants' perception is a classic study conducted by Dutton and Aron (1974). Although the experiment studied how people interpret nonspecific physiological arousal depending on its context, the results fit nicely with the discussion of experimenter effects. In Dutton and Aron's experiment, a group of male participants crossed a scary suspension bridge. On the opposite side was either an attractive female experimenter or a male experimenter. All the participants experienced arousal; however, the group that was met by the attractive female experimenter attributed the arousal to sexual feelings, whereas the group met by the male experimenter attributed the arousal to fear.

Inadvertent cues by the experimenter may also bias the participants' responses. These subtle cues, called **demand characteristics,** or *experimenter expectancy bias* (Rosenberg, 1969), are then interpreted by the participants and may alter their perception of their role in the experiment and what is expected of them. For example, the facial expression, tone of voice, gesture, or body language of the experimenter may bias the participants' response (Jung, 1971). In other words, the experimenter may give subtle cues so that the participants' behavior or response supports the hypothesis. What these expectancy biases may lead to is a *self-fulfilling prophecy;* the experimenter expects certain events or behaviors to occur and thus subtly influences the participants to fulfill these expectations.

Even if the experimenter gives no overt cues, participants may still form their own hypotheses regarding the "true" nature of the experiment, its purpose, and what is expected of them (Rosenberg, 1969).

Control Procedures

Reactive effects, whether they are due to the attitude the participant brings to the experimental session, demand characteristics, or expectancies by either the participant or the experimenter, may produce behaviors that do not reflect how the participant would act in the real world. These behaviors are known as **artifacts,** or *artifactual behaviors.* While Chapter 3 dealt with several procedures to eliminate or hold constant some of these potential sources of unwanted variance, a few additional steps may be taken.

In order to control the effects of being observed, such as the Hawthorne effect, the researcher could attempt to be as *unobtrusive* as possible while observing or recording behaviors. Unobtrusive measurement procedures will be discussed in detail under naturalistic observation, or field studies, in Chapter 15.

On the other hand, if you are concerned that the measuring device you are planning to use may produce artifactual responses, one possible solution is to use several forms or types of measuring devices. By systematically varying the types of measuring devices or procedures, you are ensuring that the behavior or response you are observing is not inherent to a particular type of measuring device.

Finally, as with any other source of unwanted variance, the researcher can always make the artifact an independent variable and study its effects systematically.

SUMMARY

- The dependent variable measure must be reliable and valid. Reliability refers to the ability of the measuring device to yield consistent results when repeated measures are taken under identical testing conditions. Validity refers to the extent to which the device is measuring what it is supposed to measure.

- Experimenters need to be aware of the adequacy of the dependent measure to detect differences between conditions. To be able to detect a significant effect of the independent variable, the choice of operational definitions for the dependent measure may be crucial.

- Range effects such as ceiling or floor effect may operate if the task is too easy or too difficult. These range effects may lead to erroneous conclusions regarding the effects of the independent variable.

- Although a researcher may choose from an almost limitless number of potential dependent variables, all dependent variable measures can fall into three major categories: behavioral measures, physiological measures, and self-report measures.

- Scales of measurement refer to the level on which the dependent variable is measured. The most appropriate scale is determined by the research design and the nature of the variables. The four major scales of measurement are the nominal, ordinal, interval, and ratio scales.

- The nominal scale is the lowest level of measurement and is typically used when the dependent measure is qualitative, or categorical. The ordinal scale of measurement is appropriate when some attribute or characteristic is being rank ordered. The distance between the ranks is not known. The interval scale of measurement is essentially an ordinal scale, but it provides information about the distance between the ranks. The interval scale does not have an absolute zero point. The highest level of measurement is the ratio scale, which is basically an interval scale with an absolute zero.

- Observation and measurement may produce reactive effects. The Hawthorne effect demonstrates how the behavior of the participants may reflect their awareness of being observed, rather than the effect of the independent variable. In addition, artifactual behavior may result from being in an experiment.

- Experimenters may influence the results of a study by cueing the participants to respond in a particular manner. These demand characteristics may cause the participants to change their behaviors according to their interpretation of the cues given by the experimenter. Additional experimenter effects may be due to characteristics such as appearance, gender, age, or race of the experimenter.

KEY CONCEPTS

Artifacts	Floor Effect	Margin of Error	Ratio Scale
Ceiling Effect	Hawthorne Effect	Nominal Scale	Reliability
Correlation Coefficient	Interrater Reliability	Ordinal Scale	Validity
Demand Characteristics	Interval Scale	Range Effects	
Experimenter Effects	Likert Scale	Rating Scale	

QUESTIONS

Short answers can be found in Appendix A.

1. Carmen is in the middle of an intelligence test, but she is wondering what the questions have to with intelligence. Carmen doubts the _____ validity of the test.

2. The ability of a measuring device to yield the same results each time it is used is called _____.

3. You're on a college admissions board and are interested in whether students who did well on the SAT will do well in college (as measured by their GPA). You are therefore interested in the SAT's _____ validity.

4. A personality test given to Ahmed identified him as withdrawn and a loner. He is, however, highly social

and has a large circle of friends. Ahmed doubts the test's _____ validity.

5. Identify the scale of measurement used in the following:

   a. Conducting research on people with varying degrees of education, comparing high school, college, and graduate school levels

   b. Judging student performance, determining who is first, second, and third

   c. Measuring the number of words recalled in a memory experiment

   d. Determining IQ scores for diverse groups of individuals

   e. Counting the number of lever presses a pigeon makes

   f. Comparing the music preferences of African-Americans and Whites

6. Identify the type of dependent variable measure used in the following:

   a. The number of errors made on a task

   b. The responses on surveys and psychological tests

   c. Comparing the MRI data from short-term and long-term memory experiments

   d. Examining whether biofeedback reduced high blood pressure

   e. Comparing the results of a personality test given to males and females

7. Explain reactive effects and give examples.

ANALYZING THE RESULTS

PRESENTING THE DATA: DESCRIPTIVE STATISTICS

▓ How do I make sense of all the data I collected?

▓ What was the typical performance or response in this study?

▨ By how much did a typical participant vary from the average performance of the group?

▨ How similar or dissimilar were the participants?

▨ What type of relationship is there between my independent and dependent variables?

▨ Should I use a line graph or a bar graph to present my results? Does it matter?

O**NCE YOU** have finished your experiment, the next step is to make sense of all the data you have collected. By using statistics, you can answer important questions such as the ones stated here. This chapter explains the role of statistics in research and demonstrates the processes by which experimenters organize, summarize, and interpret their findings.

THE ROLE OF STATISTICS IN RESEARCH

Definition of Statistics

Although the word "statistics" tends to make many students nervous, without relying on statistics the researcher could not make sense of the data collected during an experiment. There would be no way to know how a typical participant responded, how varied were the responses, or whether the independent variable had an effect. Therefore, try to get rid of any fears or discomfort you may have regarding the field of statistics, and look at it as nothing more than a tool of science that allows researchers to make sense of their data. Statistics allow the researchers to *organize and summarize* their data, and to *interpret and generalize* their findings.

Overcoming Your Fear of Statistics

One major reason students tend to fear or even dislike statistics is their feeling that they are not mathematically oriented. Some students believe that they are not good in math or that math is too abstract and hence difficult to grasp. However, if you change the way you think about statistics, you may able to overcome whatever reservations you may have.

How *should* you think about statistics? For one thing, don't think of the numbers as "math" or "abstractions." Instead, realize that they represent the actual behaviors or responses of real people: the participants in the study. The numbers may stand for the number of words recalled in a memory experiment, the number of errors made on a task, the number of women who preferred a particular story, or the IQ score received by a child on an intelligence test. If you start thinking of the numbers (data) as the actual attributes, behaviors, scores, responses, or preferences of individuals, some of your anxieties may be alleviated.

As a student, you have probably engaged in the time-honored tradition of figuring out your average in a class so that you can anticipate your final grade in the course. You have kept track of all the grades you have received, added them up, and then divided the sum by the number of exam grades you had in order to arrive at your class average. Did this procedure cause you any anxiety? Were you fearful that you didn't know what you were doing? Most likely the answer is no to both questions. Although you may not have thought of it as a statistical procedure, that is precisely what you were doing. You were calculating a measure of central tendency: the mean. However, since the numbers stood for something concrete—your grade on a given exam—you most likely did not experience any anxiety during the procedure, except perhaps worry that your grade would not work out to be as high as you would have liked.

Major Branches of Statistics

The field of statistics can be divided into two major branches or areas: descriptive statistics and inferential statistics. The researcher uses **descriptive statistics** to organize and summarize the data and **inferential statistics** to interpret the data. The present chapter deals with the descriptive branch, and the next chapter will explore the area of inferential statistics.

As the name implies, descriptive statistics describe the characteristics of your sample. For example, calculating your grade in a course from the exam grades you have received belongs in the area of descriptive statistics. The average you calculate describes your overall performance in the class. Similarly, if your professor tells you that the average grade on the last exam in the class was an 85, you can now compare your performance on the exam to that average and describe your performance as average, below average, or above average.

Two common ways of summarizing the data with descriptive statistics are to provide **measures of central tendency** and **measures of variability.** However, before describing the characteristics and uses of these measures, let's take some time to review the shape a distribution of scores may take and ways of presenting them graphically. Graphical presentation of the distribution allows the researcher to see the shape of the distribution, which in turn may determine which measure of central tendency is appropriate.

FREQUENCY DISTRIBUTIONS

Hopefully, you remember **frequency distributions** from your statistics class. Briefly, a frequency distribution is a presentation of score values and their frequency of occurrence. However, listing every single score and its frequency will often result in a lengthy list with unnecessary details, such as frequencies of 0 for certain scores. Therefore, rather than using an ungrouped frequency distribution, the researcher often divides the data into class intervals. This procedure results in what is known as a grouped frequency distribution. Once such a distribution has been constructed, it is simple to create a *frequency polygon,* which is a graphical presentation of the data.

In grouped frequency distributions, the researcher determines the number and size of the class intervals and lists the frequency of occurrence within each interval. The number and size of the intervals are arbitrary in that they are chosen at the convenience of the researcher.

TABLE 6.1 Ungrouped Frequency Distribution of Scores (f = frequency)

Score	f	Score	f	Score	f	Score	f
83	1	62	2	41	2	20	0
82	0	61	1	40	4	19	2
81	0	60	0	39	1	18	2
80	0	59	1	38	1	17	1
79	0	58	2	37	3	16	0
78	0	57	1	36	1	15	0
77	0	56	0	35	1	14	0
76	0	55	2	34	2	13	2
75	0	54	0	33	4	12	0
74	0	53	2	32	1	11	0
73	0	52	3	31	3	10	0
72	0	51	3	30	1	9	0
71	0	50	1	29	1	8	0
70	1	49	2	28	1	7	0
69	0	48	2	27	4	6	0
68	3	47	2	26	2	5	1
67	1	46	2	25	1	4	0
66	1	45	1	24	2	3	0
65	1	44	4	23	0	2	0
64	0	43	3	22	0	1	0
63	1	42	0	21	1	0	0

For example, take a look at Table 6.1, which presents the ungrouped frequency distribution of scores received on a hypothetical test. Notice that the highest score received was an 83 and the lowest a 5. However, notice also how lengthy this table is and how many frequencies of 0 are presented. In order to construct a grouped frequency distribution, take the following steps:

1. Determine the range of the scores by subtracting the lowest score from the highest score. $83 - 5 = 78$
2. Choose a convenient number of intervals. Typically, between 5 and 20 will be practical for most distributions. Let's say 9.
3. Determine the interval size by dividing the range by the number of intervals chosen. $78/9 = 8.67$ (rounded to 9).
4. List the intervals in either ascending or descending order of score values.
5. Tally the scores into the appropriate class interval.
6. Obtain the frequency for each interval by adding up the tally marks.

Table 6.2 presents the grouped frequency distribution for the data shown in Table 6.1 Notice that the unnecessary detail of frequencies of 0 have been eliminated. In addition,

TABLE 6.2 Grouped Frequency Distribution of Scores

Interval	Midpoint	Frequency
76–84	80	1
67–75	71	5
58–66	62	9
49–57	53	14
40–48	44	20
31–39	35	17
22–30	26	12
13–21	17	8
4–12	8	1

note that the midpoint, or center, of each class interval was also calculated. The midpoint of an interval is calculated by the following formula:

$$\text{Midpoint of the interval} = \frac{\text{lower limit} + \text{upper limit}}{2}$$

For example, the midpoint of the first interval, 76–84 is:

$$\frac{76 + 84}{2} = \frac{160}{2} = 80$$

Once the midpoints have been determined, it is simple to present the data graphically. Graphical presentation of the distribution allows the researcher to see the shape of the distribution, which in turn may determine which measure of central tendency is appropriate. There are two common graphical presentations: the frequency polygon and the histogram.

Frequency Polygons and Histograms

The frequency polygon and the histogram convey the same information and are frequently used by researchers to depict the data visually. By looking at the distribution, the researcher can tell whether the data are clustered together around one or more points or whether they are widely dispersed. The greater the dispersion, the more variability in the scores. In addition, the shape of the distribution also indicates whether the scores are distributed in a normal or a skewed fashion. When distribution is normal, the curve is symmetrical. When the data are distributed in an asymmetrical fashion, then the distribution is either positively or negatively *skewed,* depending on whether the majority of the scores are clustered toward the lower or higher end of the distribution. The shape of the distribution will be discussed in detail in the next section of this chapter.

The steps for constructing a frequency polygon are as follows: on the horizontal axis (the *x*-axis) is a listing of the midpoints of the class intervals, and on the vertical axis (the *y*-axis) is the listing of the frequencies. Once the axes have been labeled, the appropriate values (frequencies) are plotted for each class interval midpoint, and a line is drawn

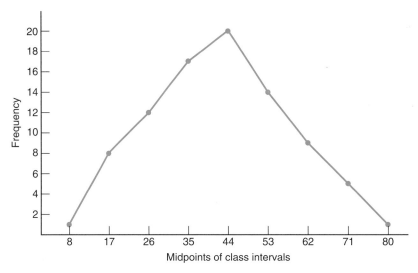

FIGURE 6.1   Frequency polygon of the grouped distribution of scores shown in Table 6.2.

to connect them. Figure 6.1 shows a frequency polygon for the grouped distribution of scores shown in Table 6.2.

The construction of the histogram rather closely follows the steps for the frequency polygon, except that with histograms bars are drawn to represent the frequencies of occurrence within a class interval. The bars drawn must touch each other in order to show that there are no gaps between adjacent intervals. The width of each bar extends from the lower to the upper limit of the interval, and its height represents the frequency of occurrences in the interval. Figure 6.2 shows the same data as Figure 6.1, except in histogram format.

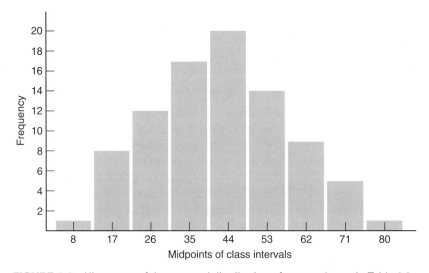

FIGURE 6.2   Histogram of the grouped distribution of scores shown in Table 6.2.

Types of Distributions

Once a histogram or frequency polygon has been constructed, the researcher can determine several important points by looking at the shape of the distribution of scores. For example, look at Figure 6.3. The first panel depicts an ideal distribution known as the *normal curve,* or the *bell curve.* Note the symmetry of this distribution, which indicates that there are an equal number of scores, both high and low, on either side of the distribution. Psychology textbooks frequently use this idealized bell curve to indicate a **normal distribution.** The second panel shows a narrower version of the normal curve, indicating less variability in

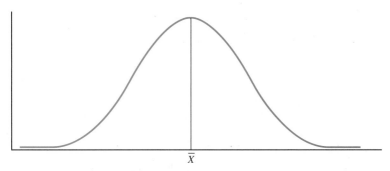

$\overline{X}$

Panel 1. Normal distribution.

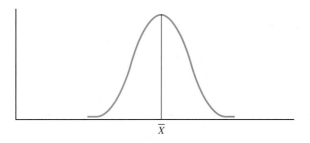

$\overline{X}$

Panel 2. Normal distribution with less variability.

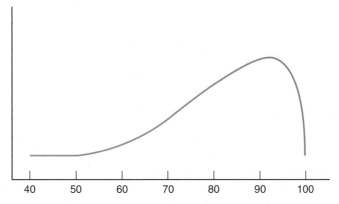

FIGURE 6.3 Panel 3. Negatively skewed distribution.

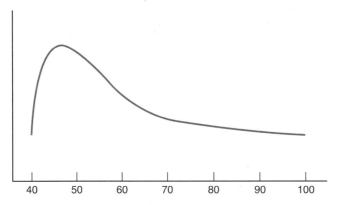

FIGURE 6.3   Panel 4. Positively skewed distribution.

the scores. The third panel depicts a negatively skewed distribution, whereas a positively skewed distribution is shown in the last panel.

Negatively skewed distributions occur when the majority of the scores are toward the higher end of the scale, but a few scores "drag" the tail of the distribution toward the lower end of the scale. For example, if the majority of the people in your class received grades in the 80s and the 90s but two or three people failed the exam, if you graphed the frequency of grades, you would have a negatively skewed distribution.

On the other hand, a *positively skewed* distribution occurs when most of the scores are toward the lower end of the scale, but a few scores pull the distribution toward the higher end of the scale. In terms of the example provided above, if the majority of the students in your class received grades in the 50s and 60s, but two or three people received 90s or even a 100, then you would have a positively skewed distribution. When the distribution is skewed, the appropriate measure of central tendency is different from the one used for normal distributions.

Now that you have reviewed the properties of distributions, it is time to take a look at the various measures of central tendency available to the researcher.

MEASURES OF CENTRAL TENDENCY

One simple way to summarize the results of an experiment is to calculate the value of the typical response, or score. The typical response, or score, shows how the average participant responded or scored in the study. Another way of looking at the typical response is to say that it represents the *average,* or the *norm,* for the sample. In fact, the terms *normal* and *abnormal* are derived from statistics. We say that a response is normal when it represents how the average or typical person responds. On the other hand, the term abnormal simply means away (ab) from the typical (norm).

There are three common measures of central tendency: the *mean, median,* and *mode.* Keep in mind, however, that the terms *average* or *typical* are theoretical concepts and therefore have their weaknesses.

The Mean

The arithmetic mean is simply the sum of all scores divided by the number of scores. It is the appropriate statistic to use when the data are on an interval or ratio scale, and it is the most widely used measure of central tendency. The statistical symbol for the mean of a sample of data is $\overline{X}$, and in scientific journal articles it is depicted as *M*. The formula for calculating the mean is: $\overline{X} = \Sigma\, X/N$, where *X* stands for each individual score; Σ means that all the scores are added together; and *N* is the total number of scores.

For example, let's say that you wish to see whether men or women make more errors on a spatial task. Table 6.3 shows the number of errors made by each participant in each condition.

To calculate the mean, the errors made by the participants in each group were added up, and the total number of errors (ΣX) was then divided by the number of scores *(N)*. For male participants, the total number of errors was 70, and for female participants the total number of errors was 66. There were 6 participants in each condition; therefore, the mean number of errors for males was 11.67 (70/6), and for females it was11 (66/6).

Although the mean is a popular measure of central tendency, it is not always appropriate. As mentioned earlier, it is used when the data are on an interval or ratio scale, and when the distribution of scores is fairly normal. When there are extreme scores, or when the distribution is skewed, the mean will reflect this and give a distorted measure of central tendency.

For example, look at the data for the male participants in Table 6.3. Suppose that the last participant made 62 errors, instead of 12. The mean error score for males would then be 20. However, the new mean would not accurately reflect the error rates for males. We could not say that the average male made 20 errors. The extreme score of 62 errors would inflate the mean so that it would no longer be representative of the distribution of scores.

For another example of the sensitivity of the mean to extreme scores consider the following. Let's say that you wished to establish the average income of a group of 10 people. Nine of those 10 individuals had an income in the $25,000–$30,000 range, but one person had an income of $1,300,000. If you simply summed up everyone's income and divided the sum by 10, the resulting average income would not be representative of the typical income in the group.

TABLE 6.3   Calculating Means

X	Males	Females
X_1	12	12
X_2	13	10
X_3	14	15
X_4	10	7
X_5	9	6
X_6	12	16
$\Sigma X =$	70	66
$\overline{X} =$	11.67	11

The Median

When you have extreme scores such as these, or the data are on an *ordinal scale,* the appropriate measure of central tendency is the median. The median is depicted as *Mdn* in scientific journals, and it represents the *midpoint* of a distribution of ordered scores. The midpoint of a distribution simply means that 50 percent of the scores are below the median and 50 percent of the scores are above it. Therefore, the median is also known as the score at the 50th percentile.

For example, let's say the following data represent the number of errors made by a group of nine participants:

21, 18, 19, 83, 20, 25, 17, 22, 16

To calculate the median, first put the scores in ascending or descending order—for example, 16, 17, 18, 19, 20, 21, 22, 25, 83—and then identify the middle score, which is 20. Note how half the scores (four) are below 20 and half the scores (four) are above 20. Note also how the extreme score of 83 errors did not artificially inflate the average score for errors.

But what if you had an even number of scores? How would you calculate the midpoint so that half the scores would be below it and half above? If that were the case, you would simply add up the two scores in the middle and divide by 2. In other words, you would calculate the mean of the two middle scores. For example, let's add the number 23 to the above distribution, so that now there are 10 scores instead of nine: 16, 17, 18, 19, 20, 21, 22, 23, 25, 83. Now add up the numbers 20 and 21, then divide by two to derive the median: 20 + 21 = 41; 41/2 = 20.5

The Mode

The final measure of central tendency is the mode; however, it is rarely used in psychological research unless the data are on a *nominal scale.* The mode is simply the *most frequent score,* or the most frequently occurring value. To derive the mode, you simply count the number of scores in your response categories, and the category with the highest frequency is the mode. For example, if you were investigating who buys more theater tickets, African-Americans, Whites, Hispanics, or Asians, you would simply count the number of people in each category who have bought theater tickets in the past year. The category with the highest number of individuals would be the mode.

The distribution will sometimes have two modes, in which case it is called a bimodal distribution, or three modes (trimodal distribution). For example, look at the following data, which represent the grades received in a class and the number of students in each category:

Grade:	A	B+	B	C+	C	D+	D	F
Number of students:	20	10	4	7	20	3	1	1

By assigning numerical values to the letter grades, such as the traditional 4.00 for the A; 3.50 for the B+; 3.00 for the B, and so on, it is easy to see how this is a bimodal distribution. Notice that an equal number of students received As and Cs, and therefore the two modes are 4.00 and 2.00, representing the As and Cs, respectively.

The mode is considered to have limited value when it comes to comparing two distributions. For example, two distributions may have identical modes, which could lead to the erroneous conclusion that they are similar, when in fact they might be very different. As an example, look at the following two distributions of grades received in two different professors' classes.

Psychology 101A

Grade:	100	95	90	85	80	75	70	65	60
Number of students:	0	0	0	6	6	7	16	10	11

Psychology 101B

Grade:	100	95	90	85	80	75	70	65	60
Number of students:	10	11	10	9	0	0	16	0	0

Notice how the mode is the same in both classes (70); however, it could not be said that the two distributions are similar. The students in the first distribution, Psychology 101A, received much lower grades overall than the students in the second distribution, Psychology 101B. In fact, none of the students in the first distribution received grades of 90 and above, whereas in the second distribution the majority of the students did.

Regardless of which measure of central tendency is used to describe the average or typical score, it cannot fully describe the data. If your professor tells you that the typical, or average, grade on the last exam was an 80, it does not tell you very much. However, if she tells you that the grades ranged from a 60 to a 100, with a mean grade of 80, you now know more about the distribution of grades. The next section discusses the second major area of descriptive statistics: measures of variability.

MEASURES OF VARIABILITY

In one psychology class or another you have most likely learned that the average IQ score in the United States is 100. However, as already mentioned, just knowing the average score does not tell you very much. What exactly does it mean to have an average score of 100? Obviously, it cannot mean that everyone scores a 100; since it's a measure of central tendency, there must be people who score below 100 and others who score above it. If you score a 95, are you below average in intelligence? In a similar vein, does a score of 105 mean that you are above average? How do we know when someone is below or above average in intelligence? We know this from the **standard deviation,** which is a popular measure of variability. If you have learned that the average IQ score is 100, then you must have also learned that the standard deviation is 15. In other words, the average IQ score is really 100 ± 15 points. This tells us that the typical, or average, person's score varies from the mean by 15 IQ points in either direction, and that is why we know that the normal range of intelligence is 85–115.

Measures of variability describe how dispersed, or variable, the scores are in a distribution. The larger the measure of variability, the more varied the scores are. Conceptually speaking, measures of variability indicate error variance, including error variance due to individual differences. Therefore, a large measure of variability is undesirable, for it would indicate a large amount of individual differences. Typically, the smaller the measure of variability, the less error variance there is due to individual differences, and the more likely it is that the hypothesis will be supported. This important concept will be covered in detail in the next chapter.

Measures of central tendency, along with measures of variability, summarize and describe the key features of an experiment. Although the standard deviation is the most commonly reported measure of variability, you should be familiar with three other measures: the **variance,** the **range** and the **interquartile range.** As you will see, the standard deviation is simply the square root of the variance.

As mentioned in the section on measures of central tendency, all analyses conducted by using statistical software provide measures of variability along with measures of central tendency.

Standard Deviation

The most common measure of variability is the standard deviation, depicted as *SD*. The standard deviation tells us how a *typical participant's score varied from the mean* in the research study. For example, if in an experiment the mean number of words recalled was 54 and the standard deviation was 4, we now know that the typical participant varied from the mean by 4 points in either direction. Therefore, the typical or average recall performance was somewhere between 50 and 58 words.

The standard deviation is the square root of the variance (S^2), and therefore to derive the standard deviation, the variance is calculated first. Chances are that you will be using one of the statistical software packages to analyze your data and therefore will not be calculating the variance or the standard deviation by hand. However, it is always a good idea to do it by hand at least once, for the following reasons. First, after you have spent time working out a problem by hand, you will probably gain an appreciation for the speed and ease with which statistical software can accomplish the same. But even more importantly, calculating statistics by hand helps you to understand the logic that underlies the procedure. In other words, by doing it yourself, it is easier to see where those numbers come from, and what they stand for.

The formula for calculating the sample variance is:

$$S^2 = \frac{\Sigma\left(X - \overline{X}\right)^2}{N}$$

where $(X - \overline{X})$ stands for the deviation from the mean and $(X - \overline{X})^2$ stands for squared deviations. The summation sign Σ simply means that you must add up all the squared deviations. Table 6.4 shows how the variance is calculated from a set of raw scores in a distribution.

Notice how the deviation from the mean is derived by subtracting each raw score (X) from the mean $(\overline{X})$. In other words, this procedure tells us how each participant's score deviates from the average or typical performance. This is why we can say that the greater the deviation, the greater the variability, including variability due to individual differences in your sample. Notice also how the deviations from the mean add up to zero. Variance is essentially the average of the dispersion of scores; however, it would make no sense to take the average of the deviations since they add up to zero. Therefore, the positive and negative signs are removed by squaring each of the deviations prior to calculating the average. Once the variance has been calculated, by taking its square root, the standard deviation is derived.

TABLE 6.4   **Calculating the Variance and the Standard Deviation**

Scores X	Deviations from the Mean $(X - \bar{X})$	Squared Deviations $(X - \bar{X})^2$
5	5–3 = 2	4
4	4–3 = 1	1
3	3–3 = 0	0
2	2–3 = –1	1
1	1–3 = –2	4
$\Sigma X = 15$		$\Sigma = 10$
$\bar{X} = 3$		
$N = 5$		

$$S^2 = \frac{\Sigma(X - \bar{X})^2}{N - 1} = \frac{10}{4} = 2.5$$

$$S = \sqrt{S^2} = \sqrt{2.5} = 1.58$$

As you can see, the calculation of the standard deviation relies on the mean of the distribution, and therefore it is also sensitive to extreme scores. In addition, just as the mean is not the appropriate measure of central tendency when the distribution is skewed, neither is the standard deviation the appropriate measure of variability for skewed distributions. With **skewed distributions** the appropriate measure of central tendency is the median, and the corresponding measure of variability is the interquartile range.

The Range

The *range* is the crudest measure of variability and is seldom used in psychological research. It is very easy to calculate, for it is simply the difference between the highest and the lowest scores in the distribution. For example, if the grades received on an exam are 45, 47, 50, 56, 67, 70, 73, 78, 79, 83, 85, 88, 90, 95, and 97, then the range is 97 – 45 = 52.

Notice how large the variability is in this particular class. The students range in ability from failure to the high 90s. Now look at another hypothetical class where the grades are 70, 72, 73, 75, 78, 80, 82, 86, 88, 90, 93, and 95. The range in this class is 25 (95 – 70), and it indicates that the students are much more similar in ability than the previous class. If you were a teacher, which class do you think would be easier to teach? That's right, it would be the second one. In the first class, if you were to teach to the students from the upper end of the range, chances are the students from the lower end would have some difficulty with the material. On the other hand, if you tailored your lectures to the lower end, the students from the upper end would not be challenged. In the second class, however, the individual differences aren't so large, so chances are that you could make your lectures challenging and yet accessible to all.

In general, the range does not tell us very much about the distribution beyond the maximum possible difference between the scores. In addition, it is very sensitive to extreme scores, and therefore, it may give a distorted idea of the variability of the scores. For example, suppose I tell you that the range in final exam grades for my class was a 65.

From this, you may conclude that the students must be very dissimilar or varied in ability. However, upon showing you the distribution of grades—32, 80, 84, 86, 88, 90, 94, 97— you realize that the students are not all that dissimilar. Only one person did poorly; everyone else did very well.

Interquartile Range

It is quite simple to calculate the *interquartile range.* The scores in the distribution are first put into order, and then the distribution is divided into four equal parts, or quartiles. The score below which 25 percent of the scores fall (Q_1) is located, as is the score below which 75 percent of the scores lie (Q_3). By subtracting Q_1 from Q_3, the interquartile range is derived.

Let's look at the following distribution of scores that have been put in order: 2, 2, 4, 5, 8, 9, 10, 12, 14, 16, 17, 18. By dividing the distribution into four equal parts, we derive the following four quartiles: 2, 2, 4 (Q_1); 5, 8, 9 (Q_2); 10, 12, 14 (Q_3); and 16, 17, 18 (Q_4). The point below which 25 percent of the scores lie is 5, and the score below which 75 percent of the scores fall is 16. By subtracting 5 from 16, we find that the interquartile range is 9.

Like the range, the interquartile range is not commonly used in psychological research. However, on occasions when the distribution is skewed, it is the preferred measure of variability.

GRAPHING THE DATA

Although earlier in this chapter you saw that frequency distributions can be depicted with histograms and polygons, neither the histogram nor the polygon can show the relationship between the independent and dependent variable. In other words, histograms and polygons are helpful in showing how the responses in the experiment are distributed; they can even show us the shape of the distribution, but they do not tell us how those responses vary as a function of the independent variable. In order to depict the relationship between the independent and dependent variables, the researcher typically graphs the data.

Whether the researcher presents the data in a line graph or a bar graph depends on the independent variable of the experiment. If the independent variable is *quantitative*, or *continuous*, typically a *line graph* is used. On the other hand, if the independent variable is *qualitative*, or *discrete*, then a *bar graph* is used.

Regardless of the type of graph used, according to convention the independent variable is represented on the horizontal axis, and the dependent variable on the vertical axis. The axes are clearly labeled, and if there are two or more independent variables, a legend is provided for clarification.

For conventional graph construction and proper labeling of axes, consult your APA manual.

Quantitative Variables

Quantitative independent variables are also said to be continuous when, theoretically, they can have an infinite number of values between adjacent units on a scale. Time, height, weight, and temperature are all continuous variables in that there could be an infinite number of values between adjacent units. For example, if you were conducting a study on the effects of study time on grades received, you might only select two levels for the inde-

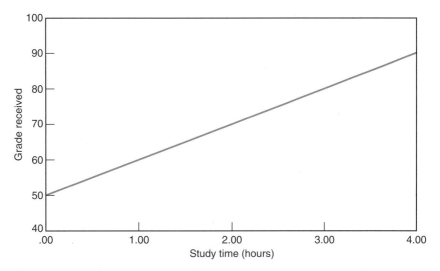

FIGURE 6.4   Grades as a function of study time in a hypothetical experiment.

pendent variable of study time: 1 hour and 2 hours. But in between these two units there could be (theoretically) an infinite number of values—for example, 1 hour, 1 second; 1 hour, 2 seconds, 1 hour, 3 seconds, and so on. Similarly, you might only select three levels of temperature—70 degrees, 80 degrees, and 90 degrees—but there could be 70.001 degrees; 70.002 degrees; and so on.

Figure 6.4 shows hypothetical data for the relationship between study time and grades received, as depicted by a line graph.

Qualitative Variables

Qualitative independent variables are discontinuous, or discrete, when there can be no possible values between adjacent units on the scale. In other words, there are only discrete categories, with no possible intermediate values. Race, gender, religion, and nationality, for example, are all qualitative variables. A participant belongs to the category of either African-American, White, or Asian. There is no continuity between the categories. Similarly, there are no intermediate values between being Catholic, Protestant, or Jewish, or between being male or female. Even if you assigned numerical values to these categories for the purpose of statistical analysis, to say that someone is 1.2 Catholic while another is 1.4 Catholic would be meaningless, not to say ridiculous.

The bar graph in Figure 6.5 shows the hypothetical data showing how participants from various ethnic backgrounds rated a task.

RELATIONSHIPS BETWEEN VARIABLES

In the beginning of this textbook, you read that scientists are primarily interested in determining the relationship between two events, or variables. How the relationship, if in fact one exists, is described depends on the nature of the independent and dependent variables

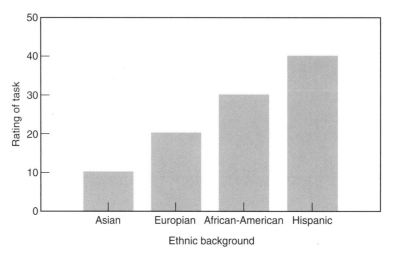

FIGURE 6.5   Rating of a task by people of various ethnic backgrounds in a hypothetical experiment.

of the study. As you will see in a moment, it would not make sense to describe a relationship between qualitative variables in the same way as you would when the variables are quantitative.

When both the independent and dependent variables are quantitative, meaning that they have true numerical value, the relationship between them may be described as a **positive linear function,** a **negative linear function,** or a **curvilinear function.**

For example, let's say that you wish to improve your exam grades and so you increase the amount of time you study. You believe that an increase in study time will lead to an increase in the grades you receive. Note that your variables are quantitative; they have true numerical value. The amount of time you study can be quantified, for instance, 1 hour, 2 hours, and your grades have numerical value as well. If you find a rise in your grades as a result of increasing your study time, then you can say that your grade is a positive linear function of study time. As one variable (study time) increased in numerical value, so did the other (grades).

However, if one of the variables in the study is qualitative and has no true numerical value, to describe the relationship in these terms would be meaningless. For instance, if you were studying the relationship between race and school performance, although you might find a relationship, to describe it as either a positive or negative linear function, or a curvilinear function, would be meaningless. If you were to find that one group had a higher grade point average (GPA) than another, to say that as race increased, GPA increased (or decreased) would be ridiculous.

When both the independent and dependent variables are quantitative, the researcher is asking, does an increase in the independent variable lead to an increase, a decrease, or no change in the dependent variable? And if there is a corresponding increase in the dependent variable, if I keep increasing the independent variable, will the dependent variable keep increasing, or will it reach a point after which it will start decreasing?

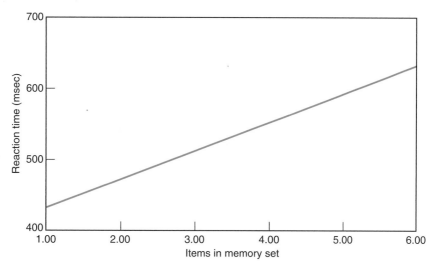

FIGURE 6.6   Positive linear relationship depicting reaction time as a function of memory set size. Based on Sternberg (1966) experiment.

Positive Linear Relationships

In a positive linear relationship an increase in the value, or levels, of the independent variable leads to a corresponding increase in the value of the dependent variable. The opposite is also true; a decrease in the value of the independent variable leads to a decrease in the value of the dependent variable.

For example, in a classic study Sternberg (1966) investigated how information is retrieved from short-term memory (STM). He was interested in seeing whether the search for a given item in STM was serial or parallel. Serial search would mean that the memory set is searched one item at a time, while a parallel search would indicate that the entire memory set is seen all at once. He presented a series of digits, for example, 1 3 4, followed by a probe, and the participant had to respond by pressing a button labeled YES if the probe was part of the original set, or NO if the probe was not part of the original set. The dependent variable was reaction time measured in milliseconds (msec). Sternberg varied the size of the memory set from one to six digits, and he hypothesized that if the search was serial, then the size of the set should matter. On the other hand, if the search through the set was all at once (parallel), then set size should not matter. Sternberg found that set size did matter: as the number of digits in the set increased, so did the reaction time. Each additional digit in the memory set added a constant 38 milliseconds to the reaction time. This finding indicates that the retrieval of items from STM is serial. Figure 6.6 shows this positive linear function.

Negative Linear Relationships

In a negative linear relationship an increase in the value, or levels, of the independent variable leads to a corresponding decrease in the value of the dependent variable. Again, the

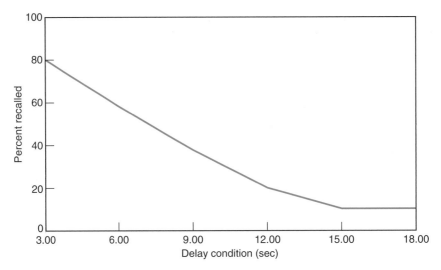

FIGURE 6.7   Negative linear relationship showing recall as a function of delay. Based on Peterson and Peterson (1959) experiment.

opposite is also true: a decrease in the value of the independent variable leads to an increase in the value of the dependent variable.

For example, Peterson and Peterson (1959) studied the ability to retrieve information from STM after short delays if rehearsal were prevented. They presented participants with a series of CCC trigrams (three consonants) such as KLH and then varied the retention interval before recall. The retention interval is the amount of time that elapses before asking a participant to recall the information that was presented. The delays between the stimulus onset (seeing the trigram) and recall were 3,6,9,12,15, and 18 seconds. During the retention interval, having the participants count backward by threes from a given number prevented rehearsal of the trigram. Peterson and Peterson found that as the length of the retention interval increased, the percent of correct recall decreased. Figure 6.7 shows this negative linear relationship.

Curvilinear Relationships

Just because a researcher obtains what is a seemingly positive linear function, it does not mean that a continuous increase in the value of the independent variable will continue to produce an increase in the value of the dependent variable. Similarly, if the function is negative, it cannot be assumed that a continuous increase in one variable will continue to produce a decrease in the other.

In Chapter 2, you read that when the independent variable has more than two levels, if the relationship between the independent and dependent variables is curvilinear, it is possible to detect it. However, if there are only two levels of the independent variable, the researcher may reach an erroneous conclusion regarding the relationship between the independent and dependent variables.

For example, let's say that you are interested in studying the effects of emotional arousal on the performance of a difficult task, and you assign three levels of arousal: low,

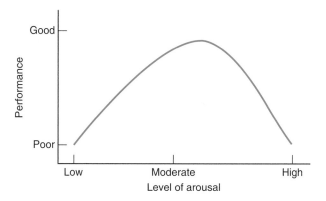

FIGURE 6.8 Depiction of a curvilinear relationship between arousal and performance.

moderate, and high. Being familiar with Mandler's theory of how the interruption of goal-oriented activity leads to emotional arousal (1975, 1984, 1990), you operationally define arousal as the number of interruptions during the task performance. You conduct the experiment on the three groups of participants who have been randomly assigned to the various arousal conditions, and then you evaluate the quality of their performance on the task. You find that there was no difference between the low- and the high-arousal conditions; the quality of the performance was equally poor. However, you also find that the participants in the moderate level of arousal condition had the highest quality performance. Figure 6.8 illustrates this finding.

As you can see, the relationship between arousal and performance in this hypothetical experiment is curvilinear. In curvilinear relationships, an increase in one variable leads to both an increase and a decrease in the other variable. The relationship will change directions at least once. Notice how an increase in arousal leads to an increase in the quality of the performance, but only up to a point. As the level of arousal increases beyond the moderate level, the quality of the performance decreases. If there had been only two levels of arousal, you might have drawn erroneous conclusions about the relationship between these variables. Look at Figure 6.8 again and suppose that there were only the low-arousal and the high-arousal conditions. If that were the case, you might have assumed (incorrectly) that there was no relationship between arousal and performance. On the other hand, if there had been only a low-arousal and a moderate-arousal condition, you might have assumed a positive linear relationship. Without the high level of arousal condition to clarify the relationship, it would have been tempting (and erroneous) to conclude that the greater the arousal, the better the performance. However, since the relationship between arousal and performance is curvilinear, the findings indicate that a moderate amount of arousal is necessary for good performance, whereas too much or too little arousal leads to poor-quality performance.

In other instances, having only two levels of the independent variable may also lead to an erroneous assumption of a negative linear relationship. For example, Gelles (as cited in Goldstein, Keller, & Erne, 1985) found that the frequency of child abuse incidents decreased as the age of the child increased. However, after age 15 the frequency of abuse once again increased. Gelles concluded that children are most vulnerable between ages 3 and 5 and between ages 15 and 17. Had Gelles only studied children under the age of 15, an incorrect assumption might have been made regarding the relationship between the age of the child and the incidents of child abuse.

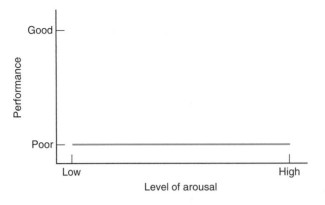

FIGURE 6.9 Depiction of no relationship between arousal and performance.

No Relationship

When there is no relationship between two variables, the line on the graph is flat. Again, caution must be used in interpreting results from experiments that use only two levels of an independent variable. Just as having only two levels may lead an investigator to erroneously conclude either a positive or a negative linear relationship when in reality the relationship is curvilinear, the researcher may conclude that there is no relationship at all. Figure 6.9 shows no relationship between arousal and performance in the hypothetical experiment mentioned earlier.

SUMMARY

- The field of statistics is a tool of science that allows researchers to make sense out of their data.
- The two major branches of statistics are descriptive and inferential statistics.
- Descriptive statistics help researchers to organize, summarize, and describe the data, whereas inferential statistics allow researchers to interpret and generalize their findings.
- One way to describe the data is to construct a frequency distribution. A frequency distribution is a presentation of score values and their frequency of occurrence. Once the frequencies of scores have been grouped into class intervals, a polygon or histogram may be used to graphically present the data.
- Graphical presentation of a frequency distribution may reveal that the data follow a normal curve or that the data are skewed. When the data follow a normal curve, the mean, median, and the mode have the same numerical value. Skewed distributions are typical when there are extreme scores, either at the high or the low end of the distribution.
- The most common way to describe the data is to calculate measures of central tendency and variability.
- Measures of central tendency describe the most typical or average response. The mean, median, and mode are all measures of central tendency. The most commonly presented measure of central tendency in psychological research is the mean. However, when there are extreme scores in the distribution the median might be more appropriate.
- Measures of variability describe how varied or dispersed the scores are. The larger the measure of variability, the more varied the scores are. Conceptually speaking, measures of variability indicate error variance, more specifically, error variance due to individual differences.

- The most commonly reported measure of variability is the standard deviation, which is the square root of the variance. The variance is the average of the sum of squared deviations from the mean. The standard deviation shows how much a typical score varied from the mean.

- Data may also be presented graphically, using either a line or a bar graph. When both the independent and dependent variables are quantitative, a line graph is appropriate. When one of the variables is qualitative, a bar graph should be used.

- Quantitative variables are also said to be continuous because, theoretically, they can have an infinite number of values between adjacent units on a scale.

- Qualitative variables are also said to be discontinuous, or discrete, because there can be no possible values between adjacent units on the scale.

- When graphing variables, the independent variable is typically placed on the horizontal axis, and the dependent variable is depicted on the vertical axis.

- The relationship between the independent and dependent variables may be linear, or curvilinear.

- In a positive linear relationship, an increase in the independent variable leads to a increase in the dependent variable. Similarly, a decrease in the independent variable leads to a decrease in the dependent variable.

- In a negative linear relationship, an increase in the independent variable leads to a decrease in the dependent variable. Similarly, a decrease in the independent variable leads to an increase in the dependent variable.

- In a curvilinear relationship, an increase in one variable leads to both an increase and a decrease in the other variable.

KEY CONCEPTS

Curvilinear Function	Measure of Central	Positive Linear Function	Range
Descriptive Statistics	Tendency	Qualitative Independent	Skewed Distribution
Frequency Distribution	Measure of Variability	Variables	Standard Deviation
Inferential Statistics	Negative Linear Function	Quantitative Indepen-	Variance
Interquartile Range	Normal Distribution	dent Variables	

QUESTIONS

Short answers can be found in Appendix A.

1. Explain the difference between descriptive and inferential statistics.

2. Describe a negatively skewed distribution and give an example.

3. Describe a positively skewed distribution and give an example.

4. Any set of scores (data) may be described by measures of _____ and _____.

5. Means and standard deviations

a. summarize the results of an experiment

b. organize the data

c. describe the data

d. all of the above

6. Which of the following is not a measure of central tendency?

a. Mean

b. Mode

c. Median

d. Standard deviation

7. In a distribution of scores: 78, 52, 89, 40, 92, 67, 90, the median is

a. 40

b. 66

c. 78

d. 89

8. In an experiment, the standard deviation was found to be 12. This means that

a. the measure of central tendency was 12

b. the independent variable had no effect

c. a typical participant varied from the mean by 12 points

d. the results were significant

9. State whether the following are quantitative or qualitative variables:

a. room temperature

b. number of words recalled in an experiment

c. the IQ score of participants

d. the race of the participants

e. reaction time on a task

f. gender of the participants

g. age of the participants

10. State whether you would use a line graph or a bar graph to present the data for the following:

a. the relationship between age and memory for words

b. the relationship between gender and task performance

c. the number of words recalled by African-Americans and Whites

d. the relationship between room temperature and learning

e. the effect of speed of presentation on the number of ideas recalled

f. the relationship between IQ and memory for abstract words

INFERENTIAL STATISTICS

- Do the results support my hypothesis?
- Are my results due to the effect of the independent variable or to chance?
- Why did my results turn out to be not significant?
- Did I make an error in rejecting the hypothesis?
- How can I maximize the probability that the results will support the hypothesis?
- From the results of my sample, can I estimate similar behavior or response characteristics for the population from which I drew the sample?

INFERENTIAL STATISTICS

In Chapter 6, you read that researchers use descriptive statistics to summarize the key features of an experiment by calculating measures of central tendency and variability. In addition, the means of the experimental conditions may be presented in a figure either by a bar graph or a line graph, depending on the nature of the variables. However, simply describing the data does not tell you whether the hypothesis was supported or whether the results can be generalized to the population. The second major branch of statistics, inferential statistics, allows you to interpret the results and to make generalizations to the population of interest. There are two major areas of inferential statistics: **parameter estimation** and **hypothesis testing.**

In *parameter estimation* population characteristics are estimated from sample characteristics. In other words, the process of parameter estimation allows us to make statistical inferences about the value of a population parameter based on our sample. A *parameter* is a number that quantifies a population characteristic. For example, you can use the mean and standard deviation of your sample as estimates of population parameters regarding the trait, behavior, or attribute that you studied in the sample. If the mean number of words recalled in the sample is 25 and the standard deviation is 5, you can estimate that the population parameter is approximately 25, or between 20 and 30.

The majority of applications in inferential statistics involve *hypothesis testing.* An important process in inferential statistics, hypothesis testing allows you to state, upon sufficient findings, that the differences observed between conditions or groups are due to the effect of the independent variable. In other words, hypothesis testing allows you the opportunity to determine the likelihood that the observed differences may have been due to chance.

For example, let's say that you are interested in studying gender differences in the performance of spatial tasks. You believe that men tend to be more spatially oriented than women, and therefore you expect that males would make fewer errors on a spatial task. Once you have collected the data and calculated the mean number of errors made by each group, you find that on average the male participants made 48 errors, while the female participants made 54. Since there is a difference of six errors between the two groups, can you conclude from those numbers alone that your hypothesis is correct and that, in general, men are more spatially skilled? The answer is no. You cannot conclude that because you do not know whether the observed difference between the two means is *significant,* meaning that it is due to gender effects and not merely to random chance or error.

HYPOTHESIS TESTING

The whole point of any experiment is to see whether the manipulation of the independent variable had an effect on the dependent variable. If the two (or more) groups or conditions appear to differ on the dependent measure, is this difference due to the independent variable or to chance? By conducting various statistical tests, you can determine whether the difference is significant or not significant. If the difference is not significant, you conclude that the independent variable had no effect and that the observed differences are due to chance. On the other hand, if the difference is significant, you conclude that the independent variable did have an effect and that the probability that the results are due to chance alone is limited.

Treatment Populations

Although most experiments involve a research hypothesis, inferential tests actually evaluate and assess statistical hypotheses. Statistical hypotheses are rooted in statistical theory and predict the hypothetical outcome for a study if, at least theoretically speaking, an infinite number of participants could participate in the project. Each participant would be assigned randomly to one of the conditions, and all the people who received the same type of treatment would belong to the same treatment population. Therefore, every experiment has at least two different populations since every experiment must have at least two conditions. At the most basic level, there might be a treatment population and a control population.

For example, if you were interested in investigating the effects of a certain drug, then theoretically speaking, the study would consist of a *treatment population* (a sample of which is exposed to the drug) and a *control population* (a sample of which is not exposed to the drug). On the other hand, if the study examined the effects of frequent, moderately frequent, and infrequent words on memory, for example, then there would be three different treatment populations.

The mean of each treatment population is designated by the Greek letter μ *(mu)*, and the differences observed between the population means are called *population treatment effects*.

Though not readily apparent, this has quite a bit to do with hypothesis testing and significant differences. Refer back to the drug study mentioned earlier. Suppose that the drug is believed to reduce schizophrenic symptoms and that one group receives the drug (treatment) and another group does not (control). After one month, the number of symptoms is counted, and it is found that the treatment group has fewer symptoms than the control group. If the number of symptoms between the two conditions is not significantly different, it means that participants in the study were in reality drawn from the same population. Therefore, the observed difference is probably due to chance or sampling error. On the other hand, if the difference between the conditions is significant, then you can conclude that the participants were in fact drawn from different populations and that the observed differences are due to the independent variable.

The statistical hypotheses mentioned above are the **null hypothesis** (H_0) and the **alternative hypothesis** (H_1). The alternative hypothesis is, essentially, the experimental or research hypothesis. The two hypotheses are mutually exclusive, meaning that if one is true, the other must be false. If the results of statistical analyses suggest that the null hypothesis is true, then the alternative or experimental hypothesis is probably false, and vice versa.

The Null Hypothesis

The *null hypothesis* states that the independent variable has no effect. In other words, it specifies that there is no significant difference between the various conditions, and any differences that are observed are due to chance alone. The prediction made by the null hypothesis is stated as H_0: $\mu_1 = \mu_2$, when there are two conditions. If there are three or more conditions, then H_0: $\mu_1 = \mu_2 = \mu_3$, and so on.

As you can see, the null hypothesis assumes that the means of the various treatment populations are the same; that is, the data are actually from the same treatment population. To refer back to the drug study, the null hypothesis assumes that the data for the two groups (drug and no drug) come from two samples of the same population. In other words, they did not come from the two separate treatment populations.

In any experiment, the researcher is always directly testing the assumption that the null hypothesis is true. If statistical analysis reveals that the means are in fact significantly different, then the null hypothesis is rejected, and the alternative hypothesis is tentatively accepted.

The Alternative Hypothesis

The *alternative, or experimental, hypothesis* is the logical counterpart of the null hypothesis. It states that the independent variable does have an effect, which means that the observed differences between the conditions are due to the independent variable manipulation and not to chance or sampling error alone. The prediction made by the experimental hypothesis is stated as H_1: $\mu_1 \neq \mu_2$, when there are two conditions, and as H_1: $\mu_1 \neq \mu_2 \neq \mu_3$, and so on, when there are three or more conditions.

Opposite to the null hypothesis, the experimental hypothesis predicts that the data are from different treatment populations. In terms of the drug study, the data for the group that receives the drug comes from the treatment population sample, whereas the data for the group that does not receive the drug comes from the control population sample.

If the null hypothesis is rejected, the experimental hypothesis is supported. On the other hand, if the null hypothesis cannot be rejected, then the experimental hypothesis is not supported.

Types of Errors

As we all know from experience, any decision-making process always involves the possibility that we will make the wrong decision. Given this fallibility in decision making, it is also possible to make an error in hypothesis testing. We may incorrectly reject either the null hypothesis or the experimental hypothesis when they are true, or incorrectly retain them when they are in fact false.

In the area of hypothesis testing, these incorrect decisions are called **Type I** and **Type II errors.** If the null hypothesis is erroneously rejected when it is true, and therefore the experimental hypothesis is supported when it is false, it is called a Type I error. On the other hand, if the null hypothesis is upheld when it is false, and therefore the experimental hypothesis is incorrectly rejected when it is true, it is considered a Type II error.

Table 7.1 shows the possible correct or incorrect decisions regarding the null and experimental hypotheses.

Decision Rule

Even if the differences between conditions turn out to be significant, and therefore the null hypothesis is rejected, there is always the possibility that the differences observed are in fact due to chance and that the null hypothesis was incorrectly rejected. If that were the case, we would be making a Type I error. However, we can limit the probability of making this error.

Before beginning the experiment, the researcher limits the probability of making a Type I error. This critical level of probability is known as **alpha,** designated by the Greek letter α, and is also known as the *level of significance*. It is called the level of significance

TABLE 7.1 Type I and Type II Errors

		Actual Status of the H_0	
		It Is True	It Is Not True
Your decision	Reject H_0	Type I error	Correct decision
	Accept H_0	Correct decision	Type II error

because it indicates whether the differences observed between conditions are large enough to be considered significant. By setting this critical probability level, the researcher acknowledges that a Type I error is possible, but its probability *(p)* is limited by alpha *(α).*

The more confident the researcher, the smaller the numerical value of alpha, since its value signifies the risk of incorrectly rejecting a true null hypothesis. In the majority of psychological research, the critical level of probability for a Type I error is set at .05. By stating that $\alpha = .05$, the researcher is saying that the probability of incorrectly rejecting a true null hypothesis cannot exceed 5 in 100. Another way of saying it is that the chance for incorrectly rejecting a true null hypothesis is 5 percent. If, after the appropriate statistical analysis, the obtained probability for error is less than or equal to the critical $p = .05$, the null hypothesis is rejected and the experimental hypothesis is supported. On the other hand, if the obtained probability for error is greater than .05, the null hypothesis is retained and the experimental hypothesis is not supported. The null hypothesis is retained because the chance for error is too great. It exceeded the acceptable or critical level for a Type I error.

Although, as stated earlier, in the majority of research the critical level of probability for error is .05, the experimenter can always set alpha at a lower level, for example, at .01, but generally does not set it at a higher level, for example, at .06. The lower the level of alpha, the more confident the researcher is in obtaining significant differences. In addition, the lower the level of alpha, the less probability there is for a Type I error. In an experiment where alpha is set at .01, the probability of incorrectly rejecting a true null hypothesis is 1 in 100.

So far, we have talked about limiting the probability of a Type I error by setting alpha, or the level of significance. But how do we limit the probability of a Type II error: the incorrect rejection of the experimental hypothesis? In the next section you will read about a very important concept called **power.** Statistical power is the ability of the experiment to detect real significant differences between conditions. If the experiment does not have enough power, real significant differences may not be detected. In that case, the experimental hypothesis must be rejected, and therefore a Type II error is possible.

Power

Suppose that your experimental hypothesis predicts that practice improves performance on some task. This prediction is perfectly reasonable; in general, the more we practice some skill, the better we tend to be. For example, musicians practice, athletes practice, dancers practice, and actors rehearse their roles prior to a performance. Students frequently take practice SAT tests before doing it for real. It makes perfectly good sense to believe that practice improves performance. Given this reasonable assumption, you set up an experiment where a group of 10 participants (Group I) receives 25 practice trials, while a second group of 10 participants (Group II) receives no practice trials. Both groups then perform the identical task, and you count the number of errors made in each condition. After analyzing the results, you find that the difference in errors made by Group I and II is not significant. In other words, the mean of Group I is not significantly different from the mean of Group II. Since the null hypothesis states H_0: $\mu_1 = \mu_2$, you must reject the experimental hypothesis (H_1) and must conclude that practice does not improve performance.

At this point, there are two possible reasons for your failure to detect a significant difference between the two groups. First, the null hypothesis may in fact be true, and practice has no effect on performance. The second possibility is that the null hypothesis is false (practice does improve performance), but the experiment did not have enough power to detect a real effect of this independent variable. Although in the above example the null hypothesis was retained, in actuality, or real life, the likelihood that people who practice do not perform any better than people who do not practice is pretty slim. Therefore, there is a very good possibility that, by rejecting the experimental hypothesis that practice improves performance, you have made a Type II error.

Power is defined as the ability or sensitivity of an experiment to detect a real effect of the independent variable. By real effect it is meant that changes in the value of the independent variable produce changes in the dependent measure. Statistically speaking, power is the probability that the null hypothesis will be rejected if it is false. If in real life the null hypothesis is false, but on the basis of statistical analysis the experimental decision is to support it, then we can say that the experiment lacked the power to reject a false null hypothesis.

The probability of making a Type II error is defined as **beta** and is designated by the Greek letter β. Furthermore, the probability of making a Type II error can be estimated by using the formula $\beta = 1-$ power. Power is essentially a probability, and therefore its value can range from 0.00 to 1.00. The larger the value of power, the greater the probability that the experiment can detect a real effect of the independent variable.

Given the formula $\beta = 1-$ power, notice that the greater the value of power, the less likely you are to make a Type II error. For example, let's say that the power of the experiment is 0.80. By using the formula, we can estimate the probability of making a Type II error: $\beta = 1- 0.80$, or $\beta = 0.20$. On the other hand, if the power of the experiment is low, let's say 0.20, then by the same formula we can calculate the probability of a Type II error to be 0.80 (1–0.20).

The actual calculation of the amount of power you need for a given experiment is beyond the scope of this textbook. However, you can take several steps to ensure that your experiment possesses enough power.

Increasing Power

In the example provided in the previous section, did you notice that the study only had 10 participants in each condition? Generally, the fewer the number of participants, the more individual differences there are, and the greater the chance for error variance. By *increasing the sample size (N),* we can increase the power of the experiment. Therefore, one way to increase power is to increase the number of participants in a study.

A second way of increasing power is to *maximize primary variance.* Do you remember Kerlinger's principles of control covered in Chapter 3? For example, if you choose extreme levels for your independent variable, your chances for treatment effects increase. As your chance for treatment effects increases, so does the experiment's power: its ability to find a real effect of the independent variable.

Taking steps to *decrease experimental errors* also increases power. Use careful control procedures, make sure all the participants are treated the same, randomly assign people into conditions, and so on. In other words, be careful and methodical. Pay close attention to the unwanted sources of variance mentioned in Chapter 3, and take every precaution to control for them. All sources of unwanted variance can lead to Type II errors in that your hypothesis may have to be rejected even if the null hypothesis is in fact false.

Finally, the *experimental design* itself can increase the power of the study. In Chapter 8, you will learn about within-subjects and between-subjects designs. Briefly, within-subjects designs use the same participants in every condition, whereas between-subjects designs use a different group of participants for each condition. Which design do you think is more powerful in that it controls for individual differences? That's right, the within-subjects design, since the participants are their own control.

Too much power is just as undesirable as too little. Increasing the power of the experiment, which leads to a decrease in the probability of a Type II error, can lead to an increase in the probability of a Type I error. In other words, if the experiment has a great deal of power, for example, by using a large sample size, then the null hypothesis might be rejected even if it is true. As Kupfersmid (1988) pointed out, given a large enough sample size, just about any null hypothesis can be shown to be false. As such, absurd as it may seem, even the experimental hypothesis that eating tomatoes increases intelligence might be supported. The following quote from Thompson (1998) regarding the ability to reject the null hypothesis illustrates this point perfectly: "Thus, statistical testing becomes a tautological search for enough participants to achieve statistical significance. If we fail to reject, it is only because we've been too lazy to drag in enough participants" (p. 799).

In closing, keep in mind that there is a tradeoff between making Type I and Type II errors: as the probability of one type of error decreases, the probability of the other type increases. As you tighten the probability of a Type I error (incorrect rejection of the null hypothesis) by using lower levels of alpha, you increase the chance that your results will not show significant differences. For example, let's say that there are two experimenters doing the identical study. Experimenter 1 sets alpha at .05, and experimenter 2 sets alpha at .01. After statistical analyses have been conducted, the obtained probability for error is found to be .03. Since the obtained *p* value (.03) is less than the critical *p* value (.05) set by the first experimenter, she can conclude that the independent variable had an effect and so she rejects the null hypothesis. On the other hand, the second experimenter cannot reject the null hypothesis since the obtained *p* value (.03) is greater than the one he specified (.01). Notice how the second experimenter increased his chance for a Type II error by decreasing the probability for a Type I error.

In addition, remember that too much of a good thing, power, may not be so great if it leads to the rejection of a true null hypothesis. In order to address this issue, in its publication manual the APA recommends that scientific reports include **effect sizes.** However, as some researchers have pointed out, this recommendation has not always been followed, and effect sizes are not reported as often as they should be (Kirk, 1996; Thompson, 1998).

Effect Size

The *effect size* indicates the magnitude of effect the independent variable has on the dependent variable. Essentially, it shows the strength of the relationship between the independent and dependent variables, and it is an additional piece of useful information that helps to clarify the impact of the independent variable. The major advantage of reporting the effect size is that it indicates the magnitude of the effect. In other words, although statistical analysis may indicate a significant effect of the independent variable, the effect size shows how strong the effect is.

For example, let's say that the statistical analysis of the data from an experiment shows that the independent variable had an effect, and therefore the null hypothesis is rejected. However, if the effect size is small, it indicates that the relationship between the independent and dependent variables is not very robust, even though the results were significant.

The effect size can be determined by calculating the Pearson r (correlation coefficient). The formula and procedure for calculating the effect size will be covered in the next chapter. Since the effect size is a square root, the value of r is always positive and can range from 0.00 to 1.00. As with the Pearson r, the greater the effect size, the greater the relationship between the independent and dependent variables.

SUMMARY

- The two major areas of inferential statistics are hypothesis testing and parameter estimation.

- In parameter estimation, the researcher estimates population characteristics from sample values such as the mean and standard deviation.

- Hypothesis testing is the application of inferential statistical procedures to see whether the independent variable had an effect. These procedures allow the experimenter to decide whether the data support the experimental hypothesis.

- Every experiment has two hypotheses: the null hypothesis and the alternative hypothesis. The alternative hypothesis is the experimental hypothesis.

- The null hypothesis predicts that the independent variable has no effect and that any differences observed between conditions are due to chance.

- The experimental, or alternative, hypothesis is the statement made by the experimenter regarding the relationship between the independent and dependent variables. Typically, the experimental hypothesis predicts that the independent variable will have an effect and that any observed differences between conditions are due to the manipulation of the independent variable.

- Every experiment begins with the assumption that the null hypothesis is true.

- At the beginning of the experiment, the researcher sets a critical level of probability that the results of the experiment are due to chance, and not to the effects of the independent variable. This critical level of probability is called alpha, and it is also known as the level of significance. By setting this critical probability level, the researcher acknowledges that a Type I error is possible, but its probability is limited by alpha.

- In the majority of psychological research, the critical level of probability for a Type I error is set at .05. By stating that $\alpha = .05$, the researcher is saying that the probability of incorrectly rejecting a true null hypothesis cannot exceed 5 in 100.

- If the researcher incorrectly rejects a true null hypothesis, a Type I error is made. If the researcher incorrectly accepts the null hypothesis when it is not true, a Type II error is made.

- The probability of making a Type II error is defined as beta, and the probability of making a Type II error can be estimated by using the formula $\beta = 1 - \text{power}$.

- Power is defined as the ability or sensitivity of an experiment to detect a real effect of the independent variable. Real effect indicates that changes in the value of the independent variable produce changes in the dependent measure. Statistically speaking, power is the probability that the null hypothesis can be rejected if it is false. If in real life the null hypothesis is false, but on the basis of statistical analysis the experimental decision is to support it, then the experiment lacked the power to reject a false null hypothesis.

- Power is essentially a probability, and therefore its value can range from 0.00 to 1.00. The larger the value of power, the greater the probability that the experiment can detect a real effect of the independent variable.
- Increasing the sample size, maximizing primary variance, minimizing experimental error, and using a within-subjects design can increase power.

KEY CONCEPTS

Alpha Level	Effect Size	Parameter Estimation	Type II Error
Alternative Hypothesis	Hypothesis Testing	Power	
Beta	Null Hypothesis	Type I Error	

QUESTIONS

Short answers can be found in Appendix A.

1. Results are said to be significant when there is a _____ probability that the results were due to chance.
   a. high
   b. statistical
   c. low
   d. significant

2. Rejecting the null hypothesis when it is true is called _____
   a. Type II error
   b. Type I error
   c. primary variance
   d. standard deviation

3. The results of the experiment were significant. Which of the following is true?
   a. The independent variable had an effect.
   b. The null hypothesis is rejected.
   c. A Type I error is possible.
   d. all of the above

4. A Type II error can only occur when the
   a. H_1 was supported
   b. H_1 was not supported
   c. H_0 was not supported
   d. difference between means is significant

5. If the results of an experiment turned out to be significant, then
   a. the independent variable had no effect
   b. the null hypothesis cannot be rejected
   c. a Type II error may be possible
   d. the independent variable had an effect

6. Alpha = 0.01 means that the chance for error is_____
   a. 1 in 100
   b. 1 in 1000
   c. 1 in 10
   d. zero

7. The area of statistics that is used for examining whether your independent variable had an effect is
   a. parameter estimation
   b. descriptive statistics
   c. hypothesis testing
   d. estimation of population characteristics

8. You can MOST limit the probability of a Type I error by setting alpha at
   a. 1
   b. 0.05
   c. 0.06
   d. 0.1

9. An experimenter investigated the effect of group size on cooperation. She predicted that participants are more likely to cooperate on a task when the size of the group does not exceed five people. Group I consisted of four participants, and Group II consisted of eight participants. Both groups were given a task to finish, and the experimenter rated each group on their cooperation on the task. Alpha was set at .05. Statistical analysis indicated that Group I had significantly higher cooperation scores than Group II. Answer the following:

a. State the null hypothesis.

b. State the experimental hypothesis.

c. Which hypothesis was rejected and why?

d. What type of error is possible at this point and why?

e. What is the probability for the error?

f. Did the experiment have enough power? Why/why not?

10. Explain the concept of statistical power and how you could increase it in a study.

STATISTICAL TESTS

▦ What statistical test should I use to analyze my data?

▦ What is the difference between *t* tests and analysis of variance?

▦ Would I get different results if I used a different statistical test?

▦ When it comes to choosing a statistical test, does it make a difference what scale of measurement I used?

STATISTICAL TESTS OF SIGNIFICANCE

The number of statistical tests available for data analysis is enormous. Selecting the appropriate one is determined by the research design and the type of data that are being collected. Different statistical tests used to analyze the same data can yield different results, and selection of the wrong procedure can lead to Type I and Type II errors. Therefore, the importance of understanding the logic of the procedures and of knowing which test is appropriate in which situation cannot be emphasized enough. Figure 8.1 presents a flowchart that should aid you in selecting the appropriate statistical test.

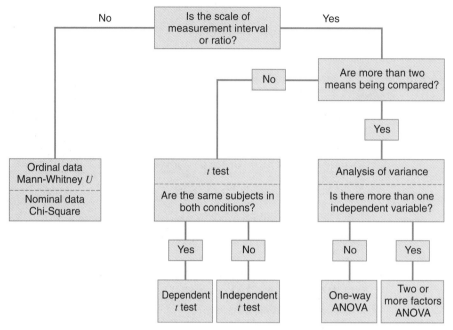

FIGURE 8.1 Decision schema for determining some statistical procedures.

The following sections cover the more common statistical procedures, stressing the conceptual rather than the computational aspects of the various tests. The computational formulas are included so that their components can be explained and clarified. However, if you wish to work through the actual analysis by hand (or your teacher wishes you to), Appendix B provides sample problems.

First, you will look at two of the most common parametric techniques used to analyze data: the *t* test and the analysis of variance (ANOVA). The logic underlying the two tests is the same: the means of different conditions are compared to see if the observed differences between them are significant. In addition, both tests take into account the ratio of "good" variance, or primary variance, due to the independent variable, and "bad" variance, or variance due to error. Generally, the *t* test and the ANOVA are appropriate when the data are on an interval or ratio scale of measurement.

When the data are below the interval scale measure, for example, when the scale of measurement is nominal or ordinal, the appropriate statistical analysis is the **chi-square** and the **Mann-Whitney *U*,** respectively. The final section of this chapter introduces you to these two nonparametric tests.

The vast majority of researchers rely on statistical software to analyze their data. While there is a variety of software available in both professional and student versions, SPSS—Statistical Package for the Social Sciences—is one of the most commonly used software in the social sciences.

TWO SAMPLES INFERENCE: *T* TESTS

When the experiment has a single independent variable with only two levels, the most frequently used statistical test is the *t* test. The *t* test compares the means of the two groups or conditions and determines whether the observed difference is significant. When the two conditions have different participants, meaning that each person only participates in one condition, we say that the samples are independent or unrelated. On the other hand, if the same people participate in both conditions, or they had been matched on some attribute prior to their assignment into conditions, then the samples are dependent or related.

Appropriate versions of the *t* test are available for independent and dependent samples, and you must be careful to select the correct one. Regardless of which *t* test is used, the logic underlying the *t* test can be conceptualized as

$$t = \frac{\text{``good'' variance (primary variance)}}{\text{``bad'' variance (error variance)}}$$

As stated previously, primary variance is the difference between the means of the two conditions due to the independent variable. As noted in Chapter 2, it is also called systematic variance or between-groups variance. The larger the obtained *t* value, the more likely it is that the difference between the means is significant. Therefore, since it is a ratio, you want a large difference between the means, or lots of "good" or primary variance, and a minimum of "bad" or error variance. A more precise conceptual formula for the *t* test is

$$t = \frac{\text{observed differences between the means}}{\text{standard error of the means}}$$

The denominator in this conceptual formula is essentially the standard deviation of the sampling distribution, called the standard error of the means, and that is why the need for a small standard deviation was stressed in Chapter 6. The larger the variability due to error, individual differences, or chance factors, the smaller the derived *t* value, and the greater the possibility that the difference between the conditions will not be significant.

In terms of the null hypothesis, the prediction is that H_0: $\mu_1 = \mu_2$. In mathematical terms, the H_0 predicts that the difference between the two means will be zero: $\mu_1 - \mu_2 = 0$.

Independent Samples *t* Test

Suppose that you wished to study the effect of story relevance on memory. You hypothesized that the more personally relevant a story is, the more ideas would be recalled. You randomly assigned 40 college students to either a relevant or not relevant condition so that there were 20 participants in each condition. You then gave each group 10 minutes to read a story. In the relevant condition, the participants read a story about the problems faced by college students, and in the not relevant condition, the participants read a story about the problems faced by senior citizens. After the 10 minutes were up, the participants were given a recall test on their respective stories. The mean number of ideas recalled in the relevant condition was 23, and in the not relevant condition it was 14. Is the difference between 23 and 14 ideas significant?

In order to answer that question, you would have to perform a *t* test for independent samples since each participant only read one type of story. In other words, you had two unrelated or independent groups. The computational formula for calculating the *t* statistic is:

$$t = \frac{\overline{X} - \overline{Y}}{\sqrt{\dfrac{\Sigma\left(X - \overline{X}\right)^2 + \Sigma\left(Y - \overline{Y}\right)^2}{N(N-1)}}}$$

where $\overline{X}$ is the mean of Group I and $\overline{Y}$ is the mean of Group II. Notice how the mean difference is derived in the numerator $(\overline{X} - \overline{Y})$. This is the difference that could be due to the independent variable. Does the formula in the denominator look familiar? It should. Remember the formula for the variance and its square root, the standard deviation, covered in Chapter 6? The underlying logic is the same here. By calculating the sum of squared deviations for each group, adding them together, dividing the total by $N(N-1)$, and taking the square root of the result, you can derive the standard deviation of the sampling distribution: the standard error of the means. The formula above can be restated as

$$t = \frac{\overline{X} - \overline{Y}}{\sqrt{\dfrac{S_1^2}{N_1}} + \sqrt{\dfrac{S_2^2}{N_2}}}$$

where S_1^2 is the variance of the first sample and S_2^2 is the variance of the second sample. By dividing the variance of each condition by the number of participants in that condition (N_1 and N_2) and taking the square root, you arrive at the standard error of the means.

Once the t statistic has been calculated, its value is compared to a set of critical values at the level of significance specified by the experimenter. In the days before computerized statistical packages, a table of critical values for t tests was consulted. If the obtained t value was equal to or greater than the critical value listed in the table, the H_0 was rejected. Today, the statistical software you are using conveniently does this for you.

According to the APA guidelines for reporting t test results, you can do it in two ways. The first simply shows whether the obtained probability for error is greater or less than the one specified by the experimenter, while the second shows the actual obtained level of probability. The second method may be preferred to the first because it shows the actual level of probability for error. The first format for reporting the t test result is

$$t\,(df) = t \text{ value}, p < \text{ or } > \text{ alpha specified by experimenter}$$

In the parentheses df stands for degrees of freedom, which will be explained in a moment. This is followed by the t value obtained and then p (probability of error), followed by either the less than or greater than sign, depending on the obtained probability for error. If the obtained probability for error is greater than the alpha specified, then the $>$ sign is used, followed by the alpha level set by the experimenter. If the obtained probability is less than what the experimenter specified, then the $<$ sign is used. The second format is identical except that the actual obtained probability for error is stated. The format is

$$t\,(df) = t \text{ value}, p = \text{ obtained level of probability for error}$$

For example, let's say that you conducted a t test to compare the two means from the story relevance experiment and your obtained t value was 4.56. In addition, let's say that the *t* test showed that there was a significant difference between the two groups, since the obtained probability for error was $p = .02$, while you set alpha at .05. You could report this finding as

$$t\,(38) = 4.56, p < .05; \quad \text{or} \quad \text{as } t\,(38) = 4.56, p = .02$$

In the first instance you are stating that your obtained probability for error was less than what you specified (.02 and .05, respectively), and in the second you are stating the actual level of probability obtained.

The second way of reporting simply gives your readers a better idea of how close to significant your findings are. If you had obtained a .04 level of probability for error, while you would be technically correct to report it as $p < .05$, by stating it as $p =. 04$ instead, your readers can see that your findings are close to being not significant. Of course, the opposite is also true. Essentially, using the "=" sign does not leave the reader wondering how close to significance your findings were.

Now look at the number 38 in the parentheses, previously referred to as the degrees of freedom *(df)*. What does it mean and how was it derived? **Degrees of freedom** refer to a statistical concept used in estimating population parameters, a concept that is beyond the scope of this chapter and as is described briefly here. More specifically, the degrees of freedom refer to the number of scores in a set of scores that are free to vary; that is, no restrictions are placed on them once the sum is known. For example, if you have a set of 10 scores that add up to 25, then the first 9 scores are free to vary but the last score is fixed: it must be a number that allows the scores to make up 25. Look at the following scores:

X_1	4
X_2	1
X_3	2
X_4	3
X_5	2
X_6	1
X_7	3
X_8	3
X_9	3
X_{10}	?
$\Sigma X =$	25

As you can see, the last number is not free to vary; it must be a 3 in order to make up the sum of 25. The first nine numbers, however, could be any value. Therefore, the *df* in the above example is 9.

To address the second part of the question, how to calculate the degrees of freedom for the story relevance experiment, simply follow the formula for deriving the degrees of freedom for independent samples *t* tests. The formula is

$$df = N_1 + N_2 - 2$$

where N_1 is the number of scores in the first group and N_2 is the number of scores in the second group. Therefore, the degrees of freedom for your hypothetical experiment is $df = 20 + 20 - 2$, or 38.

Dependent Samples *t* Test

Suppose that your experiment does not use independent groups. Remember Chapter 6, where you read that within-subjects designs have more power? Well, let's say that you did your story relevance experiment as a within-subjects design in order to increase power. If that were the case, each participant would read both types of stories. Therefore, the recall scores are now related: each pair of scores belongs to a single participant. For example, if a participant, let's call her Kim, recalled 19 ideas in the relevant condition and 12 in the not relevant condition, then the two scores are tied or related to each other since the pair of scores, 19 and 12, belongs to Kim. Similarly, if an experiment entails a pretest and a posttest, or some before and after measure, the scores will be related in that, once again, each participant would have his or her own set of paired scores.

Even if you were to use two different groups in an experiment, if you first matched the participants on some attribute, for example, IQ scores, you would still have a related groups design. By matching the participants on IQ, you would wind up with pairs of participants, each pair being comprised of two people with highly similar or identical IQ scores. One member of the pair would then be randomly assigned to one condition, and the other member to the second condition. However, even though there are different people in each condition, since the participants were first paired according to their IQ score, the two samples are related.

When dependent or related groups design is used, the pairs of scores correlate. Therefore, the *t* test used for analyzing independent samples is inappropriate. You must use the *t* test for related groups. Conceptually speaking, the two *t* tests are the same, which means that the underlying logic is identical. The computational formula is a little different, for it requires you to calculate difference scores for each participant. The computational formula for the dependent *t* test can be seen in Appendix B.

Calculating the degrees of freedom for the dependent samples *t* test is also a little different. Here, $df = N - 1$, where N stands for the number of pairs of scores. Therefore, if your experiment involved 20 participants, the degree of freedom would be 19 (20 pairs of scores minus 1).

Effect Size

You read in Chapter 7 that, in addition to reporting that the differences between the conditions were significant, it is helpful to calculate the effect size in order to determine the magnitude of the impact of the independent variable. When there are two conditions and the statistical procedure is the *t* test, the calculation of the effect size is relatively simple. The formula for deriving the effect size is

$$r = \sqrt{\frac{t^2}{t^2 + df}}$$

where t^2 is the *t* value obtained, squared.

For example, let's return to the story relevance experiment covered under the independent *t* test section. The obtained *t* value was 4.562, and the *df* was 38. By entering these values into the formula above, we obtain

$$r = \sqrt{\frac{4.562^2}{4.562^2 + 38}} = \sqrt{\frac{20.812}{58.812}} = .595$$

As you recall, the values for r can range from 0.00, which indicates no relationship between the independent and dependent variable, to 1.00. Therefore, the greater the value of r, the larger the effect size and the stronger the relationship. In the example given above, a correlation of .595 can be considered a fairly strong relationship between story relevance and memory.

THE ANALYSIS OF VARIANCE

If the experiment has only one independent variable with two levels, the t test is a perfectly adequate statistical procedure to assess the difference between the means of the two conditions. However, the majority of experiments involve more than two conditions, and frequently there is more than one independent variable. In other words, most experiments tend to be more complex than simply manipulating an independent variable on two levels. The reason for the complexity of most experiments is that a behavior or an event is rarely the function, or result, of a single factor. In addition, if you recall curvilinear functions, an experimenter needs at least three levels of an independent variable in order to be able to detect such a relationship.

When the experiment involves a single independent variable with three or more levels, it is called a single-factor, **multilevel design.** When the experiment requires the manipulation of more than one independent variable, it is called a **factorial design.** Whether the study is a multilevel or a factorial design, if the data are at least on the interval level, the appropriate statistical analysis is the **analysis of variance,** simply called ANOVA. If there is only one independent variable, the test used is the one-factor or one-way ANOVA. If there are two independent variables, the test is called a two-way ANOVA, for three independent variables, you use a three-way ANOVA, and so on.

The more independent variables there are, the more complex the statistical analysis and the interpretation of the findings. The next section covers the simplest ANOVA first. In addition, as with t tests, it does matter whether the design is between-subjects or within-subjects, and there are appropriate versions of ANOVA for each type of design, including those designs that have two or more dependent variables.

One-Way Analysis of Variance

The logic behind the ANOVA is essentially the same as that behind the t test. The means of different conditions are compared to see if there are significant differences, except with the one-way ANOVA where three or more means are being compared. The statistic that is derived is the F value, and, as with the t value, it represents the ratio of "good" variance to "bad" variance. The formula for calculating the F statistic is

$$F = \frac{MS_{\text{between}}}{MS_{\text{within}}}$$

where *MS* stands for the mean square, or variance, either between the conditions, or within the conditions. Between-conditions variance is "good" variance; as with the *t* test, it stands for variance between the conditions due to the effects of the independent variable, or treatment. On the other hand, within-conditions variance is "bad" variance, as it stands for variance within each condition due to random error, individual differences, and so on. Since the formula is a ratio, as with the *t* test, you want a large amount of between-conditions or between-groups variance and a small amount of within-conditions variance when you expect the null hypothesis to be false.

The variance due to treatment, $MS_{between}$ (MS_b), is in turn derived by dividing the sum of squared deviations for between-conditions (SS_b) by the between-conditions degree of freedom, or

$$MS_b = \frac{SS_b}{df_b}$$

Similarly, the MS_{within} (MS_w) or error variance is calculated by dividing the sum of squared deviations for within-conditions (SS_w) by the within-conditions degree of freedom, or

$$MS_w = \frac{SS_w}{df_w}$$

In order to calculate a one-way ANOVA by hand, you need the numerical values for the following: SS_t (total); SS_w; SS_b; df_t (total); df_b; and df_w. Appendix B shows how values for each of these terms are calculated.

Prior to statistical packages, once the *F* statistic has been derived, as with the *t* test, the obtained value was compared to the critical values listed in a table, according to the level of significance that was specified by the experimenter. If the obtained *F* value was equal to or greater than the critical value listed in the table, the differences between the means were significant. However, as with the *t* test, statistical software now does this for you, and the printout of the data analysis indicates whether the obtained probability for error *(p)* is greater or less than the critical level of alpha specified by you.

It might be useful to see an ANOVA summary table to clarify the concepts discussed here. For example, consider a hypothetical experiment on maze learning that had three maze conditions: a finger maze (Maze 1), an electronic stylus maze (Maze 2), and a pencil maze (Maze 3). The dependent variable was the number of errors made on each maze. Table 8.1 shows how SPSS summarizes the results of this experiment.

Notice that the sum of squares for between-conditions is 48 and the value of the degrees of freedom is 2. The mean square for between-conditions, 24, was derived by dividing the sum of squares for between-conditions by the between-conditions degrees of freedom: 48/2 = 24. The mean square for within-conditions, 3.467, was similarly calculated by dividing the within-conditions sum of squares by the within-conditions degrees of freedom: 52/15 = 3.467. Finally, it was said that

$$F = \frac{MS_{between}}{MS_{within}}$$

Therefore, by plugging in the correct numbers for each mean square, you arrive at *F* = 6.923.

TABLE 8.1   One-Way ANOVA Summary Table for Hypothetical Maze Learning Experiment

ANOVA SUMMARY

	Sum of Squares	df	Mean Square	F	Sig.
ERRORS Between Groups	48.00	2	24.00	6.923	.007
Within Groups	52.00	15	3.467		
Total	100.00	17			

POST-HOC TESTS
Tukey HSD

Maze Category *(I)*	Maze Category *(J)*	Mean Difference *(I–J)*
Finger	Stylus	–2.0000
	Pencil	–4.0000*
Stylus	Finger	2.0000
	Pencil	2.0000
Pencil	Finger	4.0000*
	Stylus	2.0000

* The mean difference is significant at the .05 level.

$$F = \frac{24}{3.467} = 6.923$$

Notice the .007 level of significance obtained in Table 8.1 which means that the differences between at least two means were significant.

According to APA guidelines, you report the results of the ANOVA as follows. Again, you have the same options as with the t test. You can either use the less than or greater than sign, or you can state the actual obtained p value.

$$F\ (df_b, df_w) = F \text{ value obtained}, p < \text{ or } > \text{ alpha specified}$$

or

$$F\ (df_b, df_w) = F \text{ value}, p = \text{obtained}$$

Therefore, in order to report the results of the ANOVA shown in Table 8.1, you could state it as $F\ (2, 15) = 6.923$, $p < .05$, or as $F\ (2, 15) = 6.923$, $p = .007$.

Although the results show a significant difference between the means of the maze conditions, since more than two means are being compared, you need to find out which pairs of means were significantly different. The ANOVA compared the mean number of errors for the three conditions, and the results indicate a significant difference between the means. However, the question is, which two mazes were significantly different? Was the performance on Maze 1 significantly different from that on Maze 2? What about the difference between Maze 2 and Maze 3? Finally, was there a significant difference between Maze 1 and Maze 3?

With the t test, there is no such problem since only two means are being compared. Therefore, if a significant difference is found, it is clearly referring to the two conditions being compared. With ANOVA however, **multiple comparison procedures** are needed to determine which pair of means is significantly different.

Multiple Comparison Tests

Multiple comparisons between pairs of means may be planned or unplanned. If the comparisons were planned prior to conducting the experiment, they are called *a priori* comparisons; if they were unplanned, then they are called *posteriori,* or *post-hoc* analyses.

Typically, comparisons are *planned* prior to the experiment when the experimental hypothesis has made specific predictions regarding the differences between the conditions. For example, the researcher may have hypothesized that there will be a significant difference between Maze 1 and Maze 2, but not between Maze 1 and Maze 3. Following the analysis of the data, you can make pairwise comparisons by conducting two *t* tests: one for comparing Maze 1 to Maze 2 and another for comparing Maze 1 to Maze 3. Note that since you made no prediction regarding Maze 2 and Maze 3, there is no reason to compare them.

Unplanned comparisons, on the other hand, take place after the data analysis has been completed. If the researcher made no specific prediction regarding the various conditions, then unplanned, or **post-hoc, tests** are in order. For example, if a teacher is interested in trying out various teaching methods but she does not know which method would be best, she could conduct an experiment in which students would be exposed to three or four different teaching methods. When the study is over, she would analyze the results, looking post hoc for differences between the various conditions.

Several good post-hoc tests are available, one of the most widely used being Tukey's Honestly Significant Difference (HSD). Most statistical software automatically conducts post-hoc analyses, and SPSS provides Tukey HSD results. By looking at the bottom panel of Table 8.1, you can see that the only two conditions that were significantly different were the finger maze (Maze 1) and the pencil maze (Maze 3) at the .05 level of significance.

Two or More Factors Analysis of Variance

If the experiment has more than one independent variable, it is called a factorial design. The type of ANOVA that is appropriate for analyzing the results depends on how many independent variables, or factors, there are in the experiment. If the experiment has two independent variables, then a two-way ANOVA is appropriate. Similarly, if there are three independent variables, then the experimenter uses a three-way ANOVA, for four independent variables, a four-way ANOVA, and so on. For simplicity's sake, this section covers the two-way ANOVA.

When a researcher designs an experiment with two independent variables, several possible results may be obtained. First, each independent variable may have an effect on the dependent variable. The effect of each independent variable is called a **main effect.** In addition, the two independent variables may interact with each other. Interactions will be covered in detail in a later chapter; for now the following example may help to explain main effects and interactions.

Let us say that you are interested in studying the effects of age and gender on shyness. You are curious to see whether there are gender differences—that is, whether one gender is shyer in general than the other—and you also wish to see whether there is a difference between children and adolescents with regard to shyness. Since you have two independent variables, you could obtain a main effect for each. A main effect of gender would indicate a significant difference between males and females in general (regardless of age), whereas a main effect of age would indicate a significant difference between children and adolescents, regardless of gender. In addition, there could be an interaction between gender and age, where you would find that the aging process affects the sexes differentially. Males may be shyer than girls in childhood, but by adolescence, girls become shyer than boys. Of course, the opposite could also be possible.

In order to analyze the results of this study, you would conduct a two-way ANOVA. The logic and procedure are the same as for one-way ANOVA, except that a different F statistic is calculated for each independent variable and for the interaction between the independent variables. Therefore, by looking at the ANOVA summary table, the researcher can tell whether there were any main effects or an interaction. As with the one-way ANOVA, each F statistic is followed by the obtained probability for error, indicating whether the differences between the means were significant or whether there was a significant interaction.

Table 8.2 shows a reproduction of SPSS analysis of the hypothetical study on the effects of age and gender on shyness. Higher scores in the cell means indicate shyness, whereas lower scores indicate being outgoing.

By looking at the summary table, you can see that there was no main effect of gender. The obtained level of significance is .91, which exceeds the maximum critical level of alpha = .05. Therefore, in this experiment, there was no gender difference in shyness. In general, boys and girls were equally shy. If you look at the age variable, you notice that there was no main effect of age either, since the obtained level of significance is .076. This finding indicates that shyness is not a function of age. However, there was a significant interaction between gender and age, as shown by the obtained level of significance .000.

TABLE 8.2   Two-Way ANOVA Summary Table for Hypothetical Study

ANOVA SUMMARY

Source of Variation	Sum of Squares	df	Mean Square	F	Sig. of F
Main Effects	14.500	2	7.250	1.813	.195
Gender	.050	1	.050	.013	.912
Age	14.500	1	14.050	3.613	.076
2-Way Interactions	252.050	1	252.050	63.013	.000
Gender Age	252.050	1	252.050	63.013	.000
Explained	266.550	3	88.850	22.213	.000
Residual	64.000	16	4.000		
Total	330.550	19	17.397		

CELL MEANS
Shyness Scores by Gender and Age

	Children	Adolescents
Male	10.40	5.00
Female	3.20	12.00

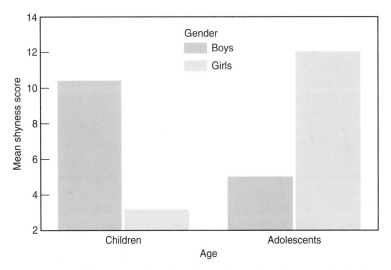

FIGURE 8.2 Shyness as a function of gender and age in a hypothetical experiment.

This interaction indicates that age affects the sexes differently when it comes to shyness. By looking at the cell means provided, you can see that boys are shyer than girls when they are children ($M = 10.40$ vs. $M = 3.20$, respectively), but girls are shyer than boys when they are adolescents ($M = 12.00$ vs. $M = 5.00$, respectively). Figure 8.2 shows the interaction between gender and age.

Reporting the results is the same as for the one-way ANOVA, except that you would state each F statistic that was obtained. For example, you would say that there was no main effect of gender, $F (1, 19) = 0.013$, $p = .91$; there was no main effect of age, $F (1, 19) = 3.613$, $p = .076$; but there was a significant gender by age interaction, $F (1, 19) = 63.013$, $p = .000$.

Even if you had obtained main effects for age and gender, since each independent variable only had two levels, there would be no need for further analysis to determine which pairs were significantly different. However, if one or both of the independent variables had three or more levels, comparison tests would be necessary. For example, if you added a young adult condition, and you obtained a main effect of age, then you would need to conduct comparison tests to see which age groups differed significantly: children from adolescents; children from young adults; or adolescents from young adults. The rationale would be the same as for the one-way ANOVA.

NONPARAMETRIC TESTS

When your data are measured on a nominal or an ordinal scale, or when the shape of the distribution is not important, the appropriate procedure for analyzing the data is to use a nonparametric test. Although there are many nonparametric tests, the following sections discuss two procedures: the chi-square and the Mann-Whitney U. If the data are measured on a nominal scale, the chi-square is appropriate. On the other hand, the Mann-Whitney U is used when the data are measured on an ordinal scale. Since ordinal scaling is fairly uncommon in psychological research, the chi-square will be covered in greater detail. For further reading on the Mann-Whitney U, consult your statistics textbook.

The Chi-Square

Suppose that you are interested in determining the most popular major on your college campus. You list all the majors available, and then you count the number of students who are majoring in each one. Notice that your dependent variable is on the nominal scale; you are stating the majors by name: English, history, mathematics, education, psychology, and so forth, and the data you will collect represent the frequency of responses for each category. In other words, each discrete category will have frequency data, representing the number of students who fall into each category. Similarly, if you were conducting a survey on which soft drink students prefer, Coke or Pepsi, you would be gathering frequency data: the number of students who prefer Coke and the number who opt for Pepsi.

When your data are frequencies, meaning the number of responses that fall into each of the discrete, nominal categories, one of the most popular statistical tests that you can use to analyze the results is the chi-square, represented by the Greek letter χ, squared, or χ^2. This section of the chapter discusses two commonly used tests: the one-group chi-square test and the two-group chi-square test. Regardless of the test used, the H_1 predicts a significant (nonchance) relationship between the variables, whereas the H_0 predicts no relationship, or a chance relationship.

The *one-group test* is appropriate if you have one group of participants and two or more response categories. Both examples given above would be analyzed using a one-group test. In the college major example, you have one group—the students on your campus—and several possible response categories—the available academic majors. Similarly, in the soft drink example you have a single group of participants and two response categories: Coke or Pepsi.

The one-group χ^2 test determines the significance of the relationship between a set of observed frequencies and a set of theoretical frequencies. The observed frequency represents the number of people who fall into a specific response category; in other words, it is what the researcher actually observes. The theoretical frequency is what is expected to occur by chance. Another way of stating this idea is that the χ^2 test determines the significance of the difference between the observed number of participants and the expected number of participants who fall into each category.

The formula for the χ^2 test is

$$\chi^2 = \Sigma \left[\frac{(O-E)^2}{E} \right]$$

where O = the number of observed frequencies in each category and E = the number of expected frequencies in each category. The summation sign means that you must add up the results for each response category.

For example, let's say that you are interested in seeing whether college students prefer Brand X or Brand Y when it comes to athletic shoes. You survey your campus and find that 120 students stated their preference for brand X and 160 students preferred brand Y. We can state the findings as:

	Brand X	Brand Y
Observed frequency	120	160
Expected frequency	140	140

The expected frequencies represent the number of students preferring each brand if the null hypothesis is true. Since the H_0 predicts no significant difference in brand preference, by chance alone we would expect that half the students would prefer Brand X and the other half would prefer Brand Y. As there were 280 participants, the expeced frequency for each brand is 140. In order to calculate the χ^2, follow the following formula:

$$\chi^2 = \frac{(120-140)^2}{140} + \frac{(160-140)^2}{140} = \frac{400}{140} + \frac{400}{140} = 2.86 + 2.86 = 5.72$$

As you see, the χ^2 test is simple to calculate. The only other information you need at this point is the degrees of freedom. The formula for calculating the degrees of freedom is: $df = K - 1$, where K stands for the number of response categories. Since there are two response categories, Brand X and Brand Y, the $df = 2-1$, or 1. Once the df is established, the derived χ^2 value is then compared to the critical values listed in a χ^2 table. As with other tests of significance, if the value of the χ^2 is equal to or greater than the critical value listed, the results are significant.

The appropriate way to report the results of the χ^2 test is: χ^2 (df, total number of frequencies) = obtained χ^2 value, p, < or > than alpha. The results of the χ^2 test performed on the hypothetical data for brand preference would therefore be stated as:

$$\chi^2 (1,280) = 5.72, p < .05$$

As with the t test or ANOVA results, if you are analyzing your data with statistical software, you may state the actual obtained p value.

The *two-group test* may be used when there are two groups of participants and two or more response categories. For example, if you were to refine the college major study mentioned earlier, and you looked at gender differences as well, you would have two groups of participants (male and female) and several response categories (the various academic majors).

For example, let's say that you investigated whether there are ethnic differences in athletic shoe preference. Note how you now have two groups of participants, African-American and White, and two response categories, Brand X and Brand Y. The observed frequencies can be placed in a matrix as follows:

	Brand X	Brand Y
African-American	120	80
White	135	65

The calculation of the χ^2 is identical to the one-group test, but the formula for the degrees of freedom is different. The formula for the degrees of freedom is: $df = (R - 1)(K - 1)$, where R = the number of rows, and K = the number of columns. In this example, the number of rows and columns is the same: two. Therefore, $df = (2 - 1)(2 - 1)$, or 1.

If you were to include a third brand, Brand Z, then you would have three columns and two rows. In terms of placing your variables into columns and rows, the conventional placement for participants is in rows, and the response categories in columns.

The Mann-Whitney U

With ordinal scales of measurement, a given score is not a measure of some ability but an indication of where the participant stands in relation to the other participants. For example, if you rank the participants in order of some skill, with 1 = highest level and 10 = lowest level, then a score of 7 does not indicate a measure of the skill per se, but merely where that person stands in relation to the rest of the group. When the data are ordinal, the Mann-Whitney U is used to see whether there is a significant difference between two groups. The test is appropriate only if the experiment is a between-subjects design. In other words, the two samples must be independent.

The test is relatively simple. The participants are first ranked on performance in both samples, and the U is calculated for one of the two groups. It does not matter which group you select. Once U_1 has been calculated, U_2 can be derived as well. The smaller of the two, U_1 or U_2, is selected as U_{obtained}. U_{obtained} is then compared with U_{critical} in the appropriate critical values table. Unlike other tests of significance, U_{obtained} must be equal to or smaller than U_{critical}.

SUMMARY

- A large variety of statistical tests are available to the researcher, and it is crucial that the data be analyzed with the appropriate test. Incorrect statistical procedures may lead to Type I or Type II errors.

- When there are only two means to compare, the most common statistical test is the t test. If the same participants participate in both conditions, or if the participants were matched on some attribute prior to random assignment into conditions, the appropriate procedure is the t test for dependent samples. If each condition has different participants, then the appropriate procedure is the t test for independent samples.

- When the independent variable has three or more levels, the experiment is called a multilevel design. The appropriate statistical analysis is the one-way ANOVA, which compares three or more means to see if there is a significant difference between the means.

- When the experiment has two or more independent variables, it is called a factorial design. In a factorial design, each independent variable may produce a main effect, which is the average effect of each independent variable. In addition, the independent variables may interact with one another. An interaction is when the levels of one independent variable have a differential effect on the scores obtained under the levels of another independent variable.

- The F statistic derived from ANOVA is a ratio of primary variance and error variance. Primary variance is variance between the conditions, while error variance is the variance within the conditions.

- When the data are on a nominal or an ordinal scale of measurement, the appropriate statistical procedures are nonparametric tests such as the chi-square or the Mann-Whitney U test.

- The chi-square test is appropriate when the data are on a nominal scale and the frequencies of responses fall into discrete categories. The one-group test is appropriate when there is one group of participants and two or more response categories. The two-group test is appropriate when there are two groups of participants and two or more response categories.

- The Mann-Whitney U test is appropriate when the data are on an ordinal scale of measurement and there are two independent samples of participants.

KEY CONCEPTS

Analysis of Variance	Dependent Samples *t* Test	Independent Samples *t* Test	Multilevel Design
Chi-Square	Factorial	Main Effect	Multiple Comparison Procedure
Degree of Freedom	Design	Mann-Whitney *U*	Post-Hoc Tests

QUESTIONS

Answers can be found in Appendix A.

1. In an experiment, a group of participants was given a pretest, then the treatment, and finally a posttest. Which statistical procedure is appropriate to see whether the treatment had a significant effect?

   a. variance

   b. independent samples *t* test

   c. dependent samples *t* test

   d. chi-square

2. In an experiment, Group I was given 25 practice trials; Group II was given 45 practice trials; and Group III was given no practice. To see which group did significantly better, you would calculate a(n)

   a. dependent samples *t* test

   b. independent samples *t* test

   c. one-way ANOVA

   d. two-way ANOVA

3. If you wanted to see whether an 8:00 A.M. English class did significantly better than a 1:00 P.M. English class (different students in each class), you would conduct a(n)

   a. dependent samples *t* test

   b. independent samples *t* test

   c. ANOVA

   d. chi-square

4. Independent samples *t* tests are appropriate when

   a. there is only one group of participants doing both conditions

   b. there are two separate groups of participants who are unrelated

   c. there are two related groups of participants

   d. there are two or more independent variables

5. In ANOVA, the *F* statistic is a ratio of

   a. primary variance/error variance

   b. error variance/primary variance

   c. secondary variance/error variance

   d. secondary variance/primary variance

6. An experimenter states that significantly more children preferred Crest to Colgate. The experimenter most likely analyzed the results using a(n)

   a. ANOVA

   b. one-group chi-square

   c. *t* test

   d. two-group chi-square

7. If you wanted to test the saying "Blondes have more fun," the appropriate thing to do would be to count the number of blondes having fun and not having fun and then compare them to the number of nonblondes having fun and not having fun by doing a(n)

   a. one-group chi-square

   b. two-group chi-square

   c. one-way ANOVA

   d. two-way ANOVA

RESEARCH DESIGNS: TRUE EXPERIMENTS

BASIC CONCEPTS IN RESEARCH DESIGNS

THIS CHAPTER introduces you to the basic concepts in research designs. All the concepts mentioned here will be elaborated on in the following chapters, and therefore the aim of the present chapter is to provide an overview of research designs rather than detailed explanations.

True experiments, as we have seen, are either single-factor or factorial designs. In single-factor experiments only one independent variable is manipulated on two or more levels, whereas in factorial designs two or more independent variables are manipulated. In addition, if the experiment has more than one dependent variable, it is called a multivariate design.

In a single-factor experiment, the levels of the independent variable may be between the subjects or within the subjects. In a between-subjects design each participant experiences only one level or condition of the independent variable, while in a within-subjects design each person participates in every level or condition.

TABLE 9.1 **Assignment of Participants in Within-Subjects, Between-Subjects, and Mixed Designs**

Within-Subjects Design		Between-Subjects Design		Mixed Design			
Condition 1	Condition 2	Condition 1	Condition 2	Cond 1	Cond 2	Cond 3	Cond 4
Luis	Luis	Luis	Harry	Luis	Luis	Harry	Harry
Carol	Carol	Carol	Lakisha	Carol	Carol	Lakisha	Lakisha
Anthony	Anthony	Anthony	Timothy	Anthony	Anthony	Timothy	Timothy
Tasha	Tasha	Tasha	Sonya	Tasha	Tasha	Sonya	Sonya
Juan	Juan	Juan	Felippe	Juan	Juan	Felippe	Felippe
Elaine	Elaine	Elaine	Debbie	Elaine	Elaine	Debbie	Debbie
Abdul	Abdul	Abdul	Ahmed	Abdul	Abdul	Ahmed	Ahmed
Carmen	Carmen	Carmen	Cynthia	Carmen	Carmen	Cynthia	Cynthia
Susanne	Susanne	Susanne	Sun Yi	Susanne	Susanne	Sun Yi	Sun Yi

The levels of the independent variables in a factorial experiment may also be between or within the subjects. However, when there are two or more independent variables, the levels of one independent variable may be between the subjects and the levels of the other independent variable within the subjects. If that were the case, the experiment would be a mixed design. Table 9.1 shows the distribution of participants in each type of experimental design.

WITHIN-SUBJECTS DESIGNS

Can you tell when someone is lying? Does body language give liars away? In other words, would you expect more fidgeting from someone who is telling the truth or from someone who is telling a lie? If you are like most people, you probably believe that liars would show more body movements than those who are telling the truth. However, that is not what Williams, Henry, Votraw, Ramharakh, and Pascalides (2001) found. In their within-subjects experiment on telling truths and telling lies, Williams et al. compared the amount of body movements demonstrated during true and false statements. The participants were given five minutes to prepare a true and a false story about themselves, and were videotaped while telling each type of story. The videotapes were later analyzed for head, hand/arm, hand/finger, and foot/leg movements, as well as for shifting position. The authors found significantly more hand/arm and hand/finger movements among the participants telling the truth. There was no significant difference for head and foot/leg movement or for shifting position. Figure 9.1 depicts hand/arm and hand/finger movements as a function of story type.

When each participant experiences every condition, the experiment is known as a **within-subjects design.** In the Williams et al. study, each participant told both a true story and a false story. If the design of the study is within subjects, then regardless of the number of conditions only one group of participants is needed, as this group will experience every condition. Since each participant's response is measured under each experimental

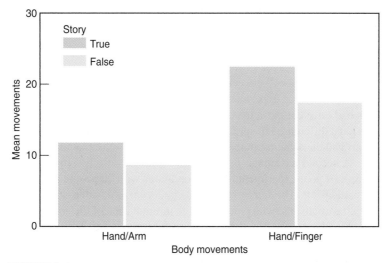

FIGURE 9.1   Mean movements during false and true stories. Based on Williams et al. (2001) experiment.

condition, the design is also known as a **repeated measures design.** In other words, repeated measures are taken on the same participants.

For another example, consider the experiment on the famous Stroop effect (1935). The effect refers to our inability to selectively attend to only one dimension or aspect of a stimulus while ignoring the other. In the Stroop task, participants are presented with a series of color words, for example, RED, GREEN, or BLUE, printed in either the same color ink or in a different color. The participants are required to ignore the meaning of the word and to respond only to the color in which the word is printed. Stroop found that participants were faster and more accurate when the ink color matched the word (for example, the word GREEN was printed in green ink) than when the color of the ink did not match the word (for example; the word GREEN was printed in red ink).

In a modern version of the original experiment, the participants are seated in front of a computer screen and presented with a series of trials. Half the trials are congruent, where there is a match between the word and the color of the ink, and half are incongruent, where the ink color does not match the meaning of the word. The participants are required to respond to the ink color by pressing the appropriate color-coded key on the computer keyboard. Typically, the results support Stroop's original discovery: the participants tend to be significantly faster in the congruent condition.

Notice that in the experiment every person participates in both the congruent and the incongruent condition, and therefore it is a within-subjects design. Note also that the significant difference between the two conditions cannot be due to better (faster) participants in the congruent condition since the same participants do both conditions. As you will see in a moment, it is precisely this ability to rule out individual differences as a source of unwanted variance that makes the within-subjects design so attractive.

Advantages of Within-Subjects Designs

The main advantage of the within-subjects design is that an important source of unwanted variance, individual differences, is eliminated. The participants are identical across conditions in terms of age, gender, ability, intelligence, personality, and so on. Therefore, observed differences between conditions cannot be attributed to subject factors. In the hypothetical Stroop experiment mentioned earlier, if the congruent and incongruent conditions had different participants, a potential source of unwanted variance could have been individual differences in speed of responding across the two conditions. Since the two conditions had the same participants, this problem was eliminated.

A second advantage is that within-subjects designs require fewer participants. For example, if your experiment has six conditions with 20 people per condition, you will need 120 participants. The same experiment conducted as a within-subjects design would require only 20 participants, who would then go through each of the six experimental conditions.

Finally, as noted earlier, a within-subjects design is more powerful because error variance due to individual differences is reduced. Since it has more power, there is a greater chance that you would be able to detect significant differences between the conditions due to the effect of the independent variable(s). Because of these advantages, a within-subject design should be used whenever possible. However, it also has some potential disadvantages that a careful researcher takes into consideration when designing the experiment.

Disadvantages of Within-Subjects Designs

Imagine that you are a participant in an experiment on maze learning. The study involves learning four different types of mazes, and each maze takes about 30 minutes to learn so that no errors are made. How do you suppose you would feel by the time the experimenter handed you the final maze? Yes, relieved that it was the last maze, but more likely bored, fatigued, irritated, and sorry that you ever signed up for this seemingly endless experiment. Since a participant must complete every condition, within-subjects designs tend to be more time consuming and demanding in terms of effort required of the participants than between-subjects designs. In addition, unless the researcher takes steps to avoid them, a potential disadvantage of within-subjects designs is the possibility of **order effects** and/or **carryover effects.**

Let us return to the Stroop study for a moment and pretend that you tried to replicate it. In your study, all the participants responded first to 50 congruent trials, then to 50 incongruent trials. You found that the participants were significantly faster in the congruent condition and concluded that hypothesis was correct: the participants' inability to selectively attend to only one dimension of the stimulus led to the slower response times in the incongruent condition. Was your conclusion correct? The answer is no. Although you can rule out the possibility that the congruent condition had faster or more capable participants, you still cannot say that the only reason they were slower in the incongruent condition was their inability to selectively attend to only one aspect of the stimulus. It is just as likely that, after responding to 50 congruent trials, by the time the 50 incongruent trials were introduced the participants were fatigued or bored with the task of pressing keys. This fatigue or boredom may have led to slower response time.

The opposite may also happen. Suppose that, contrary to your expectation, you found that the participants were significantly faster in the incongruent condition. Would that mean that the Stroop effect was absent and that the participants had no difficulty with selective attention? Yes, it could, but it is just as possible that they were so well practiced in responding from the first 50 trials that their response time was speeded up for the next 50 trials. If that were the case, the results could be due to *practice* effects.

When a previous condition alters the way a participant responds in subsequent conditions, we say that the effects of the first condition *carried over* to the subsequent conditions. In other words, having been in a prior condition changed the behavior of the participant, and this change then carried over to later conditions. Whether the change was for the better, facilitating later response through practice effects, or for the worse, hindering later performance due to fatigue, does not matter. As long as there are carryover effects, alternative explanations for your results cannot be ruled out and therefore the results cannot be said to be due solely to the effects of the independent variable. The carryover effects confounded your study.

Carryover effects are not the only potential problem with within-subjects designs. One other potential disadvantage is *order effects*. Order effects occur when a participant responds to a stimulus in a certain way simply because of the order in which the stimuli were presented. For example, let's say that you are asked to taste three different soft drinks and then state your preference. The soft drinks are presented to you in paper cups marked A, B, and C. It is very possible that you might select cup A as your preference simply because it was first or because it was marked A. In our language, the letter A carries positive connotations: it is the highest grade you can receive. We say everything is A-O.K., and a product is A-One. Similarly, the number 1 also has positive connotations: I'm number 1, my team came in first. On the other hand, you may respond to a stimulus differently simply because it is the last one in a series. For example, in a memory study you may recall the last words you have seen simply because they are most recent in your memory.

A type of order effect, called the serial position effect, is frequently observed in free-recall memory experiments (Ebbinghaus, 1885/1964; Murdock, 1962; Waugh & Norman, 1965). When participants are given a list of words to learn and then are asked to recall them in any order (free recall), recall tends to be best for the last few items and the first few items from the list. Memory for the items from the middle of the list tends to be poor. The findings that memory is best for the last few items and the first few items on the list have been termed *recency* and *primacy effects,* respectively. According to the dual memory theory (Waugh & Norman, 1965), the recency effect is due to the items' availability in short-term memory, whereas primacy effect is the result of the transfer of items to long-term memory due to rehearsal. Since items from the middle of the list are neither recent enough to be in short-term memory nor transferred to long-term memory due to limited capacity for rehearsing a large number of items, they tend not to be well recalled.

Controlling Carryover and Order Effects

In some experiments the simplest way to control for carryover or order effects is to present the conditions in a random order. For example, if you wanted to avoid carryover effects in the Stroop task, then you could randomize the presentation of the congruent and incongruent conditions for every participant. Similarly, if you wanted to avoid order effects such as primacy and recency in memory experiments, you could present the words on the word lists in a random fashion, with each participant seeing a different order. The majority of software available for designing experiments, such as MEL (St. James, Schneider, & Rodgers, 1992) or SuperLab (Cedrus, 1991; 1996), allows for the randomized presentation of trials and/or stimuli.

To illustrate this point, let's pretend that you are studying the effects of word type on memory. The levels of the independent variable are pleasant and unpleasant words, and you are interested in seeing which type of word leaves a stronger memory trace. You show a group of participants a list of 60 words, 30 of which are pleasant, for example, words such as LOVE, JOY, and ROSE, and the other half unpleasant, such as WAR, CRIME, and PAIN. By randomizing the presentation of the words, there is a very good chance that the word WAR (or LOVE, for that matter) would appear in a different position for different participants. For example, participant 1 may see WAR in the first position, so that primacy effect for the word is possible, but participant 2 may see it in the fifth position, participant 3 may see it in the nineteenth position, and so on. As you can see, by randomizing the order of presentation, you are controlling for the possibility that some words would be remembered simply because they were from the beginning or the end of the list, and not because of their pleasant or unpleasant connotation. Since each participant sees the words in a different order, primacy and recency effects are controlled for.

On the other hand, certain experiments benefit from **counterbalancing** the order of presentation. In counterbalancing, potential carryover or order effects are distributed equally across the conditions. Counterbalancing can be complete or partial. Complete counterbalancing produces every possible order of presentation of the stimuli, and each stimulus appears in every possible position, whereas partial counterbalancing provides only some of the possible orders of presentation. When the experiment has two or three treatment conditions, complete counterbalancing is the best option. However, if there are four or more treatment conditions, then partial counterbalancing is more practical. Counterbalancing can be achieved by using a **Latin square.**

For example, suppose that you are interested in seeing which type of advertisement is most effective: a product advertised by a famous actor (1), a famous model (2), or an unknown person (3). So, you design three identical ads, except that the spokesperson for the product comes from one of these categories. You wish to show the three different commercials to a group of participants, but want to avoid order effects where a particular ad would be rated as most effective simply because the participants saw it first, last, or in the middle. Therefore, you counterbalance the order of presentation by using a Latin square.

Complete counterbalancing using the Latin square can be achieved as follows. Line up the numbers so that you reverse the 3 and the 2; then complete the order of numbers by going down each column as follows:

Step 1	*Step 2*	*Step 3*	*Step 4*
1 3 2	1 3 2	1 3 2	1 3 2
	2	2 1	2 1 3
	3	3 2	3 2 1

Step 4 shows that once you are finished, there are six unique orders (O) of presentation possible. For example:

	O_4	O_5	O_6
	↓	↓	↓
$O_1\rightarrow$	1	3	2
$O_2\rightarrow$	2	1	3
$O_3\rightarrow$	3	2	1

Since six unique orders are possible, you will need a minimum of six participants so that each order may be seen once. The order in which each participant *(S)* will see the commercials is as follows:

S_1: actor, unknown person, model

S_2: model, actor, unknown person

S_3: unknown person, model, actor

S_4: actor, model, unknown person

S_5: unknown person, actor, model

S_6: model, unknown person, actor

Notice that with complete counterbalancing, each spokesperson appears in each possible position (first, second, or third). Therefore, if the participants select the commercial with the unknown person as the most effective, it could not be due to its position. Having only six participants, however, would not be enough for statistical significance; therefore, you would need to increase the number of people. You can increase to any number as long as there are an equal number of participants for each order. For example, you might consider having 24 participants, with each order being seen by four participants.

When there are four or more treatment conditions, the number of possible orders naturally increases. You can calculate the number of possible orders by using the formula, X $(X–1)$ $(X–2)$ … 1, where X is the number of the treatment conditions. Therefore, if there are three treatment conditions, then 3 (3–1) (3–2) (1) = 6 possible orders. When there are four treatment conditions, then 4 (4–1) (4–2) (1) = 24 possible orders. Keep in mind that as the number of orders increases, so does the number of participants you need for the experiment. Therefore, you might wish to limit the number of possible orders by using a partial counterbalancing procedure.

Partial counterbalancing can be done in one of two ways. You can either prepare a full set of possible orders and then randomly select a limited number of orders, or you can repeat the above procedure by reversing the last two numbers in the order. For example, to prepare a partial Latin square with four treatment conditions, do exactly as you would with three conditions. As before, reverse the last two digits and then complete the series by going down each column.

Step 1	*Step 2*	*Step 3*	*Step 4*
1 2 4 3	1 2 4 3	1 2 4 3	1 2 4 3
2	2 3	2 3 1	2 3 1 4
3	3 4	3 4 2	3 4 2 1
4	4 1	4 1 3	4 1 3 2

Notice that by doing a partial Latin square, 12 unique orders are now possible, as shown in Step 4: the four rows going across; the four columns going from top to bottom; and the same four columns in reverse order from the bottom to the top.

Counterbalancing procedures, either complete or partial, are fine when it can be assumed that the carryover effects are symmetrical. By symmetrical it is meant that condition 1 produces the same degree of carryover effect as condition 2. For example, if learning to do Task 1 first produces the same degree of practice effect or fatigue as Task 2 would if that had been learned first, then the carryover effects are the same and counterbalancing would effectively cancel them out. However, if Task 1 produces more fatigue, or leads to a greater practice effect, then counterbalancing is not going to correct for it.

For example, let's say that learning Task 1 leads to more fatigue than learning Task 2. By having half your participants do Task 2 first, you are not controlling for this asymmetry. When these participants go on to do Task 1 next, they are not carrying over the same degree of fatigue from the prior task as do the participants who completed Task 1 first. Since the two tasks produce different amounts of fatigue, counterbalancing is not effectively controlling for this differential effect. When such asymmetry is a problem, it is best to opt for a between-subjects design.

In addition, some treatment conditions lead to irreversible effects, in which case a within-subjects design is not appropriate. For example, let's say that you are studying the effects of imagery on memory. In the imagery condition you ask the participants to form an image as soon as a word appears on the computer screen. However, it would be unrealistic to expect that the participants would not continue to produce an image when they are shown words in the no-imagery condition. For instance, you could not ask them to stop imaging simply because they have now entered the no-imagery condition. Again, the appropriate experiment would be a between-subjects design.

BETWEEN-SUBJECTS DESIGNS

When the levels of the independent variable(s) are between the subjects, you will need a separate group of participants for every condition. The more conditions there are, the more participants you need. Therefore, a **between-subjects design** typically requires many more participants than a within-subjects design. However, sometimes this is the only possible route to go. For instance, when one of the variables of interest in an experiment is a subject variable such as age, gender, race, religion, intelligence, or personality characteristics, your only choice is to make that a between-subjects variable. A person cannot participate in both the male and female condition, or in both the African-American and White condition. Similarly, a participant cannot at the same time be both a child and an adolescent, or Protestant and Jewish. Naturally, there are people of mixed ethnic, racial, or religious backgrounds, but if they do not identify themselves with one of the experimental conditions, then you either do not use those participants or include another condition that reflects the ethnic or religious combination.

In addition to subject variables, when the number of treatment conditions may lead to a lengthy experimental session, the between-subjects design might be preferable to the within-subjects design. Also, as mentioned in the previous section, when the carryover effects of various treatment conditions are asymmetrical, or the treatment effect in one condition is irreversible, the between-subjects design is appropriate.

As is true of within-subjects designs, certain advantages and disadvantages are associated with the between-subjects design.

Advantages of Between-Subjects Designs

The major advantage is that since each person only participates in one condition, there are no carryover or order effects to worry about. In addition, as mentioned earlier, occasionally the between-subjects design is appropriate.

For example, let's say that you are interested in studying implicit and explicit memory. In contrast to explicit memory, where performance of a task depends on deliberate and conscious retrieval of the prior experience of having learned something, implicit memory is performance affected by prior experience without deliberate retrieval of that experience (Graf & Schacter, 1985). A typical experiment testing explicit versus implicit memory consists of two phases. During the study phase, participants are presented with information such as a list of words, and in a later test phase they are asked to perform any of a variety of tasks appropriate for either the implicit or the explicit condition. In an explicit memory task such as standard recall or recognition, participants are directed to intentionally retrieve the information learned during the study phase. Performance, therefore, depends on conscious recollection of previously seen items. In an implicit memory task, however, the participants are given a seemingly unrelated task such as word-stem completion, where they are asked to fill in the blanks with one or more letters so that it forms a word. For example, a word-stem may consist of the letters BUI————, which the participants may then complete as BUILD or BUILDING. No mention is made of the original study list. If the participants complete the word-stems with items seen on the original study list, we say that they have been primed by the original list. As such, we can say that implicit memory is a measure of transfer, or priming, from a past experience that does not require conscious recollection.

If you were to do an experiment that required the participants to deliberately retrieve information in the explicit condition, it would be difficult to assess their memory accurately in the implicit condition. Once you have asked the participants to think back to the original study list and try to retrieve as many words as possible, they may use the same deliberate retrieval strategies in the implicit condition. In other words, implicit recall may become contaminated by explicit retrieval strategies. Therefore, it would be wiser to use a between-subjects design, where one group participates in the explicit condition and a different group participates in the implicit condition.

Disadvantages of Between-Subjects Designs

A major disadvantage is that with different participants in the various treatment conditions, individual differences are always a potential source of error variance. If the individual differences are large, so is the error variance, and if you recall from the chapter on inferential statistics, the probability that you won't be able to detect significant differences between the various treatment conditions increases as the error variance increases. In other words, between-subjects designs are not as powerful in terms of their ability to detect a real effect of the independent variable.

Another potential problem is that of nonequivalent groups. For example, let's say that you wish to compare the performance of two groups, one of which receives practice on a visual discrimination task while the other group does not. If you find that the group that received practice did better than the group without practice, it is possible that the practice group had more capable or skillful participants, or the participants in the practice condition simply had better vision. In other words, there is the possibility that you had two unequal groups in terms of visual acuity or the ability to perform that particular task. If the two (or more) groups are not equal prior to the introduction of treatment, there is a risk that the treatment is confounded with the biased selection of groups. To refresh your memory, refer back to sources of secondary variance discussed in Chapter 3.

Control Procedures

One way to address these problems is to use a large sample of participants and to randomly assign them into the various experimental conditions. As you will recall, *random assignment* means that each participant has an equal chance of being assigned to any of the experimental conditions. In addition, random assignment theoretically equates the groups in terms of subject variables or characteristics. Therefore, we can assume that, theoretically, all the groups are equivalent prior to introducing the independent variable or treatment. Furthermore, the effectiveness of random assignment increases as the sample size increases.

For example, let's say that you wish to study the effectiveness of computers in teaching statistics, and 50 participants signed up for your experiment. That sample of 50 participants most likely encompasses some people who are computer whizzes, others who are just competent, and still others who are computer illiterate. By randomly assigning each participant, chances are very slim that you would end up with all the illiterate participants in one condition, and all the whizzes and competent participants in the other condition. It is much more likely that each condition would have some whizzes, competent participants, and computer illiterates. In other words, your groups would be equal in terms of computer literacy prior to the introduction of the independent variable.

If you suspect that a particular subject variable or characteristic is strongly related to the dependent variable, you may wish to *match* the participants on that characteristic prior to random assignment into conditions. This matching procedure minimizes between-groups variability prior to the introduction of treatment. In other words, if you fear that random assignment alone will not create equivalent groups, you may opt for a matched design.

For example, if you know that IQ scores correlate to your dependent measure—that is, it will affect your dependent variable regardless of the independent variable value—you may match participants on their IQ prior to the experiment. Once all the participants have been paired off according to their IQ scores, you randomly assign one member of the pair to one condition and the other member to the second condition. Table 9.2 demonstrates the steps this procedure would take.

Although matched designs ensure equivalent groups and efficiently reduce individual differences, note that the matching process sounds a lot easier than it actually is. First, you need access to prior records on the matching variable, for example, SAT and IQ scores; second, it is time consuming; and third, it can waste a lot of participants. For example, if no match is found for a particular person, then that participant has to be discarded. For these reasons, matching is not advisable unless a strong correlation exists between the matching variable and the dependent variable. For example, if the relationship between IQ and the dependent measure is not established, or if it is a weak relationship, then matching participants on IQ would be a waste of time, energy, and participants.

TABLE 9.2 Matching Subjects by IQ

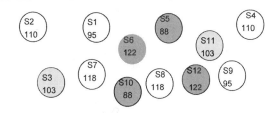

| | | Random Assignment | |
Matched Pairs	IQ	Condition 1	Condition 2
Subject 1—Subject 9	95	Subject 1	Subject 9
Subject 2—Subject 4	110	Subject 4	Subject 2
Subject 3—Subject 11	103	Subject 11	Subject 3
Subject 5—Subject 10	88	Subject 10	Subject 5
Subject 6—Subject 12	122	Subject 6	Subject 12
Subject 7—Subject 8	118	Subject 7	Subject 8

Finally, as mentioned in Chapter 3, it is crucial that all the groups be treated in the same way except for the independent variable. All extraneous variables need to be eliminated or held constant, so that only the independent variable is allowed to vary between the groups.

SINGLE-FACTOR EXPERIMENTS

As the name implies, a single-factor experiment has only one independent variable with two or more levels. The simplest design has two levels or conditions, such as treatment and no treatment (control), or two different forms of treatment. For example, you may wish to study the effect of music on learning and assign two music conditions: a music condition, where the participants learn some material while listening to music, and a no music condition, where the participants learn the material without music playing in the background.

In a multilevel design, the independent variable has three or more levels. For example, in a study on the effects of music on learning, you may wish to manipulate the type of music that the participants listen to. Therefore, the participants in one condition may learn the material while listening to jazz, in the second condition while listening to classical music, in the third condition while listening to rap, and in the fourth condition they would learn without any music.

As mentioned previously, having more than two levels of the independent variable is advantageous for two reasons: first, nonlinear or curvilinear relationships can be detected, and second, by assigning several levels, you are maximizing primary variance (see Chapter 3). The levels of the independent variable can be between the subjects, so that each condition has a different group of participants, or they can be within the subjects, where one group of people participates in each condition.

For an example of a multilevel design, consider McElwee and Farnum's study (2001) which was interested in seeing which type of information processing leads to superior memory. Their work was based on the Levels of Processing (LOP) theory proposed by Craik and Lockhart (1972), and self-referencing studies conducted by Rogers, Kuiper, and Kirker (1977). Before describing the McElwee and Farnum study, a brief review of LOP theory and self-referencing would be helpful.

According to Craik and Lockhart, information may be processed on several levels, from shallow, surface-level analysis to deep, semantic analysis. Information that is processed on a deep, semantic level tends to lead to superior recall of the information. In 1977, Rogers et al. conducted a study in which they included a self-referencing condition which required the participants to indicate the degree to which a particular trait described them. Rogers et al. found that, while semantic analysis (was a word synonymous with another word?) produced superior recall to shallow level of analysis (was a word the same size as another word?), self-referenced words were recalled the best.

Given these findings, McElwee and Farnum manipulated the independent variable (LOP instructions) on three levels: semantic (does a word mean the same thing as another word?), self-referencing (does a word describe you?), and possible future self (does the word describe you as you would like to be in the future?) The participants were given a randomly presented list of 45 traits and were asked to respond to each word according to LOP instructions. One-third of the words required semantic processing; one-third required self-referenced processing; and one-third required possible future self LOP. The authors found that the participants showed significantly better recall for words processed on a current self-referent level than on the semantic level, or on the possible future self level. On the other hand, there was no significant difference between the semantic and possible future self levels. In other words, while processing information relevant to the self produces enhanced memory, contemplating a possible future self does not. Figure 9.2 shows the results of the experiment.

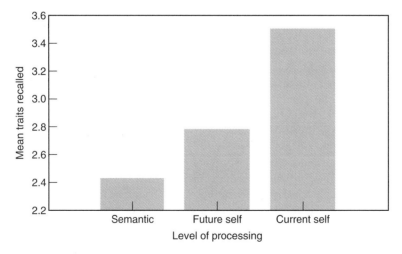

FIGURE 9.2   Mean traits recalled as a function of levels of processing. Based on McElwee and Farnum (2001) experiment.

MULTIPLE FACTORS DESIGNS

When the experiment calls for the manipulation of two or more independent variables, and all possible combinations of every level of each independent variable are represented, the experiment is called a *factorial design*. Each independent variable must have at least two levels, and therefore the simplest factorial is where there are two independent variables, each with two levels. The following experiment by Blaxton (1989) illustrates such a factorial design.

You are already familiar with the implicit-explicit memory distinction, which is what Blaxton investigated. However, her study also looked at whether the type of test used had an effect on the two types of memory processes. Prior research on implicit and explicit memory showed that, in general, explicit memory tests such as recall and recognition tend to be affected by concept-driven processes. On the other hand, implicit memory tests such as word-stem or word-fragment completions tend to be affected by data-driven processes (Craik, Moscovitch, & McDowd, 1994; Jacoby & Dallas, 1981; Kirsner & Dunn, 1985). Concept-driven tests or processes are those that access the meaning of concepts or words, whereas data-driven processes can be accomplished by merely comparing surface or feature characteristics of study and test phase items.

As an example of a data-driven process, let's say that during the study phase the participants see the word TABLET and then during the test phase they are asked to complete the word-stem TAB_____ with one or more letters so that it forms an English word. At this point, the participants may complete the stem with the word TABLET, simply because there is a match between the characteristics of the letters in the stem and the letters of the word seen previously during the study phase. Notice how the participant does not need to access the meaning of the word itself. A simple comparison between surface characteristics is enough to facilitate priming.

In her study, Blaxton manipulated two independent variables. The first independent variable, test condition, had two levels: explicit and implicit. The second independent variable, type of test used, also had two levels: concept-driven and data-driven. Blaxton found that both types of tests affected both memory conditions. In other words, explicit memory was affected by both concept-driven and data-driven tests, as was implicit memory.

The advantages of factorial designs are twofold. The first advantage is that the effects of several independent variables can be examined simultaneously and therefore you save time. Recall from Chapter 8 that each independent variable may produce its own effect, called a main effect. The second advantage is that by looking at the effects of more than one independent variable, the researcher can observe **interactions,** if there are any. Interactions were already mentioned briefly in the previous chapter and will be elaborated on in Chapter 12. To refresh your memory, an interaction occurs when the levels of one independent variable have a differential effect on the dependent variable under different levels of another independent variable. For example, if a teacher found that male students tend to do better with recognition tests such as multiple choice, but that female students do better with recall tests such as essays or fill-ins, then there would be an interaction between gender and test type. The levels of one independent variable (type of test) affect the levels of the second independent variable (males and females) differently.

Mixed Designs

As with single-factor experiments, the independent variables in a factorial design can be between-subjects or within-subjects. However, since there are at least two independent variables, factorial experiments can also have a **mixed design** (also called *split-plot design*). When one independent variable is between-subjects and one independent variable is within-subjects, the design is mixed. The mixed design combines the advantages of both the within-subjects and the between-subjects designs. The following study by Nantais and Schellenberg (1999), which investigated an interesting phenomenon called the Mozart effect, illustrates the mixed design.

The so-called Mozart effect, which was first reported by Rauscher, Shaw, and Ky (1993, 1995), refers to the experimental finding that listening to music by Mozart increases spatial-temporal performance on the Stanford-Binet intelligence test. Raucher et al. explained their results by saying that listening to music produces similar cortical firing patterns to performing spatial-temporal tasks, and therefore spatial-temporal reasoning improves by exposure to music. The implications of these findings led to a flurry of excitement over the benefit of music, to the extent that the governor of Georgia, Zell Miller, set aside a part of the budget for compact disks and cassettes for every infant born in the state.

Nantais and Schellenberg (1999) conducted two experiments to verify these findings. In Experiment 1, half the participants listened to Mozart, and the other half listened to Schubert. After 10 minutes of listening to music, the participants performed the Paper Folding and Cutting (PF & C) subtest of the Stanford-Binet. In addition, each participant also served as his or her own control by performing the PF & C task after sitting in silence for 10 minutes while wearing headphones. The order of the conditions was counterbalanced, and the music and no music conditions were tested on separate days. Nantais and Schellenberg found that there was a main effect of music: participants scored significantly higher on the PF & C test after listening to music than after sitting in silence. However, there was no difference between listening to Mozart or Schubert: both compositions increased performance on the spatial-temporal task. In other words, the effect could just as easily be termed the Schubert effect.

Notice why this experiment is a mixed design. The between-subjects variable was the type of music (Mozart or Schubert), whereas the within-subjects variable was the music condition (music or control). Each participant listened to only one type of music but was exposed to both a music condition and a control condition (silence). By having each participant act as his or her own control, individual differences in spatial-temporal abilities were eliminated. Therefore, improved performance in the music condition cannot be due to more skillful participants; rather, it seems to be due to the facilitative effects of music.

Sitting in silence for 10 minutes is pretty boring, however, and therefore Nantais and Schellenberg hypothesized that perhaps the improved performance was due to the participants' *preference* for one activity (music) over another (silence), rather than to the music itself. If that were the case, then any enjoyable activity might improve performance when paired with a less enjoyable activity. Experiment 2 was identical to Experiment 1 expect that the participants in the control condition listened to a short story rather sitting in silence. In addition, Nantais and Schellenberg asked the participants which activity they enjoyed more and which one was preferred. The results showed that the Mozart effect disappeared: there was no significant difference between the music and the short story conditions. Furthermore, there was a main effect of preference: the participants did significantly better on the PF & C task following the preferred condition. Those who preferred Mozart did better after the Mozart condition, while those who preferred the short story did better following the short story condition. Again, performance cannot be due to individual differences since the same people participated in both the music and the story conditions.

The mixed design is especially useful when one of the variables is a subject variable such as age, gender, race, or any other characteristic. Since subject variables automatically demand that the design be between-subjects, it is still possible to expose each group of participants to several levels or conditions of the second independent variable. For example, if you were interested in gender differences in the performance of spatial and verbal tasks, then the gender would be the between-subjects variable, and the task type would be the within-subjects variable. Each group (male and female participants) would perform both types of tasks: spatial and verbal. Therefore, you would need only two groups of participants.

SUMMARY

- An experiment entails the manipulation of one or more independent variables.
- In a single-factor experiment one independent variable is manipulated on at least two levels. If the independent variable has three or more levels, the experiment is a multilevel design.
- If two or more independent variables are manipulated, the experiment is a factorial design.
- In a single-factor experiment, the levels of an independent variable could be between-subjects or within-subjects.
- In a within-subjects design each person participates in every condition. Therefore, regardless of the number of conditions, only one group of participants is needed.
- In a between-subjects design each person participates in only one condition. Therefore, a different group of participants is needed for each condition.
- Factorial experiments may be within-subjects, between-subjects, or mixed designs.
- A mixed design is also called a split-plot design, where at the levels of at least one independent variable are within-subjects, and the levels of another independent variable are between-subjects.
- The major advantages of within-subjects design are that each participant is his or her own control, if offers increased statistical power, and fewer participants are needed. Potential disadvantages could be carryover and order effects.
- Counterbalancing the presentation of stimuli is a way of controlling order and carryover effects.
- The major advantage of between-subjects designs is that there are no order or carryover effects. A major disadvantage is that there are different participants in the various treatment conditions, and therefore individual differences are an ever-present source of unwanted variance. In addition, the groups may not be equivalent prior to introducing the independent variable.
- One way to control for the disadvantage of between-subjects design is to use a matching procedure. If a secondary variable is known to affect the dependent variable, the participants may be matched on that attribute prior to random assignment into conditions.
- Matching is time consuming and can waste a lot of participants. Therefore, it should be undertaken only if the matching variable correlates highly to the dependent measure.

KEY CONCEPTS

Between-Subjects Design	Interaction	Order Effects	Within-Subjects
Carryover Effects	Latin Square	Repeated Measures	Design
Counterbalancing	Mixed Design	Design	

QUESTIONS

Short answers can be found in Appendix A.

1. An experimenter studied the effects of alcohol on motor performance. Three groups received, respectively, no alcohol; 2 beers; and 4 beers. The above design is
   a. factorial
   b. multilevel
   c. within-subjects
   d. repeated measures

2. If a participant works on three mazes and performs best on the third maze, this may be due to
   a. practice effects
   b. the third maze is easiest
   c. fatigue
   d. a or b

3. An experimenter studied the effects of a major drug on schizophrenic symptoms. Group I received 0 mg; Group II received 100 mg; and Group III received 150 mg. Which of the following is true?
   a. This is a between-subjects factorial design.
   b. This is a within-subjects factorial design.
   c. This is a between-subjects multilevel design.
   d. This is a within-subjects multilevel design.

4. A study was conducted on the effects of age, gender, and social class on the buying habits of college students. Which of the following is true?
   a. The study could be a within-subjects design.
   b. The study could be either a between- or within-subjects design.
   c. The study must be a between-subjects design.

5. A multilevel design entails the manipulation of
   a. a single factor on several levels
   b. several independent variables
   c. two or more dependent variables
   d. two or more hypotheses

6. A design with two conditions with different participants in each condition is a
   a. repeated measures design
   b. within-subjects design
   c. between-subjects design
   d. factorial design

7. A design with the same participants in all three conditions is a(n)
   a. within-subjects design
   b. between-subjects design
   c. multilevel design
   d. both a and c are correct

For questions 8–10, read the following statement and then answer the questions: You wish to have people look at four different types of photographs and rate them for attractiveness.

8. In order to eliminate individual differences in taste, you should use a
   a. between-subjects design
   b. within-subjects design
   c. factorial design
   d. mixed factorial design

9. If you were to use the same group of people to judge all the photographs, you should
   a. use a Latin square
   b. vary the order of presentation
   c. show photos in same order
   d. either a or b would be fine

10. If you were to use a Latin square for the above, how many unique orders would you have?
    a. 12
    b. 6
    c. 9
    d. 1

11. A group of adolescents (Group I) rated male and female photographs, and a group of adults (Group II) rated male and female photographs. This is a _____ design
    a. mixed factorial
    b. single-factor, multilevel
    c. between-subjects factorial
    d. within-subjects factorial

12. One group performed a motor task with and without practice. Another group performed a spatial task with and without practice. In this mixed design, the between-subjects factor is _____, while the within-subjects factor is _____
    a. practice; task type, respectively
    b. motor task, spatial task, respectively

    c. task type; practice, respectively

    d. practice and no practice, respectively

13. A group of consumers tested four types of yogurts: cherry, vanilla, banana, and chocolate. The yogurts were presented to them in a counterbalanced order. The consumers preferred the cherry yogurt. Most likely this is due to

    a. order effects: the cherry was the first

    b. fatigue: by the time they tasted the chocolate, they were tired of the yogurts

    c. the cherry being the best yogurt

    d. all of the above are possible

CHAPTER 10

SINGLE-FACTOR ONE-GROUP DESIGNS

ONE-GROUP DESIGNS

Before-After Designs

Function and Advantage of Before-After Design

Limitations of Before-After Design

Solutions to Limitations

Statistical Analyses

OVER THE SUMMER, a professor develops a new method to teach advanced statistics to her students, designed to help them perform well on the final exam. She implements her new method in September and finds that the average grade on the December final exam is a 90. Since this is the highest average performance that she has seen in quite a few years, she concludes that her new teaching method is responsible for the high scores. Is this a valid conclusion? Hopefully, your answer is that it is impossible to tell.

As the have seen, the hallmark of a well-designed and well-controlled experiment is the ability to rule out alternative explanations for the results. In the present example, the treatment variable was the new teaching method, and the dependent variable was the students' final exam grade. In order for the teacher to conclude that the high level of performance was the result of the new teaching method, she would have to be able to rule out alternative explantions for the high scores. Unfortunately, alternative explanations cannot be ruled out. It is possible that the students in that particular class were exceptionally good in statistics and would have received high grades regardless of the teaching method. It is also possible that the teacher herself improved over the years and would have elicited top performance from her students regardless of what method she used to teach statistics. In other words, while the teaching method may have been the crucial variable, alternative explanations cannot be ruled out. Since the teacher used what is called a **one-shot case study,** a study without a comparison or control condition, the inference that may be drawn regarding a cause-and-effect relationship between the independent and dependent variable is seriously limited.

ONE-GROUP DESIGNS

In one-group designs, a single group of participants are observed under two or more experimental conditions. Each participant is his or her own control, and therefore the major advantage of the one-group design is the ability to control for individual differences.

The one-shot case study is certainly not recommended. It is included here merely to point out that studies without control or comparison conditions are not methodologically sound and should be avoided. In the example given here, to what is the teacher comparing the performance of her students? Since she has no prior information about the students' statistical abilities, or a control group of students who did not receive the new teaching method, she cannot establish the cause of the high exam grades. The solution to the problem is either a randomized two-group design or a before-after design. The randomized two-group design would simply mean randomly assigning half the students into the new teaching method condition while the other half would be taught using the old method. Of course, using a randomized two-group design eliminates the advantage of having each participant act as his or her own control, and therefore the before-after design might be a more desirable alternative.

Before-After Designs

In the **before-after design** version of the study, the students take a pretest in September, experience the new teaching method during the semester, and then take the final exam (posttest) in December. The teacher could then compare the before and after measures to see if there was a significant difference. Here is an example of the before-after design:

Group	Before-Measure	Treatment	After-Measure
1	Score on pretest	Teaching Method	Score on posttest

Notice how the data from the pretest can now be compared to the data from the posttest. However, even if the scores on the posttest are significantly higher than those on the pretest, the teacher still needs to be cautious when drawing causal inferences. Although the before-after design is a major improvement over the one-shot case study, it still has certain limitations, as you will see in a moment. First, let's discuss the design's function and advantage.

Function and Advantage of Before-After Designs

The primary purpose of the before-after design is to directly assess the effect of the independent variable on a participant, who is observed under two conditions. The first observation is made before the independent variable is introduced, and the second observation is taken after the participant has experienced the treatment. Before-after designs do not have to be true experiments in which an independent variable is manipulated; some might involve naturalistic observation, where the variable of interest occurs naturally. However, in the second instance, the researchers must have access to the before measures on whatever behavior they are interested in observing.

As, already mentioned, the major advantage of the before-after design is that the participants are their own control, and therefore, individual differences are eliminated. In the example of the effectiveness of the new teaching method, if the posttest scores are significantly higher than the pretest scores, the difference in the scores cannot be attributed to more mathematically capable participants in the posttest condition. The posttest score of every participant is compared to his or her own prior performance.

In addition, if pretest measures are available to the researcher and the participants are available for continuous testing, the design is particularly convenient. For example, school districts typically have access to data on student performance on a wide variety of standardized tests. If educational researchers wished to examine the effectiveness of various educational or enrichment programs, the preexisting data could be used as the pretest measure and compared to posttest scores following the completion of whatever program was under evaluation.

Limitations of Before-After Designs

In a simple before-after design, outside sources of variance are difficult to control. In other words, other, unwanted variables may be contributing to the observed differences in before and after scores. For example, let's say that you took the SAT and, unhappy with the results, you enrolled in an expensive course in order to improve your scores. Following the course, you took the SAT once more and found that your scores improved significantly. Can you conclude that it was the course alone that led to your improvement? The answer is no. Can you think of any other factor that may have contributed to the improved scores? If you said practice effects, you are correct. But practice effect is only one possible explanation; a number of other factors may have contributed to the improved SAT scores.

When the two observations are separated by a period of time, be it hours, weeks, or months, the changes in the dependent measure may be due to the passing of time, maturational factors, history, or any number of intervening variables. If, for example, a person suffering from depression enrolls in therapy, then the observed decrease in depression six months later may be due to the effectiveness of the therapy or simply to the passing of time. In other words, in time the person's depression may have lifted without the therapy. Similarly, if the reading scores of second graders improve from September to June, then the improvement may be due to the effectiveness of the program designed to improve reading (the independent variable) or to maturational factors.

Alternative explanations for changes in posttest or after measures include practice effects, maturation, history, and pretest sensitization.

Practice effects occur when performance on the posttest is better as a result of familiarity with, or practice on, the pretest. As stated above, SAT scores may have improved on the posttest due to practice effects, and not because of the intervening training program.

Maturational factors occur when the participants change from the first observation to the second, owing to internal factors and not to the effects of the independent variable.

In the preceding example, the second graders' reading scores may have improved simply because they were nine months older, and hence more mature, by the time they took the posttest. As a consequence of maturation, the students may have become more attentive, had a better understanding of what they were supposed to do on the test, or simply became better readers during the intervening time.

History effects refer to the effects of all events (aside from that of the independent variable) that occur between the two observations. For example, let's say that you are interested in assessing the attitude of participants toward police officers before and after viewing a film on the role of the police in the community. Unfortunately, a major riot breaks out in the community between the before and after observations. If the participants' attitude is different on the posttest, you have no way of knowing whether the resulting change in attitude is due to the effect of the film (the independent variable) or the riot (history).

Pretest sensitization, on the other hand, may occur if the pretest alerts, or sensitizes, the participants to the hypothesis. In a sense, pretest sensitization is a reactive effect through which the participants may alter their response on the after measure, simply because the pretest interacted with the treatment. Take the above-mentioned example of attitude change. Suppose that the participants have just taken a pretest that asked them numerous questions about capital punishment. Following the pretest, they are shown a film about an execution. Most likely, it will not take them very long to put two and two together and to realize that the film is meant to change their preexisting attitude toward capital punishment. When it is time for the posttest, the participants may resent being manipulated and may therefore stick to their original attitude, even if the film was effective in changing their original point of view. Conversely, they may wish to comply and be "good subjects," and therefore change their attitude on the posttest even if no actual change of attitude occurred. Either way, the response on the posttest may reflect pretest sensitization rather than any real effect of the independent variable.

Solutions to Limitations

The solutions to the problems mentioned above all involve additional groups of participants; therefore, the experiment can no longer be considered a one-group design.

One simple solution to the problem of practice, maturation, or history effects is to include an additional group of participants who will not receive the treatment. The participants would be randomly assigned into the treatment and no treatment conditions. For example, if you wished to see whether a training course improved SAT performance, then one group would receive the training course, while the other group would receive no training course. The design is now a randomized two-group design, as follows:

Group	Pretest	Treatment	Posttest
Group I	Yes	Yes	Yes
Group II	Yes	No	Yes

By comparing the performance of Group I to Group II, it is possible to determine whether improvement on the posttest is due to the effectiveness of the training course or to history, maturational, or practice effects. If the SAT scores of Group II also improve on the posttest, then the improvement can only be due to the effects of secondary variables, and not to the effectiveness of the treatment.

A specialized design, the **Solomon four-group design,** allows researchers to assess the effect of the independent variable alone, the effect of the pretest alone, and the potential interaction between the pretest and the independent variable. Since it is a factorial design, it will be covered in detail in Chapter 12; here is an outline of the design.

Group	Pretest	Treatment	Posttest
Group I	Yes	Yes	Yes
Group II	No	Yes	Yes
Group III	Yes	No	Yes
Group IV	No	No	Yes

Since the solutions to the limitations of the one-group design entail additional groups of randomly assigned participants, a final point needs to be mentioned. It is not always possible, or ethical, to randomly assign the participants into the various groups. For example, if the treatment involves a new teaching method, then it might not be feasible for a teacher to randomly assign half the students in her class to be taught by the new teaching method while the other half is taught by the old method. Clearly, the teacher cannot use both methods in the same class at the same time. In a similar vein, if a researcher believes that some intervention program may improve children's school performance, it may not be ethical to randomly assign children to a no intervention condition.

Statistical Analysis

The appropriate statistical analysis for the one-group before-after (or pretest-posttest) design is determined by the scale of measurement. If the scale of measurement is nominal, where the data are frequencies in discrete categories, then the one-group chi-square is the appropriate procedure. On the other hand, if the data are measured on an ordinal scale, where responses have been ranked before and after treatment, then the sign test is the correct statistical analysis for comparing the before and after measures. For data measured on the interval and ratio scales, the means of the before and after responses may be compared by using the t test for related samples.

SUMMARY

- The one-shot case study is a weak design that, due to the lack of a control or comparison condition, does not allow the researcher to draw conclusions about the effectiveness of the independent variable.

- Studies that do not allow comparisons to be made are not experiments and should be avoided.

- An inadequate solution to the one-shot case study problem is the one-group before-after design, where a single group of participants is given a pretest (before measure) prior to exposure to the independent variable. Following treatment, the group receives a posttest (after measure). The effectiveness of the independent variable is assessed by comparing the pretest and posttest scores.

- The one-group before-after design is considered inadequate because alternative explanations for changes on posttest scores cannot be ruled out. Posttest scores may have changed due to maturational factors, practice effects, history, or pretest sensitization.

- The only adequate solution to the problems posed by single-group experiments is to include additional groups of participants, such as the Solomon four-group design.

- In general, one-group experiments should be avoided, since the experimenter cannot control for the effects of outside factors.

KEY CONCEPTS

Before-After Designs   Maturational Factors   Practice Effects   Solomon Four-Group
History Effects   One-Shot Case Study   Pretest Sensitization   Design

QUESTIONS

1. Explain how practice effects differ from pretest sensitization and give examples.

2. Explain why the one-shot case study should be avoided.

3. What are the advantages and limitations of the one-group before-after design?

4. Explain how maturation differs from history.

5. On Friday, you give a pretest to evaluate the participants' attitude toward capital punishment. On Saturday, a controversial criminal case involving capital punishment receives wide television coverage. On Monday, you show a film about capital punishment, expecting that the film will change initial opinion. On the posttest, also given on Monday, you find that people's attitude toward capital punishment has changed. Explain what factor(s) may have led to the attitude change.

6. Jamal was unhappy with his SAT results, and so he enrolled in a six-week training course designed to improve performance on the SAT. He was pleased to find that his scores improved quite a bit the second time he took the test, and he recommended the training course to all his friends. Was Jamal justified in attributing the improvement on the SAT to the training course alone? Explain why or why not.

SINGLE-FACTOR TWO-GROUP DESIGNS

THE MOST basic experimental design involves the manipulation of a single independent variable on two levels. Typically, the experimental group experiences some form of treatment, while the control group receives no treatment. The performance of the two groups is then compared to see if there is a significant difference between them. The design may rely on two independent or unrelated groups, or it may require first matching the participants on some attribute prior to random assignment. In the second case, the design is a related or dependent two-group design.

INDEPENDENT TWO-GROUP DESIGNS

As already mentioned, in this design a single independent variable is manipulated on two levels, and the participants are randomly assigned to one or the other condition. Since random assignment means that all participants have an equal chance of being assigned to either of the two conditions, the procedure theoretically equates the two groups in terms of individual differences prior to introducing the independent variable. The researcher then minimizes the probability of secondary variance by ensuring that only the independent variable is allowed to vary between the two groups. That is, all potential sources of secondary variance are held constant or eliminated.

An example of the randomized two-group design is the classic bilateral transfer study that employs a mirror-tracing device similar to the one used by Starch in 1910. The study investigates the transfer of information from one hemisphere of the brain to the other, across a structure of the brain called the corpus callosum. The left hemisphere of the brain controls the right side of the body, whereas the right hemisphere controls the left side of the body. Therefore, knowledge of skills learned by the left hand is stored in the right hemisphere, while skills learned by the right hand are stored in the left hemisphere. The two hemispheres share the information by communicating with each other across the corpus callosum.

In the bilateral transfer study, the participants are randomly assigned to either a practice or a no practice condition. All participants perform a perceptual motor task by tracing a star-shaped pattern that is visible only through the mirror. The participants in the practice condition perform 25 practice trials with one hand, let's say the right hand, then five test trials with the left hand. The knowledge of the task learned by the right hand during practice is stored in the left hemisphere, which will then transfer this information to the right hemisphere. When the participants go on to do the five test trials with their left hand, the prior knowledge stored in the right hemisphere should facilitate their performance. The no practice participants perform the five test trials without any previous practice trials, and therefore, their performance is not facilitated by any prior knowledge of the task. Typically, large positive transfer effects from one hand to the other are observed, indicating that knowledge gained by one hemisphere can be transferred to, and utilized by, the other hemisphere.

The function of the two-group design is to demonstrate a significant difference between the two conditions, due to the effect of the independent variable. Since the participants are randomly assigned, and all outside factors are controlled, alternative explanations for the observed difference between the two groups can be ruled out. In the bilateral transfer study mentioned earlier, the possibility that the practice condition participants had fewer errors on the task than the no practice participants due to better motor skills is minimized by random assignment.

Advantages and Limitations

The major advantage of this design, as already noted, is that by randomly assigning the participants, the researcher may assume that the two groups are theoretically equal prior to introducing the independent variable. Provided that meticulous procedures are used to control for potential sources of secondary variance, the observed differences between the two groups can be attributed to the effect of the independent variable.

On the other hand, true random assignment may produce two groups that have an unequal number of participants. For example, the experimental group could end up with 12 participants, and the control group with 36 participants. Statistical comparison of the two means at this point may be unreliable due to the small sample size of the experimental group. A common procedure that addresses this issue is random assignment of participants within limits of equal cell or sample size. For example, if there are 48 participants, then random assignment is continued until 24 people have been assigned to one condition, and the remaining 24 participants are automatically assigned to the other condition.

A similar procedure may be used if it is suspected that gender may affect the dependent measure. For example, if 12 of the 48 participants are male, by using true random assignment all 12 males could end up in one of the conditions. In this instance, the researcher may randomly assign the males first, and once six males have been assigned to one condition, the remaining male participants are assigned to the other condition. The remaining 36 participants are then randomly assigned so that both groups have 18 female and 6 male participants.

The advantage of random assignment increases as sample size increases. The larger the sample size, the more effective the procedure of random assignment.

Statistical Analyses

The choice of inferential statistical test depends on the scale of measurement. If the scale of measurement is interval or ratio, the most common procedure is the unrelated t test. To refresh your memory, you learned in Chapter 7 that the function of the t test is to determine whether there is a significant difference between the means of the two groups. In addition, one-way ANOVA would also be appropriate. If the scale of measurement is nominal, the appropriate statistical analysis is the chi-square.

Before-After Two-Group Designs

A major disadvantage of the one-group before-after design, as shown in Chapter 10, is that changes in the dependent measure cannot be attributed to the independent variable alone. Maturation, history, and practice effects may also contribute to the observed difference between the before and after measures. One solution offered to this problem was that the researcher could include an additional group of participants which is not exposed to the independent variable. This solution is called the **before-after two-group design**.

For example, let us say that a researcher wished to study the effectiveness of an SAT training course. She randomly assigned 24 participants to the treatment condition and 24 to the control condition. Prior to beginning the training course, the SAT performance of both groups is assessed, giving the researcher pretest or before measures. One group then receives the training course, while the control group does not. Provided that the pretest scores of the two groups are equivalent, the posttest or after scores may be compared. On the other hand, if the pretest scores obtained for the two groups are not equivalent, then various procedures may be used to correct the before measures during statistical analysis. A discussion of these statistical procedures is beyond the scope of this chapter.

Advantages and Limitations   The before-after two-group design has two advantages. First, it entails random assignment of the participants, an advantage that has already been discussed. Second, it provides a measure of some behavior or trait prior to introducing the independent variable. The before measures enable the researcher to establish that the independent variable produced a difference between the two groups where little, if any, difference existed initially. For example, look at Figure 11.1, which shows the results of a hypothetical experiment studying the effectiveness of an SAT training course.

Notice that the before measures on the SAT produced equivalent scores for Groups 1 and 2; the difference between the two sets of scores is therefore not statistically significant. Group 1 then went on to receive the training course, and at its conclusion both groups were given an SAT posttest. Since only Group 1 improved, the researcher can rule out the effects of maturation, history, or practice. For example, if the improvement on the posttest scores of Group 1 was due to maturation, history, or pretest effects, then it is safe to assume that these outside factors would have also affected the performance of Group 2.

A major limitation of the design is that in order to obtain equivalent before measures a fairly large sample of participants is needed. With small samples, it is unlikely that equivalent before measures will be obtained. In addition, the before and after measures must be taken at the same time for both groups in order to control for outside influences.

Although maturation, history, and practice effects can be controlled for by having a comparison group that does not receive treatment, the design does not control for pretest sensitization. As you may recall, pretest sensitization occurs when the pretest interacts with the treatment. If the pretest alerts or sensitizes the participants to the treatment, they may act accordingly and provide unreliable posttest measures. For example, let us say that a researcher is studying the effects of propaganda on attitudes toward capital punishment. She gives both groups a survey that assesses their initial attitude toward capital punishment. Then one group watches a film on capital punishment, while the other group watches a neutral film. Following the film, each group is once more asked to fill out a survey regarding their attitude to capital punishment. If the treatment group's initial attitude toward capital punishment changed, as indicated by the posttest measure, the researcher cannot rule out the possibility of pretest sensitization. In other words, it is possible that the participants viewing the film on capital punishment "put two and two together" and concluded that the researcher was attempting to manipulate their attitude by showing the film. As a result, they may have acted accordingly and responded differently on the posttest then they would have, had they not become sensitized. Since the second group did not receive any treatment that could have interacted with the pretest, the effects of pretest sensitization cannot be assessed by comparing the two groups' posttest measures.

Assignment	Before	Training Course	After
Gp. 1	800	yes	1100
R			
Gp. 2	800	no	800

FIGURE 11.1   Design and hypothetical data for randomized two-group experiment.

Statistical Analyses   If the two groups are equivalent on the pretest or before treat-ment measures, then, as with the randomized two-group design, the appropriate statistical procedure entails comparing the posttest measures by an independent *t* test, one-way analysis of variance, or a chi-square. On the other hand, if the before measures are unequal, a simple way to "correct" the data is to calculate difference scores for each participant prior to data analysis. The difference score is obtained by subtracting the pretest measure from the posttest measure; data analysis is then performed on the mean difference scores.

Randomized-Blocks Design

In the randomized-blocks design, participants are blocked, or categorized on a particular trait or behavior that the researcher believes may have a confounding effect on the depend-ent variable. If not controlled, this confounding effect will make it difficult to separate the effect of the independent variable from the confounding variable. In other words, blocking on some variable is a control procedure, and its aim is to make the two groups in the exper-iment as equivalent as possible prior to treatment. Although students frequently confuse the blocked design with the matched design, the two are not the same. Blocked designs provide two independent or unrelated groups of participants.

For example, let us say that you are comparing the effectiveness of two diet plans: Plan A and Plan B. However, weight loss is affected not only by the type of diet plan, but also by how much a person weighs prior to beginning the diet. Typically, the more a person weighs, the more rapid and greater the weight loss. Therefore, prior to beginning the study, you weigh the 60 participants and assign them to three blocks: slightly overweight (10–20

Step 1:   Creating blocks according to weight. Sixty participants are weighed and grouped into blocks according to how much weight they need to lose.

Block 1: Slightly overweight (10–20 lbs.)	20 participants
Block 2: Moderately overweight (21–30 lbs.)	20 participants
Block 3: Greatly overweight (31–40 lbs.)	20 participants

Step 2:   Random assignment of the 20 participants from each block to either Plan A or Plan B, so that each diet plan condition has 10 participants from each block.

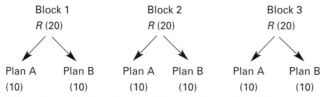

Step 3:   Notice that each diet plan condition now has 30 participants, 10 from each block. Each condition has equivalent participants in terms of their original weight. The experiment may now begin.

	Plan A	Plan B
Slightly overweight:	10	10
Moderately overweight:	10	10
Greatly overweight:	10	10

FIGURE 11.2   Randomized blocks design.

pounds), moderately overweight (21–30 pounds), and greatly overweight (31–40 pounds). For convenience sake, let us pretend that each block contains 20 participants. Once the blocking has been completed, 10 participants from each block are randomly assigned to Plan A, and the remaining 10 participants to Plan B (Figure 11.2).

Notice how each diet plan now contains people who are slightly, moderately, or greatly overweight. If, at the end of the study, you find that Plan B was more effective than Plan A, you could rule out the possibility that the result might be due to having more greatly overweight participants in this diet plan condition. Both conditions contained the same number (10) of greatly overweight participants.

In addition to blocking participants on some attribute, you could also block the experimental stimuli. For example, if you were conducting a memory study that involved a long list of 100 words, you could break the list down into four blocks (or lists) of 25 words and could have the participants recall the words at the end of each block. The blocks of words would be presented in a counterbalanced order, and the words within each block would be randomized to ensure that each participant sees the words in a different order.

Advantages and Limitations

The major advantage of this design is its ability to control for between- and within-groups variance by evenly distributing the effects of the blocking variable between the treatment conditions. By blocking the participants on some variable prior to random assignment, the researcher ensures that the two groups are highly similar in terms of that particular trait or characteristic. As such, there is good control of individual differences. In addition, since the participants are not matched one by one, the process is less time consuming and expensive than matched designs, and does not require that participants for whom no match was found be discarded.

A limitation of the design is that it requires a correlation between the blocking variable and the dependent variable. If the experimenter suspects that some secondary variable will affect the dependent variable, making it difficult to separate its effect from that of the independent variable, then blocking is a good way to control for this source of unwanted variance. However, if there is no relationship between the blocking and dependent variables, then the extra step of blocking prior to random assignment is a waste of time. Instead, the researcher should conduct a simple randomized two-group study. In addition, the procedure is more effective if a large number of participants are available for the study.

Statistical Analyses

The same statistical procedures that are used for the randomized two-group design may be used for blocked designs, including chi-square analysis, the independent t test, or one-way ANOVA. A particularly effective procedure is the randomized-blocks ANOVA.

DEPENDENT TWO-GROUP DESIGNS

As noted in Chapter 9, an important control procedure for minimizing between-groups variability due to individual differences is matching the participants on some attribute or characteristic. If you suspect that a particular subject variable or characteristic is strongly related to the dependent variable, you may wish to match the participants on that characteristic prior to random assignment into conditions. This matching procedure minimizes between-groups variability prior to the introduction of treatment. Although there are two different groups in the experiment, if you first matched the participants on some attribute, for example, IQ scores, you would have a related or dependent-groups design. Since matching provides you with pairs of participants, with each pair comprising two people with highly similar or identical IQ scores, the pairs of scores are correlated, and hence the two samples are related.

Matched-by-Correlated-Criterion Design

The **matched-by-correlated-criterion-design** is used when the experimenter knows that some factor, or criterion, is correlated with the dependent variable. The purpose of the design is to match the participants on that factor prior to random assignment into conditions. The design requires that the experimenter have access to the criterion measure prior to beginning the matching procedure.

For example, let us say that an experimenter wishes to evaluate the effectiveness of a new reading program developed for fifth graders. To ensure that the two groups of children (old program and new program) are equal in terms of reading ability, she would first match the participants on their preexisting reading skills prior to assigning them to the old or new reading program. In order to match the participants, she would need access to the children's performance on a prior reading test that had been administered by the school. Once the participants have been matched according to their individual reading scores, one member of the pair would be randomly assigned to the old reading program and the other member to the new reading program. Following the completion of each reading program, the experimenter compares the final mean reading score of the two groups.

Advantages and Limitations   A major advantage of the matched-by-correlated-criterion design is that the combination of matching and random assignment provides good control for individual differences. A second advantage is that since the matching criterion measure is available to the experimenter, and therefore no pretest is given, there is no worry that the pretest measure would sensitize the participants to the independent variable. A final advantage is that the design has more power (Chapter 7) to detect small differences due to the independent variable between the two groups of participants.

A major limitation of the design is that the researcher must have access to records on the matching variable. In addition, as mentioned in Chapter 9, matched designs are time consuming and require a large number of participants. Participants for whom no match is found are discarded, and so the procedure wastes a lot of participants. Therefore, experimenters should not use this procedure unless the matching variable is strongly correlated with the dependent variable. If the correlation between the matching variable and the dependent variable is weak, the researcher should use the randomized independent-groups design.

Before-Match-After Design

As the name implies, the difference between the **before-match-after design** and the previous one is that the experimenter must first collect measures on the matching variable by giving a pretest. Otherwise, the procedures for the two designs are identical. For example, if no reading records exist for the fifth graders in the study mentioned in the preceding section, the researcher would first administer a reading test, match the children on the basis of their reading scores, and then randomly assign them into reading program conditions.

The advantages that were mentioned for the matched-by-correlated-criterion design also apply to the before-match-after design. In terms of limitations, as with the matched-by-correlated-criterion design, there must be a correlation between the matching variable and the dependent variable, the procedure is time consuming, and it requires a large number of participants. However, as with the independent before-after design mentioned earlier in this chapter, there is the additional concern that the pretest measure may affect the participants' posttest response. In other words, the pretest may sensitize the participants to the independent variable. This problem does not exist for the matched-by-correlated-criterion design, since the measures for the matching variable are obtained unobtrusively.

An important consideration with all matched designs is that by discarding large numbers of participants for whom no match is found, the researcher may end up with a biased sample that no longer represents the population. If that were the case, the ability to generalize the findings back to the population would be limited, and the external validity of the study would be compromised. That is why it is so important that a large sample of participants be available to the researcher. The larger the available sample, the greater the probability that a match could be found for most participants, ensuring that only a few participants would need to be discarded from the study.

Statistical Analyses   For both the matched-by-correlated-criterion and the before-match-after design, if the data are on the interval or ratio scale of measurement, the appropriate statistical analysis may entail the *t* test for related or dependent samples. In addition, since each pair of participants could be viewed as a "block," the randomized blocks ANOVA may also be appropriate.

SUMMARY

- Two-group designs involve the manipulation of a single independent variable on two levels.
- The independent (or unrelated) two-group design employs two separate groups of participants who are exposed to different levels of the independent variable. The participants are randomly assigned to the conditions.
- The random assignment of the participants theoretically equates the two groups prior to the introduction of the independent variable. The larger the sample size, the more effective the random assignment.
- The function of the independent two-group design is to demonstrate a significant difference between the two conditions, due to the effect of the independent variable. If the participants are randomly assigned and all outside factors are controlled, alternative explanations for the observed difference between the two groups can be ruled out.
- The before-after two-group design entails random assignment into two conditions. Before and after measures are taken on both groups, but only one group is exposed to the independent variable.
- The before-after design has advantages because it provides a measure of some behavior or trait prior to introducing the independent variable. The before measures enable the researcher to estab-

lish that the independent variable produced a difference between the two groups where little, if any, difference existed initially.

- The limitation of the before-after two-group design is that pretest sensitization cannot be ruled out.
- The randomized-blocks design uses a limited version of random assignment into conditions. The participants are first blocked on some variable, and members of each block are then randomly assigned into one or the other condition. The blocking variable is a particular trait or behavior that the researcher believes may have a confounding effect on the dependent variable.
- The advantage of the randomized-blocks design is that it attempts to control for between and within-groups variance by evenly distributing the effects of the blocking variable between the treatment conditions.
- A limitation of the randomized-blocks design is that it requires a correlation between the blocking variable and the dependent variable.
- Dependent (related) two-group designs employ two groups of participants who have been matched on some variable prior to random assignment into conditions. Since each participant has a matched counterpart, the dependent variable measures occur in pairs.
- The matched-by-correlated criterion design is used when the experimenter knows that some factor, or criterion, is correlated with the dependent variable. The purpose of the design is to match the participants on that factor prior to random assignment into conditions. The design requires that the experimenter have access to the criterion measure prior to beginning the matching procedure.
- A major advantage of the matched-by-correlated-criterion design is that the combination of matching and random assignment provides good control for individual differences. The limitations are that matching is time-consuming and the researcher must have access to records on the matching variable.
- The difference between the before-match-after design and the matched-by-correlated-criterion design is that, in the first case, the experimenter must collect measures on the matching variable by giving a pretest. Otherwise, the procedures for the two designs are identical.

KEY CONCEPTS

Before-After Two-Group Design	Before-Match-After Design	Matched-by-Correlated-Criterion Design	Randomized-Blocks Design

QUESTIONS

Short answers can be found in Appendix A.

1. Explain the difference between the independent and dependent groups designs. Give an example for each design.

2. Explain the difference between blocking and matching participants prior to random assignment.

3. If you were interested in studying the effect of computerized instruction on statistics grades, what are some

factors on which you may wish to block participants prior to random assignment?

4. What are the advantages of matched designs? What are the disadvantages?

5. If you were conducting a study on the effect of stimulus exposure time on visual perception, what are some variables on which you may wish to match participants prior to random assignment?

6. Compare and contrast the matched-by-correlated criterion design and the before-match-after design.

7. A study was conducted to examine the effectiveness of a verbal training program that was developed to teach children with autism to speak in sentences. Sixty children were selected for the study, and prior to random assignment the experimenter grouped the children according to preexisting verbal skills. Three such groups emerged: poor speakers, medium-level speakers, and good speakers. The participants within each group were then randomly assigned to either the verbal training program or a control condition (no training). Answer the following:

a. The above design is called _____.

b. What is the independent variable?

c. State the levels of the independent variable.

d. What is the dependent variable?

e. Which two factors should correlate in order for this design to be worthwhile?

MULTIPLE FACTORS DESIGNS

SO FAR, you have learned about the most basic experiment in which a single independent variable is manipulated on two or more levels. Although the multilevel design with three or more conditions (Chapter 10) is certainly more complex than an experiment in which there are only two conditions, it is still a fairly simple design in that only a single independent variable is manipulated. The majority of studies reported in scientific journals tend to be much more complex. In order to obtain the maximum information, researchers typically manipulate several independent variables in a single study; in addition, there may be two or more dependent variable measures. For example, an experimenter may wish to examine the effects of practice and instruction on the number of errors made *and* the time it takes to complete a particular task. Notice that there are two independent variables—practice and instruction—and two dependent variables—errors made and time of task completion. When the experiment has two or more independent variables, it is called a **multifactor experiment;** when all possible combinations of all levels of each independent variable are examined, it is called a **factorial design;** and when there are two or more dependent variables, it is called a **multivariate experiment.**

DESCRIPTION AND FUNCTION OF FACTORIAL DESIGNS

In the factorial design, at least two independent variables are manipulated on at least two levels, and every possible combination of all levels is used. Therefore, the simplest factorial experiment has two independent variables, and each independent variable has two levels. For example, let us look at a hypothetical experiment that examines the effects of word type and test type on memory. The first independent variable is word type, and the levels are abstract and concrete words. The second independent variable is test type, and the levels are recall and recognition tests. The design of this experiment can be seen in Figure 12.1.

Notice that there are four conditions in this experiment. In the first condition, participants are exposed to abstract words, and their memory for the words is assessed by a recall test. In the second condition, the participants see a list of concrete words, which is then followed by a recall test. In the third condition, the participants' memory for abstract words is measured by a recognition test. In the fourth condition, the recognition test assesses memory for concrete words.

Essentially, you can look at this factorial experiment as the combination of two single-factor experiments. In fact, single-factor experiments are the basic elements, or the building blocks, of factorial designs. For example, look at Figure 12.2, where the components of this hypothetical experiment mentioned can be seen.

Notice that in Experiment 1, memory for abstract and concrete words is assessed with a recall test, while in Experiment 2, memory for abstract and concrete words is tested by recognition. However, there is no reason to conduct two separate experiments; Experiments 1 and 2 can be combined to form a factorial design.

The advantage of the factorial design is that the effects of the independent variables can be examined separately and in combination. In other words, factorial designs can demonstrate not only the individual effects of each independent variable, but also interactions between those variables, if such interactions do, in fact, exist. In the example mentioned earlier, the researcher can examine the effect of word type, the effect of test type, and the interaction (if there is one) between word type and test type.

	Word Type	
	Abstract	Concrete
Recall	1	2
Recognition	3	4

Test Type

FIGURE 12.1 Design of the hypothetical experiment investigating the effects of word type and test type on memory.

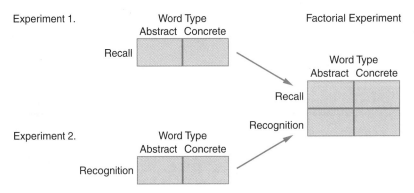

FIGURE 12.2 Components of the hypothetical word type and test type experiment.

As you can see, the main advantage of the factorial design over the single-factor experiment is that potential interactions between variables can be detected. The concept of interactions is important, since it may happen that neither independent variable has an effect by itself, yet their combination may produce a change in the dependent variable. For example, if the researcher first conducts an experiment on the effect of word type and then a second experiment on the effect of test type, it may turn out that neither variable has an effect on memory. However, it is possible that concrete words are easier to recall, while abstract words are easier to recognize, or vice versa, but this interaction between word type and test type could not be detected if two separate experiments were conducted.

As with single-factor experiments, the levels of the independent variables in a factorial experiment could be between-subjects or within-subjects design. In addition, since there are at least two independent variables, factorial experiments can also have a mixed design.

To refresh your memory, in a *between-subjects* design, each participant is exposed to only one condition. Therefore, separate groups of participants are needed for each condition. The more treatment conditions there are, the more groups of participants are needed. For example, as you can see in Figure 12.3, if the hypothetical experiment mentioned above was a between-subjects design, four groups of participants would be needed since there are four conditions. The participants would be randomly assigned to the conditions.

As illustrated in Figure 12.4, in a *within-subjects* design, only one group of participants is needed, since each participant is exposed to each treatment condition. Therefore,

| | | Word Type | |
		Abstract	Concrete
	Recall	Gp1	Gp2
Test Type			
	Recognition	Gp3	Gp4

FIGURE 12.3 Example of a between-subjects design.

		Word Type	
		Abstract	Concrete
	Recall	Gp1	Gp1
Test Type			
	Recognition	Gp1	Gp1

FIGURE 12.4   Example of within-subjects design.

in the word type and test type experiment, one group of participants would see both abstract and concrete words, and their memory would be assessed by both recall and recognition tests. The words would be presented in a randomized order, and the order in which the tests are given would be counterbalanced.

In a *mixed design,* participants would experience each level of one independent variable but only one level of another independent variable. Therefore, we could say that the levels of one independent variable are between the subjects, while the levels of another independent variable are within-subjects. For example, in the study mentioned earlier, the between-subjects variable could be either the word type or the test type. If word type is the between-subjects variable, then one group of participants sees only abstract words, while a second group of participants sees only concrete words. In this case, the within-subjects variable is test type, and each group of participants is given a recall and a recognition test (see Figure 12.5).

On the other hand, if the between-subjects variable is test type, then one group of participants is tested only on recall of the words, while the second group of participants is tested only on recognition. As you can see in Figure 12.6, in this instance, the within-subjects variable is word type, and both groups of participants would see abstract and concrete words.

		Word Type	
		Abstract	Concrete
	Recall	Gp1	Gp2
Test Type			
	Recognition	Gp1	Gp2

FIGURE 12.5   Example of a mixed design, where word type is between-subjects.

		Word Type	
		Abstract	Concrete
	Recall	Gp1	Gp1
Test Type			
	Recognition	Gp2	Gp2

FIGURE 12.6   Example of a mixed design, where test type is between-subjects.

TREATMENT EFFECTS IN FACTORIAL DESIGNS

As shown in Chapter 8, factorial experiments can result in **main effects** and **interactions.** However, in addition to main effects and interactions, the researcher can also look at **simple effects.**

Main Effects

Main effects are the average effects of the independent variables. Each independent variable may produce a main effect; therefore, there could be as many main effects as there are independent variables. In the simplest factorial where there are two independent variables, two main effects are possible.

For example, in the hypothetical study discussed in the previous section, the experimenter may observe a main effect of word type and a main effect of test type. If the researcher obtained a main effect of word type, there would be a significant difference between the mean number of abstract and concrete words remembered. Why did I say "remembered" instead of recalled or recognized? Because the main effect is the average effect of an independent variable, meaning as averaged across the levels of the second independent variable. In other words, there would be a significant difference between the mean number of concrete words and the mean number of abstract words when averaged across test conditions. On the other hand, if the experimenter obtained a main effect of test type, there would be a significant difference between the mean number of words recalled and the mean number of words recognized when averaged across word type conditions. Table 12.1 illustrates the concept of main effects.

The main effect of word type is simply the difference between the mean number of concrete words and the mean number of abstract words, after averaging across test type. Similarly, the main effect of test type is the difference between the mean number of words recalled and the mean number of words recognized, after averaging across word types. To illustrate this important concept further, Table 12.2 contains the hypothetical data collected in this experiment. The numbers represent the mean number of words in each condition.

According to the data in Table 12.2, the mean number of abstract words recalled is 10, and the mean number of abstract words recognized is 25. The mean number of concrete words recalled is 20, and the mean number of concrete words recognized is 30. Therefore, in order to determine the main effect of word type, the researcher first averaged the number

TABLE 12.1 Main Effects in the Hypothetical Experiment

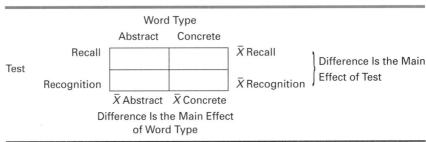

TABLE 12.2   Hypothetical Data in the Word Type and Test Type Experiment

		Word Type		
		Abstract	Concrete	
Test	Recall	10	20	$\bar{X} = 15$
	Recognition	25	30	$\bar{X} = 27.5$
		$\bar{X} = 17.5$	$\bar{X} = 25$	

Difference Is the Main Effect of Test (brace spanning Recall and Recognition rows)

Difference Is the Main Effect of Word Type (below Abstract and Concrete columns)

of abstract words across test type and then averaged the number of concrete words across test type. The mean number of abstract words remembered (recalled and recognized) was 17.5, while the mean number of concrete words remembered was 25. If the difference of 7.5 words between the abstract and concrete conditions was significant, then there was a main effect of word type. In a similar vein, to determine the main effect of test type, the number of words recalled (averaged across word type) was 15, while the mean number of words recognized was 27.5. Again, if the 12.5 difference between overall recall and overall recognition was significant, then there was a main effect of test type.

To summarize, the term *main effect* refers to the average effect of each independent variable. A significant difference between the conditions of an independent variable would indicate a main effect of that variable. Although the following example would not be a true experiment, in that nothing could be actually manipulated, students frequently find it easier to grasp difficult concepts if the research example includes subject variables.

Let us say that a researcher is interested in seeing whether gender and geographical location (South and North) have an effect on science grades. In this study, it is possible to obtain a main effect of gender and a main effect of geographical location. A main effect of gender would mean that there is a significant difference between male and female science grades, after they are averaged across the South and the North. In this instance, the science grades of males from the South and North would be averaged to derive a mean male score, and the science grades of female students from the South and the North would also be averaged to determine the mean female score. The mean male and female science scores would then be compared to see if there was a main effect of gender. Similarly, a main effect of geographical location would indicate a significant difference in science grades between students from the South and students from the North, after averaging across gender. Here, the science grades of males and females from the South would be averaged in order to determine the mean Southern grade, and the grades of males and females from the North would also be averaged in order to determine the mean Northern grade. The mean science grades from the South and the North would then be compared to see if there was a main effect of geographical location.

Interactions

Recall from Chapters 8 and 9 that an interaction occurs when the effect of one independent variable depends on the levels of another independent variable. In other words, when the

TABLE 12.3 **Hypothetical Data Showing an Interaction Between Word Type and Test Type**

| | | Word Type | |
		Abstract	Concrete
Test	Recall	10	20
	Recognition	30	15

effect of an independent variable is not the same across all the levels of another independent variable, there is an interaction. In the nonexperimental example mentioned earlier, if the researcher finds that males are better in science than females down South, but that females are better in science than males up North, then there is an interaction between gender and geographical location. This interaction indicates that the effect of one independent variable, gender, depends on the levels of the other independent variable, geographical location.

Similarly, if in the hypothetical experiment mentioned previously, recall was significantly better for concrete words than for abstract words, while recognition was significantly better for abstract words than for concrete words, there would be an interaction. Table 12.3 presents the hypothetical data that would indicate an interaction between word type and test type.

Notice how recall scores are higher for concrete words ($M = 20$) than for abstract ($M = 10$), while in the recognition condition the opposite is true: Here, the scores are higher

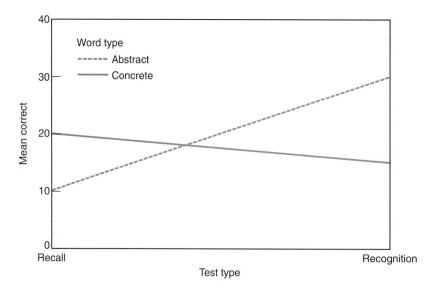

FIGURE 12.7 Interaction between word type and test type. Based on hypothetical data in Table 12.3.

TABLE 12.4 Hypothetical Data Showing no Interaction Between Word Type and Test Type

		Word Type	
		Abstract	Concrete
Test	Recall	10	20
	Recognition	25	35

for abstract words ($M = 30$) than for concrete words ($M = 15$). The interaction between word type and test type is illustrated in Figure 12.7.

Figure 12.7 shows that in the recall condition, the mean number of concrete words is higher than the mean number of abstract words. However, in the recognition condition, the opposite is true: The mean number of abstract words is higher than the mean number of concrete words. Another way to explain the interaction would be to say that abstract words are easier to recognize than to recall, whereas concrete words are easier to recall than to recognize.

When looking at the graphical presentation of data, a quick way to see whether there is an interaction between the variables is to look at the lines on the graph: If the lines are parallel, there is no interaction. In other words, the levels of one independent variable do not affect the dependent measure differently under all levels of the second independent variable. For example, let us say that there is no interaction between word type and test type. The hypothetical data are presented in Table 12.4.

Now look at Figure 12.8. Notice that the lines for abstract and concrete words are parallel, indicating that there is no interaction between the two variables. The difference in

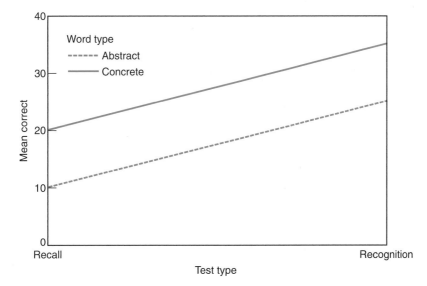

FIGURE 12.8 No interaction between word type and test type. Based on hypothetical data in Table 12.4.

recall between the abstract and concrete words is 10, and the difference in recognition between the abstract and concrete words is also 10. What the parallel lines indicate is that, theoretically speaking, regardless of how many test conditions we may add in this experiment, the difference between memory for abstract and concrete words will always remain the same: a difference of 10 words. Stated another way, the effect of word type on memory does not depend on the levels of the test variable: Memory will always remain superior for concrete words, regardless of how the participants are tested.

Although parallel lines on a graph indicate that there is no interaction and, since parallel lines never meet, there never will be an interaction. Lines that are not parallel do not automatically indicate that there is, in fact, an interaction. What nonparallel lines do indicate is that there *may* be an interaction. As you may recall from Chapter 8, the ANOVA shows an *F* statistic not only for each main effect, but also for the interaction(s). In addition, each *F* statistic is shown with *p* obtained. When looking at the obtained *p* value for the interaction, if the probability for error is greater than *p* critical (alpha), then there is no significant interaction between the variables.

The concept of interaction is important since on occasions there are no main effects, only an interaction between the variables. If researchers were only to look at main effects, they might conclude that none of the variables had an effect on the dependent measure. Therefore, they may falsely infer that there is no relationship between the independent variables and the dependent variable.

For example, if there was no main effect of word type or test type, but only an interaction between them, if the researcher were to look only at the lack of main effects, he might falsely conclude that memory was not affected by either word type or test type. In other words, the researcher might incorrectly conclude that there was no relationship between memory and word type or memory and test type. The hypothetical data in Table 12.5 indicate that there are no main effects, but an interaction between word type and test type.

Notice that there is no main effect of word type: The mean number of abstract words remembered is 15 (10 + 20 = 30; 30/2 = 15), and the mean number of concrete words remembered is also 15 (20 + 10 = 30; 30/2 = 15). Similarly, there is no main effect of test type: Averaging across word type, we find that the mean number of words recalled is 15, and the mean number of words recognized is also 15. However, this does not mean that there is no relationship between memory and word type, or between memory and test type. A look at Figure 12.9 will show that abstract words are better recognized than concrete

TABLE 12.5 Hypothetical Data Showing an Interaction But No Main Effects in the Word Type and Test Type Experiment

		Word Type	
		Abstract	Concrete
Test	Recall	10	20
	Recognition	20	10

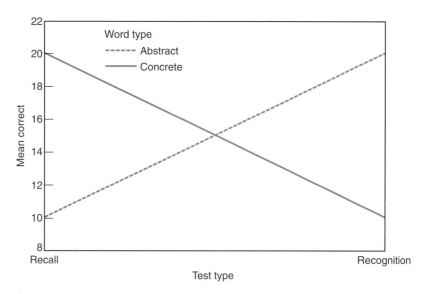

FIGURE 12.9 No main effects, but an interaction between word type and test type. Based on hypothetical data in Table 12.5.

words, whereas concrete words are better recalled than abstract words. In other words, memory for each type of word depends on how the participants are tested: Superior memory results when participants are tested with recall for concrete words and with recognition for abstract words.

Up to now, the focus has been only on crossover interactions, for example, where memory for abstract words is better under the recognition condition, while memory for concrete words is better under the recall condition. However, not all interactions are crossover interactions, which means that the lines on the graph cross each other at some point. For instance, it could very well turn out that memory for both abstract and concrete words is better under the recognition condition, and there is still an interaction. Suppose that in our hypothetical study the data shown in Table 12.6 were collected.

Notice that both abstract and concrete words were better recognized than recalled; however, notice also that the difference between abstract and concrete words in the recall condition is 10, but there is no difference between them in the recognition condition. In other words, according to our hypothetical data, memory is better for concrete words in the recall condition, but there is no difference between concrete and abstract words under the recognition condition.

In a similar vein, we could say that although memory for concrete information only increases by 5 words if a recognition test is given, memory for abstract information increases by 15 words. As you can see, test type has a greater effect on memory for abstract information than for concrete information. Although memory for both types of words increases in the recognition condition, the recognition test has a greater benefit on memory for abstract words. Figure 12.10 illustrates this interaction.

TABLE 12.6 Hypothetical Data Showing an Interaction between Word Type and Test Type

		Word Type	
		Abstract	Concrete
Test	Recall	10	20
	Recognition	25	25

Simple Effects

Aside from main effects and interactions, factorial experiments also allow investigators to examine the data for simple effects. The effects of the two levels of one independent variable under each level of another independent variable are the simple effects. For example, let us return to the original hypothetical data shown in Table 12.2. Notice that the following four simple effects could be examined:

- The effect of word type under the recall condition. Compare the mean number of abstract words recalled to the mean number of concrete words recalled ($M = 10$ vs. $M = 20$, respectively).

- The effect of word type under the recognition condition. Compare the mean number of abstract words recognized to the mean number of concrete words recognized ($M = 25$ vs. $M = 30$, respectively).

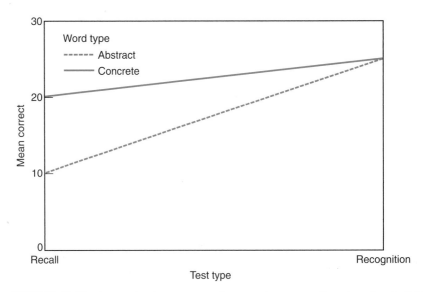

FIGURE 12.10 Interaction between word type and test type. Based on data in Table 12.6.

- The effect of test type under the abstract word condition. Compare the mean number of abstract words recalled to the mean number of abstract words recognized ($M = 10$ vs. $M = 25$, respectively).

- The effect of test type under the concrete word condition. Compare the mean number of concrete words recalled to the mean number of concrete words recognized ($M = 20$ vs. $M = 30$, respectively).

In summary, factorial experiments allow investigators to study the effects of several independent variables simultaneously, which saves quite a bit of time. The more independent variables and levels are factored in, the more complex the design and the more complex the statistical analysis.

DESIGN TYPES

If you look at the design and procedure section of a journal article, you will notice that factorial experiments are typically described in terms of numbers, for example, as a 2×2 factorial, a 2×3 factorial, or a $2 \times 2 \times 3$ factorial design. The design description can tell the reader how many independent variables were manipulated and how many levels each independent variable had. Each number stands for an independent variable, and its numerical value stands for the number of levels or conditions that particular independent variable has. For example, a design that is described as a 2×2 factorial has two independent variables, and each independent variable has two levels. Similarly, a 2×3 factorial also has two independent variables; the first independent variable has two levels, and the second independent variable has three levels. A design described as a $2 \times 2 \times 3$ factorial, on the other hand, has three independent variables: the first and second independent variables have two levels, whereas the third independent variable has three levels.

Before we go any further, see if you can identify the number of independent variables and their respective levels in the following factorial experiments:

1. 3×3
2. $2 \times 3 \times 3$
3. $2 \times 2 \times 2 \times 3$
4. 3×4

The correct answers are as follows:

1. There are two independent variables, each with three levels.
2. There are three independent variables: the first one has two levels, and the second and third independent variables have three levels.
3. There are four independent variables: the first three have two levels, and the fourth one has three levels.
4. There are two independent variables: the first one has three levels, and the second one has four.

The number of conditions in a factorial experiment depends not only on the number of independent variables, but also on the number of levels on which the variables are manipulated. To find the number of conditions in a factorial experiment, simply multiply the numbers together. Therefore, a 4×4 factorial experiment may have only two independent variables. Since each one has four levels, however, there are a total of 16 conditions ($4 \times 4 = 16$). On the other hand, while a $2 \times 2 \times 2$ factorial has three independent variables, since each variable has only two levels, there are "only" eight conditions ($2 \times 2 \times 2 = 8$).

Now that you have read the discussion between- and within-subjects designs and you are familiar with factorial experiments, you can most likely appreciate the advantage of the within-subjects design. The more conditions there are in the experiment, the more groups of participants you would need for a between-subjects design. On the other hand, regardless of the number of conditions, if the levels of the independent variable were within-subjects, you would only need one group of participants.

Finally, no matter how many independent variables there are in the experiment, the possible results include main effects, simple effects, and interactions. However, the complexity of these findings increases with the number of independent variables and their levels.

The 2 x 2 Factorial

The hypothetical experiment on the effects of word type and test type on memory was a 2 (word type: abstract and concrete) $\times$ 2 (test type: recall and recognition) factorial. Conventionally, the first independent variable is designated by the capital letter A, and its levels are depicted as A1 and A2. The second independent variable is designated by capital letter B, and its levels are identified as B1 and B2. Therefore, the results of a 2×2 factorial experiment may indicate a main effect of A, which would mean that there was a significant difference between the conditions A1 and A2, after averaging across the levels of the B variable. There may also be a main effect of B, which would be indicated by a significant difference between the conditions B1 and B2, after averaging across the levels of the A variable. In addition, there might be an A $\times$ B interaction, where the effect of one variable depends on the levels of the other variable.

The following experiment by Forgas and Bower (1987) illustrates the 2×2 factorial design. In order to study how mood affects person-perception and memory, Forgas and Bower first manipulated the participants' mood by giving them feedback on a bogus psychological test. Some participants received positive feedback, which was expected to create a good mood, while other participants received negative feedback in order to create a bad mood. In the next part of the experiment, all the participants were asked to read four realistic person-descriptions containing negative and positive details about the persons in the descriptions. There were a total of 20 negative and 20 positive details in the descriptions.

As you can see, the first independent variable manipulated was the mood created by the feedback (A), and the second independent variable manipulated was the person-description detail (B). The levels of the first independent variable were good mood (A1) and bad mood (A2), while the levels of the second independent variable were positive details (B1) and negative details (B2). Although this study involved several dependent variable measures, the focus here will be on the effect of mood on person memory.

TABLE 12.7 Number of Positive and Negative Items Recalled as a Function of Mood Based on Data from Forgas and Bower (1987)

		Mood	
		Good	Bad
Items	Positive	10.83	6.77
	Negative	5.92	8.54

To assess the effects of mood and person-description details on memory, the participants were given a recall test and were asked to recall and write down everything that they could remember about each of the characters in the descriptions. Table 12.7 shows the number of positive and negative items recalled by the participants in their respective mood conditions.

Forgas and Bower found no main effect of mood. Although participants recalled more items when they were in a good mood than in a bad mood, the difference was not significant. There was, however, a main effect of item type: The participants recalled significantly more positive than negative details ($M = 8.8$ vs. $M = 7.23$, respectively). The really interesting finding was the significant interaction between mood and item type. As Table 12.7 shows, the participants in a good mood remembered significantly more positive than negative details about the target persons (10.83 vs. 6.77, respectively), while the participants in a bad mood recalled significantly more negative than positive details (8.54 vs. 5.92, respectively). This interaction can be seen in Figure 12.11.

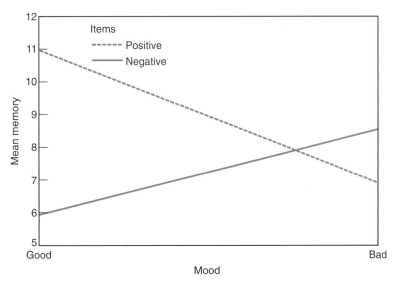

FIGURE 12.11 Interaction between mood and item type. Based on data from Forgas and Bower (1987).

The findings indicate that people tend to learn and recall more mood-congruent information than mood-incongruent information. As Forgas and Bower point out, mood tends to affect what we encode and remember about other people: Being in a good mood may bias us toward encoding and remembering positive information, while being in a bad mood may bias us toward encoding and remembering negative information.

Solomon Four-Group Design

The **Solomon four-group design** (Solomon 1949) can address the problems raised by one-group or two-groups pretest-posttest designs. The Solomon four-group design is a 2 (pretest) × 2 (treatment) factorial, in which the levels of each independent variable are the presence or the absence of the variable. The major advantage of the design is that it allows you to evaluate the effect of the treatment alone, the effect of the pretest by itself, and the interaction between the pretest and the treatment (pretest sensitization). The design can be outlined as follows:

		Pretest	
		Yes	No
Treatment	Yes	I	II
	No	III	IV

Notice that the design entails four groups of participants: Group I receives both the pretest and the treatment; Group II receives treatment without a pretest; Group III is given a pretest but no treatment; and Group IV receives neither the pretest nor the treatment. The participants are randomly assigned into conditions. For example, let us say that you obtained the following data in a Solomon four-group design:

Group	Pretest	Treatment	Posttest
Group I	60	Yes	80
Group II	—	Yes	80
Group III	60	—	60
Group IV	—	—	60

If you look at the posttest score of Group I, you can see that there was a 20-point increase from the pretest score. Is this increase due to pretest sensitization, to practice effects, or to the effect of the independent variable? By looking at the posttest score of Group II, you can rule out pretest sensitization: Group II also scored an 80 on the posttest, yet there was no pretest that could have interacted with the treatment. Next, in order to rule out practice effects due to the pretest, look at the scores of Groups III and IV. Since the posttest scores of Group III and IV are the same and the posttest score of Group III did not change, you can rule out the effect of the pretest itself.

On the other hand, the following data would indicate pretest sensitization:

Group	Pretest	Treatment	Posttest
Group I	60	Yes	80
Group II	—	Yes	60
Group III	60	—	60
Group IV	—	—	60

Notice that the change in the posttest score for Group I could not be due to the independent variable alone since Group II also received treatment, and yet the posttest score is 20 points lower than that of Group I. Similarly, the pretest alone did not produce a change in the posttest score for Group III; therefore, practice effects can be ruled out. This leaves us with pretest sensitization as the most likely explanation for the change in the posttest score of Group I.

Finally, how would the data look if changes in the posttest scores were due to the effect of the pretest itself, and not to pretest sensitization or treatment?

Group	Pretest	Treatment	Posttest
Group I	60	Yes	80
Group II	—	Yes	60
Group III	60	—	80
Group IV	—	—	60

Notice that the posttest scores for Group I and III increased from 60 to 80. However, since Group III did not receive treatment, the change in the posttest score cannot be due to the effect of the independent variable (not to mention that the posttest score of Group II is 60, even though this group did receive the treatment). Nor can the change be due to pretest sensitization; for Group III there was no treatment for the pretest to interact with, yet the posttest score increased. Therefore, the only plausible explanation is practice effect.

The 2 x 3 Factorial

In a 2×3 factorial experiment, there are still only two independent variables. However, as you can see, the second independent variable is manipulated on three levels. Such a design would entail six experimental conditions. The possible outcome of such an experiment is identical to that of a 2×2 design in that there could be main effects of A and B as well as an $A \times B$ interaction. However, since the second independent variable has three levels, if a main effect of B was obtained (as indicated by the F statistic and its corresponding p value for that independent variable), post-hoc analyses would be needed to determine which pairs of means were significantly different.

For example, let us say that a researcher is investigating the effects of modality of presentation (A) and word frequency (B) on memory. Modality of presentation refers to how the participants are exposed to the stimuli, whereas word frequency refers to the frequency with which the words are used in the English language. In this hypothetical study,

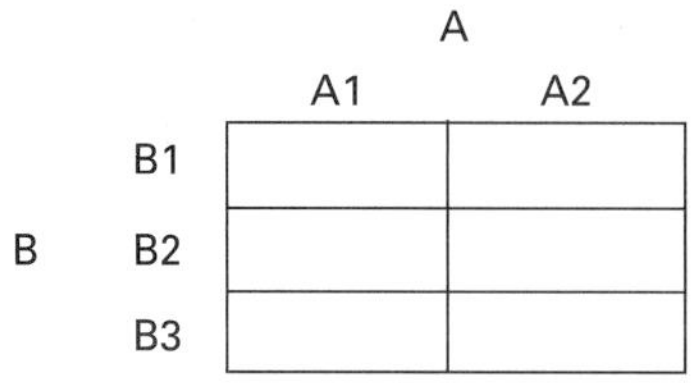

A

		A1	A2
	B1		
B	B2		
	B3		

FIGURE 12.12   Design of the 2 X 3 experiment.

the levels of the first independent variable are auditory presentation (A1) and visual pres-entation (A2), whereas the levels of the second independent variable are low-frequency words (B1), moderate-frequency words (B2), and high-frequency words (B3). The design of this experiment can be seen in Figure 12.12.

As with the 2×2 design, in order to determine the main effect of A, the means of A1 and A2 would be compared, after they were averaged across the three levels of the B vari-able. If the ANOVA indicates that the difference between the two means is significant, then there is a main effect of modality of presentation. However, in order to determine whether there is a main effect of B, three means would have to be compared: the mean number of low-frequency words recalled, the mean number of moderate-frequency words recalled, and the mean number of high-frequency words recalled. Therefore, if the ANOVA indi-cates that a significant difference between the means of conditions B1, B2, and B3, post-hoc analyses will be needed to determine which pairs are significantly different: B1 vs. B2, B2 vs. B3, or B1 vs. B3?

As an example of a 2×3 factorial, Sternberg (1966) presents a slightly modified ver-sion of a classic experiment. As noted in Chapter 6, Sternberg developed an experimental paradigm to investigate retrieval from short-term memory (STM). Part of this paradigm demonstrated a positive linear function. Sternberg's experiment was designed to answer two specific questions regarding the search through STM. (1) To locate a given item in STM, do we search the memory set item by item (serial search), or do we scan the entire memory set all at once (parallel search)? (2) Is the search self-terminating, meaning that once the needed item is located the search stops, or is the search exhaustive, meaning that even if the item is found, the search continues until all items had been scanned? His find-ings indicated that the search is serial and exhaustive. To see how he came to this conclu-sion, let us look at his experimental procedure.

You will recall that the participants were shown a series of digits, called the memory set. The size of the set varied from one to six items. On some trials the participants saw only one digit, and on others two or more digits. After each trial, the participants were pre-sented with a single digit, called a probe, and were asked to indicate by pressing the appro-priate key whether the probe was a part of the memory set. The probe was varied, so that for half the trials the digit was part of the original memory set (positive probe), and for half the trials the probe was not a part of the set (negative probe). The dependent variable was the participants' reaction time (RT) measured in milliseconds (ms).

Sternberg found that RT was a function of the memory set size. Each additional item in the set increased RT by a constant 38 ms. Therefore, he concluded that the search was serial. If the search had been parallel, then the set size would not have mattered. To see whether the search was self-terminating or exhaustive, Sternberg next looked at the effects of positive versus negative probes. Clearly, for a negative probe the search must be exhaustive, since in order to determine that a given item was not present, you would need to search through all the items in the set. For positive probes, however, it is possible that the search ends as soon as the item is located, which would indicate that for positive probes the search is self-terminating. This was not what Sternberg found; he discovered that the reaction times were nearly identical for positive and negative probes. Since the participants took just as long to decide that an item had been present as not present, Sternberg concluded that even after an item had been found the search continued through the entire set. Hence, the search through STM is exhaustive.

Now that you have an understanding of the Sternberg paradigm, let us look at the modified version presented in the student version of the MEL laboratory manual (St. James, Schneider, & Rodgers, 1992). The slight modification in the MEL version is that the memory set is manipulated on only three levels: one item, three items, and five items. Figure 12.13 illustrates the experiment.

Given what you know about the search process, what results would you predict for this experiment? For example, knowing that the search is exhaustive, would you predict a main effect of probe type (A)? If you said no, you are correct. If participants search through the entire set, regardless of whether an item was present or not present, then the mean reaction times for positive and negative probes should not be significantly different. With regard to set size, knowing that the search is serial, would you predict a main effect for this variable (B)? If you said, yes, you are correct. Since each additional item adds to the reaction time, then an increase in set size should lead to an increase in reaction time. Finally, should there be an interaction? The answer is no. Given that both positive and negative probes produce identical reaction times, set size and probe type do not interact. Figure 12.14 shows a graphical presentation of hypothetical data collected in the MEL experiment.

The 2 x 2 x 2 Factorial

The 2 × 2 × 2 factorial design involves three independent variables (A, B, and C), each manipulated on two levels. For example, in a research study, Spata (1995) investigated the effects of modality, Levels of Processing (LOP) instructions, and test type on memory.

As stated previously, modality (A) refers to how the words were presented, with A1 representing visual presentation and A2 representing auditory presentation. LOP instructions refer to how deeply the participants were asked to analyze the information. In the shallow condition (B1), the participants were asked to count the number of vowels in each

	Probe (A)	
	Positive (A1)	Negative (A2)
1 (B1)		
Set Size (B) 3 (B2)		
5 (B3)		

FIGURE 12.13 Design of a modified version of the Sternberg (1966) experiment. (*Source:* St. James. Schneider, & Rodgers, 1992.)

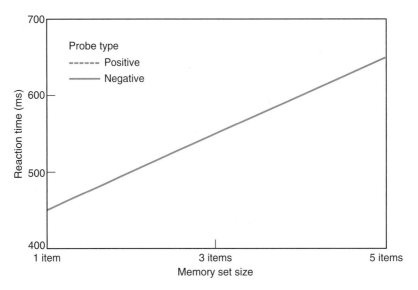

FIGURE 12.14   Showing the results of the modified Sternberg (1966) experiment. Based on hypothetical data.

word, while in the deep level of analysis condition (B2), the participants judged whether a given word was pleasant or unpleasant. Vowel counting is considered a shallow level of analysis since the actual meaning of the words does not have to be accessed to complete the task. On the other hand, in order to judge a word as pleasant or unpleasant, the participants need to think about the meaning of the word (Craik & Lockhart, 1972). The final independent variable was how memory for the words was assessed: a stem-completion test (C1) or a word-association test (C2). Figure 12.15 demonstrates the design.

Notice that there were eight experimental conditions:

1. Participants saw a list of words, processed them on a shallow level, and were given a stem-completion test.

2. Participants saw a list of words, processed them on a deep level, and were given a stem-completion test.

		A (modality)			
		A1(visual)		A2(auditory)	
		B (LOP orientation)			
		B1 (shallow)	B2 (deep)	B1 (shallow)	B2 (deep)
C (test)	C1 (stems)	1	2	3	4
	C2 (assoc)	5	6	7	8

FIGURE 12.15   Design of a 2 × 2 × 2 experiment. (*Source:* Spata, 1995.)

3. Participants heard a list of words, processed them on a shallow level, and were given a stem-completion test.

4. Participants heard a list of words, processed them on a deep level, and were given a stem-completion test.

Conditions 5–8 were identical to conditions 1–4, except the participants were given word-association tests.

As you can see, when the experiment manipulates three independent variables simultaneously, the data analysis and the interpretation of the results get considerably more complex. In a $2 \times 2 \times 2$ design such as this one, it is possible to obtain three main effects: one for each independent variable. However, since there are three independent variables, the number of possible interactions increases. It is possible to obtain an A $\times$ B interaction, a B $\times$ C interaction, an A $\times$ C interaction, and, in addition, a three-way A $\times$ B $\times$ C interaction. The interpretation of three-way interactions is quite complex.

Let us look at Table 12.8, which contains the data for the above-mentioned experiment. To analyze the results, a 2 (visual vs. auditory) $\times$ 2 (shallow vs. deep) $\times$ 2 (word stem vs. word association) ANOVA was conducted. The three-way ANOVA indicated that there was no main effect of modality. There was no significant difference between memory for visually presented items ($M = 4.18$) and auditory presentation ($M = 3.04$). There was a main effect of LOP instructions: The difference between memory for words in the shallow condition ($M = 2.85$) and the deep condition ($M = 4.37$) was significant. In addition, there was no main effect of test type: The difference between the means of the word-stem condition ($M = 3.84$) and the word-association condition ($M = 3.39$) was not significant.

There was also a significant interaction between modality (A) and test type (C). When the presentation was visual, performance was better on the stem-completion test than on the word-association test. However, when the presentation was auditory, performance was better on the word-association test than on stem completions. In other words, shifting the modality of presentation from visual to auditory had a detrimental effect on stem completions but a facilitating effect on word associations. This interaction can be seen in Figure 12.16.

This experiment revealed no significant three-way interaction between modality, LOP instruction, and test type. However, if such an interaction existed, how would it be presented graphically, and how would it be interpreted?

TABLE 12.8 **Scores on Stem Completions and Word Associations as a Function of Modality and Levels of Processing Orientation (Spata, 1995)**

| | Modality | | | | | |
| | Visual | | | Auditory | | |
Test	Shallow	Deep		Shallow		Deep
Stem	4.58	6.67		2.50		1.60
Association	1.21	4.25		3.12		4.96
$M =$	2.9	4.18	5.46	3.31	3.04	3.28

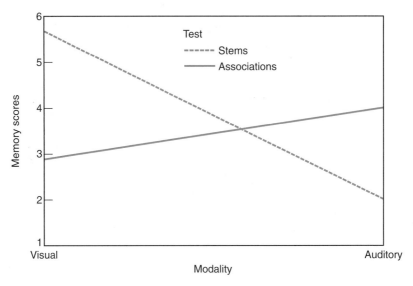

FIGURE 12.16 Modality X Test interaction. (*Source:* Spata, 1995.)

A three-way interaction is best presented on two separate graphs; that is, the effects of two variables are shown separately under each level of a third variable. For example, let us say that in the visual condition, word-stem completions benefited from shallow processing, whereas word associations benefited from a deep level of processing. On the other hand, LOP instructions had no effect in the auditory condition. If there was an interaction

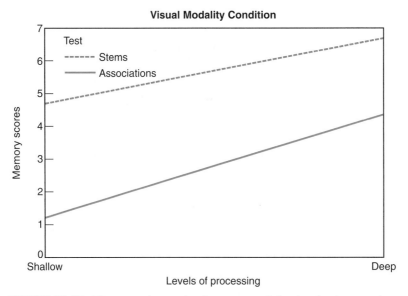

FIGURE 12.17 Three-way interaction between modality, levels of processing, and test. (*Source:* Spata, 1995.) Panel 1: Visual condition; Panel 2: Auditory condition. *(Figure continues)*

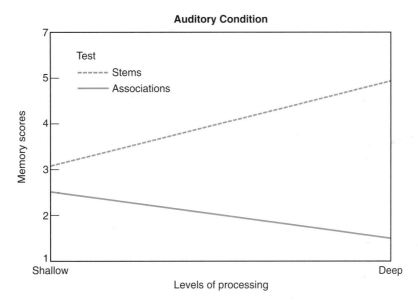

FIGURE 12.17   (Continued)

between LOP instructions and test type in the visual condition, but no such interaction existed in the auditory condition, then there would be a three-way interaction between modality, LOP, and test type. Figure 12.17 illustrates this three-way interaction. Panel 1 shows no interaction between LOP and test type in the visual condition, while Panel 2 shows an interaction between LOP and test type in the auditory condition.

This three-way interaction is only one possible example. Significant three-way interactions could take many shapes, depending on how the variables are affecting the behavior under study. For example, it is possible to obtain a three-way interaction where LOP and test type interaction under both the visual and the auditory conditions. However, if that were the case, the pattern of the interactions would be different.

Statistical Analyses

As stated previously, the appropriate statistical analysis for factorial experiments is the factorial ANOVA. When there are only two independent variables, the two-way ANOVA is appropriate; when there are three independent variables, a three-way ANOVA is used. In addition, there are ANOVA models for between-subjects, within-subjects, and mixed designs.

SUMMARY

- Complex experiments involve the manipulation of two or more independent variables and, at times, two or more dependent measures. Experiments with multiple independent variables are called factorial experiments, whereas experiments with multiple dependent variables are called multivariate designs.

- The levels of the independent variables could be between-subjects or within-subjects. In addition, factorial experiments may have a mixed design, where the levels of at least one independent variable are between-subjects and the levels of at least one other independent variable are within-subjects.

- A main effect is the average effect of an independent variable. Each independent variable may produce a main effect, and therefore, an experiment could have as many main effects as there are independent variables.

- Simple effects are the effects of the levels of each independent variable under each level of another independent variable.

- An interaction occurs when the effect of the independent variable on the dependent measure changes over the levels of another independent variable.

- The simplest factorial is the 2×2 factorial design, where there are two independent variables, each with two levels.

- The Solomon four-group design is a specialized factorial experiment. It is recommended when the experiment includes both a pretest and a posttest because it allows researchers to evaluate the effect of the treatment alone, the effect of the pretest alone, and the interaction between the pretest and the treatment (pretest sensitization).

KEY CONCEPTS

Factorial Design	Main Effect	Multivariate Experiment	Solomon Four-Group
Interaction	Multifactor Experiment	Simple Effect	Design

QUESTIONS

Short answers can be found in Appendix A.

1. How many groups would you need in a $3 \times 2 \times 2$ between-subjects design?
   a. 11
   b. 4
   c. 12
   d. 1

2. A group of college students tasted three types of yogurts in two types of containers. Which of the following is true?
   a. This is a within-subjects design.
   b. This is a 3×2 factorial design.
   c. There were six conditions.
   d. All of the above are true.

3. One group performed a motor task with and without practice. Another group performed a spatial task with and without practice. In this mixed design, the

between-subjects factor is _____, while the within-subjects factor is _____.
   a. practice; task type, respectively
   b. motor task, spatial task, respectively
   c. task type; practice, respectively
   d. practice and no practice, respectively

4. A group of participants saw both frequent and infrequent words presented slowly, and a second group saw both frequent and infrequent words presented rapidly. This is a _____ design.
   a. between-subjects, factorial
   b. between-subjects, multilevel
   c. within-subjects, factorial
   d. a mixed factorial design

5. An experimenter investigated the effects of imagery and word frequency on memory. Participants were randomly assigned into the following conditions:

Group I: high-imagery/high-frequency words

Group II: high-imagery/low-frequency words

Group III: low-imagery/high-frequency words

Group IV: low-imagery/low-frequency words

The mean number of words recalled in each condition is as follows:

Group I: 25

Group II: 20

Group III: 20

Group IV: 15

Assume that an ANOVA was conducted and that the differences between the means are significant. Answer the following:

a. Is this a between-subjects, within-subjects, or mixed design? If you said mixed, identify the between-subjects factor and the within-subjects factor.

b. What type of factorial is this? Express numerically.

c. Graph the data.

d. Was there a main effect of imagery? Explain.

e. Was there a main effect of word frequency? Explain.

f. Was there an interaction? Explain.

g. If a moderate imagery condition was added, what type of factorial would this be?

For questions 6–9, look at the following diagram (IV = independent variable):

	Pretest	IV	Posttest
Group 1	40	yes	yes
Group 2	—	yes	yes
Group 3	40	—	yes
Group 4	—	—	yes

6. If only the score of Group 1 changes on the posttest, the result is most likely due to

   a. the independent variable

   b. pretest sensitization

   c. practice effects

   d. maturation

7. If both Group 1 and Group 3 change on the posttest, the results are most likely due to

   a. the independent variable

   b. pretest sensitization

   c. practice effects

   d. maturation

8. If the independent variable alone is causing a change in the posttest scores, which group(s) should change on the posttest?

   a. Group 1 only

   b. Groups 1 and 2

   c. Groups 3 and 4

   d. Group 2

SINGLE-SUBJECT DESIGNS

BY NOW you are aware that research studies describe the typical, or average, performance of the participants. In other words, the data collected from groups of participants are analyzed in order to derive the mean response or behavior. Therefore, the mean number of words recalled in memory study, or the mean number of errors made on a task, may not accurately describe the performance of any one participant in the experiment. For example, if your teacher informs your class that the average grade received on an exam was 86, that does not mean that any one particular student in your class received an 86. In a similar vein, I frequently encounter students in my classes who, when told of the results of various studies, come up with exceptions from personal experience. If, while hearing or reading about research findings, you thought, "Not my child," "Not my friends," "Not my brother," and so on, then you were forgetting that experiments describe the average, or typical, response of the groups that were studied and not any one particular individual. Group results often mask individual performance, which is why some psychologists use single-subject designs. In a single-subject design, the individual's performance does not get "lost" in the group's data.

Single-subject designs are frequently used in clinical settings and in behavior therapy. As the name implies, the design requires taking repeated measures across time on a single individual. Each participant is his or her own control, and comparing the treatment phase to the baseline phase assesses the effectiveness of the treatment. As such, single-subject designs are a variation of the before-after designs.

SINGLE-SUBJECT DESIGNS

Contrast to Group Designs

In group designs, individual differences are controlled when the participants are either randomly assigned into conditions or first matched on some attribute prior to random assignment. In a single-subject design, the participant acts as his or her own control; therefore, individual differences and between-groups variance are not an issue.

Group designs rely on statistical tests to see whether the independent variable had an effect, and therefore they require formal hypothesis testing. In single-subject designs, instead of formal hypothesis testing the researcher typically looks for changes in the target behavior after the independent variable has been introduced. By comparing the baseline and treatment panels of a graph, for example, the researcher can see whether the behavior during the treatment phase is different from the baseline phase. Statistical tests of significance are seldom used. In fact, some researchers have argued against attempts to apply statistical procedures to single-subject designs (Michael, 1974).

In terms of reliability, both group designs and single-subject designs take care to minimize measurement error. However, group designs use a large sample size, whereas single-subject designs rely on replication to demonstrate reliability.

Elements of Single-Subject Designs

The three basic elements of a single-subject design are the **target behavior,** the **baseline phase,** and the **treatment phase.** The target behavior is what the experimenter is attempting to change or modify in some way, and therefore it is the dependent variable in the study. The term *behavior* refers to overt, as well as covert, responses. For example, if an experimenter believes that positive reinforcement will increase the rate of speech production by an autistic child, then the target behavior is speech production. Similarly, if the aim of the study is to decrease stress through relaxation training, then the target behavior is stress.

Since each participant is his or her own control, the *baseline phase* is necessary in order to establish a pattern for the target behavior. By definition, the baseline is a measure of the target behavior prior to the introduction of the independent variable, or treatment. The measure is typically the rate or frequency of the target behavior. However, it may entail physiological measures such as blood pressure or skin conductivity. During the baseline phase, multiple measures are taken of the target behavior, and the phase should be long enough for the behavior to stabilize. Any changes that are observed in the behavior during baseline should be in the opposite direction from what the experimenter expects the independent variable to produce. For example, if the experimenter believes that the independent variable will reduce the rate of the behavior, then the behavior should not be decreasing prior to the introduction of the independent variable. The baseline phase is identified by the letter A.

Once a stable baseline has been established, the independent variable is introduced. This period is called the *treatment phase* and is identified by the letter B. In most instances there is only one independent variable. However, as you will see shortly, the component analysis design assesses the effectiveness of two or more independent variables.

TYPES OF SINGLE-SUBJECT DESIGNS

The A-B Design

The simplest, but also weakest, design is the **A-B design,** which comprises a baseline phase and a treatment phase. The baseline measures are then compared to measures taken during or after the introduction of the independent variable. For example, look at Figure 13.1, which shows a hypothetical experiment using positive reinforcement to increase a student's class participation.

Notice how baseline measures were taken for class participation during a five-day period. On the sixth day positive reinforcement was introduced, and by comparing the baseline and treatment phases, you can see that the target behavior increased. At this point, can you conclude that positive reinforcement is effective in increasing class participation? The answer is no, you cannot conclude that because you cannot rule out alternative explanations for the increased participation. Remember the limitations of the one-group before-after design? Well, the A-B design is essentially the same, and has the same problems and

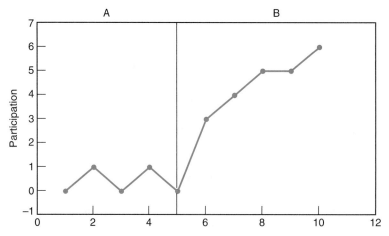

FIGURE 13.1 Hypothetical A-B design, using positive reinforcement to increase class participation.

limitations. Although the behavior clearly changed during the treatment phase, the change may be due to any number of outside factors. Although class participation may have increased due to the effect of the independent variable, it is also possible that maturation, history, or any other outside factor other than positive reinforcement caused the increase.

How can you demonstrate that it is the independent variable that is causing the increase in participation and not any other outside factor? If you said, "Remove the independent variable and see what happens to class participation," you were correct. If the behavior returns to baseline levels when positive reinforcement is discontinued, then it is unlikely that outside factors caused the increase in participation. The designs discussed in the next section are called **reversal designs,** and their purpose is to demonstrate that it was the manipulation of the independent variable, rather than outside factors, that led to the change in the behavior.

The A-B-A Design

As the name implies, in the **A-B-A design** a baseline phase is followed by a treatment phase, which is then followed by a return to baseline, or reversal phase. For example, in the above-mentioned hypothetical study, to ascertain the effectiveness of the independent variable, positive reinforcement is discontinued, and class participation is observed during a second baseline phase. If the behavior returns to the original baseline levels, then the increase in participation during the treatment phase was most likely due to the independent variable. Figure 13.2 shows the A-B-A design.

The crucial panel in Figure 13.2 is the second baseline phase, following the removal of positive reinforcement. If the behavior, in this case, class participation, does not return to the baseline rate, the researcher must conclude that some outside factor other than positive reinforcement is causing the increased rate of response. On the other hand, if the rate of class participation drops to its original baseline level, then a likely explanation for the

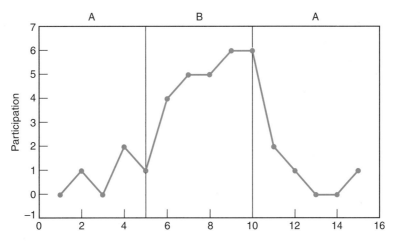

FIGURE 13.2 Hypothetical A-B-A reversal design, using positive reinforcement to increase class participation.

increased rate of participation during the treatment phase is the effectiveness of positive reinforcement.

One problem with the A-B-A design is that it leaves the participant with the original, undesirable condition; therefore, the design may be considered unethical. For example, if a particular form of treatment is effective in reducing suicidal thoughts, it would be unethical for the therapist to return such a person to his or her original state. In other words, it does not seem ethical to end the design by stopping treatment merely to demonstrate its effectiveness.

So, what is a researcher to do? What would you do if, on the one hand, you wanted to rule out alternative explanations for the change in the behavior, but on the other hand, did not want to leave the participant with an undesirable condition? That's right: reintroduce the independent variable. The following design addresses the ethical dilemma posed by the A-B-A design.

The A-B-A-B Design

This reversal design is a great improvement over the A-B-A design for two reasons. First, reintroducing the treatment eliminates the ethical dilemma, and second, the effectiveness of the independent variable can be demonstrated twice. In other words, treatment effects can be replicated. Figure 13.3 shows a hypothetical **A-B-A-B design** experiment in which high blood pressure was treated. Notice in the figure that the participant's blood pressure was high prior to treatment but decreased during the time that medication was given. When the treatment was withdrawn, the blood pressure returned to its original baseline level. However, when medication was resumed during the second treatment phase, the participant's blood pressure decreased once again. Since blood pressure only decreased during the treatment phases, the design allowed the researcher to replicate the efficacy of the medication. In addition, the resumption of treatment did not leave the participant with a dangerous condition.

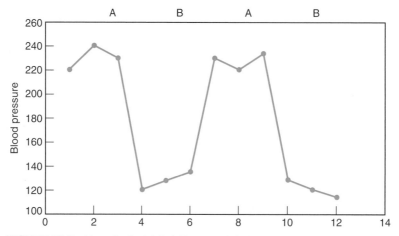

FIGURE 13.3   Hypothetical A-B-A-B reversal design, treating high blood pressure.

One major problem with all reversal designs is that the behavior may not return to baseline even if the independent variable had an effect. One problematic paradox for reversal designs is that if the behavior changes permanently due to the treatment, the effectiveness of the independent variable cannot be assumed if reversal effects cannot be demonstrated. For example, if a particular form of treatment effectively reduces blood pressure, blood pressure may never return to baseline. In other words, treatment may irreversibly change the participant's behavior so that reversal effects will not occur. The following designs attempt to address this issue.

Multiple-Baseline Designs

In **multiple-baseline designs,** the demonstration of treatment effects does not rely on reversal procedures. Instead, the researcher examines the effect of the independent variable on at least two different behaviors or participants, or looks for treatment effects in at least two different settings. The independent variable is introduced at a different time for each behavior, participant, or setting, and if the behavior changes only when the treatment is introduced, then outside explanations for the change in behavior can be ruled out. There are three types of multiple-baseline designs: across behaviors, across participants, and across settings.

In the *multiple-baseline across behavior* design, the effect of an independent variable on at least two behaviors is studied. Baselines are taken for all the behaviors of interest, but treatment is introduced sequentially. For example, let's say that a psychologist is interested in increasing both the rate of speech production and the rate of social interaction for a child with autism, using positive reinforcement. Baseline measures are taken for each target behavior: speech production and social interaction. Once stable baseline measures are obtained, the psychologist introduces positive reinforcement for only one of the behaviors—let's say speech production—but continues the baseline phase for social interaction. At this point, if the treatment is effective, the rate of speech should increase but the rate of social interaction should remain at baseline since it is not being treated. Once the rate of speech reaches a new stable rate, the psychologist introduces positive reinforcement for social interactions. If the second behavior also begins to increase when it is reinforced, the effectiveness of positive reinforcement for increasing speech and social interactions is demonstrated. Essentially, the psychologist can show that each behavior changes only when the independent variable is introduced.

As you can see, the criterion for demonstrating treatment effects is that the behavior should change only when the independent variable is introduced. In other words, although only speech is being reinforced, social interaction should not increase. If the second behavior changes along with the first behavior while only the first behavior is being reinforced, the psychologist would be forced to conclude that some outside factor was responsible for the change in both behaviors. For example, it is possible that over time the child has become more comfortable in the treatment setting. Being more relaxed, she may now become more verbal *and* more likely to engage in social interaction with others.

Figure 13.4 shows the hypothetical study in which alternative explanations for the change in the rate of the behaviors can be ruled out. Now compare Figure 13.4 to Figure 13.5, where alternative explanations cannot be ruled out. Since both target behaviors show an increased rate while only the first behavior is being reinforced, the effectiveness of positive reinforcement cannot be demonstrated.

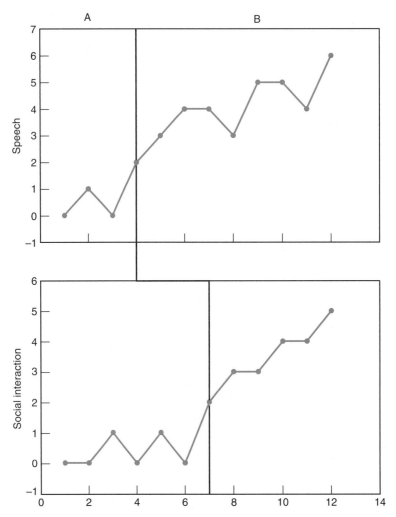

FIGURE 13.4 Hypothetical multiple baseline across behaviors design, using positive reinforcement to increase class participation and social interaction.

In the *multiple-baseline across participants* design, the researcher examines the effects of an independent variable on the target behavior of two or more participants. The logic and procedure are identical to the across behaviors design. Baseline measures of the target behavior are taken for at least two participants, but treatment is introduced at different times for each participant. As with the across behaviors design, only the behavior of the treated participant should change; the behavior of the person not receiving treatment should remain at stable baseline levels.

For example, let us say that you are interested in increasing the rate of speech of children with autism by using positive reinforcement. In this design, you would take baseline measures for each child in your study and, once stable baseline rates were obtained, you

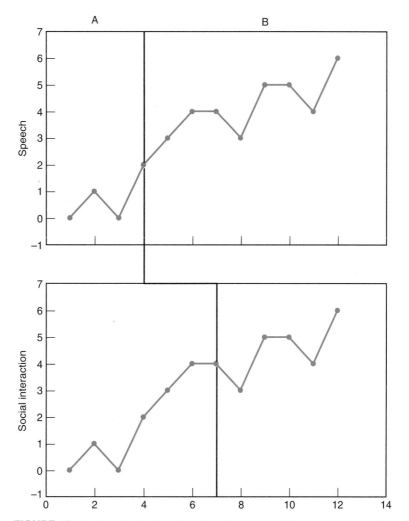

FIGURE 13.5 Hypothetical multiple baseline across behaviors design where alternative explanations cannot be ruled out.

would begin positive reinforcement for the first participant while continuing the baseline phase for the other participants. Once again, if each participant shows an increase in the rate of speech only when treatment is administered, the effectiveness of the independent variable is demonstrated. As before, the target behavior of each participant should not change until treatment is introduced. Figure 13.6 shows this hypothetical multiple-baseline across participants study.

Similar logic and procedures apply to the *multiple-baseline across settings* design. In this instance, the target behavior of a participant is treated in at least two different settings, the logic being that if the treatment is effective in modifying a behavior in one setting, it should also work in another setting. For example, if positive reinforcement truly increases

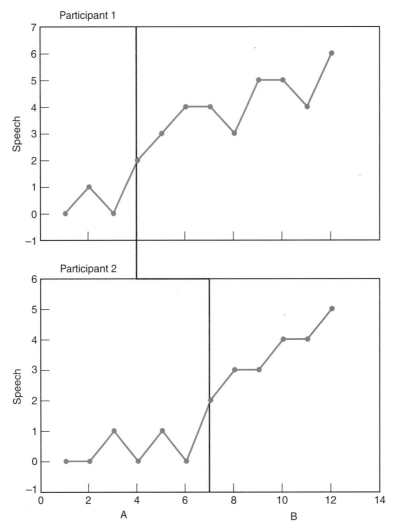

FIGURE 13.6 Hypothetical multiple baseline across participants design, using positive reinforcement to increase speech.

the rate of speech production of autistic children, then it should be effective in a wide variety of settings such as the psychologist's office, the child's school, in different classes the child attends, and so on. If the treatment only produces a change in the behavior in one particular setting, then its effectiveness cannot be demonstrated conclusively. Alternative explanations for the change in the behavior must be considered.

Component-Analysis Design

The designs mentioned so far involved only one independent variable. However, sometimes the researcher wishes to introduce several types or forms of treatment. The **component-**

analysis design allows the experimenter to assess the effects of two or more independent variables alone and in combination.

For example, let us say that a psychologist wished to examine the effects of biofeedback and medication on high blood pressure. One type of design that may be used is the *A-BC-B-BC design*. As with other single-subject designs, the client's blood pressure is monitored during the baseline phase, and once a stable baseline has been obtained, biofeedback (B) and medication (C) are introduced together. If blood pressure is reduced at this point, the psychologist cannot tell whether the change is due to the effectiveness of the medication, the biofeedback procedure, or a combination of the two. In the next phase, biofeedback is introduced alone. If blood pressure returns to the baseline level, the psychologist can assume that biofeedback alone is insufficient in reducing blood pressure. Finally, biofeedback and medication are once more introduced together, and if a reduction in blood pressure is obtained, the psychologist can assume that it is the medication that is causing the change in blood pressure, since biofeedback alone produced no change. Figure 13.7 demonstrates this hypothetical study.

The effectiveness of biofeedback alone has not been determined, and therefore the change in blood pressure may be due to an interaction between medication and biofeedback rather than to biofeedback alone. Figure 13.8 shows another type of component analysis design that addresses this issue.

The *A-B-C-BC design* is a variation on the design mentioned above. However, notice that here the effectiveness of each treatment alone, as well in combination, can be assessed. Following the baseline phase, biofeedback (B) is introduced alone, and, as before, there is no change in blood pressure. Next, biofeedback is discontinued and medication (C) is introduced alone. As you can see, blood pressure is reduced, indicating the effectiveness of medication. In the final phase, biofeedback and medication are introduced in combination. Notice that blood pressure is once more reduced to the level obtained during the C phase, indicating that the medicine alone is responsible for the change. If the combination of the

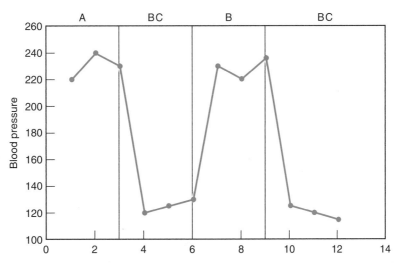

FIGURE 13.7 Hypothetical A-BC-B-BC component-analysis design, using biofeedback and medication to decrease blood pressure.

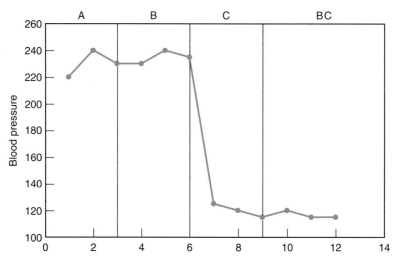

FIGURE 13.8 Hypothetical A-B-C-BC component-analysis design, where only medication works to reduce blood pressure.

two forms of treatment reduced blood pressure *below* the level obtained by medication alone, it would indicate an interaction between the two forms of treatment. Figure 13.9 shows this hypothetical interaction.

One major disadvantage of component-analysis designs is their potential carryover effect. For example, let us say that biofeedback (B) alone is able to reduce blood pressure. Next, biofeedback is discontinued, and medication (C) is introduced. If the client's blood pressure does not return to baseline level, it is impossible to tell whether the medication

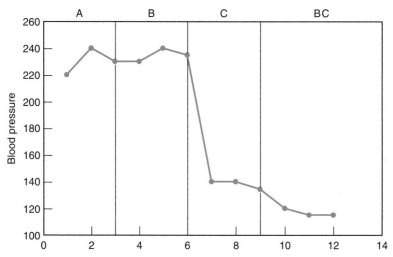

FIGURE 13.9 Hypothetical A-B-C-BC component-analysis design, showing an interaction between medication and biofeedback.

alone is also effective or whether the biofeedback training was so successful that its effects carried over into the next treatment phase. Similarly, order effects may also occur. This possibility cannot be ruled out unless the order in which the independent variables are introduced is varied for other participants. In other words, the study would need to be replicated where medication is introduced first, followed by biofeedback.

Advantages and Limitations of Single-Subject Designs

Single-subject designs have several advantages over group designs. First, while matching participants on some attribute prior to random assignment controls for between-groups variance (due to individual differences in group designs) matching is expensive, time consuming, and difficult. Obviously, the single-subject design eliminates this problem.

Second, withholding treatment may be unethical. With group designs, when testing the effectiveness of newly developed medication or treatment, it is common to use placebo and control conditions. In the placebo condition the participants may receive a sugar pill rather then the medication, while in the control condition the participants receive no treatment at all. It may be questionable whether this denial of potentially helpful treatment is ethical. With single-subject designs, there is no withholding of treatment in order to assess its effectiveness. As stated before, comparisons are made between the baseline phase, during which there is no treatment introduced, and the treatment phase. If a change takes place from baseline phase to treatment phase, it is assumed that the treatment was effective.

Third, in group designs an individual participant's response may be masked by the group average. Subtle changes in individual performance are not observed with group experiments. Therefore, if the differences between conditions in group experiments are not statistically significant, the researcher is forced to conclude that the independent variable had no effect, even though several participants may have been affected by the treatment variable. For example, if you found that a certain drug did not reduce the number of hallucinations in a group of schizophrenic participants, you would be forced to conclude that the drug had no effect, even though some participants clearly benefited from the medication. In single-subject designs, the concept of statistical significance is not important; any improvement, no matter how slight, is seen as beneficial to the participant.

Finally, single-subject designs are relatively inexpensive to conduct. Furthermore, if the experimenter finds that a particular form of treatment is ineffective, alternative treatments may be tried in succession until the desired effect is obtained.

A major disadvantage of single-subject designs is their limited external validity. To refresh your memory, external validity refers to the ability to generalize the findings to the population. Since the participant in the sample may not be representative of the population, the ability to generalize the results of the study is severely limited. For example, just because biofeedback was successful in reducing a particular client's blood pressure, the psychologist cannot assume that it would be an effective form of treatment for all individuals with high blood pressure.

Another disadvantage is the potential for carryover effects. With group experiments we do not have this problem if we use a between-subjects design. However, in single-subject designs, certain forms of treatment may produce irreversible changes in the target behavior, and therefore, returning the behavior to baseline may be impossible. Multiple-baseline designs address this problem, since they do not depend on reversal to demonstrate treatment effects.

In addition, when the design entails two or more conditions of treatment, the researcher must remain alert to the possibility of order effects. With group experiments, we can counterbalance the order of presentation in order to control for this potential confounding of order and treatment effects. In single-subject designs, one way to address this problem is to vary the order in which the independent variables are introduced with different participants.

SUMMARY

- Single-subject designs attempt to demonstrate the effectiveness of treatment for a single participant.
- Single-subject designs are most frequently used in applied clinical research and behavior modification.
- In order to establish the rate of behavior prior to introducing treatment, baseline measures should be taken over a period of time. Once the behavior has stabilized, the independent variable is introduced during the treatment phase.
- Single-subject designs do not necessitate formal hypothesis testing. In order to assess the effectiveness of treatment, the rate of the behavior during the baseline phase is compared to the rate of the behavior during the treatment phase.
- Reversal designs entail a baseline phase and a treatment phase, which is followed by the withdrawal of treatment. The most basic reversal design is the A-B-A design.
- In order not to leave the participant with the original undesirable condition, a more ethical reversal design is the A-B-A-B design, where treatment is once more introduced following the reversal.
- Multiple-baseline designs attempt to demonstrate treatment effects by introducing the independent variable at different points in time. The treatment is applied across at least two participants, two different behaviors, or two different settings. If the target behavior changes *only* when the treatment is introduced, the effectiveness of the independent variable is demonstrated.
- The component-analysis design assesses the effectiveness of two or more independent variables alone and in combination.
- A major disadvantage of the single-subject design is the inability to generalize the findings. However, these designs allow the researcher to obtain detailed information on a single participant, which is difficult with group designs.

KEY CONCEPTS

A-B Design	Baseline Phase	Multiple-Baseline	Target Behavior
A-B-A Design	Component-Analysis	Design	Treatment Phase
A-B-A-B Design	Design	Reversal Design	

QUESTIONS

Short answers can be found in Appendix A.

1. An advantage of the A-B-A-B design over the A-B-A design is that it
   a. has greater external validity
   b. is ethically superior
   c. requires fewer participants
   d. eliminates individual differences

2. In a reversal design, the second baseline period is necessary in order to
   a. rule out alternative explanation for the change in the behavior
   b. not leave the participant with the undesirable condition
   c. make results more generalizable
   d. all of the above are true

3. The problem with A-B designs is that
   a. change during the treatment phase cannot be attributed to treatment alone
   b. there are not enough participants to determine validity
   c. there is no random assignment
   d. all of the above are a problem.

4. The advantage of single-subject designs over group designs is that in the single-subject design
   a. random assignment of the participants is possible
   b. statistics may be used to detect significance
   c. results may be generalized
   d. a participant may be studied in greater detail

5. Describe, step by step, how you would attempt to increase a student's class participation using two forms of treatment: tokens and social praise.

CORRELATIONAL DESIGNS AND THE PEARSON R

IN **CHAPTER 1** you learned that scientific research falls into two basic categories: true experiments and nonexperimental studies. In nonexperimental studies, variables are not actively manipulated. Since no manipulation is involved, causality cannot be established. For this reason, nonexperimental designs are considered descriptive, in that they can describe behaviors or events, but they cannot make claims regarding the causes of those behaviors or events. The present chapter introduces you to one of the most widely used nonexpermental designs: correlational studies.

Correlational studies are useful for investigating behaviors that could not be studied otherwise, either because the variables of interest cannot be manipulated or because it would be unethical to manipulate them. For example, if you were interested in finding a relationship between IQ and school performance, it would be impossible to manipulate the participants' IQ scores and to randomly assign participants into various IQ conditions. Instead, you would need to select participants for each IQ condition on the basis of their preexisting IQ scores. Similarly, if you wished to examine the effects of x-ray exposure during pregnancy on birth defects, it would be unethical to randomly assign pregnant women into various x-ray dosage conditions.

As you can see, there are many events, or variables, that are important to study, but they cannot be investigated experimentally. Correlational studies are useful for establishing whether two (or more) variables are related, how they are related, and how strong that relationship is. In addition, correlational techniques are useful in making predictions regarding those variables. For example, if we know that a relationship exists between SAT scores and college grade point average (GPA), we can use SAT scores to predict future performance in college.

Correlational studies cannot establish causality, and alternative explanations for the results cannot be ruled out. For example, even if we were to establish a strong relationship between self-esteem and school performance, we could not say that high self-esteem causes high grades. It is equally possible that receiving high grades causes self-esteem to rise. In addition, it may be that both high self-esteem measures and high grades are caused by an outside factor such as parental involvement.

THE PEARSON CORRELATION COEFFICIENT

The Pearson product-moment **correlation coefficient,** whose symbol is *r*, describes numerically both the *magnitude* and *direction* of the relationship between two variables. The numerical value of the Pearson *r* describes the strength, or magnitude, of the relationship, whereas the positive or negative sign describes the direction of the relationship. Do you remember the discussion on positive and negative linear functions in Chapter 6? Well, a positive correlation is essentially the same as a positive linear relationship, whereas a negative correlation is the same as a negative linear relationship. When using the Pearson *r*, the underlying assumption must be that the relationship between the two variables is linear. If the relationship is curvilinear, the correlation coefficient will underestimate the strength of the relationship and may even indicate that no correlation exists between two variables that are, in fact, strongly related.

The Magnitude and Direction of the Pearson *r*

The numerical value of the correlation ranges from −1 to +1, with zero indicating no relationship between the variables. The stronger the relationship, the higher the numerical value of the Pearson *r*, regardless of the positive or negative sign. It is important to remember that with correlation coefficients, negative numbers are not automatically lower in numerical value than positive numbers. Therefore, an $r = -.7$ shows a stronger relationship between the variables than an $r = +.5$, and both a positive 1 and a negative 1 indicate perfect relationships.

The sign of the Pearson *r* depicts the type of relationship that exists between the variables. A **positive correlation** exists when an increase in the value of one variable is associated with a corresponding increase in the value of the other variable. Of course, the opposite is also true: A decrease in the value of one variable is associated with a corresponding decrease in the value of the other variable. An example of a positive correlation is the relationship between caloric intake and weight: An increase in the amount of calories consumed is associated with an increase in weight. Simply put, the more you eat, the more you weigh.

On the other hand, a **negative correlation** exists when an increase in the value of one variable is associated with a corresponding decrease in the value of the other variable. Again, the opposite is also true: A decrease in the value of one variable is associated with a corresponding increase in the value of the other variable. For example, there is a negative correlation between alcohol consumption and task accuracy: An increase in alcohol intake is associated with a decrease in task accuracy.

Graphical Presentation

The relationship between variables of interest can be depicted graphically by constructing a scatter plot. Typically, which variable is placed on the abscissa (*x*-axis) and which on the ordinate (*y*-axis) is not important. For example, if you wished to construct a scatter plot to show the relationship between grades received in an experimental psychology class and a statistics class, it would not matter which grades you placed on which axis. However, when the correlation is used for predicting some future event or behavior, then conventionally the predictor is placed on the abscissa and the criterion variable is placed on the ordinate.

Since correlational studies are nonexperimental, the variables are called not independent and dependent variables, but predictor *(x)* and criterion *(y)*, respectively. The predictor variable is the one we believe could predict some future event or behavior. The future event or behavior we wish to predict is the criterion. Therefore, we could say that we believe that the value of the future event, or the criterion, depends on the value of predictor. As such, the predictor is analogous to the "independent variable," and the criterion is analogous to the "dependent variable."

For example, in the relationship between SAT scores and college GPA, the predictor variable *(x)* is the SAT score and the criterion *(y)* is the college GPA. Why is that? Because we can expect that given a student's SAT score (the predictor) we can predict his college GPA (the criterion). In other words, what we are saying is that college GPA may depend on SAT scores, and not the other way around. Similarly, in the relationship between crack cocaine use and birth weight, we may safely assume that it is the baby's birth weight (the criterion) that is influenced by the amount of crack (the predictor) used during pregnancy, and not the other way around.

When constructing a scatter plot, each data point represents a pair of scores that belongs to a participant in the study. The more dispersed the scores, the more "scatter" there is, indicating no relationship, or at best, a weak relationship between the two variables. For example, if you were to correlate participants' IQ scores with their respective shoe sizes, you would most likely obtain widely dispersed scores. On the other hand, the less dispersed, or scattered, the scores, the stronger the relationship. Once all the data points have been plotted, a line called the **line of best fit** is drawn as close as possible to all the data points. When the correlation is positive, the line of best fit goes from bottom left to top right. When the correlation is negative, the line goes from top left to bottom right. The first panel of Figure 14.1 shows a positive correlation, while the second panel depicts a negative correlation. The scatter plot in the third panel shows that there is no relationship between the two variables.

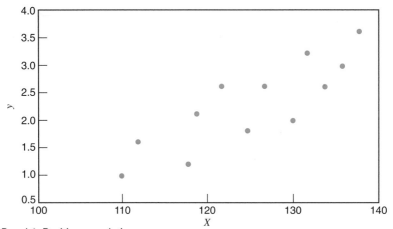

Panel 1. Positive correlation.

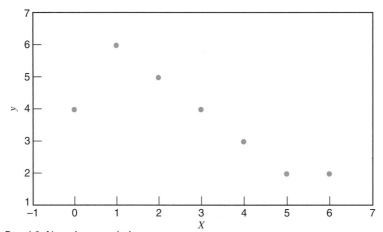

Panel 2. Negative correlation.

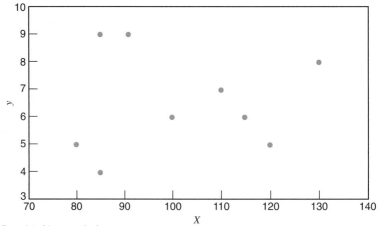

Panel 3. No correlation

FIGURE 14.1

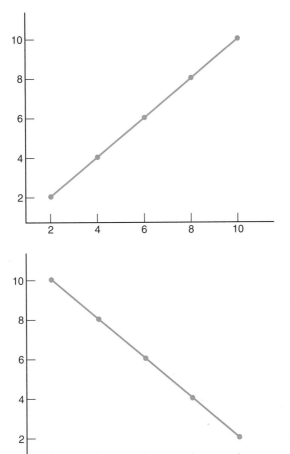

FIGURE 14.2 Panel 1. Perfect positive correlation.
Panel 2. Perfect negative correlation.

As you can see in the first panel, an increase in the value of *x* is associated with a corresponding increase in the value of *y*. The positive correlation is depicted by the direction of the line, going from bottom left to top right. On the other hand, the negative correlation shown in the second panel is indicated by the direction of the line that goes from top left to bottom right. Notice that as the value of *x* increases the value of *y* decreases.

When the relationship is perfect, as indicated by +1 or –1, all the points fall on the line, with no scores falling outside. A perfect positive correlation can be seen in the first panel of Figure 14.2, while the second panel shows a perfect negative correlation.

Calculating the Pearson *r*

Although researchers rely on statistical software to calculate the Pearson *r*, it might be useful to review the formula and to see the underlying logic of how it is performed. For example, let us say that a researcher wished to investigate the relationship between college GPA *(x)* and graduate school GPA *(y)*. Table 14.1 contains the data for this hypothetical study.

TABLE 14.1 Hypothetical Data

Subject #	College GPA (X)	Graduate GPA (Y)	X²	Y²	XY
1	2.0	2.2	4.00	4.84	4.40
2	2.5	2.7	6.25	7.29	6.75
3	3.0	3.2	9.00	10.24	9.60
4	3.2	3.2	10.24	10.24	10.24
5	3.5	3.1	12.25	9.61	10.85
6	3.7	3.5	13.69	12.25	12.95
7	4.0	3.8	16.00	14.44	15.20
	21.90	21.70	71.43	68.91	69.99

The formula for calculating the Pearson *r* is:

$$r = \frac{\sum XY - \frac{\sum X \sum Y}{N}}{\sqrt{\left[\sum X^2 - \frac{(\sum X)^2}{N}\right]\left[\sum Y^2 - \frac{(\sum Y)^2}{N}\right]}}$$

By using the data from Table 14.1, we can calculate the correlation coefficient:

$$r = \frac{69.99 - \frac{(21.90)(21.70)}{7}}{\sqrt{\left[71.43 - \frac{21.90^2}{7}\right]\left[68.91 - \frac{21.70^2}{7}\right]}}$$

$$r = \frac{69.99 - 67.89}{\sqrt{[71.43 - 68.52][68.91 - 67.27]}}$$

$$r = \frac{2.1}{\sqrt{(2.91)(1.64)}}$$

$$r = \frac{2.1}{\sqrt{4.77}}$$

$$r = .96$$

As you can see, the relationship between college GPA and graduate school GPA is a strong, positive correlation (*r* = .96). As college GPA increases, it is associated with a corresponding increase in graduate school GPA. Figure 14.3 shows the scatter plot for this hypothetical study.

Although a correlation of .96 is nearly perfect, and therefore likely to be significant, researchers need to know whether the obtained correlation between the variables is

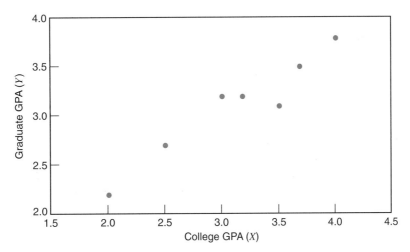

FIGURE 14.3 Correlation between undergraduate (*X*) and graduate GPA (*Y*).

significant or not significant. In other words, researchers test the null hypothesis that in the population, the correlation between *x* and *y* is zero. In the days before computerized statistical packages, a simple version of the *t* test was conducted to test the significance of *r,* but today, as with any other statistical procedure, the majority of software packages provide the obtained probability for error on the printout.

Limitations of the Pearson *r*

A basic condition necessary for calculating the Pearson *r* is a linear relationship between the variables. If the relationship is curvilinear, the correlation coefficient will be lower in value, giving a misleading indication of the strength of the relationship. As you may recall from Chapter 6, a curvilinear relationship exists when an increase in the value of one variable is associated with an increase in the other variable, but only up to a point. After a particular point has been reached, a continuing increase in the first variable is associated with a decrease in the second variable. When the relationship is curvilinear, the Pearson *r* is not appropriate. Although a full discussion of this issue is beyond the scope of this chapter, the appropriate coefficient in such cases is the correlation ratio, or the eta coefficient.

CAUSAL INFERENCES

In true experiments, the researcher manipulates the independent variable and holds constant or eliminates all other unwanted variables. By being able to rule out alternative explanations for the change in the dependent variable value, the researcher can be reasonably certain that it was the independent variable manipulation that led to the observed changes in the dependent variable measure. Typically, correlational studies do not allow the same degree of control over outside factors. Therefore, the researcher must be careful when making causal inferences on the basis of a relationship between two variables. Although it may be tempting to leap to conclusions regarding causality, especially when there is a strong, or significant, correlation between two variables, the following sections explain why the temptation should be resisted.

The Third Variable Dilemma

In order to demonstrate a causal relationship, the researcher must be able to control all variables other than the independent variable. In other words, alternative explanations for the results must be ruled out. In a correlational study, that is often impossible, however. For example, let us say that a researcher found a strong, positive correlation between IQ and school performance. Can she conclude that having a high IQ causes high grades? No, because alternative explanations for high grades cannot be ruled out. It is very possible that the relationship between IQ and school performance is caused by some third factor, such as good verbal skills. Good verbal skills certainly help when it comes to obtaining good grades, and they also allow for good performance on traditional IQ tests.

Greenwald and Gillmore (1997) addressed the third variable problem in their study on the relationship between student ratings of teacher effectiveness and expected grades for the course. Typically, course grades are positively correlated with teacher evaluations: the better the expected grade, the better the teacher evaluation (Stumpf & Freedman, 1979). However, as Greenwald and Gillmore point out, this finding does not mean that teachers can automatically improve their student evaluations by being lenient graders. In other words, the positive correlation does not imply that high grades cause high evaluations. According to Greenwald and Gillmore, outside factors such as teaching effectiveness, students' general academic motivation, and students' course-specific motivation may be causing the correlation between grades and evaluations.

In experimental studies, systematic manipulation of the independent variable, random assignment of participants into conditions, and careful control over outside variables allow for causal inferences. In correlational studies, nothing is manipulated, participants are selected for a particular trait or characteristic, and control over outside factors is limited at best. Therefore, the possibility that some unknown, third factor is causing the relationship always exists, and causal inferences are tenuous.

The Chicken or the Egg Dilemma

In addition to the third variable problem, there is also the direction of causality problem. Does *X* lead to *Y*, or does *Y* lead to *X?* In other words, which came first? For example, if we can demonstrate a relationship between heroin use and personality disorder, did the heroin use lead to the personality disorder, or did a preexisting personality disorder cause the person to turn to heroin? In a similar vein, does depression lead to inactivity, or does inactivity lead to depression?

As you can see, in correlational studies it is difficult to establish the causal variable. Even if a strong link can be established between two variables, it is difficult to determine which variable is causing the other.

CROSS-LAGGED PANEL DESIGN

Suppose you found a strong correlation between teacher warmth *(x)* and student responsiveness *(y),* and were interested in determining which came first: Did teacher warmth lead to student responsiveness, or did responsive students lead to warm and friendly teachers? Each explanation is equally plausible; however, the causal factor must have come first in time. In other words, for one factor to cause another, it must preexist the other factor. If teacher warmth is causing student responsiveness, then the teacher must have been warm and friendly *prior* to student responsiveness. On the other hand, if it were the responsive students that led to teacher warmth, then the students must have been responsive prior to the teacher exhibiting warmth and friendliness.

The **cross-lagged panel design** allows researchers to investigate the direction of causality. It is essentially a longitudinal design in that repeated measures are taken on the same participants over at least two different points in time. For the hypothetical study mentioned above, measures of teacher warmth *(x)* and student responsiveness *(y)* would be taken at least twice. A diagram of the procedure can be seen in Figure 14.4.

Let us say that the teacher's warmth and the students' responsiveness were measured for the first time in September. Teacher warmth is therefore shown as x_1 and student responsiveness as y_1. At the end of the school year in June, a second measure was taken, represented as x_2 and y_2. Notice that the design yields six correlation coefficients. The steps involved in the analysis are as follows:

First, compare the top and bottom panels: x_1y_1 to x_2y_2. If there is a relationship between the two factors (*x* and *y*), then the bottom panel (x_2y_2) must have a higher correlation than the top panel (x_1y_1), indicating that the relationship is stable over time and that the initial correlation was not due to chance.

Next compare the side panels: x_1x_2 to y_1y_2. The factor that is the suspected cause must be more stable over time and therefore have a higher correlation. If teacher warmth is the suspected cause, then panel x_1x_2 should have a higher correlation than y_1y_2. In other words, if teacher warmth is the causal factor, then the teacher who was warm in September should still be warm in June; warmth must be a stable characteristic in order for it to be a causal factor. On the other hand, if it is the student responsiveness that is causing teacher warmth, then panel y_1y_2 should have a higher correlation. If it is the student responsiveness that is the causal factor, then students who were responsive in September should still exhibit responsiveness in June.

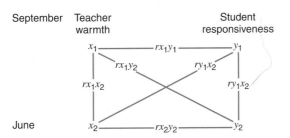

FIGURE 14.4 Diagram of a hypothetical cross-lagged panel design, investigating the relationship between teacher warmth and student responsiveness.

Finally, the crucial panels are the cross-lags. The causal factor had to have come first in time and have a higher correlation. If teacher warmth is the causal factor, then it must have preceded student responsiveness. Therefore, panel x_1y_2 should have a higher correlation than y_1x_2, since x_1y_2 represents the correlation between teacher warmth in September and student responsiveness in June, whereas panel y_1x_2 represents the correlation between student responsiveness in September and teacher warmth in June. In other words, if teachers affect students, then by June there should be a greater effect of teachers on students than the other way around. However, if it is student responsiveness that is leading to teacher warmth, then student responsiveness must have preceded teacher warmth. Therefore, panel y_1x_2 should have a higher correlation than x_1y_2, since it represents the correlation between student responsiveness in September and teacher warmth in June.

As you can see, the longitudinal nature of the cross-lagged panel design is useful for establishing the direction of causality. For example, given the increasing popularity of the Internet, an interesting question is whether spending a lot of time on the Internet leads to depression and loneliness, or do preexisting conditions of loneliness and depression lead to spending a lot of time online? In a longitudinal panel design, Kraut, Patterson, Lundmark, Kiesler, Mukopadhyay, and Scherlis (1998) addressed this question. In their study, measures on the participants' social involvement and psychological well-being were collected twice: once before Internet use (T_1) and again following one or two years of Internet use (T_3). Internet use itself as measured by mean hours per week was indicated by T_2. Their findings indicate that depression and loneliness as measured at T_1 did not predict subsequent Internet use ($r = .07$, and $r = -.09$, respectively). However, the correlation between Internet use and subsequent depression as measured at T_3 was $r = .15$ ($p = .05$). The correlation between Internet use and loneliness at T_3 was also $r = .15$ ($p = .05$).

Kraut et al. acknowledge that some outside factor may be causing both the increase in Internet use and the decrease in social involvement and psychological well-being (the third variable problem). Taking the above into consideration, the authors conclude: "Our analyses are consistent with the hypothesis that using the Internet adversely affects social involvement and psychological well-being. The panel research design gives us substantial leverage in inferring causation" (p. 1028).

Advantages and Limitations

The panel design is useful for establishing the direction of causality, but it cannot rule out the possibility that some third variable is causing the correlation between the two factors. In addition, as with any longitudinal design, it is time consuming and expensive.

SUMMARY

- In nonexperimental studies, variables are not actively manipulated. Since no manipulation is involved, causality cannot be established.

- Correlational studies are useful for investigating behaviors that could not be studied otherwise, either because the variables of interest cannot be manipulated or because it would be unethical to manipulate them.

- The Pearson correlation coefficient *(r)* describes numerically both the magnitude and direction of the relationship between two variables. The numerical value of the Pearson *r* describes the strength, or magnitude, of the relationship, whereas the positive or negative sign describes the direction of the relationship.

- When using the Pearson *r,* the underlying assumption must be that the relationship between the two variables is linear. If the relationship is curvilinear, the correlation coefficient will underestimate the strength of the relationship and may even indicate that no correlation exists between two variables that are, in fact, strongly related.

- The numerical value of the correlation ranges from –1 to +1, with zero indicating no relationship between the variables. The stronger the relationship, the higher the numerical value of the Pearson *r.*

- A positive correlation exists when an increase in the value of one variable is associated with a corresponding increase in the value of the other variable. The opposite is also true: A decrease in the value of one variable is associated with a corresponding decrease in the value of the other variable.

- A negative correlation exists when an increase in the value of one variable is associated with a corresponding decrease in the value of the other variable. Again, the opposite is also true: A decrease in the value of one variable is associated with a corresponding increase in the value of the other variable.

- Correlation is not the same as causality. The correlation between two variables may mean that *X* is causing *Y; Y* is causing *X;* or that some third variable is causing the correlation between *X* and *Y.*

- The cross-lagged panel design allows researchers to investigate the direction of causality. It is essentially a longitudinal design, in that repeated measures are taken on the same participants over at least two different points in time. The causal variable had to have come first in time.

- The major advantage of correlational designs is that certain variables are impossible, or unethical, to manipulate. A major disadvantage is that causality cannot be established due to limited control over outside factors.

KEY CONCEPTS

Correlation Coefficient	Cross-Lagged Panel Design	Line of Best Fit Negative Correlation	Positive Correlation

QUESTIONS

Short answers can be found in Appendix A.

1. A researcher found the following relationship between number of books read in a year (A) and knowledge of vocabulary words (B): $r = +.85$. Which of the following can she conclude regarding A and B?

   a. There is a fairly strong relationship.

   b. An increase in reading is associated with a decrease in vocabulary.

   c. Reading causes vocabulary scores to increase.

   d. Both a and c are correct.

2. You find that there is a positive correlation between depression and inactivity. Which of the following can you conclude?

   a. The more depressed one is, the more inactive one becomes.

   b. The more inactive one is, the more depressed one becomes.

   c. Some third outside factor could be causing both depression and inactivity.

   d. All of the above could be concluded.

3. Which of the following statements is *not* true?

a. A correlation of –0.6 is higher than a +0.4.

b. A correlation of 0 means there is no relationship.

c. A high correlation can establish causality.

d. A low correlation indicates a weak relationship.

4. A psychologist is interested in establishing whether having a lot of interests in common *(X)* leads to stable marriages *(Y)*, or if it is the other way around: having a long-term marriage leads to having a lot in common. In 1995 a group of married participants were first given a survey that measured the number of interests they had in common and later were asked to indicate how many years they were married. One year later, the participants were once more asked the same questions.

a. The design the psychologist used is called _____.

b. Draw and label each part of the diagram used in the above design.

c. Which two panels would you compare to investigate the causal factor?

d. If having a lot of interests in common leads to stable marriages, which panel should have a higher correlation? Why?

e. If having a long-term marriage leads to the development of lots of interests in common, which panel should have a higher correlation? Why?

5. For each of the following, state whether you would expect a positive or a negative correlation between the two variables:

a. Incidence of child abuse and cognitive functioning.

b. Number of cigarettes smoked and incidence of lung cancer.

c. Food intake and weight gain.

d. Hours of sunbathing and incidence of skin cancer.

e. Alcohol intake and driving ability.

CHAPTER 15

OTHER NONEXPERIMENTAL AND QUASI-EXPERIMENTAL DESIGNS

STATIC-GROUP DESIGNS

Static-Group Comparison

Limitation of the Static-Group Design

Advantage of the Static-Group Design

Before-After Static-Group Comparison

Advantages and Limitations

PROGRAM EVALUATION

▧ Are there gender differences in play behavior?
▧ How do prisoners form social hierarchies in prisons?
▧ Do mothers in Kenya socialize their children the same way as mothers do in Nigeria?
▧ What does the average college student think about politics?
▧ Do problem-solving strategies change as children grow older?
▧ What are the effects of growing up in a war-torn country?
▧ Is the program developed for senior citizens effective?

QUESTIONS SUCH as these typically cannot be answered by conducting a true experiment. Instead, various nonexperimental methods are available to the researcher such as naturalistic observation, survey research, developmental studies, and program evaluation. Although these methods cannot establish causality, they allow investigators to study behaviors and events that could not be studied otherwise.

Entire textbooks have been written on nonexperimental methods such as survey research (Judd, Smith, & Kidder, 1991), field studies (Taylor & Bogdan, 1998), and program evaluation (Rossi & Freeman, 1993). Therefore a detailed, in-depth coverage of the various methods available to the researcher is beyond the scope of this chapter. Instead, this chapter presents an overview of these techniques and introduces you to some major aspects of nonexperimental research.

NATURALISTIC OBSERVATION

If you wished to study the play behavior of children, you could simply go to a playground and observe the children at play. If you wished to study the maternal behavior of lions, you could go to Africa and observe the lions as they mother their cubs. Similarly, if you wished to study the food and beverage preference of adolescents, you could go to a high school cafeteria during lunchtime and observe what the students eat and drink.

Any time scientists observe a behavior or an event in its natural setting, they are engaging in one of the oldest methods of research: **naturalistic observation.** The method of naturalistic observation is not limited to psychologists. Researchers in zoology, astronomy, biology, sociology, and anthropology, among other disciplines, also frequently rely on naturalistic observation to gather information on particular events or phenomena.

The greatest advantage of this research method is that behaviors that occur in their natural setting tend to be more spontaneous, and therefore more natural, than behaviors observed in the laboratory. The richness and complexity of human behavior (and animal behavior for that matter) can be better observed in the real world than within the artificial constraints of the laboratory. On the other hand, a major disadvantage lies in the limited control that the researcher has over the participants' environment and behavior. Since the degree of control is so limited, it presents a greater possibility of confounding than does experimental research. As you can see, somewhat of a tradeoff occurs when it comes to internal and external validity; observational studies often have good external validity (ability to generalize) but weaker internal validity (control over variables).

There are basically two ways to conduct naturalistic observation: Researchers can observe without interacting with the group they are observing, or they can choose to interact with the group. The first method is called **nonparticipant observation.** This is the classic "field study," or what typically comes to mind when we hear the term *naturalistic observation.* For example, if you sit on a bench at a playground and observe the difference in play behavior between boys and girls, your naturalistic observation is made without participation; you are in a sense a "passive" recorder of play behavior. The second method is called **participant observation,** and the degree of participation may range from very little to full participation. For example, if in order to study the social structure of a commune you become a functioning member, the method you are using is participant observation.

In addition, the researcher may conduct *covert* observation, where the members of the group under observation do not know that they are being observed, or the observation could be *overt,* where the group members know that they are under study. Each method has its advantages and disadvantages, as you will see in the following sections.

Naturalistic observation is not the same as casual observation. In other words, it is not quite the same as when you are sitting in the library, casually observing how many people are studying and how many are talking to each other. Rather, naturalistic observation is systematic; the researcher first identifies a behavior, or a set of behaviors to be observed, selects a method of quantifying those behaviors, and decides on the most appropriate method for observation. Furthermore, observational research requires trained observers.

Selecting Behaviors for Observation

The behaviors you select for observation need to be defined clearly. For example, if you wish to observe prosocial behavior in children, you need to define what behaviors belong to the category of prosocial behavior: sharing toys and candy? comforting another child? protecting someone from a bully? In other words, you need to clearly specify which actions constitute prosocial behavior because those will be the behaviors you record during observation. For example, in a study on the relationship between prosocial behavior and academic achievement, Caprara, Barbaranelli, Pastorelli, Bandura, and Zimbardo (2000) asked children to rate their own prosocialness on a 10-item scale that assessed their degree of helpfulness, kindness, sharing, and cooperativeness. In addition, the children were asked to identify prosocial peers who cooperated, shared, consoled, and helped others. As you can see, in the Caprara et al. study the category of behaviors considered prosocial was clearly defined.

Literature review can help you to select and fine-tune your own definitions, and by going through the literature on research studies similar to your own, you can come across behavioral definitions that were used by others. An advantage of using similar (or even the same) definitions that others have used is that it enables you to make direct comparisons between your data and the data obtained by previous researchers.

Quantifying the Behavior

Once you have identified the behaviors you will observe, you need to establish a way of quantifying them. For example, you may choose to observe how often a behavior occurs and how long the behavior lasts, or you may divide the observational period into discrete time intervals.

In the first instance, you would be using the *frequency method,* where you simply record how many times the behavior occurs within a specific time frame. For example, you would record how many times a child consoles another child, shares toys or candy, or helps someone during the two-hour observational period.

If you decide to record how long the behavior lasts, you are using the *duration method* to quantify the behavior. For example, you may choose to record how long a child consoles another or what length of time the child spends helping another child.

Finally, you may opt for the *interval method,* where the observational period is divided into discrete intervals, and you record each time the behavior occurs within a given interval. For example, you may divide the observational period into a series of three-minute intervals, and record each time a child shares a toy or helps another during the three-minute time period.

Method of Observation

After you have defined and quantified the behavior for observation, you need to select which method you will use for observing and recording. As mentioned previously, you may opt for participant or nonparticipant observation, depending on the purpose of your study and on whether the participants are human or animal subjects. If you are observing animal subjects, most likely you will engage in nonparticipant observation. On the other hand, if you are observing human participants, then you will need to decide whether you will participate in the group you are observing.

In addition, you will need to decide whether your observation will be overt or covert. If the observation is overt, meaning that the participants are aware of being observed, reactive effects are a possibility. Recall from Chapter 5 that one problem with observing behavior is that participants' behavior may change as a result of knowing that they are being observed. Therefore, the behavior you observe may no longer be spontaneous or natural. On the other hand, covert observation, in which the participants do not know that they are being observed, raises certain ethical questions (provided that the participants are human, naturally), as you will see in a moment.

Reliability of Observation

It is important to establish that the recorded observations are reliable, and not affected by personal biases and expectations. In observational research you need to be especially careful to ensure that your observations are untainted by personal biases and expectancies. In addition, if you are using the frequency method you must accurately record the behavior each time it occurs. Although it may seem simple to record numbers of behaviors, when you are observing a group of people it is very easy to miss an instance of the behavior, or conversely, to be unsure whether the behavior did in fact occur.

One way to get around the problem of reliability is to use several well-trained observers. In this way, you can establish the degree to which the observations agree by calculating *interrater reliability*. A simple method of establishing interrater reliability is to calculate a percent agreement. Count how many times the observers agree, divide the number of agreements by the total number of observations, and then multiply by 100. For example, if two observers agreed on 7 out of 10 observations, then you could calculate the percent agreement as follows:

$$\frac{\text{Total number of agreements (7)}}{\text{Total number of observations (10)}} \times 100 = 70\%$$

The higher the percent agreement, the greater the reliability of the observations. In most instances, a 70 percent agreement is adequate.

Observer Bias

As noted in Chapter 5, observer bias is most likely to occur when the researcher is aware of the hypothesis and of the conditions being observed. For example, if you are aware that you are observing a group of gifted children, this awareness may taint your observations in such way that the most ordinary behavior of the children seems extraordinary. As stated in Chapter 5, one way to avoid this problem is to use blind observers who are unaware of the hypothesis and/or conditions.

Bias may also occur when the behaviors under observation are interpreted rather than merely recorded. For example, let us say that you are observing the reaction of infant girls and boys to a popup toy, such as a Jack-in-a-box. While children in both groups become startled and cry, you may interpret the boys' crying as due to anger and the girls' crying as due to fear. The best way to avoid this problem is simply to record behaviors rather than your interpretation of them; save hypothesizing until the end when you have an adequate database for interpretation.

Now that you are familiar with some of the issues involved in observational research, let us take a look at two major types of studies: nonparticipant observation and participant observation.

NONPARTICIPANT NATURALISTIC OBSERVATION

In naturalistic observation, behaviors are observed in their natural setting; no deliberate change is made in the environment, and nothing is manipulated. Since the participants' environment is not under the researcher's control and nothing is manipulated, the occurrence of the behaviors or events is not under the observer's control. The purpose of this type of research is to describe behaviors as they occur naturally, without any interference from the researcher. Since the observer does not interact with members of the group, the observation is without participation.

For an example of the naturalistic observation method, let us take a look at a study in which Goldin-Meadow and Saltzman (2000) investigated how Chinese and American mothers communicate and interact with their deaf and hearing children. According to the authors, attitudes toward children and child rearing differ between the two cultures. For instance, Chinese parents believe that they play a crucial role in effecting changes in their children, whereas American parents tend to emphasize the child's own talents and abilities. Therefore, Chinese parents tend to emphasize hard work and effort to a greater degree than do Americans, as is reflected in their interaction with their children: Chinese parents tend to be more in control of the interaction, and their communication style tends to be more instructional. Given these basic cultural differences, Goldin-Meadow and Saltzman were interested in seeing if the two groups of mothers differed in terms of (a) communication and interaction style with the children; and (b) the accommodations they make when they communicate with their deaf children.

Eight Chinese and eight American mothers were videotaped for one to two hours in their homes as they interacted with their deaf and hearing children. As you read the following brief summary of the behaviors that were observed, notice how the researchers carefully defined their terms and quantified each behavior under observation. The method used for quantifying the behaviors was the frequency method: the investigators counted each instance of the behavior under observation.
The behaviors observed were:

1. The mother's attempt to control the interaction. The interaction period began when the mother and child established joint attention that centered on a toy or a book. Control was defined as how often the mother, rather than the child, initiated an interaction.

2. The instructional purpose of the communication by the mother. Instructional purpose was defined as the number of verbal utterances made with the intention to teach or instruct the child.

3. The form of the mother's communication: verbal or nonverbal. Verbal communication was defined as the number of utterances, whereas nonverbal communication was defined as the number of attention-getting behaviors (tapping the child's arm, waving at the child, manipulating the child's arm or face) and the number of gestures (nods, pointing, hand flips).

Goldin-Meadow and Saltzman found that the mothers in both cultures initiated more interactions with their deaf children; however, Chinese mothers initiated significantly more interactions than did American mothers. In addition, Chinese mothers produced significantly more instructional utterances, regardless of the child's hearing status. In terms of verbal communication, there was no effect of culture: the mothers in both cultures produced significantly fewer verbal utterances to their deaf children than to their hearing children. Finally, culture was found to have a significant effect on the rate of gesturing: Chinese mothers were three times more likely to gesture when interacting with their children, regardless of the child's hearing ability. Based on the results of the study, the authors concluded that all the mothers in both cultures adjusted their communication style when interacting with deaf children; however, the adjustments corresponded to cultural norms governing instructional communication, body language, and gesturing.

This study entailed *overt* observation; the mothers and children knew that they were being videotaped. Therefore, it is possible that the presence of the observers altered the way the mothers normally communicate or interact with their children. For example, the lower rate of gesturing by American mothers may have been the result of self-consciousness rather than cultural restraint. In a similar vein, the Chinese mothers may have wished to appear more helpful and accommodating, and therefore increased their normal rate of gesturing.

One problem with overt observation is that reactive effects are a possibility. As noted earlier, when people know they are being observed, they may alter their behavior. This, in turn, can affect the external validity of the study. One way to get around this problem is to use covert observational techniques such as one-way mirrors, telephoto lenses, and hidden cameras. However, the use of covert techniques with human participants raises an important ethical question; just how ethical is it to observe and record people's behavior without their knowledge and permission? For example, how would you react if you discovered that someone was hiding under your dormitory bed in order to investigate what typical college students talk about? Most likely you would not be very happy; nonetheless, such a study was actually conducted by Henle & Hubble (1938).

The solutions are not simple. Although you should make every attempt to make unobtrusive observations, at times that is simply not feasible or ethical. One possible solution is to let the participants get used to your presence prior to beginning your formal observations. Once the participants have habituated to you (or the camera), they will find your presence less distracting and may behave more naturally when you begin the actual observations.

PARTICIPANT OBSERVATION

When you decide to become an active participant in the group's setting, you are engaging in *participant observation*. Again, you may choose to do so overtly, so that the members of the group know you are going to observe and record their behavior, or you may participate covertly, through which you essentially go "under cover" by pretending to be a member of the group. For example, you may overtly gain entry to a religious cult by informing the members that you wish to observe and record their meetings, interactions, and so on. Or you may pretend that you wish to join the group and become a member, in which case you may gain covert entry.

The Rosenhan (1973) study cited in Chapter 4, in which a group of graduate students gained access to mental hospitals by pretending to suffer from schizophrenic symptoms, is a classic example of covert participant observation. However, covert participant observation carries some heavy ethical implications (see Chapter 4); for one thing, the researchers are lying outright by pretending to be something they are not. For example, if you pretend to be a homeless person and live on the streets with the homeless, you are not only lying but also concealing the true purpose of your presence. In addition, when the study is completed, you can go home to your nice warm environment; the true homeless cannot. Therefore, although the behaviors observed during covert observation might be more natural and less affected by your presence, you need to keep in mind the ethical considerations raised by this method.

On the other hand, if you decide to participate overtly, remember that the same disadvantages apply as for nonparticipant observation. In fact, participant observation is even more prone to reactive effects. Your very presence may alter the way the group typically functions, or the way the members interact with one another. In addition, the more "visible" and the more intrusive you are, the more likely it is that your presence will affect the behaviors you observe.

Advantages and Disadvantages of Observational Research

Through the observational method (participant or nonparticipant), behaviors and events can be studied in their natural environment. Provided that the observation is as unobtrusive as possible, the observed behaviors will be more spontaneous, natural, and varied than what would be observed in a laboratory. Consequently, the possibility that the behavior is merely an artifact (see Chapter 5) is minimized, and the generalizability of the findings is typically good. Since the vast majority of human behavior (and animal behavior) takes place in the real world, and not within the confines of the laboratory, observing these behaviors in their natural setting can yield richer and more meaningful results. In addition, the findings in observational studies could lead to the formulation of hypotheses that could be tested by using different methods. As such, this research method can be an excellent stepping-stone for future investigation.

An additional advantage of participant observation studies is that by becoming a participating member of a group (overtly or covertly), you can observe events and behaviors from the inside. Furthermore, since you experience pretty much everything that the members of the group experience, you are more sensitive to, and aware of, environmental conditions and antecedents to events and behaviors. As mentioned above, the behaviors you observe tend to be natural. Covert participation yields the most natural behaviors; however, it carries ethical considerations.

In terms of disadvantages, the researcher needs to be aware of the possibility of observational bias and, if the observation is not unobtrusive, reactive effects. In addition, observational research may require extensive travel that could be quite expensive, and data collection can take weeks, months, or years, which makes studies like these time-consuming. Finally, keep in mind that the observational method is a descriptive method, which means that researchers should not make cause-and-effect inferences in their interpretations. Since the investigator has very little control over the participants' environment, causal relationships cannot be established.

With participant observation, gaining overt entry into the group you wish to study can be difficult and may require considerable tact and diplomacy. Also, as mentioned before, your presence may affect the ordinary functioning of the group and change the way the members typically interact. A final disadvantage is that by becoming a participating member of the group, overtly or covertly, you may risk losing your objectivity. As you become more and more involved in the daily functioning of the group, there is always a chance that you will begin to identify with the group's purpose, aims, and goals, and therefore your observations could become colored by your sense of belonging.

THE CASE STUDY

In his book, *The Mind of a Mnemonist,* the Russian psychologist Aleksandr Luria (1968) described a man called "S," who had a seemingly infinite capacity to remember a series of letters, numbers, and words, even when the series was composed of up to 70 items. According to Luria, S could:

> reproduce a series in reverse order—from end to beginning—just as easily as from start to finish.... I simply had to admit that the capacity of his memory had no distinct limits. ... He had no difficulty reproducing any lengthy series of words ... even though they had originally been presented to him a week, a month, a year or even many years earlier. (pp. 9–12).

The **case study** represents a research method that involves the in-depth investigation of an individual, a family, or even an institution. Since the key word is "in-depth," the case study is typically longitudinal. The case, be it an individual, a family, or an institution, is studied over a period of time, during which multiple observations and measurements are taken. Some of the most interesting case studies involve individuals who possess unique or unusual characteristics or experiences, such as Luria's Mr. S and "Genie," the child who was kept in isolation and never spoken to until she was 14 years old (Curtiss, 1977).

A case study may be undertaken for many reasons. For example, a clinical psychologist may wish to study a person with an usual disorder; a cultural anthropologist may wish to understand the customs and behaviors of a particular group of individuals; or an industrial-organizational psychologist may have been hired to evaluate a corporation. In addition, the case study may entail the investigation of an event, for example, a major clash between citizens and the police; or it may be used in support of a theoretical position, such as the book, *Studies on Hysteria,* published by Breuer and Freud in 1895. The book contains five case studies, including that of Anna O., and is considered by many to mark the formal beginning of the school of psychoanalytical psychology.

The means of obtaining information in a case study vary, depending on the nature and purpose of the study. For example, a specific case study may necessitate library research, review of existing records, naturalistic observation, interviews, or administration of surveys.

Advantages and Disadvantages of the Case Study

The case study permits the in-depth, detailed investigation of an individual case and the collection of a large amount of data. The knowledge gained from a case study may lead to the formulation of hypotheses that can be tested using other techniques, as well as suggest directions for future research. In addition, the insights gained through case studies may lead to the development of a theory; for example, Piaget based his theory of cognitive development on his extensive case studies of his three children.

Although the case study approach has great descriptive value, as a nonexperimental method it has limited explanatory value. As with naturalistic observation studies, the researcher may be able to describe the observed events but cannot explain why those events may have occurred. In other words, case studies cannot establish a cause-and-effect link between the events observed and what the researcher thinks might be responsible for that event. In addition, observer bias is as much of a problem in case studies as it is in naturalistic observation studies, where any biases you may have can affect not only what you observe but also how you interpret those observations.

Another disadvantage is the case study's limited ability to generalize the findings. Since case studies involve a single case (one person, one family, or one institution), it would be hasty, not to mention inadvisable, to generalize to the population from that single case. Each individual (or family, or institution) is unique; therefore, the temptation to generalize to other individuals, other families, or other institutions should be resisted.

Finally, since data typically are collected in a wide variety of settings over a long period of time, case studies can be very expensive and time consuming to conduct.

SURVEY RESEARCH

Did you ever wonder what classroom behaviors irritate professors? Williams and Smith (2001) did, and so they conducted an interesting study in which they surveyed members of the faculty at a state university and asked them to rate a series of classroom behaviors on a scale of 1 (low level of irritation) to 7 (highly irritating). Before you read any further, take a look at Table 15.1 and try to rate the behaviors listed as though you were the professor. When you are finished, compare your ratings to those of the professors' shown at the end of this chapter.

Did your ratings correspond to those of the professors? Were there any surprises, or did you anticipate the level of irritation produced by those behaviors? For example, did you anticipate correctly that wearing hats during class would be least irritating to professors ($M = 2.95$), while talking inappropriately during class ($M = 6.36$) and asking for extra credit toward the end of the semester ($M = 6.13$) would be most irritating?

Essentially, surveys are self-report questionnaires that enable researchers to assess people's attitudes and values, opinions, behaviors, likes and dislikes, demographic characteristics, and so on. As you may recall from Chapter 5, self-report measures allow the participants to report their responses to various questions or stimuli. For example, if you wished to investigate the average college student's attitude toward politics, you could administer a survey to a sample of college students. In a similar vein, if you were interested in adolescents' perceptions of authority, you could sample a group of adolescents and survey their perceptions.

Although the survey method frequently appeals to students for its apparent simplicity, in reality it is a difficult and time-consuming technique. To conduct survey research, you need to establish the objective of the study, construct the survey, identify and select a sample from the population, and decide on a method of administering the survey. Finally, keep in mind that entire textbooks have been written on the survey method; therefore, an in-depth coverage of this important technique is beyond the scope of this chapter.

TABLE 15.1   Questionnaire Asking Professors to Rate Irritating Classroom Behaviors (1 = low level of irritation; 7 = highly irritating)

Items

1. Wearing hats during class
2. Coming to class after class has begun without apologizing
3. Leaving class before class is over
4. Talking inappropriately during class.
5. Asking you, following a missed class, "Did we do anything important in class today?"
6. Leaving class for anywhere from 5–15 minutes, then returning (with soda, food, etc.)
7. Talking inappropriately with friends during class
8. Eating or drinking inappropriately during class
9. Making negative nonverbal expressions to other students during class
10. Obviously not paying attention or acting distracted in class
11. Asking for extra credit toward the end of the semester, after having not made earlier attempts to do better in the course
12. Having multiple unexplained absences from class
13. Giving insufficient advanced notice before a planned absence from school
14. Avoiding turning assignments in on time
15. Failing to prepare well enough for tests or quizzes
16. Having a minimalist ("just enough to skate by") work ethic regarding class assignments
17. Doing work from some other class during your class
18. Not taking notes in class
19. Making inappropriate or rude comments about certain material (e.g., sex, homosexuality, politics, etc.)

Source: Williams, R. W., & Smith, D. A. (2001). An analysis of irritating classroom behaviors. Questionnaire reproduced with permission.

Defining Your Objectives

Before you can conduct survey research you need to establish the *objective of the study,* since it is the objective, or purpose, that determines what questions need to be asked. In other words, it is important to determine what answers you are looking for before you can ask the right questions. For example, if the objective is to gain information about high school students' perceptions and attitudes toward illegal drugs, you need to clarify what specific aspects should be addressed by the survey. Are you interested in the students' own use of illegal drugs? the students' attitude toward drug use by others in their school? perception of drug use in the students' community? perception of and attitude toward drug use by adults?

Constructing the Survey

Once the objectives have been clarified, the survey itself must be constructed, which is a time-consuming, difficult process. First, you need to establish the format of your survey: Will the questions be open-ended or closed-ended? Will you use a rating scale, and if yes, which type? Answers to these questions depend on the purpose of your survey and on what type of information you are seeking.

Open-ended questions allow the participants to answer fully in their own words. For example: "Name the 20th century figure you most admire." Since responses are not restricted, answers to open-ended questions tend to be more complete and to reflect more accurately the participant's true response. One disadvantage, however, is that open-ended questions are difficult to score. **Closed-ended questions** are also known as forced-choice-alternatives, and an example is:

> The 20th century figure I most admire is _____
> a. Ghandi   b. Martin Luther King
> c. Mother Theresa   d. Einstein

Notice that since the response alternatives are restricted to only four choices, and regardless of how admirable each person may be, it is possible that none of them represents the participant's true choice. Therefore, a disadvantage of closed-ended questions is that the participants may be forced to select what is most (or least) appealing, or what comes closest to describing their true response. On the other hand, an advantage of closed-ended questions is that they are easier to score.

Rating scales are essentially a variation on the closed-ended question; participants are asked to grade their response to questions according to the scale provided. For examples of different rating scales and their description, refer back to Figure 5.1 in Chapter 5.

After you have determined the format of the survey, it is time to write the questions themselves. This is the tricky part since in order to obtain the information you are seeking, not only do you need to develop good questions, but you must also ensure that the questions are worded correctly. Some examples of questioning styles that you should avoid are asking two questions in one or questions that may bias the response. For example, the question, "Should college students pay a Student Center fee and be allowed to use the center whenever they wish?" contains two questions. For clarity's sake, it would be better to ask two separate questions. In a similar vein, asking, "Do you think that alcohol consumption by teenagers is reprehensible?" may bias the answer by seeming to imply the questioner's own stand on adolescent drinking. It would be less leading or biasing to ask the participants for their opinion on teenage drinking.

Sampling the Population

Once the objectives have been clarified, the researcher needs to *identify and select the sample* of people who will receive the survey. To use the example mentioned earlier, obviously the investigator cannot administer the survey to all adolescents in the country. Therefore, a representative sample of adolescents needs to be drawn from the population.

Recall from Chapter 3 the various probability (random, stratified) and nonprobability (available, quota) sampling techniques. To be able to generalize the findings of the survey, the researcher should use probability sampling. For example, to have a sample that is representative of the various ethnic backgrounds of adolescents, the researcher may use a stratified random sample.

Administering the Survey

The way you administer the survey affects the type of sample you have. For example, if you post your survey on the *Internet,* you will not have a random sample. People with access to computers and the Internet, and who actually seek out web sites with the intent to participate in surveys, are most likely not representative of the population. For instance, Media Metrix, an Internet research firm, reports that while the fastest growing group of Internet users are those in the under $25,000 income bracket, lower income households still represent less than 10 percent of the Internet-using population (Frankie, 2000). On the other hand, a major advantage of posting your survey on the Internet is that you can reach a large number of people in a relatively short period of time.

You may also choose to use a *mail survey,* where a randomly selected sample of participants receives the survey in the mail. This method of administration is fairly simple and convenient: the recipient fills out the survey and returns it to you in the self-addressed envelope provided. Although there is always the possibility that the participants who actually fill out and return your survey may not be representative of the population, your chance of obtaining a random sample is better than with the Internet method.

Similar to mail surveys is the *telephone survey,* where a randomly selected sample of participants is contacted by phone. As such, the telephone survey is essentially an interview, albeit not a face-to-face one. The questions on a telephone survey need to be kept shorter and less complex than the ones you can ask in a mailed survey, and it is better to use closed-ended questions. Keep the response categories to a manageable number; if the list of options is long, the participant may have difficulty remembering all the choices.

Again, keep in mind that those who agree to spend time on the phone to answer a series of questions may differ in important ways from those who refuse. Also be aware that neither people without telephones nor those with unlisted telephone numbers can be selected. Therefore, your final sample may not be representative of the population.

A final method of administering the survey is during a face-to-face *interview,* which may be conducted at the participant's home or place of business, your office, or any other setting. The interview may be structured or unstructured. In a structured interview you simply read a series of prepared questions, and in the unstructured interview you discuss the issues under investigation. The advantage of the structured interview is that the order in which the questions are asked is set: every participant gets the same questions in the same order. In addition, the responses are easier to code and to analyze. On the other hand, as compared to structured interviews, the unstructured interview tends to put people more at ease, the format is more flexible, and it allows participants to express their responses more fully. The disadvantage of the unstructured interview is that the responses are more difficult to code and to analyze.

An example of an open-ended, structured, in-depth interview is given in Haynes (2000). Haynes was interested in studying Black male and Black female interpersonal relationships in general and, more specifically, what Black men and women expect from marital life. She explored these questions, she said, because prior research on Black versus White families tends to suggest that Black families are either matriarchal (Murray, as cited in Haynes, 2000) or egalitarian (Blee & Tickamyer, as cited in Haynes, 2000). In addition, Haynes felt that both of these characterizations depict the Black family as "different/deviant" from the traditional norm of the White family, which defines the male as the head of the household. For comparison, Haynes used Hochschild's 1989 study of White families (as cited in Haynes, 2000.)

Participants in the Haynes study were 15 male and 19 female high school teachers, and all of them were interviewed in a classroom at their place of work. Haynes deliberately chose middle-class participants, for she believes that the majority of studies on Black family tend to focus on the poor. The interview session lasted 2 to 3.5 hours, and the participants answered questions such as the following.

- When you decide/decided to get married, what characteristics are/were you looking for in a mate?
- Do/did you want to have an equal share in household activities before marriage?
- Do you think that it is important for a husband to always be employed?
- Do/did you share your household activities with your spouse?
- How do/did you intend to raise your children during marriage?
- Define femininity and masculinity.

According to Haynes, the responses of the Black male and female participants did not vary greatly from those of the White participants in the Hochschild study. Haynes found that both male and female respondents expected the men to take on the provider role and believed the man's self-worth to be dependent on his ability to take on this provider role. In addition, both male and female respondents expected the women to be the nurturers of their families. Where the participants differed was that the Black male respondents expected their wives to work, whereas Hochschild's White male participants preferred that their wives remain at home. Haynes emphasizes that her findings contradict the popular theory that Black families are typically matriarchal.

Advantages and Disadvantages of Surveys

Once you have constructed the actual survey the survey method allows a great deal of information to be gathered on a large group of individuals in a relatively short period of time. The mail survey is the simplest and least expensive method, whereas the interview method requires trained interviewers, and is therefore the most complex and expensive approach.

The major disadvantage of the survey method is the possibility of a **response set.** For example, people's answers may reflect what they consider to be socially desirable rather than how they actually think, feel, or behave. This tendency to give socially desirable answers is greater when the questions concern "sensitive" topics such as drug and alcohol use or sexual behavior. In addition, people may tend to answer with their ideal rather than their true self in mind. In other words, the answers may reflect how the participants would like to be rather than how they actually are.

A response set also occurs when participants consistently agree or disagree with the statements on the survey. For example, people may consistently check the response "agree" or "disagree" or "true" or "false." One way to avoid this possibility is to ask the same question in several ways, varying the positive and negative directions of the questions. If someone consistently agrees (or disagrees) with opposing statements, then there is a possibility of a response set.

Obtaining responses that are socially desirable (rather than accurate) is more likely when the telephone or interview method is used. For example, if during a face-to-face interview you ask a mother whether she has ever used physical punishment with her child, she may not answer as truthfully as she would in a seemingly more impersonal mail survey. Similarly, answering truthfully about sexual behavior or drug and alcohol use may be problematic if another family member is present during the interview. For example, asking adolescents about their drug and alcohol use in front of their mother or father, or asking husbands and wives about extramarital relationships in the presence of their spouse, will most likely not yield honest responses.

In addition, if the survey is conducted over the telephone or during a face-to-face interview, you should expect the possibility of *experimenter bias* and *demand characteristics* (see Chapter 5). In other words, the interviewer (on the telephone or face-to-face) may affect the way in which participants respond.

DEVELOPMENTAL RESEARCH

Does moral reasoning change over time? How about learning and remembering? Do children solve problems in the same way as adults? Are 2-year-olds more egocentric than 8-year olds? How do various structures in the brain change as a result of maturation? Questions such as these are of great interest to developmental psychologists, and researchers in this area typically investigate the changes that take place over the course of an individual's life. More specifically, researchers are interested in determining the extent to which various cognitive, social, physiological, emotional, and behavioral processes change over time.

Since the major variable of interest is age, the research design is by necessity nonexperimental: the participants are *selected* on the basis of their age, and therefore random assignment into various age conditions is not possible. For this reason, the researcher needs to be careful when inferring a causal relationship between age and the observed changes in the processes under investigation. For example, even if the investigator finds that the moral reasoning of 12-year-olds is on a more sophisticated level than that of 6-year-olds, to attribute this difference to age or maturation alone may be hasty and unwarranted. That is, while it may tempting to explain changes in behaviors and mental processes as a function of age, it is important to keep in mind that age may have good *descriptive* value; it may not necessarily have the same degree of *explanatory* value. Therefore, you may describe *how* children of a certain age think or act, but age alone may not explain *why* they think or act that way.

Two popular methods in developmental research that allow investigators to describe the changes that take place over the course of a life span are the **cross-sectional design** and the **longitudinal design.** The cross-sectional method compares different age groups at the same time and looks for differences between groups of people. The longitudinal method follows the same group of people over an extended period and looks for changes in the behavior (or mental process) of interest at different points in time. Table 15.2 shows a comparison of the two types of designs. The numbers in the individual cells represent the age of the participants.

As you can see in Table 15.2, the row starting with the year 1980 represents a cross-sectional design, where groups of 30-, 40-, 50-, 60-, and 70-year-olds (notice that they

TABLE 15.2   **Comparison of Cross-Sectional and Longitudinal Designs**

	Year of Birth				
Year Tested	1910	1920	1930	1940	1950
1985	75	65	55	45	35
1980	70	60	50	40	30
1975	65	55	45	35	25
1970	60	50	40	30	20
1965	55	45	35	25	15

were born in different years) were tested in 1980. On the other hand, the column starting with 1950 represents a longitudinal study, where a group of participants born in 1950 were tested every five years, starting in 1965 when they were 15 years old.

Cross-Sectional Method

The cross-sectional method is used more frequently than the longitudinal design because it is more convenient, less expensive, and less time-consuming. Since individuals of different ages are compared at a single period in time, the research project can be concluded fairly quickly.

For example, Hamilton and Jordan (2000) examined the causal attribution for successful and unsuccessful performances by male freshmen and senior high school athletes. Causal attribution refers to the process by which we attempt to gain understanding of the causes of various events and behaviors. The Hamilton and Jordan study was a 2 (level of performance: most successful vs. least successful) X 2 (age: freshmen vs. seniors) factorial. The dependent variables were controllability, locus of causality, and stability. Controllability refers to the extent to which the athletes saw their performance as under their own personal control. Stability is the degree to which the causes of performance are seen as stable, meaning typical and unchanging from time to time. Locus of causality is similar in concept to controllability; if performance is seen as being under personal control, the locus of causality is said to be internal. On the other hand, if performance is seen as externally controlled, then the locus of causality is external.

The authors expected a main effect of performance, where most successful performance would be attributed to internal, stable, and controllable factors, and least successful performance to external, unstable, and uncontrollable factors. In addition, they also expected a main effect of age, with younger athletes differing from older athletes along the causal dimension. Their hypothesis was partially supported. Although there was a significant difference in attribution between most successful and least successful performances, there was no significant difference in attribution between freshmen and seniors. Both groups attributed their most successful performance to stable, controllable, and internal factors. All three dependent variable measures were significantly greater for the successful performance than for the unsuccessful performance.

In an interesting cross-sectional study that compared children's perception of peers who have lied to that of college students, a significant effect of age was found (Barnett,

Bartel, Burns, Sanborn, Christensen, & White, 2000). The authors presented a group of children (grades 4 through 6) and a group of undergraduate students with eight different lie situations described by eight different children. In each case, a fictitious child described an occasion on which he or she had lied and the reason for the lie. Barnett et al. manipulated the motive for the lie: the lie was intended to benefit the liar (self-oriented), or the lie was intended to benefit the person to whom the lie was told (other-oriented). In addition, the authors manipulated the type of benefit achieved from lying: the liar gained something tangible (material gain) or made someone else feel better (psychological benefit). After all the scenarios were presented, both groups were asked to rate on a scale various statements about the liar, such as the child is sneaky, the child is likable, or the child should be punished.

The authors found that all participants preferred children who lied for other-oriented reasons. When the children lied for self-oriented reasons, the participants rated children who lied for material gain significantly lower than when the lie was told for psychological reasons. But the most interesting finding was that children consistently rated liars more negatively than did the college students. The authors attributed this age difference to college students having had more experience with liars than did the children. Therefore, this experience may have led them to accept lying as a common component of social interaction.

That is certainly a plausible explanation. But is it possible that since the eight fictitious liars were children, the older group was more forgiving? It would have been interesting to see how the college students would have rated liars who were their own age. In other words, we may be harsher on our own peers than on those younger or older than ourselves.

For a final example, let us look at Kohlberg's (1979, 1981) theory of moral development, which proposed that changes in moral reasoning are closely related to changes in cognitive development. According to Kohlberg, people at different stages of cognitive development tend to reason differently when faced with a moral dilemma. Preadolescents and children tend to base their moral reasoning on the concrete consequences of their actions, which Kohlberg termed a *preconventional* level of moral reasoning. In adolescence, moral reasoning shifts to a more abstract level (*conventional* reasoning), where the concept of what is right or wrong is based on what is good for the community, and on law and order. Finally, older adolescents and adults whose abstract reasoning abilities are fully developed base their moral reasoning on universal principles, which Kohlberg called the *postconventional* level. As you can see, Kohlberg's proposed stages of moral development mirror Piaget's stages of cognitive development.

Although Kohlberg's theory has been widely criticized (Cohen, 1991; Conger & Petersen, 1991; Gilligan, 1982; Huebner, Garrod, & Snarey, 1990), you may want to test his ideas by selecting a group of preadolescents, a group of adolescents, and a group of adults. You give each group a series of moral dilemmas, such as the ones used by Kohlberg, and you ask the participants in each group whether they consider the actions described in the dilemmas right or wrong, and to reason why they are right or wrong. At the end of the session, you compare the responses of the three groups of participants.

Suppose that you do find that the adults are functioning on the highest level, followed by the adolescents, with preadolescents showing the lowest level of reasoning. Can you conclude that it was age alone that is responsible for the changes in the levels of moral reasoning? The answer is, no, and before you go on to the next section, can you think of reasons why you cannot conclude that?

Limitations of Cross-Sectional Research

A major limitation of the cross-sectional method is that the equivalence of the groups cannot be assumed. (Equivalence means that the groups differ only in terms of their chronological age.) To refresh your memory, in true experiments it is the random assignment of the participants into conditions that theoretically equates the groups in terms of individual differences. However, since participants in the cross-sectional study are selected on the basis of their age, the equivalence of the groups cannot be assumed. Any time that participants are selected for some characteristic rather than randomly assigned to conditions, the possibility exists that the groups differ on a wide variety of factors, not just in terms of the variable under investigation.

For example, if you were conducting an experiment on the effect of abstract and concrete word types on memory and the participants were not randomly assigned into the abstract and concrete words conditions, you could not assume that two groups were equal prior to the introduction of the independent variable. Therefore, if the participants in the concrete condition do remember more words, you could not assume that this is due to concrete words being easier; it is just as possible that the participants in the concrete condition had better memory (and vocabulary) to begin with.

To return to the question posed in the previous section, let us look at some of the problems that make the interpretation of the moral reasoning study problematic. First, as already mentioned, you cannot assume that the three groups of participants in your study were equivalent in all respects except for chronological age. In other words, the difference in moral reasoning may reflect differences in personality, environment, family background, religious training, and socioeconomic status, to name just a few factors. For example, the adolescent group may have had a more moral upbringing than the preadolescent group, which was then reflected in their moral reasoning. As such, chronological age may have had nothing to do with the level of moral reasoning.

The second problem with attributing changes in the behavior of interest to age in cross-sectional designs is the *generation effect*. You belong to a different generation than your parents, who in turn belong to a different generation than your grandparents. The experiences of each generation differ because they are shaped and influenced by the prevailing social, cultural, political, economic, and religious climate of the time. In addition, child-rearing practices and educational systems also change from generation to generation. Naturally, these different generational experiences influence people's attitudes and values, affecting how they think and behave. For example, current attitudes toward divorce and out-of-wedlock birth are vastly different than they were 50 years ago. Similarly, the old saying "Spare the rod and spoil the child" is no longer deemed good advice for raising children. Given that different generations have different experiences, and therefore different attitudes, values, and behaviors, you can see how differences observed in a cross-sectional study may reflect the generation effect and not the effects of chronological age per se.

As an example of the generation effect, consider studies on memory that compare the performance of younger and older people. Typically, these studies find a deficit in recall for the older participants. However, some investigators (Barrett, 1978; Barrett & Watkins, 1980) have proposed that this observed difference in memory may not be due to aging per se but to generational word familiarity. In his 1978 study, Barrett manipulated the generational appropriateness of the materials by preparing two word lists. One list consisted of items that favored the older participants, for example, "poultice" and "fedora," and the other list was made up of items that favored the younger participants, for example, "disco" and "afro." (Remember, this study was conducted in 1978.) Barrett found that recall of the words was a function of age and word list: The older participants remembered significantly more "old" items than the younger participants, whereas the younger participants remembered significantly more "young" items than the older participants. As you can see, the typical decrement in recall observed in older participants may very well be due to the generational effect and not to aging per se.

In terms of the hypothetical moral development study mentioned previously, the observed differences in the level of moral reasoning may reflect the generational effect rather than the effects of maturation. The adults in your study may have reasoned on a higher level than the adolescents and preadolescents because they grew up in a different era, with different moral and ethical standards. The same may be true of the adolescents as compared to the preadolescents. Furthermore, the larger the discrepancy in age between the groups being compared, the greater the generation effect. If the participants in your study were not very close in age, the observed differences may very well be due to the generation effect.

Advantages of Cross-Sectional Reseach

The greatest advantage of the cross-sectional method, as noted earlier, is that the study can be completed in a relatively short period of time. In addition, you do not need to worry about participants dropping out of your study, which can be a problem with long-term projects.

Longitudinal Design

In a longitudinal study, the same group of individuals is followed over time, and changes in the behavior of interest are measured at different points in time. For example, in order to conduct a longitudinal version of the hypothetical moral development study, you may select a group of 4-year-olds, test their moral reasoning, then test them again when they are 14, and yet again at 24. In other words, you would follow the same participants for 20 years and test their reasoning at different developmental stages.

Longitudinal studies are time-consuming. For example, if you wished to see how memory processes change from early childhood to old age, you would need to follow the same group of participants throughout their entire lifetime. Contrast this to the cross-sectional method, where you would simply test the memory of different groups ranging in age from early childhood to old age, at the same time. The cross-sectional method certainly seems more convenient, does it not? However, the longitudinal design offers some advantages over the cross-sectional approach.

Advantages of Longitudinal Research

Since the same participants are tested at different points in their lives, you do not have to worry about between-groups individual differences. In essence, the advantage is the same as it is for within-subjects design experiments: the participants act as their own control. For example, if in a longitudinal study on memory you were to find that adolescents remember more information than children do, you do not need to be concerned that perhaps the adolescent group had "better participants." In a similar vein, if you find that adolescents show higher moral reasoning than children, you need not worry that the difference may reflect a better moral upbringing for the adolescents. In other words, since the participants are being compared to themselves at different points in time, between-groups' individual differences are eliminated.

The same is pretty much true of the generation effect. For example, if you find that the moral reasoning of your participants is on a higher level when they are adults than when they were children, you need not be concerned that this change in moral reasoning perhaps reflects differences in cultural and moral climates across the generations. Keep in mind, however, that any conclusion you draw about a longitudinal study is valid only for that particular group. In other words, the generation effect may have been eliminated for the group under investigation, but it may still exist if you attempt to generalize your conclusion to another group of participants who belong to a different generation. For example, the results of a longitudinal study that ran from 1940 to 1970 may not apply to the generation you begin to study in 2000.

Limitations of Longitudinal Research

The longitudinal design is time-consuming, and the data may not be available for a very long time. In addition, the longer the study, the greater the chance that some participants will lose interest and drop out, others will move away and leave no forwarding address, and still others may die in the interim. This attrition of participants is known as **subject mortality.**

The magnitude of the problem presented by subject mortality depends on the reason participation ceased. For example, if participants stop returning because they find the study stressful or offensive, the remaining participants may no longer be representative of the population. If the remaining participants have some unique characteristics that enable them to continue in a stressful and/or an offensive study, characteristics that are not shared by those who quit, the generalizability of the study may be compromised. On the other hand, if the reason for attrition is that some of the participants have moved away, the problem is less serious because there is no reason to suspect that relocation represents any particular participant characteristic. In other words, people who move away may be no different from those who continue to participate; therefore, the external validity of the study is not compromised.

A final disadvantage is that longitudinal studies are expensive to conduct because the researchers need to keep track of a large group of people over a period of years, to keep records, and to pay personnel such as research assistants.

Sequential Designs

Sequential designs are specialized developmental studies that allow researchers to combine elements of cross-sectional and longitudinal designs. There are two basic sequential designs: the **cohort-sequential design** and the **cross-sequential design.**

The *cohort-sequential design* is essentially the replication of a longitudinal study, using participants from different cohort groups. For example, let us say that you studied

	Year Tested and Age			
Year of Birth	**1990**	**1995**	**2000**	**2005**
Cohort A 1985	5	10	15	—
Cohort B 1990	—	5	10	15

FIGURE 15.1 Cohort sequential design.

children's moral development over a 10-year period, beginning in 1990, when the children were 5 years old. At a later time, you would repeat the same procedure with a different group of participants who are 5 years old. Notice that this process enables you to study two different cohort groups from age 5 to age 15, but one group of participants was born in 1985 and the other in 1990. If both groups showed similar patterns of changes in moral reasoning from ages 5 to 15, the conclusion that these changes are age-related, as opposed to generational, would be strengthened. Figure 15.1 shows a cohort-sequential design.

Notice how the different cohort groups (A and B) constitute the cross-sectional aspect of the design, for it enables you to make comparisons across different cohort groups. It is the comparison across cohort groups that allows you to identify cohort or generation effects. On the other hand, the testing of a particular cohort group at different periods in time constitutes the longitudinal element.

In *cross-sequential designs,* the participants are retested at least once at some future time. For example, if you compared a group of 10-year-old and a group of 15-year-old participants in 1990, then you might re-measure each participant from each group five years later, and you would have a cross-sequential design. The initial comparison of the two groups comprises the cross-sectional aspect, whereas the followup measure at a later time comprises the longitudinal aspect.

STATIC-GROUP DESIGNS

In Chapter 11 you learned about the single-factor two-group design in which an independent variable is manipulated on two levels and participants are randomly assigned to the conditions. In addition, the two-group design may also entail a pretest. The static-group design is very much the same as the two-group design except that nothing is manipulated and no random assignment of participants takes place. For this reason, static-group designs are nonexperimental, presenting the weakness that is associated with having uncontrolled (and uncontrollable) secondary variables. However, sometimes there is no other way to study the effect of certain events, either because it would be impossible to manipulate the event (e.g., a natural disaster) or because it would be unethical to do so (e.g., denying treatment for a disease).

Static-Group Comparison

In a typical randomized two-group design, the experimenter manipulates an independent variable, and participants are randomly assigned to an experimental condition and a control condition. In the experimental condition, the participants are exposed to some form of treatment, whereas the participants in the control condition do not experience the treatment. Except for the lack of manipulation and random assignment, the logic of the **static-group comparison** is essentially the same: The behavior of a group of participants that experienced some event is compared to the behavior of a group of participants that did not experienced the event. The effect of the event on the particular behavior that is being measured can then be assessed.

The major difference between the randomized two-group and the static-group design is that the participants are not randomly assigned to the treatment and control conditions. As already mentioned, after some unplanned event has occurred, the researcher attempts to locate participants that did not experience the event and compares their behavior to a group of participants that did experience the event. The group that did not experience the event is called the comparison group, and for convenience's sake, the group that did experience the event can be called the treatment group. However, the treatment was some unplanned event that was not under the control of the researcher. Since the comparison is made *after* the event has occurred, the design is also known as an *ex-post-facto* design, meaning, "after the fact." The "fact" is the event the researcher was interested in studying but could not manipulate.

Limitation of the Static-Group Design

The two groups should be as similar or equivalent to each other as possible in all respects except for their experience of the event (treatment). Unfortunately, this is easier said than done. Since the participants were not randomly assigned but were selected on the basis of having experienced or not experienced some event, the researcher cannot be certain that the two groups were equivalent. For example, let us say that you are interested in studying the effect of cocaine use during pregnancy on birth weight, and you locate a group of women who used cocaine while they were pregnant and a group of women who did not use the drug. There is no way for you to be certain that the two groups of women are equivalent except for the cocaine use; most likely there are other differences between them, such as diet and nutrition, level of stress, and prenatal care. Therefore, even if you find a significant difference between the babies' birth weight, you cannot assume that the difference is due to cocaine use and not to secondary variables.

When the equivalence of the two groups is in question, the researcher must be careful in drawing conclusions on the basis of observed differences between the treatment and comparison groups. The observed differences may not be due to the effect of the treatment (experienced event) at all, but to some other unknown and uncontrolled factor. For example, let us say that you wanted to assess the effect of some disease that was left untreated, and you located a group of people who received treatment for the disease and a group that did not receive treatment. Even if you found major differences in health, you could not conclude that these differences must be due to the untreated progress of the disease. Considering that people who look after their health by going for regular medical checkups and seeking medical treatment may be very different from people who do not, the two groups may not have been equivalent to begin with. Therefore, the observed differences may be attributed to any number of factors, as well as to the lack of treatment for the disease in question. In a similar vein, if you wanted to compare the performance of children whose classrooms were fully computerized to that of children whose classrooms were not computerized, you could not assume that the two groups of children were identical in all respects except for computerized classrooms. For one thing, fully "wired" schools tend to be found in wealthier school districts, and therefore the children most likely differ from each other not only in classroom computer use, but also in terms of socioeconomic status, teachers, and so on.

Advantage of the Static-Group Design

The major advantage of the static-group design is that at times there is no way to study the effect of some event or factor experimentally. Is there a difference between the behavior of animals raised in captivity and those in the wild? Does a particular enrichment program benefit disadvantaged children? Is a drug treatment program effective? Does a parental training program reduce incidents of child abuse? What are the effects of war or terrorist attacks on child development? How do catastrophic events affect people's behavior? Questions such as these cannot be answered experimentally, yet they are important questions and need to be investigated. The static-group design allows researchers to investigate the effects of variables that cannot be manipulated.

Before-After Static-Group Comparison

In the before-after two-group design, one group of participants is randomly assigned to a treatment condition, and another group is randomly assigned to the no treatment condition. Both groups receive a pretest, and if the pretest measures are equivalent, the posttest measures may be compared to see if the treatment had an effect. The static-group version differs from that design in that, as with the comparison design discussed in the previous section, there is no random assignment of the participants.

The before-after version of the basic static-group comparison design is stronger because the pretest measure allows the researcher to assess the equivalence of the two groups. For obvious reasons, the design is appropriate only if the researcher can anticipate the event (treatment) and has access to the participants both before and after the event has occurred. For example, if the investigator has knowledge that a particular school is about to implement a new reading program in selected classes, then it is possible to obtain before measures by giving all the students a pretest to assess their existing reading skills. Once the program is concluded, all the students (those who participated in the program as well as those who did not) are again given a reading test. If the pretest scores indicate that the students were equivalent in reading skills prior to the introduction of the reading program, then the posttest measures may be compared to see whether the program had an effect on reading skills.

Advantages and Limitations

The advantages and limitations of this design are the same as for the randomized before-after design. For example, practice, history, and maturation effects can be ruled out by looking at the before and after measures of the comparison group.

A major limitation of the design is that the participants are not randomly assigned, and even though the pretest scores provide some measure of equivalence between the groups, they cannot ensure that the groups differ only in their exposure to the treatment. Any time that participants are selected, rather than randomly assigned, *selection bias* may be problem. In the example, the students may have been selected to participate in the reading program for any number of reasons: they were honors students, parents pressured the principal to include their children, and so on. Therefore, despite an initial equivalence in reading scores, it cannot be assumed that the two groups are identical. Finally, as with the randomized version of the before-after design, pretest sensitization cannot be ruled out. Changes in the posttest scores of the treatment group may be due to an interaction between the pretest and the treatment.

PROGRAM EVALUATION

Program evaluation is a major area of applied research originally developed to assess the effectiveness of various *programs* designed to benefit a specific group of individuals. Innovations in education, the health care system, the government, the criminal justice system, social services, and so on, all constitute programs. For example, Project Head Start is a compensatory preschool program that was implemented in 1965 to provide a range of services to children (and their families) from economically deprived backgrounds. Similarly, daycare and preschool for children are programs. Although the effectiveness of implemented programs needs to be evaluated so that alternative programs can be developed and implemented if the original ones are not meeting their intended goals, this outcome evaluation is only one aspect of program evaluation.

Program evaluation research consists of four phases: need evaluation, process evaluation, outcome evaluation, and cost evaluation. Figure 15.2 illustrates these phases and their purpose.

As you can see in Figure 15.2, during the *need evaluation* phase, the actual need for a particular program is assessed. For example, is there a need for a rehabilitation program for drug abusers in the community? Is there a need for an enrichment program for preschoolers in the town? Is there a need for a master's degree program in psychology at a particular college? Are there enough services to benefit the disabled? Essentially, the need

Need Evaluation	Assess the actual need for the program. Is there a sufficiently large population for the program, and will people take advantage of the program?
Process Evaluation	Assess and monitor the program after it has been implemented. Is the target population aware of the program? Has the program been implemented as originally planned?
Outcome Evaluation	Assess the effectiveness of the program. Is it meeting its intended goals?
Cost Evaluation	Assess the economic efficiency of the program. Do the benefits justify the cost? Does the cost outweigh the benefits?

FIGURE 15.2   Components of program evaluation.

assessment phase attempts to answer two questions. First, will enough people benefit from the program? And second, will a sufficient number of them actually take advantage of the program? There is not much purpose to implementing an expensive preschool program in a neighborhood that is made up mostly of senior citizens.

Need may be assessed in several ways. Demographic information may be available through archives and census data, as well as through surveying members of the target population via interviews or questionnaires. Demographic information obtained through archives and census data may indicate that a need exists, but, it will not indicate whether the target population would actually take advantage of such a program. For example, census data may show that a community has a large group of children under the age of 5. However, if their mothers are not interested in a daycare program, there is not much sense in establishing one. Therefore, an actual survey of the intended population may yield more reliable information regarding the need for a particular program.

Once the need for a particular program has been established and the program has been implemented, the second phase, *process evaluation,* begins. Process evaluation, or program monitoring, ensures that the program will be implemented as planned and will reach its intended clients. For example, if a discrepancy exists between what the program promises and what it actually delivers, there is a credibility problem. Similarly, having a suicide-prevention hotline is of no use if no one in the community is even aware of its existence. This program-monitoring phase can help catch problems early so that necessary corrections and modifications can be made as soon as possible.

The third phase, *outcome evaluation,* assesses the program's overall effectiveness. The question being asked is very simple: Is the program meeting its intended goals? For example, if the purpose of the program is to reduce the number of students who drop out of high school, then in order for the program to be effective fewer students should be dropping out than when there was no such program. Similarly, if the goal of the program is to reduce the number of fatalities in car accidents, then there should be fewer fatalities after the program has been in place.

The effectiveness of a program may be assessed based on experimental or nonexperimental methods. For example, if random assignment of participants is possible, the researcher may use a randomized two-group pretest-posttest design (see Chapter 11). When random assignment is not possible, which is frequently the case, the static-group comparison design may be used. In addition, a **time-series design** may be used.

In the time-series design, multiple observations are made before treatment (in this instance, the treatment is the program), and they are compared to observations made during or after treatment. The before observations constitute the baseline, and by comparing the trend observed during baseline to the trend observed during and after the program is implemented, the effectiveness of the program may be assessed. For example, if you wish to evaluate the effectiveness of a program designed to reduce high school dropout rates, you may compare rates for the year preceding the program and the rates for the year the program was implemented. This design is essentially a one-group before-after design and therefore has the same limitations (see Chapter 10). An improvement on this design is the **interrupted time-series design,** in which data are gathered over an extended period of time, both before and after treatment is implemented. For example, rather than just comparing the year before and the year after the dropout program is implemented, you may compare dropout rates from several years before and several years after. Unfortunately, researchers often do not have the luxury of such an extended period of time to evaluate a program's effectiveness.

The purpose of the final phase, *cost evaluation,* is to assess whether the benefits of the program merit their cost. A program may have great effectiveness but it may be so expensive that there is a cost-benefit tradeoff. For example, if a program can only benefit 10 to 12 individuals, then the expenses may be better spent elsewhere, where they could benefit more people.

SUMMARY

- Naturalistic observation entails observing behaviors or events in their natural setting. Researchers can observe without interacting with the group they are observing, or they can choose to interact with the group. The first method, so-called nonparticipant observation, is the classic "field study," or what typically comes to mind when we hear the term *naturalistic observation.* The second method is called participant observation, and the degree of participation may range from very little to full participation.

- The researcher may conduct covert observation, where the members of the group under observation do not know that they are being observed, or the observation could be overt, where the group members know that they are under study.

- Naturalistic observation is systematic; the researcher first identifies a behavior, or a set of behaviors to be observed, selects a method of quantifying those behaviors, and decides on the most appropriate method for observation.

- The case study represents a research method that involves the in-depth investigation of an individual, a family, or even an institution. Since the key word is "in-depth," the case study is typically longitudinal.

- Surveys are self-report questionnaires that enable researchers to assess people's attitudes and values, opinions, behaviors, likes and dislikes, demographic characteristics, and so on.

- Questions on a survey may be closed-ended or open-ended, or they may use a rating scale.

- Surveys may be conducted on the telephone or in face-to-face interviews; sent through the mail; or posted on the Internet.

- Developmental research focuses on determining the extent to which various cognitive, social, physiological, emotional, and behavioral processes change over time. Since the major variable of interest is age, the research design is by necessity nonexperimental: the participants are *selected* on the basis of their age.

- Two popular methods in developmental research are the cross-sectional design and the longitudinal design. The cross-sectional method compares different age groups at the same time and looks for differences between groups of people. The longitudinal method follows the same group of people over an extended period and looks for changes in the behavior (or mental process) of interest at different points in time.

- In a static-group comparison design, the behavior of a group of participants who experienced some event is compared to the behavior of a group of participants who did not experience the event. The participants were not randomly assigned into conditions prior to the occurrence of the event, and the event is not under the researcher's control.

- The before-after version of the basic static-group comparison design allows the researcher to assess the equivalence of the two groups. Since a pretest is given prior to the occurrence of the event, the design is appropriate only if the researcher can anticipate the event (treatment) and has access to the participants both before and after the event has occurred.

- Program evaluation is a major area of applied research. Although its original main purpose was to evaluate the effectiveness of various programs developed to benefit a specific group of individuals, it has since been extended to include need evaluation, process evaluation, outcome evaluation, and cost evaluation.

KEY CONCEPTS

Case Study
Closed-Ended Questions
Cohort-Sequential
 Design
Cross-Sectional Design

Cross-Sequential Design
Interrupted Time-Series
 Design
Longitudinal Design
Naturalistic Observation

Nonparticipant
 Observation
Open-Ended Questions
Participant Observation
Program Evaluation

Response Set
Static-Group
 Comparison
Subject Mortality
Time-Series Design

QUESTIONS

Short answers can be found in Appendix A.

1. Compare and contrast participant and nonparticipant observation and give an example for each.

2. Define covert observation and give an example. What are some ethical issues involved in covert observation studies?

3. What is interrater reliability, and why do we need to establish it?

4. Two observers rated the number of times a child hit another child. There were 10 observations during the day. Out of the 10 observations the two observers agreed 6 times. Calculate the interrater reliability.

5. Contrast open-ended and closed-ended questions on a survey. Discuss the advantages and disadvantages of each.

6. If you were conducting a developmental study and wished to control for individual differences, which method would be preferable: the cross-sectional or the longitudinal method? Why?

7. Compare and contrast the randomized two-group experiment to the static-group comparison design. Give an example for each.

8. List and discuss the four phases of program evaluation. Give an example for each.

Mean ratings by professors of irritating classroom behaviors (1 = low 7 = high)

Question	Mean	Question	Mean	Question	Mean	Question	Mean
1	2.95	6	6.12	11	6.13	16	5.03
2	5.05	7	6.22	12	4.99	17	5.94
3	5.68	8	4.67	13	4.33	18	4.04
4	6.36	9	5.64	14	5.27	19	5.97
5	5.38	10	5.48	15	4.65		

Source: Williams, R. W., & Smith, D. A. (2001). An analysis of irritating classroom behaviors.

SO YOU HAVE AN IDEA: GETTING STARTED ON RESEARCH

YOU HAVE a great idea for a research project and are anxious to get started. But before you can begin, you need to formulate a testable hypothesis because it is the hypothesis that determines your choice of variables, the research design, and the methodology. And before you can turn your research question or idea into a hypothesis, you need to review the existing literature on the topic. Library research is needed because hypotheses must be posited with theoretical or scientific justification, and not merely because they sound interesting or seem intuitively correct. In other words, a good hypothesis does not stand alone; rather, it is the logical extension of prior research in a particular area. Therefore, the purpose of library research is to provide you with a sufficient background for developing your hypothesis.

For example, let us say that you are interested in studying gender differences and believe that women will make more errors on a complex motor task. What is the basis for your belief? Why do you expect women to make more errors? In a similar vein, if you hypothesize that boys will be more aggressive in their play than girls, what is your justification for that prediction? After a thorough review of the literature on these topics, you may find that there really are no gender differences on motor task performance or in play behavior. On the other hand, you may find a wealth of articles that will bolster your claims regarding gender differences.

At times, the literature review will lead you to discover that very little has been done on a particular aspect of a topic. That gap in the body of knowledge might be the perfect justification for formulating a hypothesis and conducting a research study. Conversely, you may find that the topic you are interested in has been nearly exhausted; therefore, why reinvent the wheel?

SEARCHING THROUGH THE LITERATURE

When you begin your literature search on the topic of your interest, you should be aware of two major sources of information: **primary sources** and **secondary sources.** Primary sources are the original works, whereas secondary sources contain summaries or reviews of the original work, typically written by someone other than the author of the original work.

Both primary and secondary sources have their place in literature review. Secondary sources can save you quite a bit of time, and students tend to find them easier to read and to understand than the original works. On the other hand, primary sources provide you with detailed information that is typically missing from secondary sources. Therefore, it is unwise to rely exclusively on secondary sources, regardless of how convenient it may seem that someone has already summarized the works for you.

Primary and Secondary Sources

Primary sources contain the actual research article, or original work, as written by the author(s). Original research articles state the rationale for the work, cite prior research in the area, describe the participants and the procedure, report and discuss the findings, and generally provide tables, figures, and full references. For example, If you obtain a copy of *Journal of Experimental Psychology: Applied* and read the article on individual differences in responding to time-pressure situations (Joslyn & Hunt, 1998), you are reading the authors' report of the original work and are thus relying on a primary source. On the other hand, if you read *about* the authors' experiment in a textbook or in a review article, then you are getting your information from a secondary source.

Secondary sources, such as review articles and textbooks, are a good starting point for your literature review; they will cite, review, and summarize original research articles on the topic of your interest. Excellent review articles that summarize psychological research can be found in the *Psychological Bulletin* and the *Annual Review of Psychology*. However, secondary sources rarely provide all the information that will give you a full understanding of what was done, why it was done, and how it was done. Therefore, use secondary sources when you begin your literature search; then seek out the actual articles mentioned in the secondary source.

For example, if you are interested in doing research on episodic memory, by all means go to cognitive psychology textbooks and read up on the various works cited in the section on episodic memory. Next, go to the *Psychological Bulletin* and the *Annual Review of Psychology* and read good review articles that summarize a large body of important recent work done on this topic. By consulting these secondary sources, you will not only gain a deeper understanding and a sharper focus on what it is that you wish to investigate, but you will also have a long list of citations relevant to your topic. Now go and get the original articles you have been reading about: these articles are your primary sources.

As stated earlier, secondary sources are an excellent way to obtain general information and references to works that are relevant to your topic. However, relying on someone else's summary or review of a research project is not enough. First, typically there is not enough information provided, and second, the reviewer's interpretation may simply be incorrect or tainted by his or her own, and perhaps narrow, theoretical perspective. Therefore, do not rely extensively on secondary sources in your literature review; there is no substitute or shortcut to reading the original works. In addition, by using primary sources, you may come upon a great research idea. For example, while reading the original research paper, you could question whether you would obtain the same results if you were to use different participants, materials, procedures, and so on. Secondary sources such as summaries and reviews do not provide enough information for you to formulate such questions.

Scientific Journals

Scientific journals contain the most recent research on various topics and tend to be more up to date than textbooks. Therefore, with the exception of journals that focus on review articles, journals are the most valuable primary source of information on current research and theory. Literally hundreds of journals are available to the researcher. Just within the field of psychology there are large numbers of specialized journals that focus on topics such as child development, neurocognition, adolescence, educational issues, applied psychology, memory and cognition, physiology, language, personality, animal behavior, and social psychology. If you have a topic of interest, the chances are good that an existing journal specializes in that topic and regularly publishes articles on your area of interest.

It is important to be aware of the distinction between refereed and nonrefereed journals. **Refereed journals** only publish articles that have been subjected to a rigorous review process. The typical review process is as follows: The author submits the manuscript to a journal for publication. The editor of the journal sends copies of the manuscript to two or three readers, who then review and comment on the manuscript and make recommendations to the editor as to whether the manuscript should be accepted, rejected, or accepted with revisions. The editor then makes the final decision, based on the comments and recommendations of the readers, as well on his or her own judgment of the manuscript.

Since the review process is so rigorous, and the acceptance of an article frequently hinges on revisions, the quality of the works published tends to be high. For example, the

TABLE 16.1 Publications of the American Psychological Association and the Psychonomic Society

American Psychological Association Journals

American Psychologist	*Journal of Experimental Psychology:*
Behavioral Neuroscience	General
Developmental Psychology	Animal Behavior Processes
Experimental and Clinical Psychology	Applied
Journal of Applied Psychology	Human Perception and Performance
Journal of Abnormal Psychology	Learning, Memory, and Cognition
Journal of Counseling and Clinical Psychology	*Journal of Counseling Psychology*

Journal of Personality and Social Psychology
Neuropsychology
Psychological Assessment
Psychological Bulletin
Psychological Review
Psychology of Aging

Psychonomic Society Journals

Animal Learning and Behavior	*Perception and Psychophysics*
Behavior Research Methods, Instruments & Computers	*Psychobiology*
Memory and Cognition	*Psychonomic Bulletin and Review*

rejection rate for top journals is roughly 80 percent, which means that only about 20 percent of all manuscripts submitted make it to publication. The rejection, of course, does not necessarily mean that the article has no scientific value or is not sound methodologically or theoretically; often there is simply not enough room to publish all the high-quality articles that were submitted. However, the competitive and selective nature of these journals does tend to ensure that the articles that are published will be of high quality.

Nonrefereed journals publish articles on a first-come-first-served basis; the articles are printed in the order in which they are received. In addition, some nonrefereed journals charge a fee for publication. Since there is no review process, the quality of the works published is not guaranteed. Some articles may not differ in quality from those published in refereed journals, whereas other articles may be quite inferior in terms of methodology, theory, or scientific value. Therefore, when conducting your literature review, try to place greater emphasis on articles that were published in refereed journals.

Several professional organizations such as the American Psychological Association (APA) and the Psychonomic Society publish journals in the field of psychology. Table 16.1 presents a selected list of publications offered by these organizations.

Books

The books you consult during your literature review probably fall into one of the following categories: textbooks, specialized textbooks, and anthologies. *Textbooks* tend to provide the broadest and most generalized coverage of a topic or subject. For example, most cognitive psychology textbooks cover all the major areas of human cognition, such as attention, neurocognition, perception, memory, language, reading, problem solving, cognitive development, and intelligence. Generalized textbooks are rarely primary sources; however, they can provide you with a good background on particular topics and with a handy list of references.

A *specialized textbook,* on the other hand, typically focuses on one major aspect of a broader area. For example, some specialized textbooks deal only with neurocognition, psycholinguistics, or learning and memory. In addition, a specialized textbook may describe a series of research studies conducted by the author over a period of time, such as the books written by Piaget on cognitive development or Ebbinghaus's famous work, *Memory.* Specialized textbooks may or may not be considered primary sources. If you read Ebbinghaus's *Memory,* then you are reading a primary source; however, if you are reading a specialized textbook on memory, and you come across a description of the various studies conducted by Ebbinghaus, then you are still consulting a secondary source.

Finally, **anthologies** contain a collection of articles compiled by an editor (or editors) on a related topic. The articles in the anthology may have been solicited by the editor(s), or they may have been previously published elsewhere. For example, the anthology *Varieties of Memory and Consciousness* (edited by Roediger & Craik, 1989) contains a series of articles written by different authors that were originally presented at a conference at the University of Toronto. As the title of the anthology implies, the articles deal with various aspects of human memory and consciousness—for example, encoding and retrieval processes, neuropsychology, classification systems, and the role emotions and memory play in consciousness. In a similar vein, *Cross-Cultural Topics in Psychology,* edited by Adler and Gielen (1994), is an anthology that presents a collection of articles, each dealing with a particular aspect of cross-cultural research such as methodological issues, developmental issues, and the practical application of cross-cultural research findings.

Whether you can consider the articles in an anthology to be primary sources depends on how the anthology was constructed. If the article is presented in its original format, then it is a primary source; if it has been edited or revised in some way by the editor(s) of the anthology, then it is no longer a primary source. In addition, since the articles are selected (or solicited) by the editor, you should recognize that the selection process may be biased by editor's preferences, viewpoints, and theoretical orientation. Therefore, try not to rely too much on anthologies for primary sources. Treat them as a good source of information at the starting point in literature review, but be sure to seek out journal articles as you progress in your reading.

STRATEGIES OF LIBRARY RESEARCH

You can locate materials relevant to your research topic through hardbound copies of abstracts and indexes; electronic versions of abstracts and indexes; computerized databases stored on CD-ROMs; and online databases that you can access through the Internet, among other sources. As an added convenience, your home library may support various online databases that you can access from home if you have a valid library card.

Abstracts and Indexes

Abstracts are concise summaries of journal articles. By reading through abstracts, you can determine what articles are relevant to your topic and whether it is worthwhile to read a particular article. Therefore, relying on collections of abstracts can save you a lot of time. Major collections of abstracts relevant to the field of psychology include ***Psychological Abstracts,*** published by the American Psychological Association, and ERIC, published by the Educational Resources Information Center.

The hardbound volumes of *Psychological Abstracts* contain summaries of articles published in over 1000 journals in 16 areas of psychology. For example, you can access information on topics in general psychology, psychometrics, educational psychology, sport psychology, social psychology, developmental psychology, experimental psychology, and many other major areas. You can search through the abstracts by topic or by author. In order to search by topic, you would first look in the accompanying *Subject Index,* and to search by author, you would first need to access the *Author Index.*

For example, let us say that you are interested in obtaining articles on implicit memory. Following are the steps you would take to accomplish this, using the hard-copy version of the *Psychological Abstracts:*

- First, locate the topic "implicit memory" in the *Subject Index* and read the brief descriptions of the articles indexed under that topic.

- Each entry is accompanied by an abstract number. As you read the descriptions, jot down the number of the abstracts that seem relevant to your topic.

- Next, locate the appropriate volumes of the *Psychological Abstracts* that contain the particular abstracts you have selected and read the actual abstracts. Each abstract entry is headed by the name of the author(s), the title of the article, the issue, volume, and page numbers of the journal in which the article was printed. Keep a list of the articles that are most pertinent to your topic.

- Finally, obtain the articles; these are your primary sources.

In addition to using abstracts, you may wish to locate information by using indexes. *Indexes* contain an alphabetical listing of entries by topic and/or author. Two widely used indexes are the *Social Sciences Citation Index (SSCI)* and the *Science Citation Index (SCI).* Both of these publications contain three indexes: the *Citation Index,* the *Source Index,* and the *Permuterm Index.*

The *Citation Index* is helpful when you already have an article and you wish to find out what other recent publications have cited the article. The *Source Index* allows you to locate articles when you have very little information to go on—for example, you may have the name of the author but not the full reference. The *Permuterm Index* allows you to search by topic, and it is therefore similar to the *Subject Index* of the *Psychological Abstracts.* Since the *Permuterm Index* covers a greater number of journals than the *Psychological Abstracts,* it is good research strategy to rely on both resources.

In the past, researchers had no choice but to conduct manual searches through hardbound volumes of abstracts and indexes. Thanks to advances in computer technology, however, library research today tends to be faster and more convenient.

Electronic Databases

If using the hardbound volumes of *Psychological Abstracts* does not appeal to you, you can use electronic databases instead, provided that they are available at your school's library. One of the most popular electronic databases is *PsycLit,* which allows you to search for articles, books, book chapters, and *Psychological Abstracts* indexes. In addition, the previously mentioned ERIC is also available on CD-ROM.

In order to use *PsycLit,* you enter a keyword, for example, "implicit memory," and the computer searches through the *PsycLit* database, looking for abstracts, articles, books, or book chapters that contain your keyword. When the search is finished, *PsycLit* provides you with a complete reference list. Each reference, or *record,* cited on the list contains the following information:

- Document type (DT): journal article, book, book chapter, and so on
- The title (TI)
- Name of the author (AU) and the institutional affiliation of the first author (AF)
- Source (SO): publication in which the article appears
- Journal Title (JN) and publication year (PY)
- Abstract (AB) and abstract number (AN)
- Key phrases (KP): terms related to your keyword
- Major descriptors (MJ) and minor descriptors (MN)

The keyword approach is relatively simple but has one drawback: it can provide you with hundreds of citations, some of which may not be relevant to your topic. Therefore, you may wish to make the process more efficient by restricting, or refining, your search. For example, if you were interested in attention deficit disorder in adults and typed in the keyword "attention deficit disorder," you would most likely obtain a long list of citations, some of which relate to attention deficit in children. By narrowing your search to adults only, you save quite a bit of time by not having to read through abstracts that are not relevant to your topic. In this instance, you could refine your search by using the keywords "attention deficit disorder" and "adults."

The *Thesaurus of Psychological Index Terms,* which is available both in hard copy and online, provides you with a selection of keywords that allow you to narrow (or broaden) your search. The online version of the thesaurus can be accessed from the main menu of *PsycLit,* and to use it, you simply type in a keyword, for example, "attention deficit disorder."

Another popular electronic database, ERIC, provides information on literature that deals with educational issues such as higher education, vocational development, special education, literacy education, handicapped and gifted children, elementary and secondary education, and tests and measurement. The search process is similar to *PsycLit;* you type in your topic, for example, "mainstreaming," and the search provides you with a list of references (records) related to that issue. Since frequently educational and psychological issues overlap considerably, it might be a good strategy to search both *PsycLit* and ERIC for literature on your topic.

Using the Internet

The Internet is essentially a collection of computers that are connected to each other, forming networks of computers. The World Wide Web (WWW), on the other hand, is a collection of documents linked to one another. These documents are essentially home pages that contain hot links (words or pictures) and by clicking on a hot link you can access (or link to) other, typically related, documents.

In order to view these documents, or home pages, you need a browser, such as Netscape or Internet Explorer, and a search engine, such as Yahoo, Alta Vista, or Lycos. The search engines provide you with the opportunity to search for a particular topic, in either simple or advanced format. Table 16.2 gives a brief description of the various search engines available.

If you know the address, or the universal resource locator (URL) of a home page, you simply type it in the space provided by your browser. For example, the URL of the American Psychological Association is http://www.apa.org. By typing this information in the space marked "address," or "location," depending on your browser, you can access the home page of the American Psychological Association. From there, you can link to various related sites.

Searching the Internet can yield a great deal of useful information, and you can make your search more efficient by knowing where to look. One place you might start is your home library. Many libraries have electronic databases, as well electronic card catalogues. If your library supports these services and you have a valid library card, you can access online databases such as EBSCOHOST and ProQuest Direct from the convenience of your own home. Once you have accessed a particular database, you can search the literature, either by keyword, publication, or topic, depending on the database. For example, Figure 16.1 shows the first page of ProQuest Direct.

Notice how you can select which database to search: all databases, newspapers, periodicals, or peer-reviewed journals. If you wish to limit your search to refereed journals,

TABLE 16.2 A Description of Selected Search Engines

Alta Vista	Yahoo	Excite	Lycos
www.altavista.net	www.yahoo.com	www.excite.com	www.lycos.com
One of the largest search engines, it allows for both basic and advanced searches. More difficult for beginners than Hotbot but produces more precise results. If you can't find it on Yahoo, try Alta Vista.	A vast directory of web sites that allows you to research broad and general topics. Tends to produce too many irrelevant results.	Similar to Yahoo in that it allows search of general and broad topics. An added advantage is that it performs simultaneous searches of web sites and groups related results.	Similar in capability to the previous three search engines, with the added advantage of advanced search options. Its Lycos Pro version allows even more advanced search options.

Webcrawler	Infoseek	Internet Sleuth	Metacrawler
www.webcrawler.com	www.infoseek.com	www.isleuth.com	www.metacrawler.com
Provides detailed results and allows you to use "natural language searching,"—which means that you do not need to master difficult search syntax.	Allows you to link from one site to another from a given page. It has a smaller index of web sites than most other search engines.	Searches a large collection of specialized online databases. An advantage is that it can simultaneously search several sites. Best for specialized topics searches.	As its name implies, it searches simultaneously through Yahoo, Excite, and several other search engines and collates the results. A disadvantage is that search options are limited.

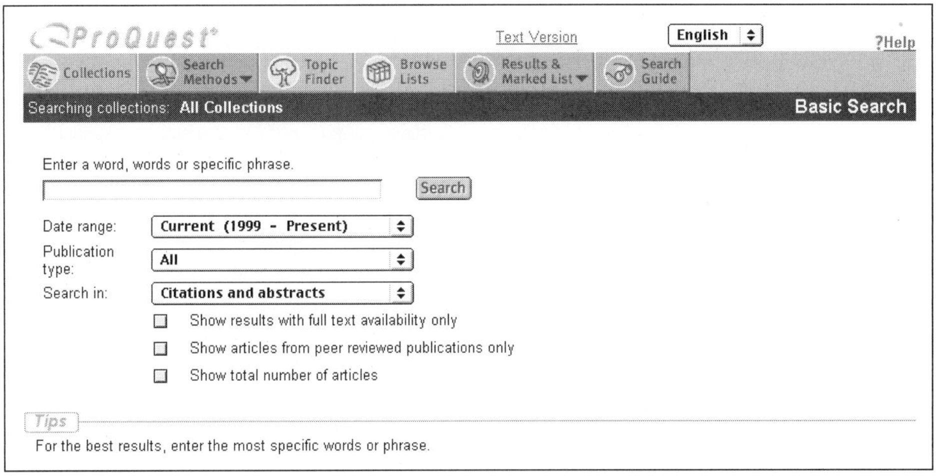

FIGURE 16.1 First page of a ProQuest search.

check the box next to "PA Research II—peer reviewed." Once you have made your choice, click "continue." The next page allows you to specify whether you wish to search by topic, publication, or word. Figure 16.2 shows the screen after you have opted to search by word.

Notice in Figure 16.2 that you are prompted to enter your keyword in the space provided. Let us say your topic is implicit memory. Simply type in "implicit memory," and then select the date range and the publication type. Figure 16.3 illustrates the result of a search, using the keyword "implicit memory."

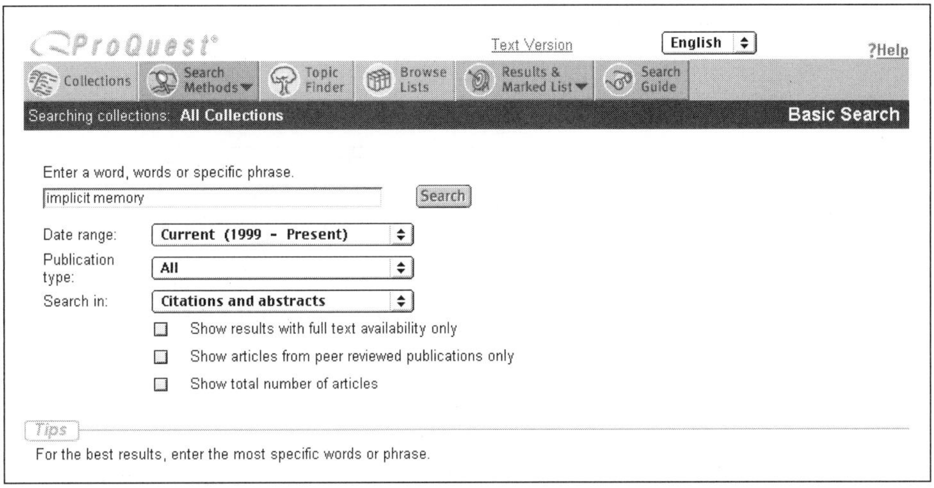

FIGURE 16.2 ProQuest search screen after opting to search by word.

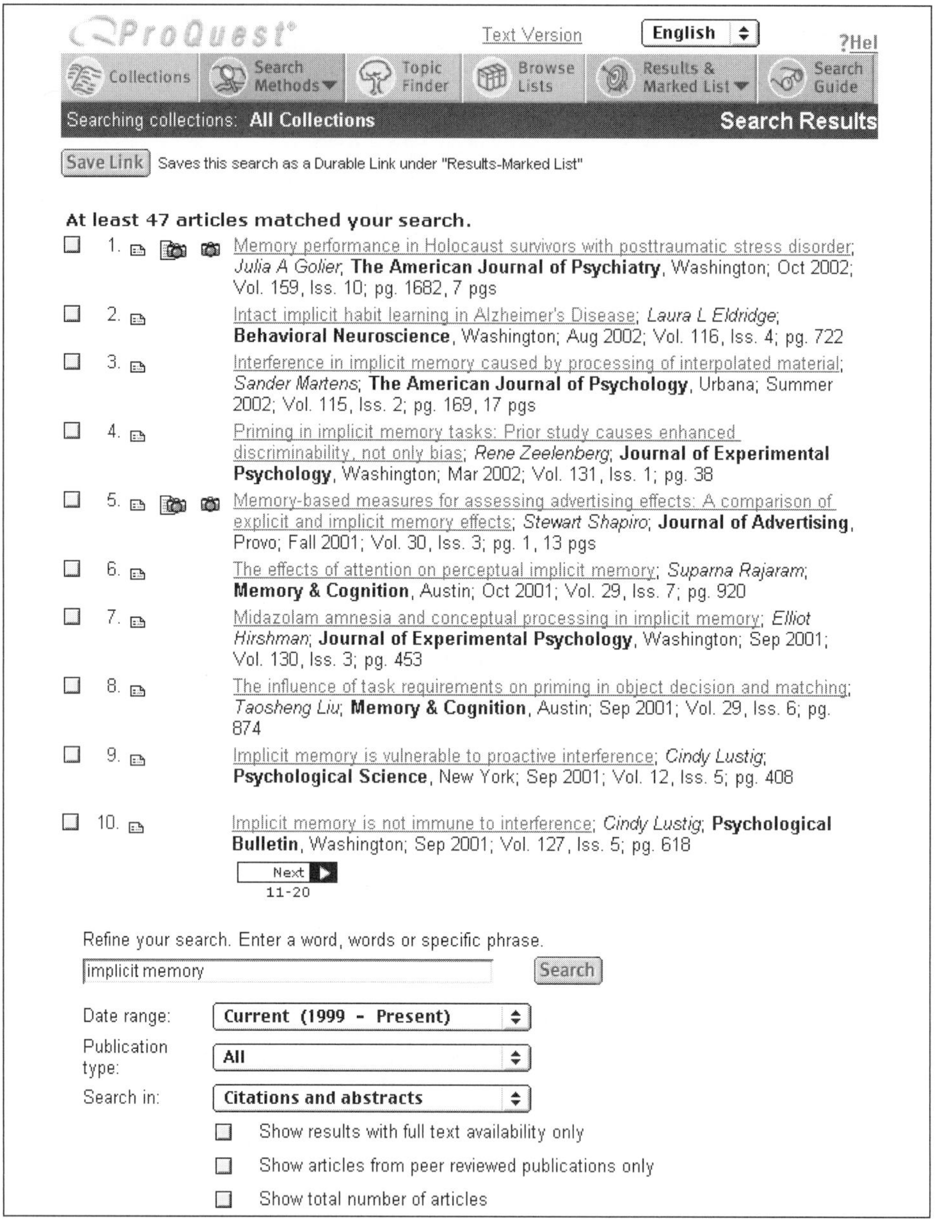

FIGURE 16.3   Screen showing the results of a ProQuest search by keyword: "implicit memory."

As you can see, the search located 34 articles from 1998 to the present that contained the keyword "implicit memory." If you wish to search for articles published before 1998, simply redefine the date range. Notice that before each citation, there is a legend. For articles 1–8, the legend is a small page, whereas for article 9 there are small and large page legends, as well as a legend for a camera. The small page indicates that only the abstract is available for viewing, whereas the large page indicates that you can view the full-text version of the article. The camera symbol indicates that the article contains graphic images, such as tables and figures. Notice that the title of each article is underlined, indicating that it is a hot link: if you wish to access the article or abstract itself, simply double click the hot link and the material will appear on the screen. If you find that the information is relevant to your topic, you can e-mail the article to yourself.

EBSCOHOST works much like ProQuest, and both databases are useful for psychological research. One additional database that you might wish to check out is the Health Reference Center: Academic. This database provides information on articles relating to medicine, nutrition, diseases, and alcohol and drug abuse.

Following are the addresses of a few select sites that you might find useful in your research endeavors. At the time of this writing, they were all in "working order"; addresses change regularly however, and the only way to know whether a URL is still in existence is to try it. As you explore these sites, notice the hot links offered to other related sites: keep on clicking.

The American Psychological Association (APA): http://www.apa.org

The American Psychological Society (APS): http://www.psychologicalscience.org

The APS Student Resources: http://psych.hanover.edu/aps/grad.html

> Along with information on graduate school and careers in psychology, this site also offers hints on doing research. In addition, there are useful links to related sites, including electronic journal services.

University of Mississippi online experiments: http://www.olemiss.edu/psychexps/

> Participate in online experiments and get some great ideas for research topics.

Longman's PsychZone: http://www.longman.awl.com/psychology/research.asp

> The online Writing and Research Center provides information on general research methods, using the Internet for research, and APA style writing.

CRITICAL READING OF RESEARCH REPORTS

Frequently, students wonder: Who am I to critique a published research article? Even though you may not have the experience of writing and publishing research papers, you should approach them with a critical eye; just because an article was published does not mean that there is no room for improvement. In addition, the fact that you are still a student of psychology, rather than a practicing professional, does not mean that you are incapable of observing flawed methodology or faulty rationale for the research project. As you are reading through each section of the article, there are several important questions that you should be asking, as discussed in the following sections.

Assessing the Introduction Section

In the introduction the researcher describes the problem under investigation, cites prior research in the area, provides a rationale for the research, states the hypothesis, and briefly describes how the hypothesis was tested. While reading the introduction section, you should be asking the following questions:

- Is the problem under investigation clearly stated?
- Is the literature review adequate and relevant to the problem under investigation?
- Did the researcher discuss prior research in sufficient detail?
- Is the hypothesis clearly stated?
- Is the hypothesis a logical outgrowth of the literature review and theoretical discussion?
- Are the variables clearly defined?
- Is there a brief discussion of the methodology?

Assessing the Method Section

The method section is divided into subsections that describe the participants, as well as the materials and apparatus that were used, and gives a detailed account of the research procedure. Remember that research studies must be replicable. Therefore, the most important question to ask while reading the method section is whether the information is presented in sufficient detail to allow replication. In other words, ask yourself: Given the details in the method section, could 1 replicate the study? Additional questions are:

- What was the sample size? Were there enough participants to allow the researcher to test his or her hypothesis?
- Were the participants adequately described? Were they diverse enough to allow the researcher to generalize the findings, or were they mostly from one gender, race, or age? Would the same results be obtained with different participants? How were the participants selected?
- Is the methodology sound? Were there any confounding variables? Were the control procedures adequate and clearly stated?
- Were the materials and procedure appropriate for testing the hypothesis?
- Would the same results be obtained if different materials were used?

Assessing the Results Section

The results section contains descriptive statistics and the inferential procedures used to analyze the data. In addition, it may include tables, figures, or both. Although many studies make are of advanced statistical procedures that may be unfamiliar to you as an undergraduate student, in general you should be able to assess the following:

- Did the results support the hypothesis? Look at main effects and interactions: were they significant? If an effect is significant, is it in the direction predicted by the hypothesis?
- At what level of alpha is the effect significant? The greater the obtained probability for error, the greater the possibility that the effect is due to chance.

- Examine the means of the various conditions: Are the obtained differences between them large or small? Even if the difference is significant, if it is a small difference, the author should be cautious in making claims about the effect of the independent variable.

- Check tables and figures for accuracy: Are the data in the tables and/or figures the same as those in the text?

Assessing the Discussion Section

In the discussion section, the author both states whether the results of the study support the hypothesis and theorizes about the findings. In addition, the researcher should state alternative explanations for the findings and elaborate on why his or her explanation is superior to the alternative ones. On the other hand, if the results were not significant, the researcher should offer possible reasons for data's failure to support the hypothesis. The discussion section should also address the implications of the findings and offer suggestions for future research. The questions you should ask while reading the discussion section are:

- Do the results merit the conclusions reached by the researcher?

- Are the explanations offered consistent with the data?

- Are the speculations made justified by the data, or does the researcher make claims that are not directly supported by the results?

- Did the researcher argue convincingly for the superiority of his or her explanation over alternative explanations?

- How do the results relate to prior findings by other researchers? Are they similar or very different? If the results are inconsistent with prior findings, how does the author address the uniqueness of the results?

- Were future studies suggested?

REFINING YOUR ORIGINAL IDEA

Now that you have thoroughly and critically reviewed the literature, it is time to formulate a testable hypothesis. Remember that your hypothesis should be a logical outgrowth of your readings and at least partially based on the findings of prior research. Although you may not want to directly replicate the work of others, you should certainly take into consideration all that was done (and how it was done) so that your own study can add another piece to the puzzle and advance the body of knowledge in a particular area. The following questions may help you in formulating your hypothesis:

- Did you find any gaps in the body of knowledge on your topic? For example, the majority of memory studies use lists of words as their stimulus materials. You might find it interesting to investigate memory for sentences or paragraphs.

- Is there a particular population that was never sampled? For example, members of minority groups are frequently underrepresented in research studies.

- As you were reviewing the literature, did you come up with alternative ways to test the authors' hypotheses? This is especially important where the authors failed to find support for their hypotheses. Perhaps approaching the problem from a different angle would yield different results.

- Was some aspect of the topic never investigated, or was it investigated superficially? This is similar to the question regarding the gap in the body of knowledge; you might find a few studies on a particular topic but not in sufficient depth or detail. For example, you may find a lot of studies on face recognition but few that investigate cross-race and/or cross-gender face recognition.

- Did you come across any flaws in methodology? For example, did any of the studies contain confounding variables? Your hypothesis may predict a very different outcome once those confounding variables are eliminated.

- Most articles suggest future research in their discussion sections; did any of them strike you as interesting and/or inspiring? Often the authors do not follow up on their own suggestions; if they did not, there is nothing to prevent you from doing so.

Let us say that you have formulated the hypothesis that the participants will remember more pleasant words than unpleasant words. Notice that the hypothesis states the relationship between word type and memory, which are your independent and dependent variables. Once you have identified your independent variable(s), consider all outside factors that may affect your dependent measure and take careful steps to control them, either by eliminating them or by holding them constant (Chapter 3).

The next step is to *operationally define* your variables. For example, how do you define "pleasant" and "unpleasant" words, and how will you measure memory? Will you be assessing recall, recognition, or both? Notice that if you are going to administer both types of tests, you have a factorial experiment.

Next, decide on the *design* type. Should it be a between-subjects, a within-subjects, or a mixed design? Remember that within-subjects designs need fewer participants and have more power to detect a real significant difference. Review the advantages and limitations of each design type (Chapter 9).

Determine the experimental *procedure.* Will the participants be tested individually or as a group? Where will you obtain the materials for the study? How will you ensure that the stimulus words will be approximately the same (in terms of length, frequency, familiarity, and so on) except for the pleasant or unpleasant quality? How many pleasant and unpleasant words will you show? How will you present the stimulus materials? For example, will the words be shown on a computer, in which case you need some programming experience, or will they be shown on index cards or on a slide projector? One relatively easy way to learn computer application is PowerPoint, which you may find to be a convenient way to present and time your stimulus materials. How will you collect the data? Have you carefully considered your *control procedures?*

Select the appropriate *statistical procedure* you will use to analyze your data (Chapter 8). Remember: the more independent variables and/or levels of the independent variable(s) you have, the more complex the data analysis.

Finally, determine who the participants will be, and where and how you will locate them. Will they be chosen on the basis of availability and willingness to participate? Will you pay them for participation? Do not overlook your friends and acquaintances; however, remember to treat them just as professionally as any other participants.

SUMMARY

- Before you can begin a research project, you need to formulate a testable hypothesis, since it is the hypothesis that determines your choice of variables, the research design, and the methodology.

- To turn your research question or idea into a hypothesis, you need to review the existing literature on the topic. The purpose of library research is to provide you with a sufficient background for developing your hypothesis. A good hypothesis does not stand alone but is the logical extension of prior research in a particular area.

- Library research may require reading primary and secondary sources. Primary sources are the original works, whereas secondary sources contain summaries or reviews of the original work, typically written by someone other than the author of the original work. Sources of information are scientific journals, textbooks, specialized textbooks, and anthologies.

- Scientific journals may be refereed or nonrefereed. Refereed journals subject the manuscript to a rigorous review process prior to acceptance and publication; nonrefereed journals tend to publish articles on a space-available basis.

- There are several ways to locate materials relevant to your research topic: hardbound copies of abstracts and indexes; electronic versions of abstracts and indexes; computerized databases stored on CD-ROMs; and online databases that you can access through the Internet.

- Abstracts are concise summaries of journal articles. By reading through the abstracts, you can determine what articles are relevant to your topic and whether it is worthwhile to read a particular article. Major collections of abstracts relevant to the field of psychology include *Psychological Abstracts,* published by the American Psychological Association, and ERIC, published by the Educational Resources Information Center.

- In addition to using abstracts, you may wish to locate information by using indexes. Indexes contain an alphabetical listing of entries by topic and/or author. Two widely used indexes are the *Social Sciences Citation Index (SSCI)* and the *Science Citation Index (SCI).*

- Information may also be located using electronic databases. One of the most popular electronic databases is *PsycLit,* which allows you to search for articles, books, book chapters, and *Psychological Abstracts* indexes. In addition, the previously mentioned ERIC is also available on CD-ROM.

- Searching the Internet can yield a great deal of useful information. In addition to college and university libraries, many community libraries have electronic databases such as EBSCOHOST and ProQuest Direct. Once you have accessed a particular database, you can search the literature, either by keyword, publication, or topic, depending on the database.

- It is crucial to read articles with a critical eye; just because an article was published does not mean that there is no room for improvement. As you are reading each section, you should be asking important questions regarding the study's hypothesis, methodology, procedure, statistical procedures, and the conclusions reached.

KEY CONCEPTS

Anthologies   Primary Sources   *Psychological Abstracts*   Secondary Sources
Nonrefereed Journals   *PsycLit*   Refereed Journals

QUESTIONS

1. Why is literature review necessary prior to formulating the hypothesis?

2. Explain the difference between refereed and nonrefereed journals.

3. What is the difference between a primary and a secondary source? Give an example for each.

4. Why is it not enough to consult only secondary sources?

5. What are review articles? Are they primary or secondary sources?

6. Give a step-by-step procedure for how you would obtain an article on infant memory.

7. What are some questions that you should be asking as you read the following sections of a research article:

   a. Introduction

   b. Method section

   c. Results section

   d. Discussion section

WRITING THE RESEARCH REPORT

RECALL FROM Chapter 1 that the criteria of scientific observation require that the observations be public and repeatable. Unless scientists report their observations, others cannot replicate them, and hence the observations cannot be considered public. Therefore, the methodology used and the results found need to be made available to other researchers in order to advance knowledge and science. Whether the results support or fail to support the hypothesis, the investigator should communicate the information to the scientific community so that knowledge about the topic under investigation may be advanced. You can look at each individual research study as a small, but important, part of a puzzle; if the researcher withholds these pieces from others, there is little hope that the puzzle may ever be completed.

The findings may be communicated in several ways: The researcher may submit the report for publication in a scientific journal, or the study may be presented at conventions or conferences. When a report is submitted for publication, the researcher must follow specific guidelines regarding the structure, format, and writing style of the manuscript. Although journals may vary slightly in their specifications, the general rules tend to be the same, and the majority of psychological journals follow the rules outlined in the *Publication Manual of the American Psychological Association* (2001).

The present chapter introduces you to the rules set out in the fifth edition of the APA manual; in no way should you consider this chapter to be a substitute for reading the manual itself when you are preparing a paper. Also, keep in mind that the guidelines for preparing research papers vary from one discipline to another other; for example, the preparation of a research paper in the field of psychology may vary from that in sociology. In addition, there are specific guidelines for reporting research studies versus theoretical papers. The guidelines presented here follow the APA style manual's specifications for reporting research studies.

INTRODUCTION TO APA STYLE WRITING

Welcome to the APA Manual

The manual is a comprehensive guide to manuscript preparation and contains detailed information about the content and organization of the paper, the expression of ideas, and the mechanical aspects of the report. The mechanical aspects of the manuscript refer to, among other things, proper spelling and punctuation, what and when to capitalize, acceptable abbreviations, the use of statistical symbols and mathematical expressions, the use of headings and footnotes, the preparation of tables and figures, and how to list references. In addition, the manual includes two sample papers: one for reporting a single experiment and the other for reporting multiple experiments.

The manual is not difficult to use. Each chapter deals with a different aspect of manuscript preparation; for example, Chapter 1 covers content and organization, Chapter 2, writing style and the expression of ideas, Chapter 3, the actual APA editorial style, and so on. Each chapter is divided into subsections, so that no matter what you need to look up, it is easy to find. In addition, each subsection is numbered, and the sample paper is annotated with these numbers, which allow you to refer back to these subsections when you are reading the sample paper.

Essentially, everything that you need to know about manuscript preparation can be found in the manual, and for that reason, it has been called the "bible" of research psychologists. Therefore, as a bit of advice, do not even *think* of sitting down and "winging" your research report; trust me, without reference to the manual, it cannot be done correctly.

WRITING STYLE

Frequently, a student is disappointed when I return a research paper with a lower grade than the student expected. "But I followed everything in the manual. I did not make a single mistake" is what the student typically says. Yes, it is true; the title page was correct, the formatting was perfect, there were no mistakes on the reference page—in other words, the paper was *mechanically* correct. However, the student had problems with how and when to start a new paragraph, spelled "they're," "their", and "there" the same way regardless of what word was intended, showed a lack of knowledge for the proper use of punctuation, and presented ideas in an unorganized and unclear manner. In other words, the quality of the paper was poor, even though the mechanics were correct.

Simply following the APA guidelines may enable you to produce a technically correct manuscript, with the correct format in terms of sections, subsections, headings, and so on. However, that alone does not guarantee that you will have a high-quality paper. Careful, methodical adherence to mechanics alone does not make up for disorganized, sloppy presentation of ideas, bad grammar, and fractured sentences. In other words, your paper may be flawless in terms of APA editorial style, but that will not make up for poor writing skills.

This section does not purport to turn a poor writer into a good writer, but it may help you with three major aspects of writing: organization, clarity of expression, and the scientific writing style.

Organization

Most writers find it helpful to outline their ideas prior to beginning the actual writing. By constructing an outline, you are organizing your thoughts as well as the materials. Although writing an outline takes extra time, it can help you to see whether your paper "flows". By "flow" I mean that there is a logical sequence to the presentation of ideas; each paragraph is a logical extension of the preceding one. One of the most common mistakes that I encounter in student papers is that while each paragraph might be technically correct, there is no continuity between the paragraphs. This lack of continuity makes the paper choppy, disjointed, and difficult to read. Outlining your ideas first will help you to organize the material and to show you whether the progression of ideas (eventual paragraphs) is logical. It will also point out where you might need transitional sentences that link one paragraph to another.

Once you have prepared the outline, write a first draft. Yes, I said a draft, and yes, that means extra work; but even the best writers do not turn out a perfect paper without revisions. When you read your draft, questions that you may ask yourself include the following: Did I present my ideas clearly and in an organized manner? Could others follow and understand what I wrote? Is there a logical progression of ideas, or do the paragraphs seem disjointed, with no connection between them? If your answers are unsatisfactory, make the necessary revisions. The following may help you with paragraphing and organization:

- Each paragraph should discuss a major concept or idea, with the first sentence of the paragraph introducing the theme, or topic, of the paragraph. Subsequent sentences then elaborate on the topic. For example, in the introduction section of your paper, the first paragraph should describe in general terms the issue or topic under investigation. The second paragraph can then discuss a previous research study in the area. Once prior research has been discussed (in several paragraphs), you should begin a new paragraph, explaining the rationale for your research.

- A new idea or concept should not be introduced into a given paragraph that is discussing another topic. For example, if you are discussing the characteristics of short-term memory in one paragraph, when you are ready to discuss long-term memory, start a new paragraph. In a similar vein, if you finished discussing Sternberg's experiment on retrieval from short-term memory, begin a new paragraph if you next wish to discuss experiments that studied retrieval from long-term memory.

- Transitional phrases or sentences can help to link the paragraphs. For example, you might begin a new paragraph by saying, "While Sternberg found that retrieval from short-term memory is serial and exhaustive, this finding does not apply to retrieval from long-term memory." Notice how the sentence links the concept discussed in the previous paragraph (retrieval from short-term memory) to what you are going to discuss in the present paragraph (retrieval from long-term memory).

- Do not make the paragraphs too long or too short. Lengthy paragraphs are tedious to read, and overly brief paragraphs make the paper "choppy." If you see that there are hardly any breaks on the pages, chances are your paragraphs are too long. On the other hand, if your paragraphs contain only one or two sentences, then your paragraphs are too short, this indicates that you are not developing the concept or idea stated in the paragraph sufficiently.

Clarity of Expression

The best way to see whether you are writing with sufficient clarity is to read your paper from your audience's point of view. Even if your "audience" is your professor, write as though he or she is unfamiliar with your work. For example, after you have finished the method section of your paper, a good question to ask is, could a reader replicate my experiment on the basis of my description?

Some issues to keep in mind when striving for clarity are grammar and sentence structure, word choice, and brevity. For example, if you wish to convey that a child's play behavior was videotaped, do not write, "The experimenter recorded the child's play behavior with a video camera." Notice how unclear the sentence is; while you may know exactly what you meant by the sentence, your reader could just as well assume that what you actually recorded was a child playing with a video camera. An unambiguous way to state the sentence would be to say, "Using a video camera, I recorded the child's play behavior."

One common mistake I frequently encounter in student papers is the phrase, "This experiment," when the student wished to refer to his or her own work. The phrase tends to start a new paragraph, typically after the student has finished discussing prior research in the area. However, since the student just finished writing about a prior study, it is unclear whether "this experiment" is referring to the one just discussed or to the one he or she is about to discuss. A way to clarify the ambiguity is to say "The present experiment" or "My experiment" when switching from discussing prior research to your own work.

A final common error that I wish to discuss stems from an attempt to reduce sexist language, and for that it is commendable. However, good grammar need not be sacrificed in order to avoid using the pronoun "he." For example, students often write something like this: "The participant was seated in front of the computer, and they were told to make their way…" Notice how the singular term "participant" does not agree with the plural "they" and "their." In attempting to avoid saying "he" was told to make "his" way, the writer made a major grammatical error. Keep in mind that there must be an agreement between singular and plural usage; if you are discussing a single participant, subsequent references to the participant must be singular as well. You can avoid this problem by using the plural form of the term: students, experimenters, scientists, and so on. For example, you could rephrase the above-mentioned ungrammatical sentence to read, "The participants were seated in front of a computer…" In this instance, the subsequent references "they" and "their" would be correct.

Scientific Writing

Often students assume that scientific writing relies on terms such "heretofore," "thusly" or "aforementioned," and so they tend to pepper their paper with such terminology. In a similar vein, using words such as "consume" instead of "eat," or "utilized" instead of "used," does not constitute scientific writing. So, what are the characteristics of scientific writing? Scientific writing should be accurate, complete, concise, and clear.

By *accurate* I mean that the information included in the report should be correct in terms of theoretical discussions, citations, and results reported. For example, if you are writing up an experiment that you did in class, or if you are unsure about the underlying theory or about the procedure itself, be sure to ask your professor to explain and clarify. There is no sense in writing an erroneous research paper.

The second characteristic refers to the previously mentioned term "specificity." In other words, the report should be *complete* enough to allow replication. This concept is especially important when writing your method and results sections. Always keep in mind that those sections should be detailed enough to allow replication of your experiment, including how the data were analyzed.

Although it may strike you as a contradiction, a paper can be accurate and complete and still meet the criterion for *brevity*. You can make your paper more concise by eliminating redundancies, verbose sentences, adjectives, and detailed descriptions. When you are finished with your paper, read it carefully and weed out all unnecessary adjectives such as "great," "very," and "extremely." Is it necessary to say that Sternberg's experiment was *extremely* important? No, it isn't; it is enough to say that it was important. Similarly, even if you obtain a level of probability of .0001, it is not necessary to say that the difference was *very* significant.

Next, get rid of redundancies. Common redundancies include the terms "exactly the same" or "previously found." Simply eliminate the first term; the meaning conveyed remains the same if you say, "The two word lists were the same" or "Context effects have been found." Again, read through your paper and root out these redundancies by asking, would the meaning of the sentence remain the same if I eliminated this term?

Your paper can also be made more concise if you leave out detailed description, especially regarding the methodology or instruments used by other investigators. Rather than spending several pages on description, simply cite the original study and let the reader go to the original source for the details.

The final criterion, *clarity,* has been covered in the previous section.

What to Avoid

There is one final pitfall to avoid: biased language. It is quite simple to convey a bias, albeit unconsciously, about gender, age, race, sexual orientation, and so on. For example, by saying, "Autistic children were compared to normal children," you are implying that the autistic children are inferior to children without autism. Similarly, by saying that 25 Asians participated in the study, you are unintentionally denying the participants' individuality.

According to the APA manual, the writer could avoid biased language by writing at the appropriate level of specificity, being sensitive to labels, and acknowledging participation. The appropriate **level of specificity** issue addresses the bias raised by the previous example on Asian participants. If possible, describe the people in your sample specifically: were they Vietnamese, Korean, Japanese, Chinese? Similarly, some participants prefer the term "Hispanic," while others use the term "Latino."

Being sensitive to labels means that you should avoid broad generalizations that take away the participants' individuality. For example, by saying that your sample contained 25 depressives, you are objectifying the participants by using the term "depression" as a noun. Instead, you could write that 25 people diagnosed with depression participated. In addition, as you will see in the next chapter, bias may be promoted when investigators use their own culture as the standard against which people from other cultures are measured. As a result of such a comparison, participants from other cultures may be labeled in such a way as to imply inferiority.

The third guideline instructs writers to *acknowledge participation.* The people in your sample should be seen as active participants. Therefore, use the active rather than the passive term when describing the experimental procedure. For example, say, "the participants completed the survey," instead of "the participants were given the survey." Again, the idea is to acknowledge that participants are individuals who *act,* and not objects that are *acted upon;* for this reason, the term "participant" is now preferred to the term "subject."

THE STRUCTURE OF A RESEARCH PAPER

The research article is composed of five major sections: abstract, introduction, method, results, and discussion. In addition, all articles have a title page and a reference section, and some may contain tables and figures. The correct order of the sections is as follows:

- Title page
- Abstract
- Introduction
- Method
- Results
- Discussion
- References
- Tables
- Figure captions page
- Figures
- Appendixes

The following sections discuss each component; however, for full coverage refer to your APA manual. The numbers in parentheses next to each section heading indicate the pages in the APA manual where you can find further information about the particular topic covered.

Title Page (10–12)

The title page contains the page header, page number, running head, title, author(s), and institutional affiliation(s). An illustration of the title page can be seen in Figure 17.1.

The *page header* contains the first two or three words of the actual title and appears on every page of the manuscript except figures. The header allows readers (and editors) to

Modality Effects 1

Running head:IMPLICIT MEMORY

Modality Effects on Implicit Word-Stem Completions

Jane Doe
Any University

FIGURE 17.1   Sample APA style title page.

identify pages of the manuscript in case they become separated. The *page number* may be placed on a separate line below the header, or it may be placed about 5 spaces to the right of the header.

The *running head* is a short version of the title, and it should not exceed 50 characters, including letters, spaces, and punctuation. Note that the letters in the running head are capitalized. While you type the running head only once, it appears on the top of every page of a published paper to help readers to identify the article. Therefore, it is used for publication purposes.

The actual *title* of the article should be informative and communicate to the reader what was investigated. When readers scan the table of contents of a scientific journal, a title that fails to capture their attention may remain unread. Unread articles do not advance science, no matter how important the topic or how striking the findings. Therefore, make sure that your title informs the reader about your topic and the variables under investigation. A good title reveals the independent and dependent variables, as well as the relationship between them. For example, the title, "Mood Effects on Person-Perception Judgments" (Forgas & Bower, 1987) informs the reader of the topic of the paper and also states the variables under investigation.

Good titles are neither so lengthy that they cause confusion nor so brief that they are uninformative. For example, the title "An Experimental Study of the Effects of Related Words and Unrelated Words on Reaction Time in a Lexical Decision Task" is a bit too long, while the title "The Effects of Word Relatedness" is a bit too concise. In the first instance, the words "An Experimental Study" are superfluous, and "Related Words and Unrelated Words" are redundant. In the second instance, the title is so brief that it tells the reader nothing regarding the relationship between the variables under investigation. The "Effects of Word Relatedness" on what? However, the title "Lexical Decisions: The Effects of Word Relatedness on Reaction Time" is about right. In fact, you may even want to leave out the words "on Reaction Time."

The title is centered between the margins, and the first letter of each word is capitalized. Articles and prepositions such as to, an, of, a, and the are not capitalized.

The *author's name* follows the title. If there are multiple authors, typically the first author listed is the one who made the most contributions to the paper. The *institutional affiliation*—usually the college or university where the research was conducted—appears below the author's name. For example, if you submit your research paper to your professor, the name of your college or university will be stated below your name.

Abstract (12–15)

The second page of your manuscript contains the **abstract,** which is a single-paragraph summary of the research paper. The word "Abstract" is centered at the top of the page, and the summary is written in block paragraph format without indentations. Figure 17.2 illustrates the format and content of the abstract.

The abstract is difficult to write because it must summarize an entire research project in 120 words or less. The abstract should include the hypothesis that was tested, a description of the sample, the variables under investigation, a brief description of the method, what was found (including statistical significance levels), and major conclusions based on the results. Most authors find it easier to write the abstract last, once the entire paper has been written.

Modality Effects 2

Abstract

The present study investigated modality effects in an implicit memory task. Twenty participants were randomly assigned to either a visual or an auditory presentation condition. Following the visual or auditory presentation of 40 words, the participants were given a word-stem completion task and asked to complete each stem with one or more letters so that it formed an English word. The results indicated significant priming effects in the visual condition, but no priming effects were found in the auditory condition.

FIGURE 17.2   Sample abstract page.

According to the APA manual, the abstract should reflect only the information that is contained in manuscript; information that is not mentioned in the body of the paper should not be included in the abstract. The abstract should be nonevaluative; in other words, do not comment on the information in your manuscript, just report the information. In addition, the abstract must be self-contained in that all abbreviations and unique terms must be defined, and the names of tests should be spelled out.

Abstracts are listed in the *Psychological Abstracts,* as well as in online databases such as *PsycLit* and *PsycINFO.* Therefore, as with titles, it is important for the abstract to be informative, so that readers can understand what you did and decide whether to read the full article. Remember that your abstract is frequently the first encounter readers have with your research, either as they are thumbing through the *Psychological Abstracts* or as they are scrolling through entries on a computer screen. If your abstract is poorly written or uninformative, the reader is not going to be motivated to read the full article.

Introduction (15–17)

The third page of your manuscript begins the **introduction section.** Write the exact title of the article on the top of the page and center it. The first letter of each word is capitalized, as it is on the title page.

As the name implies, the introduction section introduces the topic under investigation, reviews prior research relevant to the topic, and states the purpose and rationale of the present research study. In addition, the introduction section specifies the variables under study, a brief description of the method, and a prediction regarding the outcome of the project.

The order in which the components are listed above may be used as a guideline for organizing your introduction section. In other words, when writing the introduction, go from the broad to the specific: Start with a general discussion of the topic and end with describing what you did and why. Figure 17.3 illustrates the content and organization of the introduction section.

Modality Effects 3

Context Effects and Retrieval in Short-Term Memory

In memory research, context can be defined as the semantic contextual cues provided by verbal items within which an item is embedded (Lewandowsky, Kirsner, & Bainbridge, (1989) or as the environmental cues that are operating at the time of study and testing (Smith, Glenberg, & Bjork, 1978).

It has long been known that the more the learning context matches the retrieval context, the greater the recall performance (Tulving & Thomson, 1972). Glenberg and Kraus (1981) found that when other, more salient cues are not available, recall is dependent on contextual cues. By changing the environmental context from time of encoding to the time of retrieval, a decrease in recall perfromance was obtained. Southard (1982) reported similar findings in short-term memory (STM) performance.

The purpose of the present study was to test the hypothesis that in STM a recall decrement would be observed when the encoding context differed from the retrieval context. This hypothesis is based on the rationale that in STM, recall is mediated both by active semantic attributes and context (Gorfein, 1987).

The participants were shown a series of word-pairs drawn from taxonomic categories. A semantic shift occurred after every second trial. Two retention interval durations were used: 4 seconds and 13 seconds. During the retention interval, a Stroop color-naming task served as the encoding context. It was expected that at short retention intervals context would have no effect since recall would be mediated by semantic activation. At long intervals, however, semantic attributes would have decayed, and therefore consistency in context would facilitate recall.

FIGURE 17.3   Sample introduction section page. (*Source:* Gorfein and Spata, 1987.)

The opening paragraph discusses the issue at hand and its significance. This is followed by a review of theories and previous research related to the study. The review of relevant literature need not be exhaustive; assume that the reader is familiar with your topic. However, it should include important prior findings, as well as pertinent recent developments in the area. When discussing prior research, remember that it should have a direct bearing on your topic and justify the rationale for your research project. In other words, when trying to decide whether to include a particular study, ask yourself: "How can I relate this finding to my own research? How does this study tie in with my own project?"

Remember that the rationale for your research must be rooted in previous findings and theories. Therefore, concentrate on studies that help you to demonstrate how your own investigation evolved from prior knowledge in the area. As your APA manual states, there should be a logical continuity between prior work and your own work.

There are three ways to cite previous research, depending on how the sentence with the citation is constructed. (1) You can state the name(s) of the investigator(s) and the date within parentheses; (2) you can cite the name(s) first, followed by only the date in parentheses; and (3) you can state the name(s) and date without parentheses. An example of each is as follows:

1. Some investigators have found levels of processing effects as a function of experimental design (Challis & Brodbeck, 1992).
2. Challis and Brodbeck (1992) report levels of processing effects as a function of experimental design.
3. In their 1992 study, Challis and Brodbeck found levels of processing effects as a function of experimental design.

Notice that in the first instance, when the authors' names are listed within parentheses, they are separated by the ampersand symbol (&). However, when the names appear outside of the parentheses, as in example 3, the word "and" must be used. In addition, when multiple studies are cited within parentheses, the listing is in alphabetical order by first author, and each citation is separated by semicolon. For example:

> On conceptual implicit tests, modality was found to have no effect (Blaxton, 1989; Srinivas & Roediger, 1990).

When an article has three or more authors, the first time it is cited all the names must be listed. For example:

> Craik, Moscovitch, and McDowd (1994) investigated the effects of surface and conceptual attributes on implicit and explicit memory tests.

On subsequent citations you can refer to the study by citing the first author's name, followed by et al. For example:

> Craik et al. found that conceptual attributes did not have an effect on data-driven, implicit tests.

For further detail on correct citations, see your APA manual.

Once you have discussed the pertinent literature, introduce what you did and explain why you did it. Describe the purpose of the study and the underlying rationale. Give a brief description of your method, including how you manipulated the independent variable(s) and how the dependent variable was measured. State your hypothesis, what you expected to find, and why you expected those findings. In other words, you should carefully elaborate on the rationale for your hypothesis and your expectations. The following is a brief summary of the introduction section.

- Introduce the topic.
- Review previous research and theories.

- Relate the literature review to your topic.
- State the rationale for your hypothesis and briefly describe what you did.
- State your expectation(s) for the experiment's outcome.

Method (17–19)

The **method section** describes in detail how the study was conducted. Separate subsections describe the participants, the materials and apparatus, and the experimental procedure. When writing the method section, keep in mind that it must be sufficiently detailed and precise to allow replication. After you have finished writing it, ask yourself whether readers would be able to replicate your study. An example of a method section can be seen in Figure 17.4.

Levels of Processing 6

Method

Participants

Twenty-four Adelphi University undergraduates participated to partially fulfill a course requirement. All participants were native English speakers.

Materials

A pool of 80 word pairs were selected from the University of South Florida word-association norms (Nelson, McEvoy, & Schreiber, 1994). The stimulus words ranged in frequency of occurence from 24–50, with a mean frequency of occurence of 34 (Kucera & Francis, 1963).

Procedure

The participants were tested individually, and the materials were presented on a computer controlled monitor with timing and randomization of stimuli controlled by the MEL system (Schneider, 1988). Prior to the study phase, each participant was given practice trials in counting vowels in words, word-stem completion and word-association. During the study phase, participants were shown a list of words, one word at a time, for 4 seconds each, and told to indicate the number of vowels in each word by pressing the appropriate number on the keyboard. Each word was preceded by a "get ready" signal (####) for 500 ms, and participants were told to respond quickly while being as accurate as possible. The words on the lists were presented in random order for all participants.

FIGURE 17.4 Sample method section. (*Source:* Spata, 1995.)

Where the introduction section ends, the method section begins. Do not start a new page. Type the word "Method" and center it. Notice that the headings for each subsection are flush against the margin and italicized. The first subsection describes the *participants*. Give all relevant detail regarding the number of participants, their age and gender, and how they were selected from the population. In other words, were the participants randomly selected? Is participation part of a course requirement? Are they receiving payment? Were they selected on the basis of their willingness to participate? Other demographic characteristics, for example, race or ethnic background, need not be mentioned unless the participants were selected for the study precisely for those characteristics.

Materials and equipment used are described in the next subsection, under the heading *Materials and Apparatus*. Apparatus refers to actual equipment—for example, a mirror-tracing device, tape recorder, or computer—while materials refer to tests, surveys, word lists, pictures, and so on. The experiment may entail the use of both materials and apparatus, or it may involve just the use of materials. For example, if you are showing word lists on a computer, then your subsection heading would read "Materials and Apparatus," and you must describe both the materials (word lists) and the apparatus (computer). When describing the apparatus, you should state the model and the manufacturers. On the other hand, if you are showing the participants a series of pictures printed on index cards, then your subsection heading would read "Materials," below which you discuss the nature of the pictures. Frequently, it is helpful to include examples of your materials in an appendix, in which case you would refer the reader to the appendix.

The *procedure* subsection that follows is crucial. It must give a step-by-step, detailed description of what you did throughout the experiment. It needs to include the following:

- What the participants were told prior to beginning the study.
- Whether they were tested individually or as a group.
- How the participants were assigned to conditions.
- Practice trials given, if any.
- What instructions were given: They can either be paraphrased or given in a quotation.
- Manipulation procedures and how they were introduced.
- All control procedures, such as counterbalancing the order of stimuli.
- What data were collected and how they were collected.
- Debriefing procedures, if any. Remember that debriefing must follow all studies involving deception.

Results (20–26)

Where the method section ends, the **results section** begins. Do not start a new page. Type the word "Results" and center it. As the heading implies, the purpose of this section is to report your findings. You would typically state all descriptive and inferential procedures and their calculated values, including alpha and obtained probability levels. Figure 17.5 shows a sample results section for a single-factor experiment.

As you can see in Figure 17.5, the section starts with descriptive statistics, stating the derived means and standard deviations, and ends with a statement regarding the results of

Practice Effects 11

Results

For each condition: practice and no practice, the means and standard deviations were calculated and are presented in Table 1. In the
practice condition, the mean number of errors was 12.3 (*SD* =
2.10), and in the no practice condition the mean number of errors
was 17.5 (*SD* = 2.23). Figure 1 shows the number of errors made as
a function of practice.

The difference between the means was significant, *t* (20) = 4.56,
p = .002.

FIGURE 17.5   Sample results section for a single-factor experiment.

the *t*-test. Notice how the author refers the reader to tables and figures. (Tables and figures
will be discussed later in this chapter.)

When the experiment is more complex, the results section becomes more complex as
well. For example, let us say that an experimenter manipulated word frequency and test
type, and found main effects for both variables as well as an interaction. One way that the
results could be presented is as follows:

*Alpha was set at .05 for all statistical tests. Table 1 shows the mean number of frequent
and infrequent words recalled and recognized. A 2 (word frequency) X 2 (test type)
ANOVA revealed a main effect of word frequency, F (1, 22) = 73.75, p = .001, with significantly greater memory for high-frequency words than low-frequency words (M = 23
vs. M = 17, respectively). There was also a main effect of test type, F (1, 22) = 34.55, p
= .02, with significantly more words recognized than recalled (M = 22 vs. M = 18). In
addition, there was a significant word frequency by test type interaction, F (1, 22) =
12.34, p = .001. As can be seen in Figure 1, high-frequency words were better recalled
than recognized, while for low-frequency words recognition was superior to recall.*

In the case of more complex factorial experiments and/or statistical analyses, or
where there were several dependent variable measures, it may help the reader if you
divided this section into several subsections and stated the various statistical procedures
and findings for a given variable. For example, in the Forgas and Bower (1987) experiment
described in Chapter 12, the researchers investigated the effects of mood (good and bad)
and person-descriptions (positive and negative) on reading time, impression formation,
judgment latencies, recall, and recognition. To present their findings in a clear, organized
manner, the results section of their paper was divided into five subsections, one for each
dependent measure. Under the appropriate heading, the authors then described how their
manipulations affected each dependent variable.

The results section should state the statistical procedures you used and what you found; you should not comment on or interpret the findings in this section. The interpretation of the results belongs in the discussion section.

Discussion (26–27)

Now is the time to interpret and evaluate the results of your experiment. How you go about interpreting the findings depends on which aspect(s) of your results you wish to emphasize and clarify. The **discussion section** immediately follows the results section. Do not start a new page. Type the word "Discussion" and center it. A sample discussion section can be seen in Figure 17.6.

Recall and Recognition 14

Discussion

The hypothesis was that participants' expectation as to the method of how retention will be tested determines how the information will be processed, which in turn affects retention. The significant difference between expected and unexpected recall and recognition scores supports the hypothesis. The participants in the expected test condition recalled and recognized a significantly greater number of words ($M = 9$ and $M = 15$, respectively) than participants in the unexpected test condition ($M = 5$ and $M = 12$, respectively).

Since the two conditions (expected vs. unexpected) varied only in the instructions of how retention would be tested, the differences in the scores can be attributed to the encoding of information according to test demand. Different retrieval strategies alone would not explain why the participants' performance was superior on both recall and recognition when they were tested by the expected, as opposed to the unexpected, method. It seems, therefore, that encoding and retrieval strategies are interdependent, and that efficient retrieval depends on the appropriate encoding of information. The poorer performance in the unexpected condition can be attributed to inappropriate encoding strategies: Participants who expected a recall test used different encoding strategies than what is required for efficient recognition, and vice versa.

Tversky (1973) stated that rather than needing more information for recall than recognition, it is different kind of information, encoded and organized in a different way, that is appropriate for

---

FIGURE 17.6 Sample discussion section.

The structure of the discussion section is the opposite of the introduction section. You begin with the specific—what you found—and you conclude with the general—implications of your findings and suggestions for future research. As shown in Figure 17.6, begin by stating your original hypothesis, and discuss whether your findings support the hypothesis. Refer back to the statistics obtained and show why the data support or do not support the hypothesis.

Next, relate your findings to previous research and theory. Are your findings similar to, or different from, the results of others investigating this topic? How do your results fit in with existing theoretical perspectives? If your results are different from what others have found, or cannot be explained within a theoretical framework, hypothesize about why this may have occurred. For example, if your hypothesis was not supported, it may be that your sample size was too small, or your experiment did not have sufficient power to detect a real effect. Incidentally, discussing problems or shortcomings in the experiment, such as those mentioned above, can be appropriate, especially if it helps to clarify nonsignificant or negative results. However, remember that this is a discussion section, not a whining section; do not catalogue a list of woes and ills. Nor should you offer vague, unsupported speculations. Try to remember that even if your data do not support the hypothesis, it may still be important information.

Finally, discuss the implications of your study. You may wish to include here why studies like yours are important; state what potential "real-life" application it may have; and suggest future research that would address issues raised, but not answered, by your project. While you are free to interpret your results and their implications, you must base your interpretations on your findings, the findings of others, and/or within an established theoretical framework. In other words, try to avoid unwarranted speculations that go beyond what the design and the data are able to indicate.

References (207–281)

The **reference section** begins on a separate page. Type the word "References" and center it. List all works cited in your paper, and *only* those that were cited. There must be a match between the works cited in the body of the manuscript and the works listed in the reference section. If an article or book appears in the body of the text, it must appear in this section as well; similarly, if a work is listed in this section, it must appear somewhere in the body of the manuscript. Figure 17.7 shows a sample reference section.

List all works alphabetically by first author. The format is called a hanging indent, where the first line of each reference is flush against the margin and subsequent lines are indented five spaces. Start with the last name of the author, followed by their initials. Next state the year of publication within parentheses. For journal articles, state the title of the article, the title of the journal, the volume, and the page numbers. As you can see in Figure 17.7, the titles of journal articles are not italicized; however, italicize the title of the journal itself and the volume. Only the first word of a journal article title is capitalized, but capitalize each word in the journal title. The title of books is italicized as well.

The APA manual devotes 74 pages to how different types of materials are referenced. So a full discussion of the various formats is clearly beyond the scope of this chapter. However, a list of some commonly encountered instances can be seen in Table 17.1.

Modality Effects 12

References

Blaxton. T. A. (1989). Investigating dissociations among memory measures: Support for a transfer-appropriate processing framework. *Journal of Experimental Psychology: Learning, Memory, and Cognition, 15,* 657–668.

Clifton. C. Jr. (1966). Some determinants of the effectiveness of priming word associates. *Journal of Verbal Learning and Verbal Behavior, 5,* 167–171.

Jackson. A., & Morton, J. (1984). Facilitation of auditory word recognition. *Memory and Cognition, 12,* 568–574.

Kucera, M., & Francis, W. (1967). *Computational analysis of present-day American English,* Providence, RI: Brown University Press.

FIGURE 17.7   Sample reference page.

TABLE 17.1   A Sample of APA Style Reference Formats

Journal Article: Single Author	More, A. J. (1969). Delay of feedback and the acquisition and retention of verbal materials in the classroom. *Journal of Educational Psychology, 60,* 339–342.
Journal Article Multiple Authors	Graf, P., & Ryan, L. (1990). Transfer-appropriate processing for implicit and explicit memory. *Journal of Experimental Psychology: Learning, Memory, and Cognition, 16,* 978–992.
Books	Kucera, M., & Francis, W. (1967). *Computational analysis of present-day American English.* Providence, RI: Brown University Press.
Article in an Edited Book	Kirsner, K., & Dunn, J. C. (1985). The perceptual record: A common factor in repetition priming and attribute retention. In M. I. Posner and O. S. M. Marin (Eds.), *Attention and performance XI.* (pp. 547–556).
Computer Software	St. James, J., Schneider, W., & Rodgers, A. (1992). Experiments in perception, cognition, social psychology, and human factors (version 1.6) [Computer software]. Pittsburgh, PA: Psychological Software Tools, Inc.
Internet Sources Articles	Jacobson, J. W., Mulick, J. A., & Schwartz, A. A. (1995). A history of facilitated communication: Science, pseudoscience, and antiscience: Science working group on facilitated communication. *American Psychologist, 50,* 750–765. Retrieved September 12, 1999, from the World Wide Web: http://www.apa.org/journals/Jacobson.html.
Paper Presented at a Meeting	Westrup, D. A., Keller, S. R., Nellis, T. A., & Hicks, R. A. (1992). Bruxism and arousal predisposition in college students. Paper presented at the Western Psychological Association meeting, April 1992, Portland, OR.

Tables and Figures (147–201)

Tables and figures can often help to clarify the information that the results section presents in sentence format. Tables efficiently summarize the main findings, whereas figures illustrate the results in a graphical format. Figures are especially helpful in presenting interesting or unusual functions, as well as interactions. Each table and figure is prepared on a separate page, and you must refer to them in the body of the results section. Tables and figures are placed at the end of the manuscript, and a figure caption page precedes all figures.

According to the APA manual, each table is numbered and is given a title. The title explains what is contained in the table. Note that the table page also has a header (the same as the rest of the manuscript) and the appropriate page number. Figure 17.8 illustrates the table referred to in the results section, depicting the hypothetical data collected in the word frequency and test type experiment.

Although the most common purpose of a figure is to present graphically the findings of the experiment, on occasion the researcher may use figures to illustrate the stimulus materials, such as word lists, or to clarify a complicated experimental procedure. As stated above, figures also have titles; however, they are listed separately on a figure caption page. The figure caption page precedes the figure(s). Whereas the figure caption page contains the manuscript header and a page number, the figure itself does not. In other words, the page containing the figure does not have a page number, nor does it have a header; the only thing that appears on the page is the figure itself. A sample figure caption page can be seen in Figure 17.9.

For further information on the construction of tables and figures, consult your APA manual.

Word Frequency 10

Table 1

Mean Recall and Recognition as a Function of Frequency.

	Word Frequency	
Test	High	Low
Recall*	30	6
Recognition**	16	28

* $p < .01$

** $p < .01$

FIGURE 17.8 Sample table page.

The Effect of 14

Figure Caption

Figure 1   Mean recall as a function of test type.

FIGURE 17.9   Sample figure caption page.

Appendixes (205–207)

Materials that would be too distracting to the reader if they were included in the main body of the manuscript may be presented in an appendix. For example, the appendix may contain a sample of the stimulus materials used, such as surveys, psychological tests, or word lists. As with tables and figures, in the main text refer the reader to the appendix. If the paper contains only one appendix, then simply say, "A complete list of the target words can be seen in the Appendix." If there is more than one appendix, each appendix is labeled with a letter, for example, Appendix A, Appendix B, and so on. When referring to a specific appendix, you say, "A complete list of the target words can be seen in Appendix A."

PRESENTING THE RESEARCH PAPER

Writing for Publication

Once your manuscript has been prepared, you may wish to submit it to a journal for publication. Which of the many journals you decide to submit it to depends on the topic of your research. There are specific journals that publish articles on learning and memory, sensation and perception, abnormal psychology, personality, social behaviors, and so on. In addition, the length of your paper may also influence your decision; some publications such as the *Journal of Experimental Psychology,* or *Memory and Cognition,* accept long, multiple-experiment papers, whereas others such as the *Psychonomic Bulletin and Review* prefer shorter, more concise papers. The final consideration may be whether to submit to a refereed or nonrefereed journal.

The editors of refereed journals send the manuscript out to several reviewers, who then comment on the manuscript and make recommendations as to whether it should be accepted, rejected, or accepted with revisions. On the basis of these reviews, the editor then makes an ultimate decision. The review process is fairly lengthy, and it may take several months before you hear from the editor. Even if you are fortunate and your manuscript is accepted for publication, it may be a year (or longer) before you see your work in print.

Getting a manuscript accepted for publication is typically very difficult for you as an undergraduate student, especially if you are the sole author of the paper. That does not mean, however, that there are no venues for you to share your research with the scientific community.

Conventions and Conferences

The majority of psychological associations such as the American Psychological Association (APA), the Eastern Psychological Association (EPA), the Midwestern Psychological Association (MPA), and the American Psychological Society (APS) hold annual conferences or conventions. At these conventions scientists present their research, hear or see other colleagues' presentations, and meet and discuss topics of mutual interest. Research papers are typically presented orally or in poster sessions. Many professional organizations encourage students to submit their paper for potential oral or poster presentation. Once the work is submitted, a panel of judges reviews your manuscript and makes a decision to accept it or to reject it. As you can see, there is no way to escape the review process.

Oral presentations are typically limited to 15–25 minutes, depending on the professional organization and/or the paper session. Making an oral presentation can be fairly difficult for a "beginner" because the rationale for the research, the hypothesis, method, results, and discussion must all be presented in a brief period of time. In addition, tables and figures are also typically included in a presentation. Given the limited amount of time, seasoned participants frequently prepare slides, transparencies, or a PowerPoint presentation and use these as guides for further explanation and clarification. For example, rather than attempting to explain complex procedures and results, which most listeners would have difficulty following, you may want to prepare a set of slides or transparencies so that your audience can visually follow what you are saying.

Finally, nothing can be more boring for a listener than to have the presenter stand there for 15 minutes, reading the paper. Remember that you were invited to *present* your paper and not to read it. Therefore, make sure that you speak to your audience, make frequent eye contact, and use your notes only for brief references.

According to my students who have presented their research during *poster sessions,* the poster format of presentation is more relaxing and less anxiety-producing for the undergraduate presenter. A poster session typically lasts an hour and a half, and each session consists of papers that are related in topic. For example, one session may present posters mostly on animal research, another on human learning and memory, and a third may deal with topics in social psychology.

As the name implies, you present your research on a poster that outlines the main aspects of your paper. Typically, the poster is an abbreviated version (seldom exceeding a single page) of your paper's abstract, introduction, method, results, and discussion section. Since you will be on hand to explain your research, the poster should include only the most essential information. The pages (components of your paper) may be arranged on a poster board, which in turn is attached to a large board provided by the organization. Although each organization has its own guidelines for preparing the poster, a sample of the American Psychological Society's (APS) guideline to how a poster should be organized can be seen in Figure 17.10.

According to the APS, posters should be easy to read and organized in a logical fashion. In addition, your poster should be visible (and readable) from a distance. Therefore, use at least a 12-point font and even a larger font for section titles. For the paper's title, authors, and affiliation, the letters should be at least 1 inch to 1.5 inches in height.

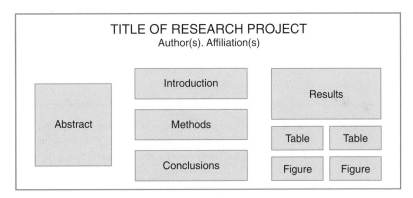

FIGURE 17.10   APA guideline for poster presentation.

Once the poster session is underway, people will stop by and read your poster, and ask questions regarding your research. In addition to answering the questions, it is helpful to have a handout ready to give to interested readers, complete with your name, institutional affiliation, phone number, and e-mail address.

The majority of the presenters (oral and poster format) at conventions are professional psychologists and graduate students. As such, the quality of the presentations is high, and most likely you will be in illustrious company. Therefore, do not think for a moment that presenting your work at a convention is in any way less "professional" than having it published in a journal. Quite the contrary: conventions typically showcase the most current and cutting-edge research. In addition, researchers frequently present their work at conventions or conferences prior to submitting it for publication. Presenting first often allows researchers to rely on fellow colleagues' comments and suggestions to make modifications and/or to refine their work.

Special Forums for Undergraduates

Many professional organizations such as the EPA, MPA, APA, and APS welcome student submissions. Of course, there is no guarantee that a proposal will be accepted, but all undergraduate students should be encouraged to submit their work. First, it is a wonderful experience in and of itself. Second, getting into graduate school is highly competitive; demonstrating that you are capable of professional quality research will give you an edge.

In addition to the organizations already mentioned, many colleges and universities have forums designed specifically for undergraduate presentations. Typically, these colleges and universities send out information, as well as application forms, to the chairs of psychology departments in other colleges and universities. If your professor or the chair of your department brings these forums to your attention, you should consider submitting your work.

Finally, a publication of the APS, the *Observer*, has a section specifically for and by students, called the Student Notebook. This section frequently prints information on upcoming conferences and conventions (specially geared toward student research) complete with a "call for papers." You may consider checking out the APA Student Caucus web site at http://www.psychologicalscience.org/apssc/index.html.

SUMMARY

- The criteria of scientific observation require that the observations be public and repeatable. Unless scientists report their observations, others cannot replicate them; hence, the observations cannot be considered public. Therefore, the methodology and the results found need to be made available to other researchers in order to advance knowledge and science.

- The findings may be communicated in several ways: The researcher may submit the report for publication in a scientific journal, or the study may be presented at conventions or conferences.

- When a report is submitted for publication, the researcher must follow specific guidelines regarding the structure, format, and writing style of the manuscript. Although journals may vary slightly in their specifications, the general rules tend to be the same, and the majority of psychological journals follow the rules outlined in the *Publication Manual of the American Psychological Association.*

- The manual is a comprehensive guide to manuscript preparation and contains detailed information about the content and organization of the paper, the expression of ideas, and the mechanical aspects of the report.

- Following the APA guidelines may enable you to produce a technically correct manuscript, but that alone does not guarantee that you will have a high-quality paper. Adherence to mechanics alone does not make up for disorganized, sloppy presentation of ideas, bad grammar, and fractured sentences.

- Writing an APA-style paper requires organization, clarity of expression, and a scientific writing style.

- The four criteria of scientific writing style are accuracy, completeness, brevity, and clarity.

- The elements of a research report are title page, abstract, introduction, method (participants, materials, apparatus, and procedure), results, discussion, and references. In addition, there may be a tables and figures and appendixes.

- The research article may be submitted for publication or presented at a conference. Presentation may take place during a paper session or a poster session.

- The majority of professional conferences and conventions welcome student presentations.

KEY CONCEPTS

Abstract	Introduction Section	Method Section	Results Section
Discussion Section	Level of Specificity	Reference Section	

QUESTIONS

1. What are the four criteria of the scientific writing style? List, discuss, and give an example for each.

2. What does the APA manual mean by "level of specificity"? Explain and give an example.

3. Give three examples for how you would avoid biased language in your research paper.

4. Dr. Terrence described his participants as "twenty manic-depressives." Which aspect of the APA manual was violated? How might Dr. Terrence comply with the manual and at the same time correctly describe his participants?

5. Which section of the research paper contains an interpretation of the findings and the implications of those findings?

6. Which section of the research paper contains a detailed description of how the study was designed and conducted?

7. Discuss how researchers may share their findings with the scientific community.

CHAPTER 18

METHODOLOGICAL ISSUES IN RESEARCHING HUMAN DIVERSITY

- Are there gender differences in the expression of emotions?
- How does the performance of African-Americans on tests compare to that of Asians?
- Do Hispanic children use the same strategy to solve a problem as non-Hispanic children?
- Is the incidence of personality disorders the same in other countries as in the United States?
- Do people from around the world engage in the same types of cognitive processes?
- Do memory processes decline as we age?

THESE QUESTIONS are essentially asking the following: How do people differ in terms of gender, age, ethnicity, and culture? The study of human diversity in behavior and mental processes is the aim of researchers in cross-cultural psychology. Before you read any further, let's clarify the use of the term *cross-cultural*. Traditionally, the term refers to studies that compare people from different cultures, for example, China and the United States. However, since diversity can exist within a dominant culture, the term is used here to include comparative studies that examine differences between people who may belong to the same dominant culture, for example, the United States, but are members of different subcultures within that dominant culture, for example, teenagers and senior citizens. In addition, although traditionally the term *comparative psychology* refers to cross-species research on animals, research in human diversity is also comparative in nature; it involves the comparison of people from different cultures and subcultures.

Comparative research on human diversity may examine differences and similarities between males and females; North American mothers and South American mothers; African-American college students and European-American college students; Hispanic children and non-Hispanic children; or senior citizens and young adults. In sum, the comparison groups may be selected on the basis of any participant characteristic that is of interest to the researcher. Whether the study focuses on gender, ethnicity, or culture, certain important methodological concerns are unique to studies in cross-cultural psychology. The chief concern is, to what extent can we say that the tasks, materials, and methodologies developed by, and for, one group (typically White, male, and middle class from the United States and Europe), are equally appropriate for studying or assessing the members of another group? For example, is a personality test developed in the United States a valid tool of personality assessment in India? Is a memory task developed in the laboratory of a Western culture equally appropriate or valid in a non-Western culture? Even the equivalency of participants arises when we consider whether a 20-year-old college student from Cairo is essentially the same as a 20-year-old college student from New York.

As you are probably beginning to realize, conducting comparative research on people from diverse cultures is far more involved than merely taking established materials, tests, and methods, and using them to assess people from a wide variety of backgrounds. The researcher in this fascinating and important area must take into consideration the appropriateness of his or her materials, the experimental tasks and procedures, and also the characteristics of the participants themselves.

PARTICIPANTS

Equivalence of Groups

As we have seen, participants in a typical experiment are randomly assigned into conditions, thereby creating (at least theoretically) equivalent groups of participants prior to introducing the independent variable or treatment. However, in cross-cultural research the "treatment" typically involves some participant characteristic of interest such as gender, ethnicity, or cultural background; therefore, random assignment is not possible. How do we ensure that the comparison groups are equivalent in all other factors or dimensions? For example, when comparing a student from India to her U.S. counterpart, the differences between them will not be limited to their country of origin but will instead encompass a wide range of differences in terms of language, upbringing, schooling, experiences, traditions, beliefs, and values, just to name a few extraneous variables. Similarly, African-

American children may differ from European-American children in more ways than just skin color; they may share the same dominant culture, but their experiences, and the meaning and value they attach to those experiences, may be vastly different.

Suppose we tested a group of participants with schizophrenia, compared their performance to participants who do not have schizophrenia, and concluded that people with schizophrenia do not do as well on a categorization task *because* they are schizophrenic. The problem with this conclusion is that alternative explanations cannot be ruled out due to the presence of extraneous, confounding variables that could not be controlled. The participants with schizophrenia may have been less motivated to do well; they may have been less able to concentrate on the task; or they may have been adversely affected by the experience of having schizophrenia. The point is that any one of these factors, or a combination of factors, could have contributed to the differential performance. Since the two groups were not equivalent in all other aspects aside from schizophrenia, we cannot rule out the possible effects of those other aspects. However, even if every effort is made to use groups that could be considered equivalent, when researchers attempt to go beyond describing behavior to explaining the underlying causes of those behaviors, they still need to be careful when drawing inferences about group differences based on differential performance.

The following example illustrates the importance of looking at alternate hypotheses before drawing conclusions. In a series of experiments, Claude Steele, an African-American professor of social psychology, addressed the question of why African-Americans score significantly worse on standardized tests than Whites (Steele, 1995; 1997). Rather than attempting to explain the differences in performance by focusing on variables such as family structure, economic status, and educational opportunity, Steele suggested that the observed differences may be due to the effects of what he termed **stereotype vulnerability** in test-taking situations. Stereotype vulnerability is the detrimental effect that negative stereotypes can have on the performance of individuals who are aware of the existence of these stereotypes. In other words, the negative stereotype can lead to a self-fulfilling prophecy. Therefore, a "real" difference (due to various ethnic or cultural variables) may not even exist, except as an artifact of taking standardized tests by those vulnerable to certain negative stereotypes. In one experiment, Steele (1995) gave a test made up of the most difficult questions on the verbal part of the Graduate Record Exam (GRE) to two groups of Black and White Stanford University students. One group was told that the exam's purpose was simply to research factors underlying verbal problem-solving strategies, while the other group was told that the test was diagnostic of their intellectual abilities and limitations. Steele found that the group of Black students who thought the test's purpose was merely to look at problem-solving approaches did just as well as the White students, but the group of Black students who believed that the test actually measured their intellectual ability did significantly worse. There was no difference in the performance of the two groups of White students.

The stereotype vulnerability hypothesis has been supported with similar findings in studies on women and mathematical ability (Spencer, Steele, & Quinn, 1994, as cited in Steele, 1997). Spencer et al. found that when women were told that the advanced mathematics GRE produced gender differences, they performed worse on the test than male participants. However, when the women were told that the test was insensitive to gender differences, they performed as well as the men.

Matching, Equivalence, and Representativeness

To increase the probability of obtaining equivalent groups, the researcher may turn to matching participants on a series of relevant characteristics. Notice the choice of word—*increase* rather than *ensure*. That is because no matter how carefully the experimenter may go about matching participants, in comparative cross-cultural research it can never be assumed that the groups have been matched on all important variables, and therefore it cannot be assumed that the equivalence problem has been solved. For example, the participants may have been matched on age, education, income, and social status, but that does not ensure that all relevant uncontrolled variables have been eliminated.

The following study using the Muller-Lyer illusion (shown in Figure 18.1) demonstrates the matching problem. The Muller-Lyer task entails judging which line is shorter than the other, when in reality both lines are identical in length.

Cross-cultural studies have found that Europeans were more likely than non-Europeans to perceive the top line as shorter—in other words, to "fall for" the illusion (Segall, Campbell, & Herskovits, 1966). One widely held explanation was that the difference in performance was based on the different perceptual experiences of Europeans and non-Europeans. European participants lived in *carpentered* worlds, where their environment was comprised of angles, corners, and straight lines, whereas the non-European participants had less experience with carpentered environments. If the hypothesis regarding carpenteredness and perceptual experience is correct, then groups from within the *same* culture but with different experiences with carpenteredness should also be susceptible to the illusion. This, however was not found. When a group of Africans from a rural area (noncarpentered) were compared to a group of Africans living in a city, neither group perceived the illusion. In other words, both groups reported that the lines were equal in length. Clearly, the carpenteredness hypothesis failed to be supported. The question of why Europeans see the illusion while non-Europeans do not remains to be answered.

Berry (1971) proposed that perhaps the prior studies failed to match participants on perceptual development, and since the susceptibility to the illusion diminishes with age, it is an important variable to control for. Berry's study compared two groups of Eskimo participants who differed in terms of carpenteredness but were matched on age, gender, and perceptual development. Significant differences were found between the groups' perception of the illusion, and the carpenteredness hypothesis was supported. As Berry later found out, however, the participants were not matched on an important variable: density of eye pigmentation. Eye pigmentation density is negatively correlated to seeing the Muller-

FIGURE 18.1   The Muller-Lyer illusion.

Lyer illusion; the denser the eye pigmentation, the less likely someone is to perceive the illusion. The dark-skinned individuals' more densely pigmented eyes may explain why there was a difference between Europeans and non-Europeans but no difference between the two groups of Africans. With regard to the Eskimo study, Berry found that the participants from the carpentered environment had lighter skin than participants from the noncarpentered one. Therefore, the same difference in performance was observed as between Europeans and non-Europeans.

Thus, even the most careful attempt to match participants on seemingly important variables may fall short of obtaining equivalent groups, and the false sense of security regarding the assumption of the participants' equivalence may lead to an erroneous conclusion. As Berry later found, the susceptibility to perceiving the illusion is more a function of eye pigment density than experience with carpentered environments.

In addition to the problem of perhaps neglecting to match on crucial variables, matching also involves the problem of representativeness. As you have learned, for a study to have good internal and external validity, the sample on which the study is conducted should be unbiased and representative of the population. In cross-cultural research, that is a bit tricky to achieve, especially in light of the previous section on equivalence. Frequently, the more representative the sample is of the culture or subculture studied, the less equivalent it is to the sample of comparison. For example, let us say that a cognitive psychologist wishes to compare the recall performance of children from Thailand to children in the United States. The more the psychologist attempts to match the children on various attributes such as schooling, vocabulary, intelligence, family background, and so on, the less representative of its own culture the sample becomes. No matter how we look at it, the average child in Thailand has vastly different experiences from his or her counterpart in the United States, and the more the psychologist attempts to find children in Thailand whose experiences and backgrounds most closely resemble the American children's, the less likely it is that the Thai children selected would represent their own culture.

So what are researchers to do? Seemingly, the more they strive for equivalent samples, the less representative of the population those samples become. On the other hand, if the researcher strives for representativeness, the samples obtained may not be equivalent; hence, meaningful comparison between them becomes difficult. Some researchers (Osgood, May, & Miron, 1975) suggest that whether the researcher stresses equivalence over representativeness, or vice versa, depends on the purpose of the study. If the purpose of the research is to *describe* a culture in terms of opinions, beliefs, or traditions and, therefore, the study is primarily a survey or opinion poll, then representativeness is more important than equivalence. However, if the primary aim of the study is to *compare* two or more cultures on some variable or performance, then equivalence is more important than representativeness. Osgood et al. state that striving for representativeness is inappropriate in the majority of instances, and they favor the maximization of equivalence between comparison groups.

MATERIALS AND TASKS

Language

If we were to take materials such as word lists, personality inventories, surveys, or IQ tests developed in one culture, translated them into the language of the culture we wished to study, and then administered them in that culture, could we assume that the materials would be essentially the same except for the language? Do the experimenter's questions translated into another language still convey the same original meaning?

An important aspect of language to consider is **connotative meaning**—the feelings and images that words arouse (Osgood, 1964). In his comprehensive cross-cultural research study, Osgood investigated language and thought, but more specifically, he tested the generality of the connotative aspects of language. In other words, he wished to see the extent to which words across languages aroused the same feelings and images. His findings indicated that, while cultures may share the same concepts, the connotative meaning of those concepts is culture-specific. For example, the concept of "marriage" may exist across a wide variety of cultures, but the feelings and images aroused by that particular word may be culturally determined by factors such as: are marriages arranged by parents, or do the partners choose each other? Is the woman considered her husband's equal or his subordinate? Are marriages monogamous, or can husbands have many wives?

One way to ensure the equivalence of translations is to employ a method called **back-translation.** Back-translation is accomplished as follows: A bilingual individual translates the material from the original language (let us say English) into the language of interest (let us say Spanish). Next, another bilingual working independently from the first translator translates it back from Spanish to English. This process is repeated several times with different translators, and then the original English material and its final English back-translation are compared. Concepts that are not readily translatable show up as discrepancies between the original and final English versions and are discarded. The back-translation method is an excellent way of ensuring that the original meaning or concept is retained in the translation. Brislin (1976) notes that this approach *decenters* the material away from the original source, so that the product in the second language is not stilted and artificial, yet still conveys the original meaning or concept.

Another frequently used methodological approach to cross-cultural research is the *etic-emic* distinction developed by Pike (1966). According to Pike, the *emic approach* studies behavior from within the system (culture) and examines only one culture. As such, this approach is *culture-specific;* it describes behavior from within a particular culture and takes into account what the people of that culture consider meaningful and important. Emics are therefore culture-specific concepts. On the other hand, the *etic approach* studies behavior from the outside, generalizes across cultures, and takes into account all human behavior. Etics are not specific to any given culture but are *universals* across all cultures. This distinction between culture-specific concepts and universals should be taken into consideration when constructing materials. For example, cross-cultural research that entails the use of questionnaires or surveys could benefit greatly from the etic-emic approach. Przeworski and Teune (1970) suggest that the researcher could develop a set of core items that are meaningful and answerable by members of all cultures under study. These core items would tap the etic aspects of a culture, namely, those concepts that are universal and shared across cultures. In addition, a set of culture-specific items could also be devised. These items would be different for each culture examined and would address the emic aspects of the culture. Using this procedure, one could formulate initial general statements regarding the culture under study **(etics),** which could then be clarified and made more specific by the responses made to culture-specific items **(emics).** The major advantage of this approach is that it would allow cultural similarities and differences to be identified at the same time.

The previously mentioned back-translation method may also be employed to yield etic-emic dimensions. Material that is retained during the back-translation process could be said to reflect the etic aspects of the material; the concepts retained are shared between the two cultures or languages. On the other hand, material that is eliminated would reflect the emic, or culture-specific aspects.

Experiences

According to Brislin (as cited in Gorfein & Spata, 1989), materials that are developed in typically middle-class American culture may have limited usefulness in another culture. This may be true, since during the development of materials the experimenter draws upon the common experiences shared by the people of the culture in which the instrument is being developed. On the other hand, the participants used as a comparison may not have had those experiences, or they may not attach the same value and meaning to those experiences. Not surprisingly, problems may arise when instruments or tasks designed, pretested, revised, and validated in one culture are used in another, and then attempts are made to reach conclusions about the second culture based on the norms developed in the first.

Since words do not always evoke the same feelings or meanings in people from different cultural backgrounds, it stands to reason that the same experience in two different cultures may not be valued in the same way, or have the same meaning attached to them. People in all cultures and subcultures may experience depression, but the way that experience is interpreted and talked about will vary. Therefore, depression inventories developed in one culture may not be appropriate for assessing depression in another. For example, Ebigno (as cited in Mrinal, Mrinal, & Takooshian, 1994) found that a depressed North American will talk about hopelessness, feelings of worthlessness, loss of interest, and thoughts of suicide, and questions relating to these symptoms can be found on depression inventories. On the other hand, a depressed Nigerian counterpart will express feelings of a burning sensation in the body, a crawling sensation in the head, and feelings that the stomach is bloated with water. If the researchers were unaware of these differences in the experience of depression, they might have concluded that, based on the results of depression inventories, depression was much less prevalent in Nigeria than in North America.

In a similar vein, J. G. Miller (1999) states that researchers in cross-cultural psychology must be made aware of the fact that "the response options permitted on many standardized instruments inadvertently exclude the perspectives of certain populations" (p. 89). Miller offers the example that psychologists frequently treat a high self-image as a sign of healthy psychological functioning. However, according to Miller, commonly used instruments that measure self-image and the self-concept do not take into consideration that certain cultures value self-effacement. Therefore, the existing measures of self-image and the self-concept are inappropriate tools of assessment for "cultures that embody a relational view of self" (p. 89).

Levenson, Ekman, Heider, and Friesen (1992) have demonstrated the important role that cultural determinants play in the interpretation of experiences. In their study, the Minangkabau people of West Sumatra were asked to pose various facial expressions, such as anger, fear, disgust, happiness, and sadness. Levenson et al. found that the Minangkabau experienced the same physiological arousal while posing as their American counterparts; however, the Minangkabau did not interpret their arousal as emotional. For the Minangkabau another person must be present in order to experience emotion; if no meaningful "other" is present, there is no fear, happiness, sadness, or disgust. In other words, in the Minangkabau culture, emotionality is relational; it is defined by the nature of the interaction between at least two individuals.

As an example of how cultural experiences shape our outlook and world-view, consider the following study conducted by Trice (2000) on male and female children's perception of gender-appropriate occupations. Trice compared children from the United States, Italy, and Bulgaria. He selected Bulgaria because "during 50 years of socialist education, gender differences were deliberately minimized" (p. 661) and Italy because of "continuing gender differentiation in Mediterranean cultures" (p. 661.) The children were presented with 20 occupations and were asked whether the occupations should be held by men, women, or be open to both. The occupations were: elementary school teacher, college professor, scientist, police officer, soldier, waiter, secretary, salesclerk, hotel cleaner, bookshop owner, carpenter, cab driver, cook, musician, painter, librarian, veterinarian, automobile factory worker, bank teller, and newspaper reporter. Figure 18.2 shows the results of the study.

Trice found that the girls from each country held fewer gender-stereotyped perceptions than did boys, that Italian children held the most stereotypical perceptions, followed by children from the United States, and that Bulgarian children were the least gender stereotyping. As you can see in Figure 18.1, some interesting cultural differences emerged with regard gender-neutral occupations. (Gender-neutral occupations are those that could be performed by either a man or a woman.) Italians saw the smallest percentage of jobs as gender-neutral (boys: 27%, girls: 33%), whereas Bulgarians saw the largest number of jobs as gender-neutral (boys: 63%, girls: 72%). Children in the United States showed the largest

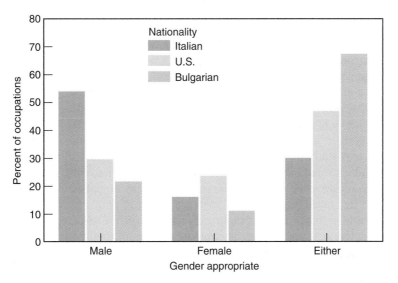

FIGURE 18.2   Italian, Bulgarian, and U.S. children's perception of gender-appropriate occupations.

disagreement between the sexes, with boys indicating 35 percent of the occupations as gender-neutral and girls 59 percent. In addition, U.S. children viewed occupations such as waiter, librarian, and secretary as female occupations, Bulgarian children did not consider those occupations gender-specific, and Italian children considered those male-oriented occupations. The author suggests that the relatively low level of gender stereotyping by Bulgarian children is the result of years of socialist goals for gender equality, whereas the high level of stereotyping by Italian children indicates that occupational stereotyping continues in Italy. In addition, Trice sees the significant difference between U.S. male and female perceptions regarding gender-neutral occupations as an indication of continuing gender conflict in the workplace.

Whether or not we agree with those conclusions, and there very well could be alternative explanations such as economics, the job market, the availability of child care, and so on, it is clear that our culture exerts its influence on how we perceive the world and our place in it. Our everyday experiences shape our concepts, determine what roles and behaviors we deem appropriate and desirable, and affect how we process information about one another.

Familiarity and Meaning

Closely related to the issue of experiences is the issue of the familiarity and meaning of various materials and tasks. Clearly, the more experience you have with a certain task or procedure, and the more familiar you are with it, and the more meaning it has for you. Suppose you were given a task that was not only unfamiliar to you but, from your point of view, made very little sense. Furthermore, let us say that you did not perform well on this strange and bewildering task, and then your performance was unfavorably compared to the performance of another person who was highly familiar with the task and the procedure. Would it be valid to conclude that you lack some ability necessary for the completion of the task? Stimulus materials, whether we are talking about a list of words in a memory experiment, an IQ or personality test, or a series of geometric figures that must be sorted into categories, may not be equally familiar or meaningful to the groups we are wishing to compare. Helms (1992) cautions that in the area of testing, cultural equivalence has not been achieved. According to Helms, a test has cultural equivalence if all items on the test have the same meaning to different cultures and subcultures. In a similar vein, Merenda (1994) states that before we attempt to use materials developed in one culture on another culture, it is necessary to revise those materials by dropping some items or tasks that are inappropriate and adding others that are culturally relevant.

A study of the Kpelle people in Liberia illustrates the importance of taking task familiarity and meaning into consideration when conducting comparative research. Cole and colleagues (1968) used a *free-recall* technique to study cultural differences in memory. In a free-recall task, the participants are presented with a list of words and are then asked to recall as many as they can, in any order. According to Cole, the free-recall procedure is an appropriate approach to determining how people in different cultures go about a memory task. Since the participants are free to recall the material learned in any manner they choose, insight into organizational processes may be gained. In other words, if the participants recall the material in the order of original presentation, we can say that memory is by rote. On the other hand, if the material is recalled by categories, then we may infer that the material has been actively reorganized by meaning. Typically, if the list is comprised of items drawn from categories, such as animals, vegetables, or fruits, participants from Western cultures tend to recall words in *clusters* from within the categories. In their study, Cole and colleagues presented the Kpelle participants with a list of words and then asked them to recall the words in any order. As compared to their American counterparts, the Kpelle recalled fewer items and did not show any evidence of clustering, or reorganization of the material. However, when the to-be-remembered items were incorporated into folk stories, performance improved.

This study demonstrates that materials and tasks must be familiar and serve some meaningful purpose before we can make any type of comparison between the performance of diverse groups. Since memorizing isolated bits of information (words) is neither a familiar nor a particularly meaningful part of Kpelle life, performance was not up to Western standards, where isolated facts or bits of information are frequently memorized for exams in school. However, once the same material was presented to the Kpelle in some meaningful and familiar way, such as telling stories, performance improved.

Simmons (1979) suggests that when conducting comparative research, the **cultural salience** of materials must be taken into consideration. Cultural salience is the degree to which words, objects, tests, or activities are highly familiar to, and/or valued by, a particular culture or subculture. Given that people from different cultures and subcultures value and are familiar with different things, it is safe to assume that not all materials and activities are equally salient to groups. For example, some cultures value *collectivism,* while others value *individualism.* Individualistic societies such as the United States and most European countries value and strive for self-reliance, independence, and personal achievement, sometimes at the expense of a larger group such as the family or work group. On the other hand, collectivist societies such as those found in parts of Africa, Latin America, and Asia value harmonious social relationships and strive for the "common good." In other words, individualistic cultures encourage individual action and decision making, whereas collectivist cultures favor group input and cooperation. Given this cultural difference, it is possible that participants from individualistic societies would interpret performing a task as, "I must do well even if others don't," whereas participants from collectivist societies would interpret it as, "We must do well as a group," and would be mystified by the need to accomplish the task alone, without cooperation and group input.

Familiarity with materials is a concern not only when conducting research across cultures, but also when comparing different subcultures within a particular society. For example, in memory studies poorer performance may result when the to-be-remembered material is not representative of things that are important, meaningful, or familiar to members of a particular subculture. Let us say you wish to compare senior citizens to young adults on a memory task, and so you construct a word list, present it to both groups, and then ask them to recall as many items as they can. If the young adults recall more items than the senior citizens, can you safely assume that decrease in memory performance is a function of age? No, you could not, not even if the participants had been matched on all important variables such as education level, vocabulary, and intelligence. You could not attribute poor performance to aging because you could not assume that the words on the list were equally familiar and meaningful to both generations. As noted earlier, Barrett (1978) manipulated the generational appropriateness of the materials by constructing two different lists: an "old" list, comprised of words such as "fedora" and "poultice," and a "young" list made up of words such as "disco" and "afro." When the "old" list was presented, older participants showed higher recall than younger participants, whereas when younger participants were shown the "young" list, they remembered more than the older participants. In other words, each generation remembered more generationally appropriate than inappropriate material. Given these findings, it the same principle would likely operate not only when comparing older and younger participants, but also when comparing men and women, African-Americans and European-Americans, participants with high and low socioeconomic status (SES), and urban and rural dwellers.

Intelligence, IQ, and Testing

Since scores obtained on intelligence tests are frequently used to make comparisons between groups, or as the basis for matching groups in comparative research, a brief discussion of this topic is important. Let us, for a moment, suspend the controversy regarding intelligence, intelligence testing, and the meaning of the IQ score, and assume that intelligence tests are a valid measure of intelligence. Even if we make this assumption regarding validity, quite a few important factors must still be taken into consideration before reaching a conclusion regarding the performance of one group in comparison to another. Performing well on an intelligence test is not just a function of being intelligent. Motivation to do well, low levels of anxiety at the time of testing, socioeconomic status, and even the experience of working within time limits contribute to optimum performance. For example, studies show that highly anxious individuals do not perform as well as those lower in anxiety (Hubble & Groff, 1982), nor do individuals who are not motivated to do well (Sewell, Farley, Manni & Hunt, 1982). Even the social class in which one is raised contributes to performance. Roberts and DeBlossie (1983) found that, in general, people from low SES families, and members of minority groups who are also from lower SES families, tend to be handicapped by their experiences with language, symbols, and concepts when taking a test constructed according to White, middle-class standards. In addition, individuals raised in rural environments, such as many Native Americans, do not perform as well on tests with a constraining time limit since, typically, they are not used to having to complete tasks within a strict time frame. When given unlimited time to complete the test, their scores improve dramatically.

Although these factors are only a few of the many outside variables that contribute to scores on intelligence tests, we can see how easy it would be to reach a hasty, and most likely erroneous, conclusion on the basis of performance that a particular group is not as intelligent as another group. Triandis (1994) gives an excellent description of all the factors to be considered when comparing the performance of two distinct cultural groups. Although he speaks of intelligence tests in particular, the points he raises could be applied to all tests, materials, and tasks used in comparative research. Possible alternative explanations for differences in performance between two hypothetical groups are as follows.

Definition of concept: The definition of *intelligence* may not be the same for both groups. The characteristics that a culture considers important and valuable aspects of intelligence are not universal but culture-specific. Therefore, applying the same definition and measuring instrument to both groups may be inappropriate.

Instructions: One culture may be more familiar with the format, aim, or technique of the testing situation, as well as with the responses the investigator considers appropriate. Therefore, the instructions for the test (or task) may not be understood the same way by both groups. The culture more familiar with the test or situation has the advantage.

Motivation: Different cultures are motivated by different tasks; what is interesting and motivating in one culture may be in another culture puzzling at best and pointless at worst.

Experimenter effects: Cultural norms regarding interaction with "authority figures," "distinguished visitors," or "suspicious outsiders" may influence people's responses. An experimenter may be viewed with suspicion, hostility, friendship, or neutrality, and the participants' cooperation and performance may be affected by their reaction to the experimenter. If one group views the experimenter with suspicion while the other group views him or her with neutrality, the performance of the groups might differ due to their differential attitude rather than their differential ability.

Meaning of test: How a particular group interprets the test and its purpose may also affect their performance. People's responses may vary depending on whether the test is used solely for research purposes or for sharing with family members. The concept of confidentiality in test situations is not universally understood; therefore, responding may be influenced by misunderstandings regarding the ultimate use or aim of the test.

Anxiety: Anxiety is present in all cultures, but levels of nervousness, test anxiety, and the need to perform well may vary among cultures.

Response set: Once more, cultural norms may dictate that participants answer in a polite way, a defensive way, a hostile way, or a cooperative way. For example, in order to be polite and helpful, people may answer the way they think the researcher wants them to answer. This is an example of social desirability.

Sample Equivalence: This aspect is covered in detail in the present book, but Triandis also points to the importance of having two comparable groups in terms of age, gender, education, environment, and so on, before any meaningful interpretation of performance is possible.

Ethics: Certain topics and questions may be taboo to some cultures or, at the very least, offensive. Questions that may be part of ordinary social interaction in one culture may be offensive or rude in another. Also, the way the experimenter interacts with members of a given culture may be considered too personal or objectionable by that culture.

Drawing Conclusions and Generalizing

Any comparative research always bears the risk of making sweeping generalizations based on inconclusive findings. This problem becomes especially troubling if a group's poor performance on some task leads the investigator to conclude that the group tested lacks the skills or processes necessary for successful completion of that task. In other words, rather than stating that the group did not *demonstrate* those skills or processes in *that* particular situation, the researcher draws the conclusion that there is a complete absence of those skills or processes.

Cole and Means (1981) caution that poorer performance by a particular group should not be interpreted as the result of some sort of "deficiency." According to Cole and Means, the poorer performance of a specific group of people is often taken as support for what has been referred to as the **deficiency hypothesis** (Scribner & Cole, 1972). In other words, the poorer performance is interpreted to mean that the members of the group are deficient in some specific ability or skill. However, remember that the specific goals and aims of cultures and subcultures vary, as do experiences and familiarity with materials and tasks. Therefore, when interpreting the performance of a special group under study, it would benefit the researcher to go beyond the deficiency interpretation and to look for alternative explanations such as perhaps the group does not utilize that skill or ability in *this* task, under *these* circumstances.

In the free-recall study conducted with the Kpelle people, if Cole et al. had not thought of incorporating the words into stories, they might have reached the erroneous conclusion that the memory processes of the Kpelle were not only different from, but actually *worse* than, those of their Western counterparts. The effects of culture on memory have been investigated by several researchers, (D'Azevedo, 1982; Mistry & Rogoff, 1994). Mistry and Rogoff point out that learning and remembering take place within a specific context, and therefore these processes are affected by the values and customs of a particular culture. For example, Western cultures tend to prize the ability to learn and recite long lists of words, remember minute details of various events, and memorize a large amount of historical facts. All these abilities are seen as indications of having a "good memory." However, these abilities are most likely the result of Western-style education, which tends to emphasize strategies such as rote learning and categorization. It is not surprising, therefore, that participants from Western cultures tend to perform well on memory tasks that tend to "tap into" such learning strategies. On the other hand, people from other cultures that do not emphasize such processes may not perform as well on Western-style memory tests. However, they may demonstrate equally impressive memory for material that is culturally relevant and meaningful, such as remembering a great deal of information about crops, the migratory pattern of animals, and the life cycle of plants and other food materials.

In a similar vein, let us consider the findings that American students do not perform as well in mathematics as Chinese and Japanese students (Stevenson, 1992, 1993; Stevenson, Chen, & Lee, 1993). American students' performance ranked third (Stevenson et al.). Since the investigators made certain that the measurements were taken at the same time during the school year, under identical testing conditions, and with equivalent materials, the poorer performance of Americans does not appear to be caused by factors that may have put these students at a disadvantage. Given that the assessment process was not biased toward American students, should you conclude that American students have an innate deficiency in mathematical ability? Perhaps not.

One possible explanation for the American students' underperformance points to cultural attitudes toward ability and effort. According to Stevenson et al., when the students who had participated and their mothers were questioned, the majority of the Americans attributed mathematical ability to innate intelligence, whereas the majority of the Chinese and Japanese believed that high scores on mathematical tests were the result of hard work and effort. In light of this cultural emphasis, it is possible that the American students, believing that hard work and effort would have little or no impact on their academic achievements, did not try as hard to learn and to succeed. In contrast, the Asian students, convinced that academic success is mostly the result of hard work and discipline, may have as a result made an extra effort when studying.

Hopefully, this chapter has helped you to see the various factors that need to be considered in comparative research before any meaningful comparisons or generalizations can be made. While pointing out the difficulties and possible "pitfalls" of cross-cultural research, the intention was not to discourage such research but to encourage responsible and thoughtful research. Human diversity is one of the most exciting, interesting, challenging, and important topics there is for scientists to investigate, and by understanding how we, as human beings from different cultures and subcultures, differ as well as how we are alike, we advance psychology as a science of behavior and mental processes. Since culture influences both behavior and mental processes, in order to broaden our understanding and to go beyond the confines of any one particular culture, it is a factor that must be studied extensively. However, the approach we take must be based on sound methodology and take into account all the possible factors that could lead us to make the wrong inference or reach the wrong conclusion.

SUMMARY

- Comparative research with human participants requires studying the similarities and differences in behavior and mental processes between cultures and subcultures.
- In studying human diversity, the researcher must consider methodological issues unique to comparative research.
- Equivalence of groups is crucial if the researcher is to make valid and meaningful comparisons.
- Equivalence may be attempted by matching participants on important variables. However, this does not guarantee that all important variables have been considered and controlled for.
- Equivalence of material and task means that both comparison groups are equally familiar with, and attach the same value and meaning to, the stimuli and procedures.
- Since people from different cultures and subcultures have different experiences and, in turn, may interpret those experiences differently, the value and meaning they attach to those experiences may also differ.
- The issue of language is especially important when conducting research across cultures, and the materials and instructions have to be translated. In order to ensure that the translation conveys the same meaning and/or information, researchers frequently use the technique of back-translation and the etic-emic approach.
- Cultural salience is an important consideration. It refers to the degree to which words, materials, or tasks are highly familiar to, and valued by, a culture or subculture.
- When drawing conclusions based on the differential performance of groups, it is important to go beyond the deficiency hypothesis and to look for alternative explanations.

KEY CONCEPTS

Back-Translation	Cultural Salience	Emics	Stereotype
Connotative Meaning	Deficiency Hypothesis	Etics	Vulnerability

QUESTIONS

Short answers can be found in Appendix A.

1. A researcher translated a list of English words into Chinese, and then had another person translate the Chinese list back into English. After several trials, the words from the last translation that did not match the original English list were discarded. The technique used is called _____

2. In order to compare male and female participants, a researcher constructed a list comprised of words frequently used by, and therefore familiar to, both sexes. This approach represents

   a. etics

   b. emics

   c. cultural salience

   d. connotative meaning

3. A study found that, while words such as "freedom," "love," and "respect" were used in both cultures investigated, the words elicited different imagery and emotions from the participants in the two different groups. This is due to difference in the _____ of words.

4. Prior to taking a difficult mathematics test, a group of White male participants were told the following: "Research shows that Asian participants do significantly better on this test than Whites, but we would like you to try and do your best." Another group of White males were simply told to do their best. The first group did significantly worse than Asian participants, while the second group did equally well. The poorer performance of the first group was most likely due to:

   a. the deficiency hypothesis

   b. stereotype vulnerability

   c. lack of cultural salience

   d. unequivalence of materials

5. Briefly explain when it would be more desirable to obtain groups that are equivalent than groups that are representative of the population from which they were drawn.

6. Briefly explain how you would go about obtaining samples of children for a study that compares the verbal skills of South and North Americans.

SHORT ANSWERS TO END-OF-CHAPTER QUESTIONS

Chapter 1

2. a. method of authority   b. experimental method   c. common sense
   d. Rationalism   e. common sense
3. a. experimental   b. nonexperimental   c. nonexperimental   d. experimental
   e. nonexperimental
4. a. Population: All fifth graders in New York State. Sample: The 50 fifth graders
   b. Population: All college freshmen. Sample: The 120 college freshmen
   c. Population: All dentists in Detroit. Sample: The 120 dentists surveyed.
5. Scientific observation is empirical, public, and repeatable.

Chapter 2

1. a. constant   b. variable   c. variable   d. variable   e. variable   f. variable
   g. constant

2. **Independent variable**   **Dependent variable**
   a. weather   participants' mood
   b. print size   memory for words
   c. software   statistics grade
   d. training   errors
   e. race (subject variable)   product preference
   f. absence   fondness
   g. verbal feedback   performance
   h. gender (subject variable)   reaction time

4. **Experimental group**   **Control group**
   a. group 1   group 2
   b. group 2   group 1
   c. group 1   group 2
   d. group 1   group 2
   e. group 2   group 1

    6. b. (packaging info is confounded with box color)

    7. a. stress   b. being interrupted   c. stress and no stress (interruptions and no interruptions)   d. number of errors made

Chapter 3

    1. a. external   b. external   c. internal   d. internal   e. external   f. internal

    2. a, b, c, and d

    4. Use placebo and a double-blind study.

    6. a. random assignment of participants; same words were shown to both groups; presentation rate was held constant; time allowed for recall and recognition was held constant

       b. computerized presentation, timing, and response recording

    7. a. available   b. available   c. random   d. stratified random   e. available f. available

Chapter 4

    5. c. (allowed only if justified by educational/scientific/applied value)

    6. b. (used mostly in social psychological research)

    7. d. (all of the above)

    8. b, c, d, and f

Chapter 5

    1. face validity

    2. reliability

    3. predictive validity

    4. construct validity

    5. a. nominal   b. ordinal   c. ratio   d. interval   e. ratio   f. nominal

    6. a. behavioral   b. self-report   c. physiological   d. physiological   e. self-report

Chapter 6

    4. measures of central tendency and measures of variability

    5. d. (all of the above)

    6. d. (standard deviation)

    7. c. (78)

    8. c. (typical participant varied from the mean by 12 points)

    9. a. quantitative   b. quantitative   c. quantitative   d. qualitative e. quantitative   f. qualitative   g. quantitative

   10. a. line   b. bar   c. bar   d. line   e. line   f. line

Chapter 7

    1. c. (low)

    2. b. (Type I error)

3. d. (all of the above)

4. b. (H_1 was not supported)

5. d. (the independent variable had an effect)

6. a. (1 in 100)

7. c. (hypothesis testing)

8. b. (0.05)

9. a. No significant difference between the cooperation scores of Group I and II.

b. Group I will have significantly higher cooperation scores than Group II.

c. The null hypothesis was rejected. Group I had significantly higher cooperation scores than Group II.

d. Type I. A true null hypothesis may be rejected.

e. 0.05

f. Apparently, it did have enough power because a significant difference was found.

Chapter 8

1. c. (dependent samples t test)

2. c. (one-way ANOVA)

3. b. (independent samples t test)

4. b. (there are two separate groups of participants who are unrelated)

5. a. (primary variance/error variance)

6. b. (one-group chi-square)

7. b. (two-group chi-square)

Chapter 9

1. b. (multilevel)

2. d. (a or b)

3. c. (between-subjects, multilevel)

4. c. (study must be a between-subjects design)

5. a. (a single factor on several levels)

6. c. (between-subjects design)

7. d. (both a and c are correct)

8. b. (within-subjects design)

9. d. (either a or b would be fine)

10. a. (twelve)

11. a. (mixed factorial)

12. c. (task type; practice, respectively)

13. c. (the cherry being the best yogurt)

Chapter 11

7. a. randomized-blocks design

b. verbal training program

c. training and no training

d. speaking in sentences

e. preexisting verbal skills and speaking in sentences

Chapter 12

1. c. (12)
2. d. (all of the above)
3. c. (task type; practice, respectively)
4. d. (mixed factorial)
5. a. between-subjects
   b. 2×2
   d. Yes. Significantly more words were recalled in the high-imagery condition.
   e. Yes. Significantly more high-frequency words were recalled.
   f. There was no interaction.
   g. 3×2
6. b. (pretest sensitization)
7. c. (practice effects)
8. b. (groups 1 and 2)

Chapter 13

1. b. (ethically superior)
2. a. (rule out alternative explanations for the change in behavior)
3. a. (change during the treatment phase cannot be attributed to treatment alone)
4. d. (a participant may be studied in greater detail)

Chapter 14

1. a. (there is a fairly strong relationship)
2. d. (all of the above can be concluded)
3. c. (a high correlation can establish causality)
4. a. cross-lagged panel design
   b.
   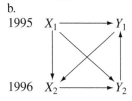
   c. $X_1 Y_2$ and $Y_1 X_2$
   d. $X_1 Y_2$. Interests in common came first (1995) in time.
   e. $Y_1 X_2$. Stability in marriage came first (1995) in time.
5. a. negative
   b. positive
   c. positive
   d. positive
   e. negative

Chapter 15

4. $6/10 \times 100 = 0.6 \times 100 = 60\%$
6. Use a longitudinal study. Since the participants are their own control/comparison, individual differences and generational effects are controlled.

Chapter 17

5. discussion section
6. method section

Chapter 18

1. back-translation
2. a. (etics)
3. connotative meaning
4. b. (stereotype vulnerability)

COMPUTATION OF SELECTED STATISTICAL TESTS

INDEPENDENT SAMPLES *T* TEST

Recall from Chapter 8 that the computational formula for the independent samples *t* test is

$$t = \frac{\bar{X} - \bar{Y}}{\sqrt{\dfrac{\Sigma\left(X - \bar{X}\right)^2 + \Sigma\left(Y - \bar{Y}\right)^2}{N(N-1)}}}$$

where $\bar{X}$ is the mean of Group I, $\bar{Y}$ is the mean of Group II, and $\bar{X} - \bar{Y}$ represents the difference between the two means. Notice that the formula also requires you to calculate the sum of squared deviations for each group.

Let us say that an investigator was interested in seeing whether men would make significantly fewer errors on a spatial task than women. The following data represent the number of errors made in each group.

Group I: Women *(X)*   **Group II: Men *(Y)***

X	$(X - \bar{X})$	$(X - \bar{X})^2$	Y	$(Y - \bar{Y})$	$(Y - \bar{Y})^2$
50	5	25	52	13	169
49	4	16	49	10	100
51	6	36	41	2	4
31	−14	196	42	3	9
47	2	4	37	−2	4
51	6	36	36	−3	9
28	−17	289	21	−18	324
41	−4	16	31	−8	64
54	9	81	38	−1	1
$\Sigma X = 402$		$\Sigma = 699$	$\Sigma Y = 347$	$\Sigma = 684$	
$\bar{X} = 45$			$\bar{Y} = 39$		
(44.67)			(38.56)		
$N = 9$			$N = 9$		

At this point, you have all the information to calculate t:

$$t = \frac{\overline{X} - \overline{Y}}{\sqrt{\dfrac{\sum(X - \overline{X})^2 + \sum(Y - \overline{Y})^2}{N(N-1)}}}$$

$$t = \frac{45 - 39}{\sqrt{\dfrac{699 + 684}{9(8)}}}$$

$$t = \frac{6}{\sqrt{\dfrac{1383}{72}}}$$

$$t = \frac{6}{\sqrt{19.2}}$$

$$t = \frac{6}{4.4}$$

$$t = 1.36$$

In order to determine whether the difference between the means is significant, you will need to consult a critical values table. If the obtained value for t is equal to or greater than the critical value stated in the table, then the difference between the two means is significant. In this instance, the critical value listed in the table under $p = .05$ is 1.746. Since the obtained value (1.36) is smaller than the critical value (1.746), the difference between the errors made by men and women is not significant.

DEPENDENT SAMPLES T TEST

Suppose that a researcher tested participants who were either matched on some attribute prior to random assignment or participated in both conditions. If that were the case, the two samples would be related. In other words, the pairs of scores would be correlated, and the appropriate statistical test would be the dependent samples t test.

The computational formula for the dependent samples t test is

$$t = \frac{\overline{X}D}{\sqrt{\left[\dfrac{N\left(\sum D^2\right) - \left(\sum D\right)^2}{N}\right]\left[\dfrac{1}{N(N-1)}\right]}},$$

where $\overline{X}D$ is the mean of difference scores. Notice that in one instance, the difference scores are first squared and then added, as indicated by: $(\sum D^2)$; in the other instance, the difference scores are first added and then squared, as indicated by: $(\sum D)^2$.

For example, let us say that children were first measured for aggression, and then they watched a violent television show. Following the show, the number of aggressive acts was again counted. Did the television show significantly increase the number of aggressive acts? The following data represent the number of aggressive acts before *(X)* and after *(Y)* viewing the violent television show.

Before X	After Y	Difference X–Y = D	D2
5	7	−2	4
3	3	0	0
7	9	−2	4
5	7	−2	4
6	8	−2	4
4	6	−2	4
8	10	−2	4
5	9	−4	16
6	8	−2	4
1	3	−2	4
$\Sigma X = 50$ $\bar{X} = 5$	$\Sigma Y = 70$ $\bar{Y} = 7$	$\Sigma D = -20$ $\bar{X}D = -2$	$\Sigma D^2 = 48$

Before X	After Y	Difference *(D)* X − Y = D	D2

Given the information above:

$\bar{X}D = -2$
$\Sigma D^2 = 48$
$(\Sigma D)^2 = (-20)^2 = 400$
$N = 10$

You are now ready to plug in the appropriate values in order to calculate *t*.

$$t = \frac{XD}{\sqrt{\left[\frac{N(\Sigma D^2) - (\Sigma D)^2}{N}\right]\left[\frac{1}{N(N-1)}\right]}}$$

$$t = \frac{-2}{\sqrt{\left[\frac{10(48) - 400}{10}\right]\left[\frac{1}{10(10-1)}\right]}}$$

$$t = \frac{-2}{\sqrt{\left[\frac{480 - 400}{10}\right]\left[\frac{1}{90}\right]}}$$

$$t = \frac{-2}{\sqrt{\left[\dfrac{480-400}{10}\right]\left[\dfrac{1}{90}\right]}}$$

$$t = \frac{-2}{\sqrt{\left[\dfrac{80}{10}\right]\left[\dfrac{1}{90}\right]}}$$

$$t = \frac{-2}{\sqrt{[8][0.01]}}$$

$$t = \frac{-2}{\sqrt{0.08}}$$

$$t = \frac{-2}{.283}$$

$$t = 7.067$$

Again, in order to see whether there was a significant increase in aggression after viewing a violent television show, the obtained t value is compared to the critical value in the table. Under $p = .05$, the critical value in the table is 1.833. Since the obtained t value (7.067) is greater than the critical value (1.833) listed in the table, the difference between the before and after scores is significant.

ONE-WAY ANALYSIS OF VARIANCE

When the independent variable has three or more levels, the appropriate statistical analysis is the one-way analysis of variance. Recall from Chapter 8 that the formula for calculating the F statistic is

$$F = \frac{MS_{between}}{MS_{within}}$$

where MS stands for mean squares. $MS_{between}$ (MS_b) represents variance between the conditions (variance due to treatment), and MS_{within} (MS_w) represents variance within a condition (error variance). The variance due to treatment (MS_b) is in turn derived by dividing the sum of squared deviations for between-conditions (SS_b) by the between-conditions degrees of freedom, or

$$MS_b = \frac{SS_b}{df_b}$$

Similarly, the MS_w, or error variance is calculated by dividing the sum of squared deviations for within-conditions (SS_w) by the within-conditions degree of freedom, or

$$MS_w = \frac{SS_w}{df_w}$$

Therefore, in order to calculate a one-way ANOVA by hand, what you need are the numerical values for the following: SS_t (total); SS_w; SS_b; df_t (total); df_b; and df_w.

Let us say that an experimenter wished to see whether there was a significant difference in the number of errors made on three different types of mazes: a finger maze (maze 1), an electronic stylus maze (maze 2), and a pencil maze (maze 3). The following data represent the number of errors made on each maze.

Maze 1 (Finger)			**Maze 2 (Stylus)**			**Maze 3 (Pencil)**		
X1	$(X-X)$	$(X-X)2$	X2	$(X-X)$	$(X-X)2$	X3	$(X-X)$	$(X-X)2$
3	3	9	8	0	0	7	–3	9
6	0	0	8	0	0	10	0	0
6	0	0	11	3	9	10	0	0
5	–1	1	6	–2	4	10	0	0
7	1	1	7	–1	1	10	0	0
9	3	9	8	0	0	13	3	9
36		20	48		14	60		18
X=6	SS1		X=8	SS2		X=10	SS3	

Based on the above, you now have the following information:

$$\Sigma X1 = 36 \qquad \Sigma X2 = 48 \qquad \Sigma X3 = 60$$
$$\bar{X}1 = 6 \qquad \bar{X}2 = 8 \qquad \bar{X}3 = 10$$
$$SS1 = 20 \qquad SS2 = 14 \qquad SS3 = 18$$
$$N = 6 \qquad N = 6 \qquad N = 6$$

Calculating SS_w

Add the three sums of squared deviations: $SS1 + SS2 + SS3 = 20 + 14 + 18 = 52$; $SS_w = $ **52**

Calculating SS_t

1. Square each of the 18 raw scores ($3^2 + 6^2 + 6^2 \dots + 13^2$), then add = 1252.
2. Next, add the sums of all the raw scores: $\Sigma X1 + \Sigma X2 + \Sigma X3 = 36 + 48 + 60 = 144$.
3. Square the result from step 2: $144^2 = 20{,}736$.
4. Divide the result from step 3 by N: $20{,}736/18 = 1152$.
5. Subtract the result of step 4 (1152) from the result of step 1 (1252): $1252 – 1152 = 100$; $SS_t = $ **100**.

Calculating SS_b

$$SS_b = SS_t – SS_w$$
$$SS_b = 100 – 52$$
$$SS_b = \mathbf{48}$$

Now the only thing left is to calculate the various degrees of freedom:

Total $df = N - 1$, or $18 - 1 = \mathbf{17}$
Between-conditions $df =$ Number of conditions $- 1$, or $3 - 1 = \mathbf{2}$
Within-conditions $df =$ total $df -$ between conditions df, or $17 - 2 = \mathbf{15}$

Recall that $MS_b = SS_b/df_b$ and $MS_w = SS_w/df_w$. Now simply plug in the values obtained:

$$MSb = \frac{48}{2} = 24$$

$$MS_w = \frac{52}{15} = 3.47$$

The final step is to calculate the F statistic:

$$F = \frac{MS_{between}}{MS_{within}}, F = \frac{24}{3.47} = 6.92$$
$$F = 6.92$$

As with the t statistic, you would need to compare the obtained value for F to the critical value listed in the table. If the obtained value is equal to or greater than the critical value listed, the differences between the means are significant.

MANN-WHITNEY *U* TEST

When the data are measured on an ordinal scale, the appropriate test of significance is the Mann-Whitney U test.

For example, let us say that a psychologist is interested in seeing whether there is a difference in social skills between transfer students and students who stayed in the same school. The following data represent the scores the students received on the social skills inventory, with higher scores representing higher level of skills and their rank based on test scores. An asterisk next to a student's name indicates transfer status.

Score	Student	Rank
25	Judith	1
23	Sam	2
21	Kenny	3
18	Shaq*	4
17	Mirza	5
15	Marilyn	6
14	Emilio	7
12	Elaine*	8

10	Holly*	9
9	Hope	10
8	Grant*	11
6	Bob*	12
5	Tony	13
3	Meredith*	14
2	Stu*	15

At this point, form two groups, with one representing the transfer students and the other representing nontransfer students. Include their rank order based on test scores.

Nontransfer	Rank	Transfer	Rank
Judith	1	Shaq	4
Sam	2	Elaine	8
Kenny	3	Holly	9
Mirza	5	Grant	11
Marilyn	6	Bob	12
Emilio	7	Meredith	14
Hope	10	Stu	15
Tony	13		
$N_1 = 8$	$\Sigma = 47$	$N_2 = 7$	$\Sigma = 73$
	$R_1 = 47$		$R_2 = 73$

Steps for calculating U_{obtained} (U_{obt}):

1. First you need to calculate U_1. Choose one group; it does not matter which one you choose. Let us say that you picked the nontransfer group. The formula for calculating U_1 is:

$$U_1 = N_1 N_2 + \frac{N_1(N_1 + 1)}{2} - R_1$$

$$U_1 = (8)(7) + \frac{8(8 + 1)}{2} - 47$$

$$U_1 = 56 + \frac{72}{2} - 47$$

$$U_1 = 56 + 37 = 92 - 47 = 45$$

$$U_1 = \mathbf{45}$$

2. Next, calculate U_2. The formula for calculating U_2 is:

$$U_2 = (N_1)(N_2) - U_1$$

$$U_2 = (8)(7) - 45$$

$$U_2 = 56 - 45$$

$$U_2 = \mathbf{11}$$

3. The one yielding the smaller value (U_1 or U_2) is the U_{obt}. Since U_2 (11) is smaller than U_1 (45), $U_{obt} = 11$.

4. Finally, you would consult the appropriate table for critical values of U. U_{obt} must be equal to or smaller in value than $U_{critical}$ (U_{crit}). In this instance, at $p = .05$, $U_{crit} = 13$. Since U_{obt} (11) is smaller than U_{crit} (13), there is a significant difference in social skills between transfer and nontransfer students.

GLOSSARY

A-B-A Design   A reversal design that entails a baseline measure, the treatment phase, and withdrawal of treatment, or reversal.

A-B-A-B Design   A reversal design in which treatment is reintroduced following the reversal. Its major advantages are that it can demonstrate treatment effects twice, and it does not leave the participant in an undesirable condition.

A-B Design   A weak single-subject design that entails a baseline phase and a treatment phase. Essentially, it is the single-subject version of the one-group before-after design.

Abstract   A single-paragraph summary of the entire research report.

Alpha Level   The probability of making a Type I error.

Alternative Hypothesis   The experimental hypothesis stated by the experimenter. It is the experimenter's prediction for the relationship between the independent and dependent variable.

Anthologies   A collection of articles compiled by an editor (or editors) on a related topic.

Applied Research   Type of research conducted in order to predict behavior in the real world (as opposed to the laboratory) or to solve real-life problems.

Artifacts   Behaviors that are the result of being in an experiment and may not reflect how the participant would act in the real world.

Available Sample   Also called a haphazard sample, or a convenience sample. This sample may consist of psychology students at colleges and universities who are required to participate for course credit, or it may depend on volunteers who are willing to participate in the study.

Back-translation   A procedure used in order to achieve equivalent translations of materials.

Bar Graph   Graphical presentation of the data when one of the variables is qualitative.

Baseline Phase   A phase in which repeated measures are taken on the behavior prior to introducing treatment. The purpose is to establish a stable rate for the target behavior.

Basic Research   Research that involves the testing of hypotheses generated by a particular theoretical framework. The purpose of basic research is to gather a body of "evidence" or knowledge that supports a given theoretical position.

Before-After Designs   A design that entails administering a pretest in which treatment, and a posttest (after measure) to a group of participants.

Before-After Static-Group Comparison   An independent two-group design in which the participant cannot be randomly assigned into conditions. A pretest measure is taken prior to the occurrence of an event of interest.

Before-After Two-Group Design   An independent (unrelated) design in which both groups of participants are given a pretest and a posttest, but only one group is exposed to the treatment.

Before-Match-After Design   A dependent (related) design in which the participants are given a pretest, so that the scores obtained on the pretest can be used to create two matched groups.

Beta   The probability of making a Type II error.

Between-Subjects Design   A type of experimental design in which each person only participates in one condition. In between-subjects designs, a different group of participants is needed for every condition.

Carryover Effects   Results that occur when a previous condition alters the way a participant responds in subsequent conditions. The effects of the first condition are said to be carried over to the subsequent conditions.

Case Study   An in-depth study of a person, group, or institution.

Ceiling Effect A range effect in which all the participants quickly reach their maximum level of performance due to the simplicity of the task.

Chi-Square A nonparametric procedure used when the data are on a nominal scale of measurement. The chi-square test compares observed frequencies and theoretical frequencies within discrete categories.

Closed-Ended Question A type of survey question in which the response options are restricted.

Component-Analysis Design A single-subject design that assesses the effects of two or more independent variables separately and in combination.

Confound A secondary variable that interacts with the independent variable, either enhancing or lessening its effect. Confounding makes it difficult to separate the effects of the independent variable from that of the confounding variable.

Connotative Meaning The feelings, images, and associations that words arouse.

Constants Events, objects, or situations that do not vary in quantity and/or quality.

Construct Validity The extent to which a measuring device produces results that are consistent with the construct being measured.

Content Validity The extent to which the items on a test or survey constitute a representative sample of all the possible items for a given category or area.

Control Group The group that is not exposed to the independent variable (treatment).

Correlation Coefficient A coefficient that can be used to describe the relationship between two variables. A commonly used coefficient is the Pearson *r*.

Correlational Studies A nonexperimental research method that entails observing the relationship between two or more events. The events occur naturally, meaning that the researcher does not manipulate one event in order to observe its effect on the other event. This method is frequently used when the variable of interest cannot be manipulated, or if it would be unethical to manipulate it.

Cost Evaluation A program evaluation phase that assesses whether the benefits of the program merit their cost.

Counter Balancing A procedure for controlling order and carryover effect.

Criterion-Related Validity Correlation of performance on a test with other measures used to assess the behavior or characteristic.

Cross-Lagged Panel Design A longitudinal correlation analysis that enables researchers to investigate the direction of causality.

Cross-Sectional Design A type of developmental study in which different age groups are compared at the same time.

Cultural Salience The degree to which words, objects, tests, or activities are highly familiar to, and/or valued by, a particular culture or subculture.

Curvilinear Function A function in which an increase in one variable leads to both an increase and a decrease in the other variable. The relationship will change directions at least once.

Data The empirical evidence gathered during a scientific study. Data are typically some measure of behavior, such as the number of words remembered during a memory experiment. The singular for data is datum.

Debriefing Informing the participants about the true nature of the study and revealing any deceptive practices that may have occurred during the experiment. Debriefing takes places after the experimental session has been completed.

Deception Deliberately misleading the participant in order to conceal the true nature of the study.

Deficiency Hypothesis A tendency to explain the poorer performance of a culture or subculture in terms of some lack or deficiency in skills or ability needed for optimal performance.

Degrees of Freedom A term used to refer to the number of scores in a set of scores that are free to vary, once the sum of the scores is known.

Demand Characteristics A type of experimenter effect in which cues given by the experimenter, deliberately or inadvertently, may bias the participants' behavior.

Dependent Samples *t* Test A two-sample inference test to see whether the means of the two samples are significantly different. It is used when the same participants participated in both conditions, or when the participants were matched on some attribute prior to random assignment.

Dependent Variable The dependent variable is the suspected "effect" in the relationship between two events. It is the behavior, or event, that the experimenter thinks will be affected, or changed in some way, by the manipulation of the independent variable.

Descriptive Statistics A branch of statistics that organizes, summarizes, and describes the data.

Determinism   An assumption of the scientific method that all events have causes or are determined by some previous event.

Discussion Section   The part of the research paper that discusses the findings stated in the results section. Included are whether the data support the hypothesis and how the findings are similar to, or different from, the results of others investigating this topic.

Double-Blind   An experimental procedure in which neither the participant nor the experimenter knows which condition the participants are in.

Effect Size   The magnitude of effect the independent variable has on the dependent variable.

Emics   Culture-specific concepts that do not generalize across cultures or subcultures in terms of importance or value. Emic concepts are shared by members of a particular culture or subculture.

Error Variance   Also called within-groups variance. Error variance affects the dependent variable measure in an inconsistent, unpredictable manner.

Etics   Universal concepts that do generalize across cultures or subcultures in terms of importance or value. Etic concepts are shared by all cultures and subcultures.

Experimental Group   The group of participants who are exposed to the treatment condition.

Experimental Studies   Also called true experiments in which one or more variables are manipulated and the effects of this manipulation on another variable (or variables) are observed. Control over outside factors is good; cause- and-effect relationships can be inferred or established.

Experimenter Effects   The behavior of the experimenter, or experimenter characteristics such as age, race, gender, or appearance that may affect or bias the behavior of the participants.

External Validity   The extent to which the observed relationship between the independent and dependent variables in the experiment can be generalized to other settings, other people, and other circumstances.

Face Validity   The extent to which the device appears to measure what it is supposed to measure from the participant's perspective.

Factorial Design   An experimental design in which there are two or more independent variables, with all possible combinations of every level of each independent variable.

Factorial Experiment   An experiment in which two or more independent variables are manipulated and every possible combination of the variables is represented.

Floor Effect   A range effect that occurs when the task is so difficult that no one can do well, regardless of the independent variable manipulations.

Frequency Distribution   A summary of the data that shows the number of cases or frequencies of responses that fall into specific categories.

Frequency Polygon   Graphical presentation of a frequency distribution using line graphs.

Histogram   Graphical presentation of a frequency distribution using a bar graph.

History   A source of secondary variance referring to the passing of time between experimental sessions. All events other than the independent variable are part of history and may affect the dependent variable.

Human Factors   An area of applied research. It is the application of knowledge regarding human abilities, such as memory, learning, perception, and attention, to the design of tools, machines, or manuals used by people in the real world.

Hypothesis   A tentative statement regarding the relationship between the variables of interest. Hypotheses are either supported or not supported by the data.

Hypothesis Testing   A statistical process that allows the experimenter to decide whether the results of the experiment support the experimental hypothesis.

Independent Samples *t* Test   A two-sample inference test to see whether the means of the two samples are significantly different. It is used when different people participated in each condition.

Independent Variable   A factor or event that the experimenter thinks will affect another factor or event. It is the variable that the experimenter manipulates; it is also called the treatment variable.

Individual Differences   Subject factors that serve as a major source of unwanted variance. Participants as individuals come with their own unique history, characteristics, traits, and abilities, and ways of seeing and analyzing information.

Inferential Statistics   A branch of statistics that enables researchers to interpret and generalize their findings.

Informed Consent   Requirement, according to the APA, that participation in research be voluntary, and participants must be informed about the purpose and nature of the study prior to giving their consent to participate.

Institutional Review Board   An institutionwide ethics committee that must review and approve all research proposals and ensure ethical research practices.

Interaction   In a factorial design, a condition that occurs when the levels of one independent variable have a differential effect on the dependent variable under different levels of another independent variable.

Internal Validity   The researcher's ability to state that the relationship she or he predicted between the independent and dependent variables does indeed exist and that this relationship is due to the effects of the independent variable and not to extraneous, uncontrolled variables.

Interrater Reliability   The degree to which two or more observers agree in their description or quantification of the behavior(s) under observation.

Interrupted Time-Series Design   A variation on the time-series design whereby data are gathered over an extended period of time, both before and after treatment is implemented.

Interval Scale   A level of measurement that has the mathematical properties of magnitude and equal interval spacing. However, there is no absolute zero point.

Introduction Section   A major element of the research project that introduces the topic, cites relevant research in the area, states the hypothesis, identifies the variables, and provides a brief description of the method.

Latin Square   A counterbalancing procedure used to control order and carryover effects.

Level of Significance   A probability level set by the experimenter for rejecting the null hypothesis when it is true. See also alpha level.

Line Graph   Graphically summarizes the findings of an experiment when both variables are quantitative.

Line of Best Fit   A line on the graph drawn as close as possible to all the data points.

Longitudinal Design   A type of developmental study in which the same group of individuals is followed over a period of time. Several measures are taken on the same group at different points in time.

Main Effect   The average effect of each independent variable in a factorial design.

Mann-Whitney *U* Test   A nonparametric procedure used when the data are on an ordinal scale to see whether there is significant difference between two independent groups.

Matched-by-Correlated-Criterion Design   A dependent groups design in which the participants are matched, one by one, on some factor or criterion that is correlated with the dependent variable prior to random assignment. The design requires that the experi-

menter have access to the criterion measure prior to beginning the matching procedure.

Matching   A procedure used for controlling individual differences. Prior to random assignment, the participants are matched on some attribute that is known to affect the dependent variable.

Maturation   A source of secondary variance that refers to how participants may change over time. Maturation is a potential problem with lengthy experiments or with studies that involve several sessions.

Mean   A measure of central tendency. The mean is the arithmetic average of the scores.

Measure of Central Tendency   The average, typical response or score in a distribution.

Median   A measure of central tendency. The median is the midpoint of a distribution.

Method of Authority   An approach to knowledge that relies on the word of experts or authorities on the topic of interest. Hypotheses generated from the statements of authorities must be testable through empirical research.

Method Section   Part of the research paper that describes, in separate subsections, the participants, materials and equipment, and step-by-step procedure.

Mixed Design   A type of factorial design in which the levels of one independent variable are between the subjects and the levels of another independent variable are within-subjects. Also called a split-plot design.

Mode   A measure of central tendency. The most frequent score in a distribution.

Multilevel Design   A single-factor experiment in which the independent variable has three or more levels.

Multiple Comparisons   Following ANOVA, tests that allow the researcher to determine which pairs of means were significantly different when there were more than two levels of an independent variable.

Multiple Factors ANOVA   A statistical procedure used with factorial design to see whether there are main effects and interactions.

Multiple-Baseline Design Across Behaviors   The same independent variable administered sequentially in order to treat at least two behaviors.

Multiple-Baseline Design Across Participants   The same independent variable administered sequentially to at least two participants.

Multiple-Baseline Design Across Settings   The same independent variable administered sequentially in at least two different settings.

Multiple-Baseline Designs   A variation on the A-B design, in which treatment is introduced sequentially across two or more participants, behaviors, or settings.

Multivariate Design   An experiment in which there are multiple dependent variables.

Naturalistic Observation   A nonexperimental method that involves the systematic observation of some event or behavior in its natural setting.

Need Evaluation   A phase of program evaluation where the actual need for a particular program is assessed.

Negative Correlation   A linear relationship in which an increase in one variable is associated with a decrease in the other variable, and vice versa.

Negative Linear Function   A type of relationship between the independent and dependent variables, in which an increase in the independent variable leads to an increase in the dependent variable. Similarly, a decrease in the independent variable leads to a decrease in the dependent variable.

Nominal Scale   The lowest level of measurement, typically used with variables that are qualitative rather than quantitative. Nominal scales do not possess any mathematical attributes; they have no magnitude, equal interval spacing, or an absolute zero. They merely label or define discrete categories to which the variables can be assigned.

Nonexperimental Designs   Research methods that do not involve experimental manipulation of variables. Control over outside factors is poor; cause- and-effect relationships cannot be inferred or established.

Nonparametric Tests   Procedure used when the data are measured on a nominal or an ordinal scale, or when the shape of the distribution is not important.

Nonparticipant Observation   A type of naturalistic observation study in which the researcher observes and records behaviors without participating in the group's activities.

Nonprobability Sampling   In nonprobability sampling, the unknown probability of a given member of the population being selected for participation because the sampling is based on convenience. Therefore, there is always a possibility that the sample is not truly representative of the population.

Nonrefereed Journals   Journals that publish articles on a first-come-first-served basis; the articles are printed in the order in which they are received. In addition, some nonrefereed journals charge a fee for publication.

Normal Distribution   A symmetrical distribution of scores, also known as the normal curve, or the bell curve. In a normal distribution, the mean, median, and the mode have the same numerical value.

Null Hypothesis   A statistical hypothesis that predicts that the independent variable has no effect.

One-Shot Case Study   Nonexperimental design that lacks a comparison or control condition.

One-Way ANOVA   Statistical procedure used with multilevel designs. Compares three or more means to see if the observed differences are significant.

Open-Ended Questions   Items on surveys that allow participants to record their responses without having to select from alternatives.

Operational Definitions   Definitions that give clear, precise definition to theoretical concepts and variables, including how they were measured.

Order and Pretest Effects   Sources of secondary variance that may occur when performance on a second test is affected by the first test regardless of the independent variable.

Ordinal Scale   A level of measurement that allows for the ranking or rank ordering of variables according to how much of the attribute that is being measured they may possess.

Outcome Evaluation   A program evaluation phase that assesses the program's overall effectiveness.

Parameter Estimation   An area of inferential statistics that involves estimating population characteristics from sample characteristics. The process of parameter estimation allows the experimenter to make statistical inferences about the value of a population parameter based on the sample.

Participant Observation   Naturalistic observation method in which the observer becomes a member of the group and participates in the group's activities.

Population   A set of all the events, people, objects, and so on, that the researcher is interested in studying—for example, all working women in the United States.

Positive Correlation   A linear relationship in which an increase in one variable is associated with an increase in the other variable, and vice versa.

Positive Linear Function   A type of relationship between the independent and dependent variables, in which an increase in the independent variable leads to a decrease in the dependent variable. Similarly, a decrease in the independent variable leads to an increase in the dependent variable.

Post-Hoc Tests   An unplanned multiple comparison test used when the researcher made no specific prediction regarding the various conditions.

Power   The ability of the experiment to detect real significant differences between conditions.

Practice Effect   In before-after design experiments, improved performance on a posttest as a result of having experienced the pretest.

Predictive Validity   Ability of a measuring device to predict a future event or behavior.

Pretest Sensitization   A source of secondary variance that occurs when a pretest alerts the subject to the hypothesis. If the treatment interacts with the pretest, the participants' responses may be altered.

Primary Sources   Sources that contain the actual research article, or original work, as written by the author(s).

Primary Variance   The observed differences in the dependent variable scores due to the manipulation of the independent variable; also called systematic variance, or between-groups variance.

Probability Sampling   The probability that a specific member of the population will be selected to participate in the study.

Process Evaluation   A program evaluation phase that monitors the program and ensures that the program is implemented as planned and that it is reaching its intended clients.

Program Evaluation   An area of applied research that requires assessing the need for a particular program, monitoring the program, evaluating the outcome of the program, and assessing the effectiveness of the program in terms of cost and benefit.

Psychological Abstracts   Concise summaries of journal articles published by the American Psychological Association (APA). There is a hardbound as well as an electronic version.

PsycLit: A computerized database that searches for abstracts, journal articles, and book chapters.

Qualitative Variables   Discontinuous variables in that there can be no possible values between adjacent units on the scale.

Quantitative Variables   Variables that are also said to be continuous when, theoretically, they can have an infinite number of values between adjacent units on a scale.

Quota Sampling   Sampling that is similar to stratified sampling, except that the members of the subgroups of interest are not randomly selected from the various strata.

Random Assignment   Theoretically, a technique that equates the groups prior to introducing the independent variable. By definition, random assignment means that every member of the sample has an equal chance of ending up in any of the conditions.

Random Sampling   Sampling in which every member of the population has an equal chance of being selected for participation.

Randomized-Blocks Design   An independent groups design in which the participants are first blocked on some variable prior to random assignment.

Range   A measure of variability derived by subtracting the lowest score from the highest score.

Ratio Scale   The highest level of measurement. The ratio scale has the same mathematical properties as the interval scale, but there is an absolute zero point.

Rationalism   An approach to knowledge whose roots are in philosophy. It states that truths can be arrived at through reasoning and logic alone. Empirical support is not necessary, for truths derived from reason and logic are said to be self-evident.

Reactive Effects   A source of secondary variance that may occur when the participants alter their behavior due to being observed or measured.

Refereed Journals   Scientific publications that submit a manuscript to rigorous evaluation prior to acceptance for publication.

Reference Section   An alphabetical listing by first author of all works cited in the research paper.

Reliability   The ability of the measuring device to yield similar results when repeated measures are taken under identical testing conditions.

Repeated Measures Design   See within-subjects design.

Representative Sample   Sample of participants who were selected in an unbiased manner and who are representative of population characteristics.

Response Set   A pattern of responding on self-report surveys that is not related to the content or the items on the survey.

Results Section   The part of the research paper that contains descriptive and inferential statistical procedures and findings.

Reversal   A control procedure in single-subject designs where the treatment phase is followed by the withdrawal of the independent variable. The target behavior is then assessed in order to measure the effect of the loss of treatment.

Sample A subset of the population that the researcher is interested in studying. The participants selected for a research project are the sample.

Scientific Method An approach to knowledge used by all scientists in which hypotheses are tested through empirical research.

Scientific Observation The systematic observation of an event or behavior of interest and the collection of data that will be analyzed at the end of the study.

Secondary Sources Summaries of the original work, typically written by someone other than the author of the original.

Secondary Variance Variance caused by extraneous, outside factors that were not recognized and/or controlled for by the experimenter. These extraneous variables have a consistent effect on the dependent variable.

Self-Fulfilling Prophecy A phenomenon whereby the experimenters expectation that certain events or behaviors will occur may subtly influence the participants to fulfill these expectations

Single-Blind An experimental technique used to eliminate subject expectancies. In a single-blind experiment, the participants do not know to which treatment condition they were assigned.

Skewed Distribution An asymmetrical distribution. If the "tail" of the distribution is pointing toward the higher scores, it is positively skewed. If it points toward the lower scores, it is negatively skewed.

Solomon Four-Group Design A factorial experiment that allows researchers to assess the effect of the independent variable alone, the effect of the pretest alone, and the potential interaction between the pretest and the independent variable.

Split-Plot Design See mixed design.

Standard Deviation A measure of variability that shows how much a typical response varied from the mean. It is the square root of variance.

Static-Group Comparison Design A research design where the participants are selected, rather than randomly assigned. The purpose of the study is to compare two or more groups of participants after the uncontrolled occurrence of an event (treatment).

Stereotype Vulnerability A hypothesis proposed by Steele stating that negative stereotypes about one's group could lead to self-fulfilling prophecy and confirmation of the stereotype.

Stratified Sampling Sampling technique that ensures that the sample matches the population on certain characteristics such as gender, race, ethnicity, religion, or any other factor that is known about the population.

Subject Mortality The loss of participants in longitudinal studies.

Subject Variables Individual characteristics such as age, gender, race, ethnic background, motivation, intelligence, and personality. These variables are by definition nonexperimental in that the researcher selects for these characteristics rather than manipulates them.

Theory An organized body of knowledge that generates hypotheses and explains behaviors within a specific framework. Theories are said to be dynamic, in that they are continually tested, refined, and revised in light of new experimental evidence.

Time-Series Design A research design that entails making multiple observations before treatment and comparing them to observations made during or after treatment.

Treatment Phase An element of the single-subject design and the period during which the independent variable is introduced.

Type I Error Incorrect ejection of the null hypothesis when it is true.

Type II Error Incorrect acceptance of the null hypothesis when it is not true.

Validity The extent to which a measuring device measures what it is designed to measure.

Variables Any condition, situation, object, event, or characteristic that may change in quantity and/or quality.

Variance A measure of variability that is the average of the sum of the squared deviations from the mean.

Within-Subjects Design An experimental design in which every person participates in every condition. Also called a repeated measure design since repeated measures are taken on the same participant.

REFERENCES

ADAIR, J. G. (1973). *The human subject: The social psychology of the psychological experiment.* Boston: Little, Brown.

ADLER, L. L., & GIELEN, U. P. (Eds.). (1994). *Cross-cultural topics in psychology.* Westport, CT: Praeger.

American Psychological Association. (1992). Ethical principles of psychologists and code of conduct. *American Psychologist, 47,* 1597–1611.

American Psychological Association. (2001). *Publication manual of the American Psychological Association* (5th ed.). Washington, DC: Author.

ANDERSON, C. A., LINDSAY, J. J., & BUSHMAN, B. J. (1999). Research in the psychological laboratory: Truth or triviality? *Current Directions in Psychological Science, 8,* 3–9.

AZAR, B. (1999). Destructive lab attack sends a wake-up call. *Monitor, 30,* 16.

BARNETT, M. A., BARTEL, J. S., BURNS, S. R., SANBORN, F. W., CHRISTENSEN, N. E., & WHITE, M. M. (2000). Perception of children who lie: Influence of lie motive and benefit. *Journal of Genetic Psychology, 161,* 381–383.

BARRETT, T. R. (1978). *Aging and memory: Declines or differences?* Paper presented to the Psychonomic Society, San Antonio, Texas.

BARRETT, T. R., & WATKINS, S. K. (1980). *There are age-related declines in recall following semantic processing: True or false?* Paper presented to the Psychonomic Society, St. Louis, Missouri.

BARTLETT, F. C. (1932). *Remembering: A study in experimental and social psychology.* Cambridge, England: Cambridge University Press.

BERRY, J. W. (1971). Muller-Lyer susceptibility: culture, economy, or race? *International Journal of Psychology, 6,* 193–197.

BERSCHEID, E., BARON, R. S., DERMER, M., & LIBMAN, M. (1973). Anticipating informed consent: An empirical approach. *American Psychologist, 28,* 913–925.

BLAXTON, T. A. (1989). Investigating dissociations among memory measures: Support for a transfer appropriate processing framework. *Journal of Experimental Psychology: Learning, Memory, and Cognition, 15,* 657–668.

BRAUN, A. R., & HERSOVITCH, P. (1998). Dissociated pattern of activity in visual corties and their projections during human rapid eye movement sleep. *Science, 279,* 91–95.

BREUER, J., & FREUD, S. (1895). *Studies on hysteria.* In Standard edition (vol. 2.). London: Hogarth Press.

BRIDGMAN, P. W. (1927). *The logic of modern physics.* New York: Macmillan.

BRISLIN, R. (1976). Comparative research methodology: Cross-cultural studies. *International Journal of Psychology, 11,* 215–229.

CAMPBELL, D. T. (1969). Prospective: Artifact and control. In R. Rosenthal and R. L. Rosnow (Eds.), *Artifact in behavioral research* (pp. 351–382). New York: Academic Press.

CAPRARA, G. V., BARBARANELLI, C., PASTORELLI, C., BANDURA, A., & ZIMBARDO, P. G. (2000). Prosocial foundations of children's academic achievement. *Psychological Science, 11,* 302–306.

CARPENTER, S. (1999). Freud's dream theory gets boost from imaging work. *Monitor, 30,* 19.

CHALLIS, B. H., & BRODBECK, D. R. (1992). Level of processing affects priming in word fragment completion. *Journal of Experimental Psychology: Learning, Memory, and Cognition, 18,* 595–607.

CHRISTENSEN, L. (1988). Deception in psychological research: When is its use justified? *Personality and Social Psychology Bulletin, 14,* 644–675.

COFER, C. N. (1971). Conditions for the use of verbal associations. *Psychological Bulletin, 68,* 1–12.

323

COHEN, L. D. (1991). Sex differences in the course of personality development: A meta-analysis. *Psychological Bulletin, 109,* 252–266.

COLE, M., GAY, J., & GLICK, J. (1968). A cross-cultural investigation of information processing. *International Journal of Psychology, 3,* 93–102.

COLE, M., & MEANS, B. (1981). *Comparative studies of how people think.* Cambridge, MA: Harvard University Press.

CONANT, J. B. (1951). *On understanding science: An historical approach.* New Haven, CT: Yale University Press.

CONGER, J. J., & PETERSEN, A. C. (1991). *Adolescence and youth* (4th ed.). New York: HarperCollins.

COZBY, P. C. (1997). *Methods in behavioral research.* (6th ed., p. 92). Mayfield Publishing Company.

CRAIK, F. I. M., & LOCKHART, R. S. (1972). Levels of processing: A framework for memory research. *Journal of Verbal Learning and Verbal Behavior, 11,* 671–684.

CRAIK, F. I. M., MOSCOVITCH, M., & MCDOWD, J. M. (1994). Contributions of surface and conceptual information to performance on implicit and explicit memory. *Journal of Experimental Psychology: Learning, Memory, and Cognition, 20,* 864–875.

CURTISS, S. R. (1977). *Genie: A psycholinguistic study of a modern-day "wild child."* New York: Academic Press.

DARLEY, J. M., & LATANE, B. (1968). Bystander intervention in emergencies: Diffusion of responsibility. *Journal of Personality and Social Psychology, 8,* 377–383.

D'AZEVEDO, W. A. (1982). Tribal history in Liberia. In U. Neisser (Ed.), *Memory observed: Remembering in natural contexts,* 258–268. San Francisco: Freeman.

DENMARK, F., RUSSO, N. P., FRIEZE, I. H., & SECHZER, J. A. (1988). Guidelines for avoiding sexism in psychological research: A report of the Ad Hoc Committee of Nonsexist Research. *American Psychologist, 43,* 582–585.

DENNIS, W. (1960). Causes of retardation among institutional children: Iran. *The Journal of Genetic Psychology, 96,* 47–59.

DUTTON, D. G., & ARON, A. P. (1974). Some evidence for heightened sexual attraction under conditions of high anxiety. *Journal of Personality and Social Psychology, 30,* 510–517.

EBBINGHAUS, H. (1964). *Memory: A contribution to experimental psychology* (H. A. Ruger and C. E. Bussenius, Trans.). New York: Dover. (Original work published 1885.)

EPLEY, N., & HUFF, C. (1998). Suspicion, affective response, and educational benefit as a result of deception in psychological research. *Personality and Social Psychology Bulletin, 24,* 759–768.

FORGAS, J. P., & BOWER, G. H. (1987). Mood effects on person-perception judgments. *Journal of Personality and Social Psychology, 53,* 53–60.

FRANKIE, C. (2000). Bit by bit, digital divide narrowing. *Newsday,* Tuesday, August 22.

GAMSON, W. A., FIREMAN, B., & RYTINA, S. (1982). *Encounters with unjust authority.* Homewood, IL: Dorsey Press.

GILLIGAN, C. (1982). *In a different voice: Psychological theory and women's development.* Cambridge, MA: Harvard University Press.

GOLDIN-MEADOW, S., & SALTZMAN, J. (2000). The cultural bounds of maternal accommodation: How Chinese and American mothers communicate with their deaf and hearing children. *Psychological Science, 11,* 307–314.

GOLDSTEIN, A. P., KELLER, H., & ERNE, D. (1985). *Changing the abusive parent.* Champaign, IL: Research Press.

GRAF, P., & SCHACTER, D. L. (1985). Implicit and explicit memory for new associations in normal and amnesic subjects. *Journal of Experimental Psychology: Learning, Memory, and Cognition, 11,* 501–518.

GRAHAM, S. (1992). Most of the subjects were white and middle class. *American Psychologist, 47,* 629–639.

GRAZIANO, W., VARCA, P., & LEVY, J. (1982). Race of examiner effects and the validity of intelligence tests. *Review of Educational Research, 52,* 469–498.

GREENBERG, D. S. (1999). When institutional review boards fail the system. *The Lancet, 353,* 1773.

GREENWALD, A. G., & GILLMORE, G. M. (1997). Grading leniency is a removable contaminant of student ratings. *American Psychologist, 52,* 1209–1217.

HALL, J. F. (1954). Learning as a function of word frequency. *American Journal of Psychology, 67,* 138–140.

HAMILTON, P. R., & JORDAN, J. S. (2000). Most successful and least successful performances: Perceptions of causal attribution of high school track athletes. *Journal of Sport Behavior, 23,* 245–254.

HARLOW, H. F., & HARLOW, M. K. (1962). The effect of rearing conditions on behavior. *Bulletin of Menninger Clinic, 26,* 213–224.

HARLOW, H. F., & ZIMMERMAN, R. R. (1959). Affectional responses in the infant monkey. *Science, 130,* 421–432.

HAYNES, F. (2000). Gender and family ideals: An exploratory study of black middle-class Americans. *Journal of Family Issues, 21,* 811–837.

HELMS, J. E. (1992). Why is there no study of cultural equivalence in standardized cognitive ability testing? *American Psychologist, 47,* 1083–1101.

HENLE, M., & HUBBELL, M. B. (1938). "Egocentricity" in adult conversation. *Journal of Social Psychology, 9,* 227–234.

HUBBLE, L. M., & GROFF, M. G. (1982). WISC-R verbal performance IQ descrepancies among Quay-classified adolescent male delinquents. *Journal of Youth and Adolescence, 11,* 503–508.

HUEBNER, A. M., GARROD, A., & SNAREY, J. (1990). *Moral development in Tibetan Buddhist monks: A cross-cultural study of adolescents and young adults in Nepal.* Paper presented at the meeting of the Society for Research in Adolescence, Atlanta, GA.

JACOBY, L. L., & DALLAS, M. (1981). On the relationship between autobiographical memory and perceptual learning. *Journal of Experimental Psychology: General, 3,* 306–340.

JAMIESON, D., LYNDON, J. E., & ZANNA, M. P. (1987). Attitude and activity preference similarity: Differential bases of interpersonal attraction for low and high self-monitors. *Journal of Personality and Social Psychology, 53,* 1052–1060.

JOSLYN, S., & HUNT, E. (1998). Evaluating individual differences in response to time-pressure situations. *Journal of Experimental Psychology: Applied, 4,* 16–43.

JUDD, C. M., SMITH, E. R., & KIDDER, L. H. (1991). *Research methods in social relations* (6th ed.). Ft. Worth, TX: Holt, Rinehart & Winston.

JUNG, J. (1971). *The experimenter's dilemma.* New York: Harper & Row.

KELMAN, H. C. (1967). Human use of human subjects: The problem of deception in social psychological experiments. *Psychological Bulletin, 67,* 1–11.

KEPPEL, G., & SAUFLEY, W. H. (1980). *Introduction to design and analysis: A student's handbook.* San Francisco: W. H. Freeeman.

KERLINGER, F. N. (1973). *Foundations of behavioral research.* New York: Holt, Rinehart and Winston.

KIRK, R. (1966). Practical significance: A concept whose time has come. *Educational and Psychological Measurement, 56,* 746–759.

KIRSNER, K., & DUNN, J. C. (1985). The perceptual record: A common factor in repetition priming and attribute retention. In M. I. POSNER and O. S. M. MARIN (Eds.), *Attention and performance XI.* (pp. 547–556). Hillsdale, NJ: Erlbaum.

KOHLBERG, L. (1979). *The meaning and measurement of moral development* (Clark Lectures). Worcester, MA: Clark University.

KOHLBERG, L. (1981). *The philosophy of moral development* (Vol. 1). San Francisco: Harper & Row.

KOSSLYN, S. M., THOMPSON, W. L., COSTANTINI-FERRANDO, M. F., ALPERT, N. M., & SPIEGEL, D. (2000). Hypnotic visual illusion alters color processing in the brain. *The American Journal of Psychiatry, 157,* 1279–1284.

KRAUT, R., PATTERSON, M., LUNDMARK, V., KIESLER, S., MUKOPADHYAY T., & SCHERLIS, W. (1998). Internet paradox: A social technology that reduces social involvement and psychological well-being? *American Psychologist, 53,* 1017–1031.

KRUPAT, E., & GARONZIK, R. (1994). Subjects' expectations and the search for alternatives to deception in social psychology. *British Journal of Social Psychology, 33,* 211–222.

KUPFERSMID, J. (1988). Improving what is published: A model in search of an editor. *American Psychologist, 43,* 635–642.

LEVENSON, R. W., EKMAN, P., HEIDER, K., & FRIESEN, W. V. (1992). Emotion and autonomic nervous system activity in the Minangkabau of West Sumatra. *Journal of Personality and Social Psychology, 62,* 972–988.

LURIA, A. R. (1968). *The mind of a mnemonist.* New York: Basic Books.

MACCOBY, E. E. (1990). Gender and relationships: A developmental account. *American Psychologist, 45,* 513–520.

MANDLER, G. (1975). *Mind and emotion.* New York: Wiley.

MANDLER, G. (1984). *Mind and body: Psychology of emotion and stress.* New York: Norton.

MANDLER, G. (1990). A constructivist theory of emotion. In N. S. Stein, B. L. Leventhal, & T. Trabasso (Eds.), *Psychological and biological approaches to emotion* (pp. 21–43). Hillsdale, NJ: Erlbaum.

MARTIN, S. (1999). Revision of ethics code calls for stronger former client sex rule. *Monitor, 30,* 44.

MCELWEE, R., & Farnum, J. (2001, April). *Updates about the self-reference effect in memory: Possible selves and individual differences measures.* Paper presented at the Eastern Psychological Association meeting, Washington, DC.

MERENDA, P. (1994). Cross-cultural testing: Borrowing from one culture and applying it to another. In L. L. ADLER and U. P. GIELEN (Eds.), *Cross-cultural topics in psychology* (pp. 53–58). Wesport, CT: Praeger.

MEYER, D. E., & SCHVANEVELDT, R. W. (1971). Facilitation in recognizing pairs of words: Evidence of a dependence upon retrieval operations. *Journal of Experimental Psychology, 90,* 227–234.

MEYER, J. P., & PEPPER, S. (1977). Need compatibility and marital adjustment in young married couples. *Journal of Personality and Social Psychology, 35,* 331–342.

MICHAEL, J. (1974). Statistical inference for individual organism research: Mixed blessing or cure? *Journal of Applied Behavior Analysis, 7,* 647–653.

MILGRAM, S. (1963). Behavioral study of obedience. *Journal of Abnormal and Social Psychology, 67,* 371–378.

MILLER, E. (1999). Research on the Web. *Observer, 12,* 4.

MILLER, J. G. (1999). Cultural psychology: Implications for basic psychological theory. *Psychological Science, 10,* 85–91.

MISTRY, J., & ROGOFF, B. (1994). Remembering in cultural context. In W. W. Lonner & R. Malpass (Eds.), *Psychology and culture* (pp. 139–144). Boston: Allyn & Bacon.

MRINAL, N. R., MRINAL, U. S., & TAKOOSHIAN, H. (1994). Research methods for studies in the field. In L. L. Adler and U. P. Gielen (Eds.), *Cross-cultural topics in psychology* (pp. 25–40). Wesport, CT: Praeger.

MURDOCK, B. B., Jr. (1962). The serial position effect in free recall. *Journal of Experimental Psychology, 64,* 482–488.

NANTAIS, K. M., & SCHELLENBERG, E. G. (1999). The Mozart effect: An artifact or preference. *Psychological Science, 10,* 370–373.

OLIANSKY, A. (1991). A confederate's perspective on deception. *Ethics and Behavior, 1,* 253–258.

ORTMANN, A., & HERTWIG, R. (1997). Is deception acceptable? *American Psychologist, 52,* 746–747.

OSGOOD, C. E. (1964). Semantic differential technique in the comparative study of cultures. *American Anthropologist, 66,* 171–200.

OSGOOD, C. E., MAY, W. H., & MIRON, M. S. (1975). *Cross-cultural universals of affective meaning.* Urbana: University of Illinois Press.

PETERSON, L. R., & PETERSON, M. J. (1959). Short-term retention of individual verbal items. *Journal of Experimental Psychology, 58,* 193–198.

PIKE, K. L. (1966). *Language in relation to a unified theory of the structure of human behavior.* The Hague: Mouton.

PRZEWORSKI, A., & TEUNE, H. (1970). *The logic of comparative social inquiry.* New York: Wiley.

RAUSCHER, F. H., SHAW, G. L., & KY, K. N. (1993). Music and spatial performance. *Nature, 365,* 611.

RAUSCHER, F. H., SHAW, G. L., & KY, K. N. (1995). Listening to Mozart enhances spatial-temporal reasoning: Towards a neurophysiological basis. *Neuroscience Letters, 185,* 44–47.

ROBERTS, E., & DEBLOSSIE, R. R. (1983). Test bias and the culturally different early adolescent. *Adolescence, 61,* 260–262.

ROEDIGER, H. L., & CRAIK, F. I. M. (Eds.). (1989). *Varieties of memory and consciousness: Essays in honor of Endel Tulving.* Hillsdale, NJ: Earlbaum.

ROETHLISBERGER, F. J., & DICKSON, W. J. (1939). *Management and the worker.* Cambridge, MA: Harvard University Press.

ROGERS, T. B., KUIPER, N. A., & KIRKER, W. S. (1977). Self reference and the encoding of personal information. *Journal of Personality and Social Psychology, 35,* 677–688.

ROSENBERG, M. J. (1969). The conditions and consequences of evaluation apprehension. In R. ROSENTHAL and R. L. ROSNOW (Eds.), *Artifact in behavioral research.* New York: Academic Press.

ROSENHAN, D. L. (1973). On being sane in insane places. *Science, 179,* 250–258.

ROSENTHAL, R. (1966). *Experimenter effects in behavioral research.* New York: Appleton.

ROSENTHAL, R. (1969). Interpersonal expectations: Effects of the experimenter's hypothesis. In R. ROSENTHAL and R. L. ROSNOW (Eds.), *Artifact in behavioral research.* New York: Academic Press.

ROSENTHAL, R., & ROSNOW, R. L. (1975). *Primer of methods for the behavioral sciences.* New York: Wiley.

ROSSI, P. H., & FREEMAN, H. E. (1993). *Evaluation: A systematic approach* (5th ed.). Newbury Park, CA: Sage.

SCHULTZ, D. P., & SCHULTZ, S. E. (1992). *A history of modern psychology.* New York: Harcourt Brace Jovanovich.

SCRIBNER, S., & COLE, M. (1972). Effects of constrained recall training on children's performance in verbal memory task. *Child Development, 43,* 845–857.

SEARS, D. O. (1986). College sophomores in the laboratory: Influences of a narrow data base on social psychology's view of human nature. *Journal of Personality and Social Psychology, 51,* 515–530.

SEGALL, M. H., CAMPBELL, D. T., & HERSKOVITS, M. J. (1966). *The influence of culture on visual perception.* New York: Bobbs-Merril.

SEWELL, T., FARLEY, F. H., MANNI, J., & HUNT, P. (1982). Motivation, social reinforcement, and intelligence as predictors of academic achievement in Black adolescents. *Adolescence, 17,* 647–656.

SHARPE, D., ADAIR, J. G., & ROESE, N. J. (1992). Twenty years of deception research: A decline in subjects' trust? *Personality and Social Psychology Bulletin, 18,* 585–590.

SIMMONS, W. (1979). The effects of the cultural salience of test materials on social class and ethnic differences in cognitive performance. *The Quarterly Newsletter of the Laboratory of Comparative Human Cognition, 1,* 43–47.

SINGER, P. (1990). *Animal liberation: A new ethics for our treatment of animals* (Rev. ed.). New York: Avon Books.

SMITH, S. L. (1996). Neither victim nor villain: Nurse Eunice Rivers, the Tuskegee Syphilis experiment, and public health. *Journal of Women's History, 8,* 95–113.

SMITH, S. S., & RICHARDSON, D. (1983). Amelioration of deception and harm in psychological research: The important role of debriefing. *Journal of Personality and Social Psychology, 44,* 1075–1082.

SOLOMON, R. L. (1949). An extension of control group design. *Psychological Bulletin, 46,* 137–150.

SOLSO, R. (1998). *Cognitive psychology* (5th ed.). Boston: Allyn and Bacon.

SPATA, A. V. (1995). *The word-association test as a conceptual implicit memory task.* Unpublished doctoral dissertation, Adelphi University, New York.

SRINIVAS, K., & ROEDIGER, H. L. (1990). Testing the nature of two implicit tests: Dissociations between conceptually-driven and data-driven processes. *Journal of Memory and Language, 28,* 389–412.

St. JAMES, J., SCHNEIDER, W., & RODGERS, A. (1992). Experiments in perception, cognition, social psychology, and human factors (version 1.6) [Computer software]. Pittsburgh, PA: Psychological Software Tools, Inc.

STARCH, D. (1910). A demonstration of the trial and error method of learning. *Psychological Bulletin, 7,* 20–23.

STEELE, C. M. (1995). Stereotype threat and the intellectual test performance of African Americans. *Journal of Personality and Social Psychology, 69,* 797–811.

STEELE, C. M. (1997). A threat in the air: How stereotypes shape intellectual identity and performance. *American Psychologist, 52,* 613–629.

STERNBERG, S. (1966). High-speed scanning in human memory. *Science, 153,* 652–654.

STEVENS, S. S. (1946). On the theory of scales of measurement. *Science, 103,* 677–680.

STEVENS, S. S. (1951). *Handbook of experimental psychology.* New York: Wiley.

STEVENS, S. S. (1975). *Psychophysics.* New York: Wiley.

STEVENSON, H. W. (1992). Learning from Asian schools. *Scientific American,* 70–76.

STEVENSON, H. W. (1993). Why Asian students still outdistance Americans. *Educational Leadership,* 63–65.

STEVENSON, H. W., CHEN, C., & LEE, S. Y. (1993). Mathematics achievement of Chinese, Japanese, and American children: Ten years later. *Science, 259,* 53–58.

STROOP, J. R. (1935). Studies of interference in serial verbal reactions. *Journal of Experimental Psychology, 18,* 643–662.

STUMPF, S. A., & FREEDMAN, R. D. (1979). Grades, learning, and student evaluation of instruction. *Research in Higher Education, 7,* 193–205.

SUOMI, S., & HARLOW, H. (1972). Social rehabilitation of isolate-reared monkeys. *Developmental Psychology, 6(3),* 487–496.

TAVRIS, C. (1999). Science and pseudoscience. *Observer, 12,* 27.

TAYLOR, S. J., & BOGDAN, R. (1998). *Introduction to qualitative research methods* (3d ed.). New York: Wiley.

THOMPSON, B. (1998). In praise of brilliance: Where that praise really belongs. *American Psychologist, 53,* 799–800.

TREASTER, J. B. (1994, February 1). Survey finds marijuana use is up in high schools. *New York Times,* p. A1.

TRIANDIS, H. (1994). *Culture and social behavior.* New York: McGraw Hill.

TRICE, A. D. (2000). Italian, Bulgarian, and U.S. children's perceptions of gender-appropriate occupations. *The Journal of Social Psychology, 140,* 666.

U.S. Department of Health and Human Services. (1982). Protection of human subjects. HHS Document 4.108:45, Pt. 46. Washington, DC: Author.

VELLEMAN, P. F., & WILKINSON, L. (1993). Nominal, ordinal, interval, and ratio typologies are misleading. *American Statistician, 47,* 65–72.

WAUGH, N. C., & NORMAN, D. A. (1965). Primary memory. *Psychological Review, 72,* 89–104.

WILLIAMS, R. W., HENRY, R. M., VOTRAW, L. M., RAMHARAKH, R., & PASCALIDES, S. F. (2001, April). *Telling truths and telling lies: Differences in non-verbal behavior.* Paper presented at the Eastern Psychological Association meeting, Washington, DC.

WILLIAMS, R. W., & SMITH, D. A. (2001, April). *An analysis of irritating classroom behaviors.* Paper presented at the Eastern Psychological Association meeting, Washington, DC.

AUTHOR INDEX

SUBJECT INDEX

Note: Page numbers followed by f indicate figures; those followed by t indicate tables.